NOT IN THE FACE OF THE ENEMY

OTHER BOOKS BY HUGH A. HALLIDAY

Terrebonne: From Seigneury to Suburb
(self-published, Niagara Falls, 1971)

The Wreck of the "Lady of the Lake"
and Other Stories from the Age of Sail
(self-published, Niagara Falls, 1973)

Chronology of Canadian Military Aviation
(National Museums of Canada, Ottawa, 1975)

The Tumbling Sky
(Canada's Wings, Stittsville, 1978)
Studies of Canadian fighter pilots of the Second World War

242 Squadron: The Canadian Years
(Canada's Wings, Stittsville, 1981)
History of a Canadian unit in the Royal Air Force

The Little Blitz
(National Museums of Canada, Ottawa, 1984)
History of the German bombing campaign, January-May 1944,
with the emphasis on Canadian contributions to the
air defence of Britain

Woody: A Fighter Pilot's Album
(CANAV Books, Toronto, 1987)
An illustrated biography

The Royal Canadian Air Force at War, 1939-1945
(with Larry Milberry; CANAV Books, Toronto, 1990)
One-volume history of the RCAF at home and abroad
during the Second World War

Typhoon and Tempest:
The Canadian Story
(CANAV Books, Toronto, 1992)
Canadians flying these types, with emphasis
on aerial tactical warfare achievements

Wreck! Canada's Worst Railway Accidents
(Robin Brass Studio, 1997)
Thirty rail disasters, 1854-1986

Canada's Air Forces, 1914-1999
(with Brereton Greenhous, Art Global, 1999)
Seventy-fifth anniversary of the RCAF

Murder Among Gentlemen:
A History of Duelling in Canada
(Robin Brass Studio, 1999)
A history of a curious practice

NOT IN THE FACE OF THE ENEMY

CANADIANS AWARDED THE AIR FORCE CROSS AND AIR FORCE MEDAL, 1918-1966

Hugh A. Halliday

ROBIN BRASS STUDIO

Toronto

Published 2000 by
Robin Brass Studio Inc.,
10 Blantyre Avenue, Toronto, Ontario M1N 2R4, Canada
Fax: 416-698-2120 • e-mail: rbrass@total.net
www.rbstudiobooks.com

Distributed in the United States of America by
Midpoint Trade Books,
27 West 20th St., Suite 1102, New York, NY 10011
Fax: 212-727-0195 • e-mail: midpointny@aol.com

Printed and bound in Canada by AGMV-Marquis,
Cap-Saint-Ignace, Quebec

Thanks to F.J. Blatherwick for the loan of colour photographs of the Air Force Cross and Air Force Medal. Thanks to Larry Milberry for the loan of a number of aviation photographs. Thanks to Molly Brass for the cover design concept.

Canadian Cataloguing in Publication Data

Halliday, Hugh A., 1940–
   Not in the face of the enemy : Canadians awarded the Air Force Cross and Air Force Medal, 1918-1966

Includes bibliographical references and index.
ISBN 1-896941-19-2

1. Air Force Cross (Great Britain : Medal). 2. Air Force Medal (Great Britain). 3. Great Britain. Royal Air Force – Medals, badges, decorations, etc. 4. Canada. Royal Canadian Air Force – Medals, badges, decorations, etc. 5. Canada. Royal Canadian Air Force – History. I. Title

UG979.C3H34 2000   358.4'11342'0971   C00-932505-0

A wise nation preserves its records, gathers up its muniments, decorates the tombs of its illustrious dead, repairs its great public structures, and fosters national pride and love of country by perpetual references to the sacrifices and glories of the past.

– JOSEPH HOWE (1804-1873), ADDRESSING
THE HOWE FESTIVAL, FRAMINGHAM,
MASSACHUSETTS, AUGUST 31, 1871

Without heroes we are all plain people and don't know how far we can go.

– BERNARD MALAMUD (1914-1986),
AUTHOR OF *THE NATURAL*

Example is the school of mankind, and they will learn at no other.

– EDMUND BURKE (1729-1797),
LETTERS ON A REGICIDE PEACE

Heroism, whether masculine or feminine, is ultimately, however, of limited usefulness on the battlefield, and even its most powerful verbal celebration of limited effect. For in the midst of fear, which is the fighting man's psychological element, it is example which counts.

– JOHN KEEGAN,
THE NATURE OF WAR (1981)

CONTENTS

PREFACE 9

1 ORIGINS AND PROCEDURES 13

2 THE EARLY YEARS 27

3 INTERREGNUM 55

4 SECOND WORLD WAR AWARDS 65
Canadians in the Royal Air Force 68
Home Front Operations 71
Mercy and Rescue Work 78
Meteorological Flying 87
Test and Development 98
Training 112
Ferry Operations 143
Transport 149
Fighter Pilot AFCs 159
Exceptional Men – Exceptional Cases 160

5 "BRAVERY IN THE PERFORMANCE OF DUTY":
1947–1966 173

6 POSTWAR AWARDS 189
Operation POLCO 190
With the Royal Air Force 196

Search and Rescue 204
Operation HAWK: No. 426 Squadron on the Pacific Airlift 221
Fighter Awards 229

7 A NEW GENERATION OF AWARDS 237

APPENDICES 245
A: Canadian Recipients of the Air Force Cross as
Members of the Royal Air Force, 1918–1920 245
B: RCAF Air Force Cross Recipients in the Second
World War 249
C: RCAF Air Force Medal Recipients in the Second
World War 255
D: CAN/RAF Recipients of the Air Force Cross and
Air Force Medal, 1941–1956 256
E: Air Force Cross Awards – RAF, RAAF, RNZAF in
Canada, 1942–1946 257
F: Air Force Medal Awards – RAF in Canada, 1942–1946 258
G: Postwar RCAF Awards 258
H: Location of Selected AFC Medals 259

ENDNOTES 261

INDEX 279

Student pilots and instructors walk out to their de Havilland Tiger Moths at No. 20 Elementary Flying Training School, Oshawa, during the Second World War. (Canadian Forces Photograph PL 5356)

PREFACE

Many authors have a compulsive need to justify their works. I am no exception. I wish to explain how this book came about, what I hope to have accomplished and the limitations of its contents.

Late in 1992 I began a compilation of RCAF honours and awards of the Second World War. This task was largely completed at the time I retired from the Canadian War Museum, but work continued to fill in gaps or expand on information already transcribed. The database created was so large as to make it unpublishable by traditional means; if printed, the text would run to some 6,000 single-spaced typed pages. Nevertheless, the information is there and available as a starting point for other projects by myself and others.

With some 7,600 citations or recommendations, I could have written about persons decorated for work in a specific field (such as medicine or radar). Alternatively, I could have written about awards of a specific type, such as the George Medal. This latter approach appealed to me. It became a matter of choosing which medal. I eliminated the Distinguished Flying Cross as being too large a subject (more than 4,000 RCAF recipients alone). The Air Force Cross (awarded to officers and warrant officers) and Air Force Medal (for other ranks) looked more manageable, with fewer than 500 awards to RCAF personnel. Even including Canadians who had enrolled directly in the Royal Air Force ("CAN/RAF Personnel"), First World War awards and post-1945 awards, the numbers were practical.[1]

With respect to First and Second World War awards I chose to relate *representative* stories of Air Force Cross and Air Force Medal recipients. As the reader may soon appreciate, I could not describe the careers of all these people (although all are listed in appendices) as that would have been repetitious. I undertook to deal with themes by which persons received these awards. In the case of persons whose AFC or AFM was part of a much larger array of decorations (e.g., G/C J.A. Kent) I have dealt with the award in question and mentioned their other honours only in passing.

The case of AFCs and AFMs awarded between 1948 and 1966 to members of the RCAF was different. There were only 26 of the former and four of the latter, and although some exploits resembled others, each was unique; most represented incredible feats of professionalism tinged with exceptional courage. Moreover, I had already concluded that the postwar RCAF was a field that had been badly "under-written" by both popular and academic historians; to my knowledge, no television docu-dramas have been contemplated about Operation CANON, much less Operation HAVEN. There was, in short, an excellent argument to tell all the postwar AFC and AFM stories without risking repetition or redundancy.

This book has changed considerably in the course of writing, for it was apparent that awards of the Air Force Cross and Air Force Medal were in many ways representative of Canada's ambivalent attitudes towards formal national honours. At various times we have accepted, then spurned British decorations (and the AFC and AFM were essentially British medals,

available to a limited international community that was both Empire and Commonwealth). Following generous awards during the Second World War, Canada restricted them severely thereafter. The last AFC was awarded to a member of the Canadian Forces in 1966; six years passed before a new set of distinctive Canadian gallantry awards was created. The practical story of the AFC and AFM in a Canadian context is thus part of a larger tale of evolving national consciousness.

A note on sources is in order, to explain the limitations of the book. When I began the original project in 1992, I compiled my lists from documents titled "Supplements to Air Force Routine Orders" (otherwise known as "Green Sheets"). These gave the names of recipients but did not always provide a citation describing their accomplishments. Archival material held by the Directorate of History (notably biographical files) filled many gaps; other files in the National Archives of Canada provided more.[2] Information of post-1945 AFC and AFM awards to RCAF personnel was also readily available, thanks in part to the fact that the RCAF had one of the best public relations offices in government during the 1950s and 1960s. There were also scores of files in the National Archives of Canada dealing with such diverse subjects as McKee Trophy nominations, honours, search and rescue, prime ministerial correspondence, and so on. Indeed, reading lists of files prompted me to think of Zsa Zsa Gabor's frustrated cry, "So many men – so little time."

Access to personal documents was allowed in some instances. The Government Personnel Records Centre (a division of the National Archives of Canada) operates under Protection of Privacy legislation which allows limited viewing of such material, and only if the file concerns a person who has been dead for at least twenty years; in many cases it was not known whether a person was deceased or when. Even if a file could be seen, there were restrictions on what could be copied. Nevertheless, those files which I was permitted to see proved useful to confirm dates and add details about such things as performance assessments and crashes.

Occasionally it was possible to consult the logbooks of AFC recipients, either directly, through next-of-kin, or at museums. Researchers familiar with these will know how varied they are. Some men turned their logbooks into diaries, rich in details of flights and aircraft. Others recorded the minimum of information. That of A/C G.G. Diamond, for example, was most interesting for his activities in 1941 and early 1942, which were unrelated to the transport work that gained him his AFC. The logbooks of F/L Charles G.R. Dyer were remarkable for being so dull – 43 months of monotonous instructing with the names of pupils, flying times and sequence numbers, but absolutely no adventures. Dyer was awarded an AFC for his instructional work, and the fact that his career was so uneventful was an indication of how good he was at his business.[3]

Some information could be found only in Britain, notably on awards from the First World War, awards to RCAF personnel serving in RAF units during the Second World War and CAN/RAF personnel. Four trips to the Public Records Office in London (three with generous help from the Air Command Heritage and History Fund) yielded considerable information on Second World War awards, but relatively little on First World War awards.[4] Some of the information missing from this book may still be traceable; any person or institution prepared to write me a $10,000 cheque for another three-week research expedition to Britain (which might or might not fill in the gaps) should note my address.

Readers who discover that their particular family member or friend has not been the subject of extended treatment (or even persons seeking more information than is in this book) can consult the websites which now distribute the basic material gathered in the course of my research: <www.airforce.ca/citations/wwii/index.htm> for awards to members of the RCAF for Second World War services, and <www.airforce.ca/citations/postwar/index.htm> for awards to members of the Canadian Forces for air or air-related duties in the postwar period up to 1970. I hope omissions on my part will be forgiven.

No preface would be complete without acknowledging the help of my wife, Monique. On successive visits to archival sources, and most notably the Public Record Office in London, we have worked with ever greater efficiency and studied our subjects in greater detail. Her familiarity with the work has been matched by her understanding of the documents, and her sense of organization has saved me from the chaos that would otherwise dominate my work habits.

HUGH A. HALLIDAY
Orleans, Ontario
October 2000

Chapter 1

ORIGINS AND PROCEDURES

Show me a republic, ancient or modern, in which there have been no decorations. Some people call them baubles. Well, it is by such baubles that one leads men.

– NAPOLEON BONAPARTE, ON ESTABLISHING
THE LEGION OF HONOUR, MAY 19, 1802

Praise is the sure bait to catch a soldier and sometimes to push him along.

– JAMES WOLFE, WRITING TO AN UNNAMED LADY,
DECEMBER 14, 1758

I received orders for France, accompanied by the usual twenty-four hours' leave. Having made up my mind that some heroic experiences in the field were ahead of me, I immediately went to a tailor and had the pilot's wings moved a good quarter-inch higher above the pocket of my tunic to leave room for impending decorations! What price the confidence of youth?

– WALTER E. GILBERT (1899-1986), RECALLING HIS BRIEF
FIRST WORLD WAR FLYING CAREER[1]

For much of the First World War, the British had two distinct flying services – the Royal Naval Air Service (directed by the Royal Navy) and the Royal Flying Corps (the army's air arm). Personnel who distinguished themselves were honoured with a variety of awards. Some were common to the army and navy: the Distinguished Service Order was the same for both services, as was the Victoria Cross (although naval VCs were awarded with a blue ribbon, whereas army VCs had a crimson ribbon). Other awards, though of equal status, differed from army to navy. Thus, a "good show" might bring an army officer a Military Cross while an equivalent act would bring a naval officer the Distinguished Service Cross. Junior ranks in these services might receive a Military Medal (army) or a Distinguished Service Medal (navy).

The events leading to the formation of the Royal Air Force by merging its two predecessors need not detain us here. Suffice to say that in the spring of 1918 authorities were considering what decorations might be awarded to members of the new service. The initiative came from within the Admiralty. On May 6, 1918, Sir Frederick Ponsonby (Keeper of the Privy Purse) wrote to Commodore Sir Geoffrey Paine (Air Ministry), advising him that the King had approved a proposal for four new awards, to be announced on the monarch's birthday.[2]

The official voice of the Crown was the *London Gazette*. Its edition of June 3, 1918, published details of the new honours "signifying Our appreciation of acts of valour, courage and devotion to duty performed by Officers and Men of Our Air Force and in the Air Forces of Our Self-governing Dominions beyond the Seas."[3] They would be:

The **Distinguished Flying Cross**, "granted only to such Officers and Warrant Officers of Our Said Forces as shall be recommended to Us for an act or acts of valour, courage or devotion to duty performed *whilst flying in active operations against the enemy.*"

The **Distinguished Flying Medal**, "granted only to such Non-Commissioned Officers and Men of Our Said Forces as shall be recommended to Us for an act or acts of valour, courage or devotion to duty performed *whilst flying in active operations against the enemy.*"

The **Air Force Cross**, "granted only to such Officers and Warrant Officers of Our Said Forces as shall be recommended to Us for an act or acts of valour, courage or devotion to duty performed *whilst flying though not in active operations against the enemy.*"

The **Air Force Medal,** "granted only to such Non-Commissioned Officers and Men of Our Said Forces as shall be recommended to Us for an act or acts of valour, courage or devotion to duty performed *whilst flying though not in active operations against the enemy.*" [emphasis added by the author in all cases].

The design of the new awards was spelled out in heraldic terms. The Air Force Cross was to be silver, "a thunderbolt in the form of a cross, the arms conjoined by wings, the base terminating with a bomb surmounted by another cross composed of aeroplane propellers, the four ends inscribed with the letters G.V.R.I.[4] In the centre a roundel thereon a representation of Hermes mounted on a hawk in flight bestowing a wreath. On the reverse the Royal Cypher above the date 1918. The whole ensigned by an Imperial Crown and attached to the clasp and ribbon by two sprigs of laurel."[5]

The ribbon for the AFC was originally to be of red and white horizontal stripes, one-eighth inch thick (the DFC was to have similar blue and white stripes). On July 24, 1919, this was amended to diagonal stripes and the DFC underwent a similar change.

On August 27, 1919, eligibility was extended to army and navy personnel as well as civilians "who render distinguished service to aviation in actual flying."[6] Over the years other amendments were made to the regulations. Thus, on March 23, 1932, the standard for an award was altered to those who showed "*exceptional* valour, courage or devotion to duty," and the reference to civilian eligibility was omitted; up to that point, 14 AFCs and three AFMs had been granted to civilians including two to foreigners (Charles Lindbergh and the Marquis F. de Pinedo).[7] On March 7, 1938, the inscription at the four ends of the cross was changed to "G.VI.R.I." while on July 15, 1955, this inscription was changed to "E.R.II" (reflecting the succession of new monarchs to the throne). An amendment on March 11, 1941, extended eligibility to members of the Fleet Air Arm serving with the RAF and dominion air forces. A further amendment on February 23, 1942, allowed for recommendations in respect of dominion personnel to be made by the appropriate dominion ministers. Thus, the way

The Air Force Cross, clearly showing heraldic symbols denoting flight, with Hermes (Mercury), god of roads, communications, invention, cunning and theft. The reverse bears the royal cypher as it existed in 1918. The obverse (front) of the cross has each of the four arms of the cross inscribed differently – "G" (George), "R" (Rex or King), "I" (Impereator or Emperor) and "VI" (this example dating from the reign of George VI). (Photos courtesy F.J. Blatherwick)

The Air Force Medal, awarded to personnel below the rank of warrant officer. Hermes (Mercury) riding an eagle can be discerned more readily than on the Air Force Cross. When Britain abolished medals based upon distinctions of rank (1993), award of the Air Force Medal was discontinued; thereafter, aerial gallantry "not in the presence of the enemy" would be recognized through the Air Force Cross, regardless of the recipient's rank. (Photos courtesy F. J. Blatherwick)

was cleared for Canadians serving in Canada to be recommended for an AFC through a purely Canadian channel of communications.

The Air Force Medal was of a simpler design. It was to be silver, oval in shape, and bear the effigy of the reigning monarch on one side. The reverse was to have a laurel wreath around a representation of Hermes mounted on a hawk in flight bestowing a wreath. Originally, the ribbon was to have red and white horizontal stripes, one-sixteenth inch thick (the DFM had similar horizontal stripes, blue and white). As with the AFC, diagonal stripes were substituted for horizontal stripes on July 24, 1919. Civilian eligibility was added on August 27, 1919; Fleet Air Arm eligibility expanded on March 11, 1941, and provision made for dominion (as opposed to British) recommendations on February 23, 1942.

C.G. Grey, the noted British aviation author, applauded the new awards, particularly because they drew a distinction between combat and non-combat service. He admitted, however, that it might not always be possible to define certain flying (such as coastal patrols) in terms of one or the other. He also noted the potential for confusion in that the letters "AFC" had also been assigned to the Australian Flying Corps[8] Grey subsequently wrote (not quite accurately) that the Distinguished Flying Cross was given for "war flying" and the Air Force Cross was for "civil flying, such as great pioneer flights, or the testing of experimental aeroplanes over a long period." He then added an informal comment that circulated in the RAF between the world wars: "Recalling the danger of flying experiments, a humorist remarked that 'the DFC was for flying in the face of the enemy, whereas the AFC was given for flying in the face of Providence.'"[9]

Provision was made in the original regulations for the possible forfeiture of awards should the recipient subsequently be deemed unworthy. This was rarely done, although on January 25, 1921, the *London Gazette* announced cancellation of an AFC bestowed 18 months earlier on Major Edward E. Clark (RAF), "in consequence of his having been convicted by the Civil Powers." This drastic move was facilitated by the fact that Clark was still a serving officer; it is unlikely that similar action would have been taken had he previously returned to civilian life.[10]

The eligibility of Royal Naval personnel for what were essentially RAF awards occasionally caused some confusion and consternation; in 1940 the Admiralty expressly declined a DFC for Lieutenant Richard Cork (recommended for Battle of Britain services) and substituted the naval equivalent, the Distinguished Service Cross.[11] Similar problems do not appear to have dogged the AFC, but between 1949 and 1953 the Admiralty considered instituting Fleet Air Arm versions of the AFC and AFM, to be styled the Naval Flying Cross and Naval Flying Medal. The more the idea was discussed, the greater were the objections raised. Ultimately, it was decided that AFC and AFM awards would continue, but that efforts would be made to secure more George Medals for hazardous non-combat deeds performed by naval aviators.[12]

As of early 1919 Air Force Crosses (and their belligerent companions, the Distinguished Flying Crosses) were seldom seen; the actual medals were still being struck. When the DFC of a deceased officer (Lieutenant V.H. McElroy) was late in reaching Canada, the Governor General inquired of the Colonial Office, which duly reported that the decoration would be forwarded about May 1; the explanation was: "The new Air Force decorations are now in process of manufacture, and it is not expected that any will be completed for at least another month."[13]

How quickly the McElroy family received their son's DFC is

The medals of Douglas Muir Edwards, showing his Air Force Cross, 1939-45 Star, France and Germany Star, Defence Medal, Canadian Volunteer Service (with Clasp for overseas service), War Medal (with Oak Leaf denoting a Mention in Despatches), Queen Elizabeth II Coronation Medal, Canadian Forces Decoration (long service), Legion of Honour, Croix de Guerre, American Air Medal.

not certain, but by mid-1919 the air force awards were slowly being distributed. A visit by the Prince of Wales to Canada was an opportunity for presenting hundreds of decorated servicemen (or their next-of-kin) with their honours, including DFCs and AFCs. Another Colonial Office despatch made this clear: "The Prince of Wales will present Air Force decorations, viz Distinguished Flying Crosses and Air Force Crosses, to demobilized officers of the Royal Air Force now residing in Canada on the occasion of his forthcoming visit."[14]

The distribution of service honours continued well into the 1920s, sometimes through the mail, sometimes at formal investitures. A ceremony in Vancouver on March 5, 1920, saw Brigadier J.M. Ross pin awards on seven veterans, including a Victoria Cross (to Captain E.D. Bellow) and an Air Force

Cross (to Captain L.E. Best). The award of one AFC (to the next-of-kin of a deceased officer) was delayed by a row involving a widow and a mother who questioned the validity of her late son's marriage!

Thousands of servicemen were recommended for awards during the Second World War; British authorities were reluctant to approve excessive numbers, lest the value of such honours be debased. On the other hand, good work deserved recognition. In 1941 two new awards were created: the King's Commendation for Brave Conduct and the Kings's Commendation for Valuable Services in the Air. Neither included a decoration; instead a small oak leaf emblem (identical to that denoting a "Mention in Despatches") was worn on the ribbon of the War Medal 1939-1945. Nearly 300 members of the RCAF were accorded such Commendations. Their full scope lies beyond this book, but it is worth noting that approximately 24 Commendations began as recommendations for Air Force Crosses, while at least one RCAF AFC started life as a Commendation. In the course of a few incidents some participants received the AFC while others in the same episode were accorded Commendations. Similarly, the occasional AFC nomination was downgraded to a Mention in Despatches for little apparent reason other than that quotas for awards had been filled.

An explicit instance of this involved F/O Peter Gower Hughes (Courtney, British Columbia), who was put up for an AFC in the autumn of 1942 for services as a navigator in No. 113 (Bomber Reconnaissance) Squadron; up to that point he had taken part in four attacks on submarines off Canada's east coast. On November 26, 1942, Air Force Headquarters advised Eastern Air Command that the proposed award had been shot down because "too many recommendations were being received from No. 113 Squadron, thereby lessening the number of awards available to other units in this Command"; AFHQ was also critical in that the reference to four attacks on U-boats took no account of whether or not these had been successful. Hughes was accorded a Mention in Despatches in May 1943 and a DFC for work with No. 10 (BR) Squadron in June 1944.[15]

Clearly, a Mention in Despatches or a Commendation for Valuable Services in the Air was akin to an award without an actual decoration. One wartime incident illustrates the problems that confronted authorities when trying to decide what type of recognition should be granted.

On April 9, 1945, P/O John Bryden was giving instruction in a Mosquito of No. 8 Operational Training Unit (Greenwood, Nova Scotia). Just after takeoff his port engine burst into flames. Bryden took over from his pupil and hit the extinguisher; the fire persisted. He then executed a gentle 170-degree turn and crash-landed on the airfield; neither he nor his pupil were injured. Bryden was recommended for an AFC, but Eastern Air Command Headquarters queried this; they were inclined to charge him with dangerous flying. According to accepted procedure, he should have climbed the aircraft or made a straight-ahead forced landing rather than risk a turning stall at low level. His immediate superior, S/L H.C. Stewart, angrily wrote that "the book" did not apply – in part because "Mosquito landings away from aerodromes are practically always fatal crashes" and partly because the widely spread out town of Kingston, Nova Scotia, lay directly in the path of the aircraft. The unit CO, G/C E.M. Reyno, concurred, adding, "If this aircraft, which is of wooden construction throughout, had crash landed in or even near a populated area, with a full load of fuel on board, the results would have been most disastrous." Eastern Air Command Headquarters relented, but the AFC recommendation was downgraded to a Commendation.[16]

The case of P/O Bryden was repeated frequently in many theatres throughout the war, in circumstances that ranged from recommendations for Victoria Crosses down to the most humble awards. When did "bravery" become "foolhardiness"; where did "good work" become "superior work"? And should a man's good work be recognized if he showed failings in other ways? A case in point was F/O Robert Anthony Butts, who in August 1942 was recommended for an AFC for services with No. 10 (BR) Squadron. His superiors noted that he had flown 115 sorties (851 operational hours) on anti-submarine patrols; Eastern Air Command Headquarters raised the point that he had recently been posted following a court martial for low flying. The Air Force Cross did not go through, but in December 1945 F/L Butts was awarded a Distinguished Flying Cross on completion of a tour on heavy bombers (34 sorties, 212 hours 50 minutes operational flying) with No. 582 Squadron.

How did one receive a decoration – Air Force Crosses and Air Force Medals included? The process was complex, and essentially it was played by British rules with which Canadians seldom argued and never fundamentally questioned. An award began with a recommendation, usually drafted by the nominee's immediate superior, which found its way through successive layers of approval (station followed by command headquarters, Air Ministry in Britain, the Department of National Defence in Canada) until finally the monarch consented and the award was duly announced in Air Force Routine Orders as well as official publications: the *Canada Gazette* and the *London Gazette*. As awards progressed through channels, the decoration might be altered (as with Bryden's AFC downgraded to a Commendation), and the texts of citations would be tightened up and edited. An example is that of P/O Alan M. James, awarded an AFC for services in No. 145 (BR) Squadron. When first recommended on March 11, 1943, his superior, S/L E.M. Williams, wrote:

> This officer has completed 1,240 hours of flying, of which 735 hours are operational. He has successfully carried out 183 operational sorties over the North Atlantic. He is a brilliant Captain whose determination and devotion to duty has been outstanding.
>
> During a flight in February, 1943, when attempting a landing at night in zero conditions, he encountered severe carburettor icing. One engine iced up completely and jammed the throttle and it was only by back-firing the second engine every few minutes and exercising great skill that he managed to reach an alternative aerodrome and land safely.
>
> His outstanding coolness in an emergency doubtless saved the aircraft and the lives of his crew and his example has won him the admiration of all.[17]

When the recommendation finally reached the Governor General in late 1943 this had been abbreviated to a bare-bones text:

> This officer during his many operational flying hours has displayed great devotion to duty and exceptional flying ability. He has contributed excellent and extremely valuable work on convoy patrols and anti-submarine sweeps.

There were many types of honours and awards, but for the purposes of this book one need look only at the rules governing the AFC and AFM. Both were classed as "gallantry" awards. Within that category there were two categories – "immediate" and "periodic." Immediate awards were for acts of outstanding courage and daring; in theory no limit was placed upon their numbers, and the time elapsed between recommending and gazetting was often very brief. It took less than two months to process the AFCs associated with the Trans-Atlantic glider tow of 1943.

Periodic awards (also called "non-immediate awards") constituted the bulk of AFCs distributed during the Second World War. Initially they were gazetted (with many other honours) in January and June of each year (the New Year's List and the King's Birthday List). From 1942 to late 1945 this was altered to four lists. The initial reason was to speed up awards to the growing body of flying instructors in the Commonwealth Air Forces; however, in 1944 the intermediate lists (March and September) were expanded to honour a wider range of duties. Periodic awards were for long-term good work in tasks that did not necessarily include dramatic incidents. However, what most marked periodic awards was that they were rationed and distributed on a quota basis.

The quotas varied with time and circumstance. They were extremely generous for combat formations with high casualties (Bomber Command), less so for operational organizations whose members ran lower risks (Coastal Command, Aden). In theory they were fairly restricted for training and transport formations, but the large numbers of hours flown offset to some degree the limits on distribution. Thus, when Britain's Air Ministry Awards Committee was contemplating a quota of honours to be issued in the autumn of 1944, they were dealing with 159 submissions distributed among their various commands as follows:[18]

	Bar to AFC	AFC	AFM	Commendation
Flying Training	1	23	11	11
Transport Command	–	19	3	22
Technical Training	–	6	–	–
Rhodesian Air Training Group	–	4	–	6
Bomber Command	–	21	–	–
Coastal Command	–	7	–	–
Tactical Air Force	–	21	4	–

On February 12, 1943, A/C F.S. McGill (Air Officer Commanding, No. 1 Training Command, Toronto) despatched a letter to all units under his jurisdiction. The document bore on many aspects of honours and awards in Canada. At one point he wrote: "All Honours and Awards at the present time are placed on a quota basis for the Commands in Canada. These quotas are not liberal and consequently Commanding Officers should only recommend the most outstanding personnel."

McGill did not describe the quotas in detail, save for one type. Recommendations for flying instructors were to be submitted twice yearly (the deadlines were January 1 and July 1). On each occasion the quota per training command was to be for three AFCs (two for SFTS instructors, one for an EFTS instructor), three AFMs (two for SFTS instructors, one for an EFTS instructor) and four Commendations (divided equally between elementary and service flying training schools). However, McGill suggested that if many deserving cases were submitted, the quotas might be exceeded. The AOC was clearly anxious to see more awards granted within his command; towards the close of his letter he noted:

In the past, Commanding Officers have not been sufficiently aware of the value of an award to individuals on stations. If the right individual is selected, recommended and subsequently receives an award, the morale and esprit de corps of the entire personnel on the station will receive impetus. It also brings to realization the fact that the airmen or officers who have, of necessity, been stationed in Canada can achieve awards for meritorious service and devotion to duty.[19]

Correspondence in other commands explains in more detail the quotas which applied to those formations. On February 3, 1943, A/V/M J.A. Sully (Air Member for Personnel) wrote from Air Force Headquarters, Ottawa, to the Air Officer Commanding, Western Air Command (Vancouver). He explained that, in consultation with the British Honours and Awards Committee, AFHQ had settled upon a quota of honours for Western Air Command, based upon operational hours flown within WAC. For gallantry awards (DSO, DFC, DFM, AFC, AFM, CGM), some 2,500 command operational hours would be the basis for one award. As Western Air Command had flown about 25,000 operational hours in 1942, the expected quota for 1943 would be ten gallantry awards. However, Sully made it clear that only in exceptional circumstances involving combat rather than prolonged patrols would such awards as DFCs and DFMs be contemplated. Sully's letter advised AOC Western Air Command that unit commanders might be made aware that award quotas existed, but the specific numbers involved were not to be disclosed to them. In this way AFHQ hoped to encourage meritorious recommendations and limit frivolous ones.[20]

On June 6, 1944, Sully sent out another letter on behalf of the Chief of the Air Staff. It was directed to the Air Officers Commanding seven major air commands in Canada (EAC,

WAC, Northwest Air Command, plus Nos. 1, 2, 3, and 4 Training Commands). The letter began by explaining a problem besetting those in Ottawa who had to decide on the allocation of awards – too many submissions: "Recent submissions from commands have in some cases numbered between 50 and 80 recommendations from which only a tenth may be granted under present quota restrictions."[21]

G/C John A. Sully, AFC, 1941. Much of the correspondence respecting Second World War awards policies passed through his hands. (Canadian Forces Photograph PL-1202)

Sully went on to instruct each command to establish an honours and awards committee. This was to consist of the chief staff officer, senior air staff officer, senior administration officer and senior personnel officer. Each committee was to ensure that units within the command were informed about the criteria for awards and the proper procedures for submitting recommendations. The command honours and awards committees were also to vet and prioritize the recommendations so that the number of submissions did not exceed the quota by more than 50 per cent. In other words, if the command's quota was ten awards, and unit COs sent up 25 recommendations, the command committee was to cut this back to a maximum of 15 for transmission higher up.

In his letter of June 6, 1944, Sully clearly expressed two points which were often brought out in other correspondence:

Quotas for chivalry awards are established by United Kingdom authorities for each Periodic List and are based on total non-operational strength.

Immediate awards for specific acts of gallantry are free awards and not subject to any quota.

In laying out these points, Sully described the limits for *flying awards* that had been established for 1944. Even though these were for the whole of Canada, they were very generous. There were to be four lists in all: a King's Birthday Honours List, New Years Honours List and two Intermediate Lists. The limits in each were to be as follows:

	AFC or AFM	Commendation
Birthday Honours List	24	24
New Years Honours List	24	24
Spring Intermediate List	12	12
Autumn Intermediate List	12	12

Because flying awards in Canada tended to be approved in clumps, it is both simple and interesting to note the numbers actually gazetted for Canadian service between 1 January 1944 and 1 January 1945:

	AFC or AFM	Commendation
January 1944	13	11
May 1944	15	13
June 1944	17	4
November 1944	23	20
January 1945	41	23

It is obvious, then, that the "quotas" laid down at various times were not followed strictly. Further proof is that the Sully letter of June 6, 1944 indicated the maximum number of *submissions* that would be entertained from Western Air Command (remember that the submissions would exceed actual awards by some 50 per cent). For the autumn Intermediate List, WAC could submit only one AFC/AFM recommendation and one Commendation; for the New Years List it could submit only two AFC/AFM recommendation and two Commendations. In other words, in these two lists WAC could expect fewer than six flying awards; the honours actually granted numbered 11.

Another example of modified quotas, once more drawn from Western Air Command, was the rush to grant awards at the war's end. In a letter dated October 26, 1945, from AFHQ to the AOC Western Air Command, it was announced that the quotas prevailing for the first half of 1945 were to be increased by 75 per cent for the last half of 1945. It translated into the following numbers:

Quota	Jan-July 45	Late 1945
Flying Awards	12	21
Chivalry Awards	2.4	4
Mentions in Despatches	36	63

Apart from quotas to formations and attempts to spread awards around various schools and squadrons, it was also expected that individuals would meet certain minimal standards of activity. Thus, in August 1944 and again in December 1945 the RAF Awards Committee suggested that AFC and AFM candidates should have flown about 100 hours or more in the previous six months, to ensure that decorations did not go to people engaged mainly in administrative duties. Yet every guideline had an exception; the "100-hour" rule was clearly waived when lesser time had been logged in very dangerous work. Attempts were also made to factor in the *conditions* under which instructional flying was conducted. At one point officials cut back recommendations for instructors in Rhodesia because the excellent flying weather there was not deemed very challenging. Bomber Command instructors at operational training and heavy conversion units were also considered to be having an easy time of things (and hence less deserving of Air Force Crosses) because they were dealing with pupils who were more experienced than those in ordinary flying schools.[22]

Amid the voluminous correspondence that passed back and forth about decorations, one finds the authorities struggling to define what constituted deserving conduct or circumstances for an award; what kind of "service" should be rewarded? How could one distinguish between levels of gallantry? In his letter of June 6, 1944, A/V/M Sully advised field commanders that recommendations should *not* stress any of the following:

(a) that an officer or airman was well liked by his associates,
(b) that the person had athletic interests or abilities,
(c) that an airman was filling an officer's position (however, the same fact could be stated in terms such as that the airman was performing duties beyond those normally expected),
(d) service in the last war.[23]

However, the most striking feature of Sully's instructions was an attempt to quantify courage and relate it to specific medals:

Citations covering specific acts of gallantry should be accurate and so worded that inference may be drawn from the citation as to the degree of gallantry performed so that the correct award may be determined.

Deeds of gallantry in non-operational units usually fall into one of the brackets listed below:

(a) 85/100%   GC   Acts of gallantry having entailed the supreme sacrifice or degree of risk equal to this condition.

(b) 50/85%   GM   Risk of life being extremely great but less than the degree covered in (a).

(c) 25/50%   AFC,   The degree of gallantry being
              AFM,   less than that of (b).
              OBE,
              MBE,
              BEM

(d) 1/25%   Commendation[24]

One might sympathize with an officer agonizing over recommendations following a brave act, especially an incident which had more than one participant; how was he to distinguish between one man's bravery and another? How could anyone calculate risk as a percentage? Moreover, those reviewing award submissions had to guard against the undue influence of unit commanders or adjutants who were especially skilful in composing recommendations. In May 1942, Britain's Chief of the Air Staff noted that, of nine awards emanating from Flying Training Command, six had been divided between two units. He asked if this distribution was fair, or whether it was "attributable to the greater skill of certain Unit Commanders in writing recommendations."[25]

The manner in which awards were handled after the Second World War differed greatly from wartime practice (it was

A typical investiture on an RCAF station. F/O Richard J.E. Barichello had been a pilot at No. 1 General Reconnaissance School, Summerside, Prince Edward Island. On one occasion he dropped his dinghy to a downed crew, even though his own engines were faltering. Here he receives his AFC from G/C B.D. Hobbes, Commanding Officer at Patricia Bay, British Columbia, January 19, 1945. (National Archives of Canada C.144693)

thoroughly Canadian and very strict); this is best described in the context of chapter 5.

The events relating to an AFC award to S/L (later W/C) Robert Byers may be deemed typical. He was among the first nine RCAF recipients of the AFC. Born in Massena, New York, but raised around London, Ontario, he had been a mechanic, instructor and commercial pilot before the war. In spite of an injury sustained in a parachute jump (August 1935), he had logged 1,000 hours on various duties before his acceptance by the force in October 1939. On June 11, 1942, he received a telegram from the Air Officer Commanding, No. 4 Training Command, congratulating him on having been awarded the

Air Force Cross (the *Canada Gazette* of that day officially reported the honour). From that moment forward, Byers (like other decorated personnel) was entitled to wear the ribbon, even though months would pass before he received the decoration itself. Numerous other telegrams poured in from friends and family; in August be received a congratulatory letter from the Minister of National Defence for Air, Charles G. "Chubby" Power which gave the citation for the award:

This officer has been in charge of the Ferry and Communications Flight at these Headquarters [No. 4 Training Command] for more than a year, and during this time it has been necessary to ferry a very large number of aircraft long distances, in some cases from the Atlantic seaboard. Due to the persistent energy, resourcefulness, and devotion to duty of this officer these aircraft have been ferried very successfully in nearly every case. This officer has also been called upon to test Flying Instructors and potential Flying Instructors and to fly communication aircraft under adverse conditions. This officer has shown marked ability and devotion to duty and it is strongly recommended that his services be recognized by the award of the Air Force Cross.[26]

RCAF personnel received their various awards in many ways, usually in a manner in which they had some choice. Some stepped forward to be decorated by King George himself, sometimes months after the award had been authorized. Warrant Officer Percy L. Buck, for example, was notified in July 1943 that he had been awarded an AFC for services as an instructor in Canada; a year later, on August 11, 1944, Flying Officer Buck received the cross itself from King George VI during the monarch's visit to Linton.[27] Others were invested by a senior officer or (in Canada) by the Governor General or a provincial Lieutenant Governor. Hundreds chose simply to receive their honours by registered mail.

A standard investiture (if such an event existed) was a parade held at Station Patricia Bay on January 19, 1945. A total of 1,497 officers and men (half the personnel on base) paraded in the afternoon and watched as A/V/M F.V. Heakes presented three decorations: a British Empire Medal to Sergeant R.R. Barker, a Distinguished Flying Cross to F/L W.A.

Patricia Bay, January 19, 1945. Following the investiture ceremony on the tarmac, three members of the RCAF wear their newly acquired decorations: Sergeant Ronald R. Barker (awarded BEM), who had rescued a comrade from a burning aircraft; F/L William A. Armstrong (awarded DFC), who had shown heroism attacking enemy shipping overseas; and F/O R.J.E. Barichello. (National Archives of Canada C.144688)

Outside Buckingham Palace, London, 1943, seven Canadians who have just received their decorations from the hands of King George VI. From left to right they are W/C R.C. Fumerton (Fort Coulonge, Quebec, DFC and Bar), F/L N. Smith (Arnprior, Ontario, DFC), S/L B. Walker (London, Ontario, DFC), F/O D. Berry (Ottawa, AFC), F/O S.O. Aistrop (Sudbury, Ontario, AFC), W/C R.J. Lane (Victoria, DSO) and F/L J.W. Draper (Toronto, DFC). Aistrop and Berry had both been decorated for instructional services in Canada prior to being posted overseas. (Canadian Forces Photo PL-29326)

Armstrong, and an Air Force Cross to F/O R.J.E. Barichello.[28] On the other hand, when W/C Gordon G. Diamond was invested with his AFC, he was one of 127 persons (army, navy, air force, and civilian next-of-kin) present to receive decorations from the Governor General on June 27, 1945. Among those witnessing the event were his wife and son; the latter was destined to become a brigadier-general in the integrated Canadian Forces.[29]

Some honours were a long time getting to their recipients, in part because the individuals moved frequently. F/L Joseph Dutchak was awarded the Air Force Cross in November 1944; he was finally invested with the honour at a Government House ceremony held on January 26, 1954. F/L Earle F. O'Mara, awarded his AFC in December 1945, received the decoration as a similar ceremony on February 7, 1955. F/L Delford H. Kenney was a particularly difficult case. The Department of National Defence finally sent his DFC, Bar to DFC and AFC to the Department of External Affairs on August 9, 1955, and on February 13, 1956, External reported that Kenney had been presented with his awards at his home in Bronxville, New York.

Delivery of S/L Edward Bagley Gale's AFC was especially trying. Although it had been awarded to him in May 1944, he had not been invested with the decoration when it was sent from Britain to Canada in 1945. By then he had been posted to Britain. The AFC recrossed the ocean, but Gale was killed in a flying accident before it could be presented. His mother finally received it from the hands of the Governor General on November 14, 1950.

Chapter *2*

THE EARLY YEARS

I know that I shall meet my fate
Somewhere among the clouds above;
Those that I fight I do not hate,
Those that I guard I do not love.

> – WILLIAM BUTLER YEATS (1865-1939),
> *AN IRISH AIRMAN FORESEES HIS DEATH* (1919)

Everyone who takes up flying becomes converted from disbelief into enthusiasm. Shortly after his conversion, he may, or may not, kill himself.

> – ROYAL FLYING CORPS MAXIM, CIRCA 1915

Oh, mother, put out your Golden Star,
Your son's gone up in a Sop.
The wings are weak, the ship's a freak,
She's got a rickety prop;
The motor's junk, your son is drunk,
He's sure to take a slop;
Oh, mother, put out your Golden Star,
Your son's gone up in a Sop.

> – RFC MESS SONG, CIRCA 1917, EXTOLLING
> SOPWITH AIRCRAFT[1]

No Canadian was awarded an Air Force Medal during or immediately after the First World War, but many were recipients of Air Force Crosses.[2] The award of the first AFCs was announced in the *London Gazette* of June 3, 1918; two Canadians were included in the lists (Captain John R.S. Devlin and Lieutenant Lawrence N. Mitchell). Up to July 1920 a total of seventy Canadians had been so honoured. Unhappily, no citations were published and documentation of these early AFC winners is exceedingly poor. The stories that follow must be taken as representative of the group.

The first two Canadian AFC winners differed markedly in their experiences. A native of Ottawa, Devlin had enlisted in the Royal Naval Air Service in 1915 and received a Distinguished Service Cross in June 1917 for bombing Turkish bridges in the Balkans. He was posted to Canada in late 1917, becoming an instructor at the School of Artillery Co-Operation, North Toronto. Evidently he was a diligent officer to receive an AFC.

Mitchell, who came from Liverpool, Nova Scotia, had begun his military service with the Canadian Army Medical Corps, switching to the Royal Flying Corps in November 1916. From May 1917 to June 1918 he was a test and acceptance pilot at Hendon. These were routine duties which would nevertheless have entailed many hours of flying. He also had at least one brush with the enemy; on the morning of July 7, 1917, the Germans mounted a daylight Gotha bombing raid on London. The RFC put up 78 aircraft; one of these was a DH.5 (serial A9408) piloted by Mitchell. At 15,000 feet he attacked a bomber which appeared to have one engine stopped, but his own gun jammed, foiling his attempt to deliver a *coup de grace*.[3]

Many appear to have received their AFCs (like Devlin) for instructional work, either in Britain (Lieutenant James G. Crang, awarded AFC on November 2, 1918) or with the Royal Air Force training program in Canada (Major Albert E. Godfrey, who was on the staff of the School of Aerial Fighting, Beamsville, Ontario). Lieutenant Alfred H. Hinton's award may have been connected as much to instructional work as to coastal patrols. Lieutenant Wilfred L. Rutledge of Fort William, Ontario, had been decorated with the Military Medal and Bar while serving with the 28th Battalion in France before transferring to the RFC in April 1917. He saw action as an observer, then retrained as a pilot, instructed in England and flew coastal patrols. His last flying duties (November 1918 to July 1919) were with No. 1 Squadron of the nascent Canadian Air Force in Britain.

S/L George M. Croil, AFC, wearing RCAF formal mess kit, 1927. Note the uncomfortable high collar, based on a similar design used by the Royal Flying Corps during the First World War. Croil's career had included working with Lawrence of Arabia, yet he was best remembered as a stiff, humourless staff officer. (Canadian Forces Photo RE 75-316)

Major George M. Croil and Lieutenant David Allen Harding had both been instructing in Egypt, but had also flown occasional sorties in support of Arab guerillas under the general direction of T.E. Lawrence. The former is mentioned briefly in *Seven Pillars of Wisdom* as having transported Lawrence of Arabia. On December 6, 1917, flying a BE.2c, he made repeated searches for an aircraft that had gone missing near Akaba. Another search, on December 23, 1917, was vividly described in RAF documents:

One of the machines of the search party, having had engine failure, landed in the desert about half-way between Suez and Akaba. Captain Croil showed great resource in flying out himself in a high wind and sandstorm and conducting three other machines carrying mechanics and a large number of spares, tools, and fuel for the disabled machine; landing these beside the disabled machine, which enabled repairs to be carried out, and safely conducting back the three machines under the greatest difficulties against a gale of wind with much sand blowing and obscuring the whole countryside, and seeing them safely landed. As the only two available pilots for two of the machines were pupils, Captain Croil had to fly behind and keep them on the right compass course. In doing this he showed great skill. The journey, which should occupy about an hour, took three hours owing to the gale. Owing to his actions the disabled machine, which would otherwise probably have been lost, was saved and brought in later.[4]

Croil attained the rank of air vice-marshal; he was Chief of Air Staff from 1938 to 1940 but was too formal for the wartime Minister of National Defence for Air, Charles G. Power, who replaced him with the more colourful Lloyd Breadner. Croil became Inspector-General of the RCAF (grand title, little authority); he was promoted to air marshal upon retirement.[5]

Like Croil, Lieutenant David Allen Harding (Petrolia and Sarnia, Ontario) was instructing in Egypt; his specialty was scout (fighter) aircraft, and he was injured in a flying accident on October 4, 1918. Apart from his AFC he was Mentioned in Despatches by General Allenby, but why is uncertain; he may also have been flying air support on behalf of Arab irregulars. Harding served in the RCAF until January 1946, rising to group captain in the process. He was a skilled instructor and participated in many pioneering flights. Harding might have gone further had he not periodically bent regulations (particularly flying rules) between the wars.

Croil and Harding may have met another Canadian, Lieutenant Lewis E. Best, during their operations in Egypt. A native of Victoria, he went overseas with the Canadian Expeditionary Force in 1915, then transferred to the Royal Naval Air Service. His flying career took him to Aboukir and Port Said. In February 1919 he was awarded an AFC. No citation accompanied the announcement, but the origi-

nal recommendation, drafted three months earlier, indicated why he had been singled out for distinction:

> This officer has been one of the most regular seaplane pilots at Port Said, and has carried out long sea patrols in a most satisfactory manner, both as regards escorting convoys and also submarine patrols.[6]

Lieutenant Herbert Asher Vineberg (born September 1893 in Montreal) trained in Canada as a pilot in the summer of 1917 (his only crash was on his first solo flight). He was posted to Britain in September. He took a further course to become an instructor, and in June 1918 was assigned to No. 13 Train-

(Left) Lieutenant David Harding, AFC, wearing Canadian Air Force uniform of 1921. (Right) Harding, photographed in 1941 when he was a wing commander on the staff of No. 16 SFTS, Hagersville, Ontario. For services in the Second World War he would be awarded the OBE. (Canadian Forces Photograph PL-5247)

ing Depot Station, Ternhill, Shropshire. Vineberg ran up nearly 400 hours teaching others to fly Handley-Page bombers, particularly at night. He wrote a handbook on the care and piloting of these machines, for which he was commended. He took refresher training with the Canadian Air Force in the spring of 1921 but did not further pursue flying. Between the wars Vineberg was an investment broker, but he rejoined the RCAF in 1940 and served until 1944 as a Link instructor.

Captain Ellis Anthony (Maitland, Nova Scotia) had a particularly varied career. He joined the Royal Naval Air Service in February 1916 and served in France as a fighter pilot (Nieuports and Sopwith Triplanes) until he was wounded whist strafing enemy troops. Upon recovery, he became a ferry pilot, delivering Camels and DH.4s to France. In a 1921 document he stated that he had lost one machine (type unspecified) in the Channel. His last posting involved anti-submarine patrols with No. 251 Squadron; he commanded a flight. Like many Canadian veterans of RAF service, Anthony took a pilot refresher course at Camp Borden in 1921. He sought to make the air force his career but was refused because of his age (he was 30 in 1924). Between the wars he worked as a coal merchant, but during the Second World War he obtained an RCAF commission and served as a flying control officer at Calgary and Pennfield Ridge. Anthony died in March 1975.

In the case of some Canadian AFC recipients the records are so sketchy that it is difficult to say what marked them out for distinction. Captain Geoffrey Stuart O'Brian (Toronto) was a ferry pilot in 1916 and 1917 and an instructor on JN-4s in Canada in 1918 (200 hours on that type). Frederick P. Holliday (Australian by birth, Canadian by choice), after a distinguished career on Bristol fighters (DSO, MC), spent most of 1918 at training units in Britain. A particularly intriguing case is that of Lieutenant Harvey A. Miller; he appears to have been decorated with both the AFC and a French Croix de Guerre for services in North Russia (late 1918 and early 1919) but what they may have been has not been determined. Miller's credentials as a Canadian are difficult to assess; some sources declare he was from Idaho; a colleague wrote that Miller knew "more of New York than he does of maple leaves."[7]

Lieutenant Herbert A. Vineberg, AFC, was an expert at teaching others to fly Handley-Page bombers in 1918.

Captain Ellis Anthony, AFC, photographed while taking Canadian Air Force refresher flying training, Camp Borden, Ontario, 1921.

Another intriguing award is the AFC to Major Douglas G. Joy of Toronto. In May 1918 he had been commanding No. 105 Squadron, one of two units flying RE.8 army co-operation aircraft, which had been despatched to Ireland at the request of the new Lord Lieutenant, Lord French. The "Irish troubles" were coming to a boil, and French was prepared to use aircraft to police the rural areas. Bombs and machine guns, he declared, "ought to put the fear of God into these playful Sinn Féinners." The British government refused to sanction such extreme measures. Joy's RE.8s flew reconnaissance and communications sorties on behalf of the army but did not undertake any offensive action. Nevertheless, aircrews carried a rifle and at least 250 rounds of ammunition should they force-land in a hostile countryside.[8] The timing of Joy's AFC indicates an association with this work. In August 1920, as a member of the Canadian Air Force, he flew the first air ambulance mission in Canada, transporting a Lieutenant Townley from Camp Borden to Toronto; the passenger was described as suffering from "old war wounds."[9] For most of the interwar period he was a prominent supporter of Canadian flying clubs.

S/L Douglas Joy, AFC, in RCAF uniform, 1929. His work was performed in the context of brewing Irish rebellion in 1918-1919. (National Archives of Canada PA-53741)

G/C John G. Ireland, about 1941. A flying boat pilot on anti-submarine patrols in 1917-18, Ireland was one of many veterans who volunteered again to "do their bit" during the Second World War.

Several Air Force Crosses were awarded for anti-submarine patrols and attacks around the North Sea and English Channel. The manner in which they were granted appears odd; it would seem that such missions, if flown from a base in France, would bring a Distinguished Flying Cross, but when undertaken from a British base they would merit an AFC. This was exactly the inconsistency that C.G. Grey had foreseen when the awards were created.

Captain Jack Graham Ireland of Montreal was one of many Canadians who first learned to fly in the United States before joining the Royal Naval Air Service; he trained at the Wright School, Dayton, Ohio. Subsequently he spent most of his service time on flying boats at Calshot, Felixstowe and Dundee. Although he flew some anti-submarine patrols, the greater part of his time was likely spent instructing. However, he may also have been engaged in experimental work.

Lieutenant Alfred H. Hinton (born in Ottawa, June 1896) had a longstanding interest in aviation, including glider building as early as 1910. He went overseas in September 1916 as a member of the Canadian Field Artillery, but transferred to the Royal Flying Corps in April 1917. He spent six months in France as an observer, then took pilot training. He subsequently flew anti-submarine patrols with No. 36 Squadron, commanding a detached flight of that unit. Between the wars he was a surveyor and mining engineer. From September 1940 to January 1946 he served as a provost officer with the RCAF. He died at Sunnybrook Hospital, Toronto, in 1966.

Captain Kenneth G. Boyd (Goderich and Toronto), another pilot on anti-submarine duties, flew DH.4s. He had one brush with a U-boat, on August 12, 1918. Piloting D8065 off the Belgian coast, in company with three other aircraft, he attacked his target with two 230-pound bombs, at heights varying from 200 to 1,000 feet. He and his gunner also fired 500 rounds of ammu-

nition. The formation dropped a total of eight bombs and claimed direct hits. Although it was believed they had damaged the submarine, the assessment was too optimistic.[10]

The ungainly Blackburn Kangaroo was used in limited numbers but had the most outstanding record of all First World War aircraft in the anti-submarine role. This was partly due to the conditions where it was used – hunts where submarines were known to be. Nevertheless, it offered excellent forward visibility and a rapid rate of turn. In only 600 hours of flying, Kangaroos spotted 12 submarines, attacked 11, damaged four and were instrumental in the destruction of one which was crippled from the air and finished off by a patrol vessel.[11]

Lieutenant Robert R. Richardson (Guelph, Ontario) had been wounded with the Canadian Expeditionary Force in 1916 before transferring to the Royal Naval Air Service. He

The Blackburn Kangaroo looked odd, but it was among the most successful anti-submarine aircraft flown from British bases. Lieutenant Robert R. Richardson made five attacks on enemy U-boats flying this type. (National Archives of Canada PA-6361)

was finally posted to Seaton Carew flying Kangaroos in No. 246 Squadron. Richardson made no fewer than five attacks on submarines, on June 8 and 13, July 26 and 28, and September 3, 1918, but on July 28 his bombs failed to explode while on September 3 there was no surface vessel on hand to exploit his attack. Although his successes were limited, Richardson's enthusiasm was not and his AFC was undoubtedly for this work.[12]

Lieutenant Frederick H. Prime (Toronto) had joined the RNAS in 1916. He spent the war at various seaplane and flying boat stations around Britain. One adventure occurred on July 8, 1918, when he was based in the Scilly Isles. His fellow pilot that day was Captain C.R.H. Stewart. They had taken off in a Large America flying boat (N4234) and had been airborne three hours when engine trouble compelled them to alight on the sea. A hospital ship stood by while the crew attempted to make repairs, but after another two and a half hours, rising seas had so damaged the aircraft that it was finally abandoned. The vessel picked up the crew.[13]

Captain Archibald C. Reid (Winnipeg) had joined the RNAS after attending the Curtiss Flying School in Toronto. He was posted to Dover in May 1917 and served as a seaplane pilot until the end of the war. A contemporary intelligence report describes the most eventful sortie of his career:

June 28th [1918]: Whilst carrying out W/T [wireless telegraphy] test flight a periscope was observed by Seaplane N.2966, pilot Captain Reid, just awash, slowly moving S.W. in position 51 deg. 04 min. 30 sec. N.; 1 min. 18 sec. E. at 1245. When periscope was sighted, machine had passed over spot, and on turning to attack, periscope disappeared. Surface craft informed, and P.57 dropped depth charge in approximate position. Nothing further seen.[14]

Lieutenant Stuart Graham of Wolfville, Nova Scotia, Canada's first bush pilot, did not make much of his First World War adventures. When nominated in 1948 for the McKee Trophy, his sponsors could provide only the briefest description of that portion in his career:

Mr. Stuart Graham was studying electrical engineering at the outbreak of World War I and decided to forgo a degree for uniform. He joined the 5th Canadian Mounted Rifles at Montreal in 1915 and went overseas as a machine gunner.

Wounded in action at Ypres, he spent a year in hospital in England and then obtained transfer to the Royal Naval Air Service, was selected for pilot training in France and eventually on completion of this training was posted to [anti] submarine duties as pilot of a Short seaplane. In due course, he transferred to the Royal Air Force and for successful anti-submarine activities was awarded the Air Force Cross. After the Armistice, he continued for several months with the RAF engaged in mine destruction patrol work over the English Channel.[15]

Fortunately for historians, his logbook has survived, although it shows a career somewhat different from that just cited. His training commenced on November 14, 1917, flying Caudron biplanes; Graham soloed December 3 after five hours 56 minutes of dual instruction. He went on to Calshot, logging time on such types as the FBA and Norman Thompson flying boats and Short 184 seaplanes; on three occasions he had to force land after engine trouble.

Late in March 1918 he was assigned to the Cattewater Air Station in Devonshire to conduct anti-submarine patrols, searches and occasional exercises with the Royal Navy. He continued to fly Short 184 seaplanes until July 9, when he re-

Norman Thompson flying boat. Among Canadian AFC winners who flew this type was Stuart Graham (National Archives of Canada PA-6379)

turned to Calshot and was given the equivalent of operational training on Felixstowe F2A flying boats. However, his log entries suggest he had difficulties with this type, which he described as "no good for school work." He was given a passing mark, but when he returned to Cattewater on July 28 it was to resume flying on Short seaplanes. His logbook confirms that he was awarded the AFC for anti-submarine patrols. However, contrary to the 1948 account, Graham recorded no mine-detection sorties after the Armistice, although he did report a successful search for a missing DH.9 and continued fleet manoeuvres. By the time he was demobilized he had flown 355 hours.

A few entries from Stuart Graham's logbook, however understated, show the nature of his work and the adventures that could befall a pilot far from the European battlefields:

[April 22, 1918 on Short N2832 – five hours in the air]: Sighted large enemy submarine at 1544 in "41 H" [a map reference, precise location unknown]. Dropped 230 [pound bomb] and 100 lb. 230 fell 50 feet to starboard 10 seconds after submergence. 100 lb 50 feet ahead of wake 2 seconds later.

[May 17, 1918 on Short C1984 – airborne one hour 30 minutes]: Visibility very good. Vibration set up owing to unbalanced engine (five magneto leads adrift). Forced to land in 59B. Taxied home arriving 0300.

[May 19, 1918, on Short B1624 – airborne one hour 35 minutes]: Visibility very good. Main petrol feed adrift. Forced landing. Towed by destroyer #108; arrived home 1800.

[May 27, 1918, on Short N1258 – airborne six hours, flying at 1,400 feet]: Visibility poor. Sighted and bombed super-submarine at 1715 BST [British Summer Time] in 49.17. First bomb burst 70 feet to starboard quarter 10 seconds after submersion. Second bomb burst 30 feet to starboard quarter two seconds later. Large air discharge immediately ahead of point of submersion commencing about 7 seconds after submersion continuing for 45 seconds.

[June 6, 1918, on Short N2836, airborne four hours 10 minutes]: Forced to land in 71 DRE. Repaired engine trouble and took off again. Met destroyers in 59 VST but not convoy.

[June 27, 1918, on Short N2836, airborne three hours 35 minutes]: Visibility very good. Sighted what appeared to be upturned submarine. Landed and on examination proved to be large whale (dead).

[July 7, 1918, on Short N1762, airborne 20 minutes]: Observer began unwinding aerial in harbour; cleared mast of ship by 15 feet and had aerial carried away.

[August 31, 1918, on Short N2799, airborne five hours 45 minutes]: Visibility fair. Struck coast of Guernsey and Alderney. Machine OK. Used up all petrol.

Some First World War fliers subsequently became pioneers of commercial aviation. Stuart Graham, AFC, photographed here about 1928, was Canada's first "bush pilot." (National Aviation Museum of Canada)

Although his attack of May 27 appeared promising, the submarine escaped undamaged. What stands out from Graham's logbook is the duration of his patrols; most were slightly over three hours long, but it was not uncommon to be airborne more than five hours. In light of his future as Canada's first bush pilot, an interesting entry is that of November 6, 1918, when an American naval ensign took him for a short hop in a Curtiss HS2 flying boat; Graham wrote, "Found HS2 very nice to fly and very stable."[16]

Unwittingly, Graham played a role in a small incident which underlined Canada's "colonial" status in the eyes of British authorities. In the summer of 1918 a force was being organized to fly anti-submarine patrols from Canadian bases; it was to be named the Royal Canadian Naval Air Service. He applied to transfer to the new organization, but the switch did not go through. His request had generated concern in British officers who perceived a problem of principal – "whether the Air Ministry will allow RAF officers to transfer to the Royal Canadian Naval Air Service." That Graham was a Canadian attempting to join a Canadian formation seemed irrelevant to those in authority. In fairness to the British, it appears that some officers feared a mass exodus of Canadians from the

Short 225 torpedo bomber and anti-submarine patrol aircraft. The type was flown by many Canadians, including Stuart Graham. (National Archives of Canada PA-6420)

Royal Air Force at a time when they constituted 35 per cent of the flying personnel of that organization.[17]

In the matter of records (or lack thereof), Captain Reginald Sheridan Carroll of London, Ontario, was an exception, both as to duties and to documentation. He had been employed by the Canadian Bank of Commerce in 1915, prior to his enlistment in the Royal Flying Corps. Soon after the war the bank compiled a two-volume study of its employees' military services, which was published under the title *Letters from the Front*. Thanks to this project, Carroll's recollections have come down to us.

He had joined the RFC on December 7, 1915, sailed to England, and received training as a Corps pilot, specializing in co-operation with army units. With only 17 hours 44 minutes flying time, Carroll had gone to France to fly BE.2c biplanes with No. 4 Squadron. The commanding officer insisted that he fly as much as possible for a week before even allowing him over the lines. In all, he served nine months in combat, directing artillery fire, conducting occasional reconnaissance flights, and surviving mercifully rare scraps with enemy fighters. He returned from one flight with his aircraft riddled by machine gun fire; during another flight an ack-ack burst severely wounded his observer and bloodied Carroll about the nose and right eye.

The work that eventually led to his receiving an AFC was described by him in a long epistle to the compilers of *Letters from the Front*; his own account is worth quoting:

At the close of the Somme campaign, I was recalled to England to take up the duties of a ferry pilot between Farnborough, Hants, England, and St. Omer, France. My new duties consisted of flying new machines to the Expeditionary Force in France, and flying back the old time-served machines from France to England, where they were finally dismantled and scrapped. During the time I was engaged on this work I made 130 cross-channel flights, and delivered 100 new machines to the Expeditionary Force.

In June 1916 [sic – he more likely means June 1917] I was posted as a test pilot to No. 8 Aircraft Acceptance Park, Lyminge, Kent. Here my duties consisted of testing new machines for the first time after erection at the aircraft factories. After about three months' service in this capacity, I was posted as Officer-in-Charge of Experimental Tests and Despatch, to No. 1 Southern Aircraft Repair Depot, Farnborough, Hants. I was greatly elated over receiving this important appointment, as it carried with it promotion to the rank of Captain. My new duties, however, were extremely responsible, and, to say the least, very arduous. They consisted of carrying out experimental, production, demonstration and performance tests on all types of aircraft.

No. 1 Southern Aircraft Repair Depot was the principal Aircraft Experimental Station in England; consequently numerous inspections were made of the Depot, by their Majesties the King and Queen, also inspections by Ministers and Delegates from all the Allied foreign countries. On three occasions I had the honour of giving exhibition flights before their Majesties the King and Queen, after which I was duly presented. On another occasion I took a Japanese delegation for a flight in a Handley-Page machine, and another time an Italian delegation on a machine of the same type.

Carroll's work hitherto was interesting enough, but not the stuff for an award. However, he was about to become involved in work associated with British parachutes. Such devices had been known for years: 19th-century balloonists had often spiced up their acts with a parachute descent, and in wartime the crews of vulnerable kite balloons, directing artillery fire, had routinely been issued with parachutes; at least 800 British and American observers were said to have saved their lives after their platforms had been shot down burning, to say nothing of the uncounted French, Italians and Germans who had survived through the same device. By 1917 parachutes were being used to drop spies behind German lines, and on occasion supplies were being delivered to isolated units in the same manner.

Nevertheless, parachutes were not issued to crews of powered aircraft. In 1914 and 1915 there were good reasons; the devices were bulky, difficult to store in the cockpit of an underpowered airplane, unreliable, and almost impossible to use in an emergency. Initially, too, there was the feeling on the part of senior officers that aircrew who had parachutes would somehow fly and fight less enthusiastically than those without an escape mechanism; early pilots may also have felt that the man with a parachute was something of a "sissy." The fighting man's opinion changed as more and more comrades perished in burning aircraft, and no one viewed the balloon observer to be an inferior being for having saved himself by parachute as his blazing gas bag plunged to the ground.

By 1917 there were fewer excuses; proper parachutes had been developed, but authorities, particularly in Britain, seemed to invent reasons for not making them part of general issue. Two forceful but tactless individuals were pressing for the adoption of parachutes. Everard Calthorpe had invented one which, with a pitchman's skill, he had dubbed the "Guardian Angel." He had been testing it, principally with his own funds, since 1915. He enlisted the support of a Royal Marine officer, Major T. Orde-Lees, a man so unlikeable that, as one of 22 men marooned for three months during the Shackleton Antarctic Expedition of 1913-1915, he had been considered the first candidate for devouring should the party have had to resort to cannibalism. Orde-Lees demonstrated the early "Guardian Angel" by jumping from London's Tower Bridge. When the Air Ministry established a parachute committee in June 1918, he was selected to chair it.

Unfortunately, the Air Ministry insisted upon a rigid and comprehensive test program, even after August 1918 when it became clear that German aircrew were now routinely using parachutes. Although Orde-Lees conducted scores of trials – in at least five instances he personally jumped from under 300 feet – authorities insisted upon comparisons of several 'chutes involving numerous aircraft. In fact, the only airplane that seemed to be difficult to reconcile with parachutes was the Sopwith Camel, and the only major hitch occurred when a parachute with a dummy weight attached snagged briefly on the tail hook of a Bristol Fighter. The over-testing of parachutes – an excessive quest for perfection – delayed their introduction into the RAF until 1922. Even in the last year of the war, hundreds of pilots and gunners might have survived, but for bureaucratic stalling and indifference.[18]

However, let us resume with Reginald Carroll's account of his wartime services:

One of the most interesting, and at the same time most important series of experiments I carried out comprised the release of parachutes from aircraft. Just prior to the Armistice the German Flying Corps had adopted a very crude knapsack type of parachute, but despite its poor workmanship this parachute functioned most successfully, and reduced the casualties among their pilots and observers by nearly 60 per cent.

Up to this time no attempt had been made to adopt parachutes on British aircraft, although our casualties were in proportion nearly 25 per cent heavier than the infantry.

However, the insistent propaganda on the part of Major Orde-Lees, who for two years had been agitating for the adoption of parachutes on aircraft, eventually found its reward, and I was asked to undertake the carrying out of these experiments, which involved at the start the release of dead weights attached to the harness of the parachute, and later the release of "live loads."

I released parachutes to which were attached dead weights from all of our principal service machines, both of the single and two-seater types, and these experiments having proved eminently successful, I continued same with Major Orde-Lees, who on numerous occasions made jumps at varying altitudes from the De Havilland 4 and De Havilland 9 machines, and it was while thus demonstrating in France, before Major-General Trenchard – General Officer Commanding Independent Air Force – that the Armistice was signed.

On August 8, 1918 I made formal application to the Air Ministry – in view of American intentions – for permission to attempt the Atlantic flight on any type of aeroplane or seaplane that might be deemed suitable for an expedition of this character. A week later I was ordered to report to the Air Ministry for the purpose of an interview re this flight. During the interview I was informed that my application, which was the first of its kind, so I was advised, had been accepted, and I was then requested to apply myself to the study of the Atlantic charts and to hold myself in readiness to leave England for America at 48 hours' notice. However, I heard nothing more of this project until after the Armistice, when I was informed that owing to the exceptionally keen competition on the part of the civil aircraft manufacturers, the Air Ministry had abandoned the Atlantic expedition so far as "heavier-than-air" machines were concerned, and would concentrate entirely upon the organization of an Atlantic flight by "lighter-than-air" craft.

Whilst I was in command of the Tests and Despatch at No. 1 Southern Aircraft Repair Depot, I carried out 1,302 test flights on all types of aircraft, and tested a total of 1,046 new machines. I have flown 86 distinct types of aircraft and 143 types of aircraft engines.

I have now been flying for four years and two months, and have flown for a period of 1,386 hours.

In January of this year [1919] I was posted to No. 1 Communication Squadron, Hendon, to take up duties of "Peace Conference Pilot" between London and Paris. I had the honour of conveying the first official Government mails and despatches by air to the headquarters of the Peace Conference, Hotel Majestic, Paris. On other occasions I have piloted Major-General [J.E.A.] Seely, Mr. Bonar Law, Lord Londonderry, and many other celebrities, on various expeditions to France in connection with the Peace Conference.[19]

Captain Carroll was awarded his AFC on January 1, 1919. Immediately after the war he made several pioneering flights in India, Malaya and Singapore. His airfields were race courses and golf greens; his trademark was aerobatics before crowds still unaccustomed to aircraft; his most significant flights saw him scattering advertising leaflets over Penang and transporting a modest cargo from Klang to Kuala Lumpur, some 20 miles distant. His barnstorming "east of Suez" was cut short when his employer, the Nieuport Aircraft Company of Great Britain, folded. By April 1921 he was back in the RAF, first on temporary duty, then with a short service commission. As of 1923 he was serving again at the Experimental Section, Farnborough. He relinquished his commission and was placed on the Reserve List in June 1926. The subsequent career of this itinerant Canadian is unknown.[20]

The records respecting Captain Alexander M. Shook, DSO, DSC, are detailed in some respects, sketchy in others. Born in Peel County, Ontario, in 1888, he had been teaching school at Red Deer, Alberta, when the war broke out. After obtaining a pilot's certificate at the Curtiss Flying School, Toronto, he had joined the Royal Naval Air Service and flown extensively from Dover and Dunkirk. He received a French Croix de Guerre in July 1917, a Distinguished Service Cross in August 1917 for "repeatedly attacking and destroying hostile aircraft," and the Distinguished Service Order in January 1918, "in recognition of services in the prosecution of the war." As of the spring of 1918 he was with No. 5 Group (headquarters at Dover, responsibilities on both sides of the Channel). On May 30 he was made responsible for discipline and flying of the group pilots pool. His orders read: "Captain Shook will endeavour to start a system of training with a view to teaching the new pilots the country, showing them the various aerodromes and position of the lines in this area."

He took up his duties on June 5 and soon recognized an array of problems. Pilots trained at large airfields such as Cranwell adjusted poorly to cramped operational bases; several overshot the new fields and crashed into obstacles beside the airstrips. Shook had a poor opinion of their formation flying skills – "Instead of one formation of five machines here were five formations of one machine" – and increased this type of training with himself as the chief instructor. New pilots had scant knowledge of engines, and although they had fired thousands of Lewis rounds at gun butts, they had received almost none on Vickers machine guns. They also lacked air-to-air firing experience. He proposed a radical expansion of firing drill, both on the ground and in the air, including use of a derelict airplane for shooting at gun butts. This would familiarize pilots with the sense of sitting and firing from a stationary aircraft before doing the same thing airborne.[21]

On July 1 he filed a report on his accomplishments the previous month. It constitutes the fullest account of the work which brought him an AFC a year later. It also demonstrates the nature of what was virtually operational training in 1918. After summarizing June figures (323 hours flown, 40 pilots sent to squadrons, 33 still under instruction), he went on:

Fifty-one pilots have been given formation practice and have been shown the lines and the aerodromes in the vicinity of Dunkirk. Whenever weather permits formation patrols take the following course: Audembert along the coast to Nieuport, along the lines to Dixmude, back over aerodromes at Dunkirk, inland to St. Omer and back to Acceptance Park Aerodrome.

Considerable practice has been done on machine guns, and an endeavour has been made to have all pilots leave the Pool with at least a working knowledge of his guns.

An average of only eight men a day has been available for working on Pool machines with the result that pilots have had to push machines in and out of the hangars, and start all engines. Two pilots have been injured while starting engines due to there being an insufficient number of experienced officers to take charge.

An endeavour has been made to give all pilots at least three hours local flying and from three to five hours formation practice, and all Camel pilots are given practice in running engines to ensure that they are able to adjust the mixture readily.

An attempt has been made by means of pictures, drawings, silhouettes and verbal descriptions to enable pilots to readily recognize machines, both Allied and enemy, in the air.

Huffing [stalling] practice and maneouvering machines in the air is practised on all local flights and considerable proficiency has been shown by all pilots before leaving the Pool.

Nearly all these branches of instruction have not received the attention at training schools in England that they should have. Pilots invariably express a strong desire for more practice, and more instruction, but owing to the limited staff available at Pilots Pool they are not getting anything like the instruction they show the need of.

It is submitted that the minimum formation practice be placed at five hours; that no pilot should go to a squadron with less than 50 hours flying; that the gunnery course be extended and at least a limited degree of proficiency obtained; and that the Pool be provided with an Armament Officer and at least another experienced Flying Officer for instructional purposes.[22]

The timing of Shook's AFC (June 1919) clearly shows that it was for more than his activities with No. 5 Group Pilots Pool, but subsequent records are sketchy. He was given charge of Leysdown Station in July 1918 and went to No. 2 School of Observation (Manston) in mid-September. He was repatriated to Canada in February 1919 and discharged the following month.

Charles Eardley Wilmot had an exceptionally varied career between 1917 and 1922. A native of Newcastle, Ontario, he joined the RFC in late 1916, trained in Canada, and subsequently instructed at Camp Mohawk (Deseronto) and in Texas, logging about 500 hours on JN-4s. Proceeding overseas early in 1918, he continued as an instructor, first at Cranwell and then Gosport; during these assignments he flew Avro 504s (approximately 200 hours), Sopwith Camels (200 hours), Sopwith Pups (100 hours) and De Havilland 4s (50 hours). He was awarded the AFC in June 1919.

Wilmot could have obtained a commission in the RAF. Instead, he chose demobilization (November 1919) and joined a Handley-Page Company mission to South America, demonstrating British aircraft and training Argentinian air force pilots. Over two years he logged 200 hours on Sopwith Dragonflies, about 150 hours on SE.5s, plus lesser times on Handley-Page bombers, Martinside Scouts and Norman Thompson flying boats. The adventure ended when an aircraft caught fire in the air. Wilmot force-landed and escaped with burns to his face and arms; soon after returning to Canada the mission was disbanded.

Between the wars he sold automobiles, farmed, helped organize the Kingston Flying Club and later the Norfolk County Flying Club. He joined the RCAF in 1939 and became an instructor once more, first at Camp Borden and then Uplands. Sadly, he was killed on October 15, 1941; taking a shortcut across the tarmac, he was struck by a taxiing Harvard.

Albert Earl Godfrey of Vancouver was one of the most remarkable officers ever to serve in the RCAF. A friendly, popular figure (long known as "Father Godfrey"), he was proud of two accomplishments above all else. One was having held, from 1910 to 1944, virtually every rank from bugler to air vice-marshal; the other was that in September 1943, manning a machine gun aboard an Eastern Air Command Liberator attacking a U-boat, he became the most senior Canadian officer to fire directly on the enemy during the Second World War.

A veteran of trench warfare and expert with machine guns, Godfrey transferred from the Canadian Expeditionary Force to the Royal Flying Corps in July 1916. He flew as an observer until December, when he was posted to England, trained as a pilot, then returned to France. Flying Nieuport 17s with No. 40 Squadron, he shot down 13 enemy aircraft and earned the Military Cross.

From September 1917 to April 1918 Godfrey flew with Home Defence squadrons, operating Sopwith Camels in futile attempts to intercept nocturnal German bombers. "During all my night flying I never saw a Hun machine," he later wrote. He did, however, have a novel idea about how nocturnal raiders *should* be intercepted. He suggested that rather than having London blacked out, the city should be illuminated so that bombers would be silhouetted and evident to fighters patrolling higher up! Several years later, while commanding the Air Board station at Jericho Beach, he tested his theory with aircraft flying over Vancouver at night and concluded that he had been correct.

In the spring of 1918 Godfrey was posted to Canada, first as an instructor, then assuming command of No. 1 Squadron, School of Aerial Fighting, at Beamsville, Ontario. He was promoted to major in September 1918 and made chief instructor of the whole school.[23] The School of Aerial Fighting was a very large establishment, with roughly 100 JN-4 trainers, one Camel, and one Avro 504 (a type which would have supplanted the "Jenny" had the war gone on). It was a finishing school for aircrew trained in Canada. Cadets arrived with some 30 hours of aerial experience and were taught bombing, gunnery and air fighting tactics for about ten hours before being shipped overseas. Preparations for winter training were cut short by the Armistice.

Aircraft overhead were now a familiar sight in much of Canada, but when one actually *landed* in a town it might still be considered as newsworthy. Thus the Welland *Telegraph* of

August 7, 1918, printed a headline, "FIRST PASSENGER REACHES WELLAND BY AIR PLANE," followed by the story of "Instructor Godfrey," on August 4, flying Captain J.R. Reilly from Beamsville to Welland, some 20 miles away. They had some difficulty selecting a landing site (the local fair grounds had too many poles) and finally alighted in a soft field of buckwheat. Reilly was left behind; Godfrey returned to base.[24]

Just after the Armistice, the school was visited by Brigadier C.G. Hoare, the British officer in charge of all RAF training in Canada. He had never seen Niagara Falls, some 40 miles distant, and asked Godfrey to fly him over the cataract. They used the Avro 504, cruising over at 3,000 feet. Hoare banged on the fuselage and motioned for a descent; Godfrey dropped to 2,000 feet, then 1,000 feet, but his superior still seemed dissatisfied with the view. Finally, Godfrey circled near the head of the falls, put the nose down, and dived into the gorge, sailing under the Honeymoon Bridge (located where the Rainbow Bridge now stands) before being trapped in the gorge by eddies and downdraughts. The Avro shuddered on the edge of a stall; it was a stunt that had been forbidden to cadets.

A second bridge offered less clearance; Godfrey made a hair-raising 180-degree turn, narrowly missing rock walls, then hauled the Avro out of the gorge, skimming rooftops as he did; Hoare shouted for a return to base. When they touched down, the general was furious, frightened and profane. Hurling his helmet to the ground, he swore he would never fly again. He soon broke his vow, and evidently forgave his pilot by recommending Godfrey for an AFC.[25] Late in November 1918, writing to Air Ministry, Hoare described Godfrey as "a remarkably fine pilot himself and a very fine officer." He also pointed out that Godfrey, an acting major, had succeeded a British lieutenant-colonel "who could not begin to take on the job." This is probably as close as one may get to the original recommendation.[26]

In a paper he wrote while attending RAF Staff College, Godfrey described the School of Aerial Fighting but said little of his own meritorious role. Nevertheless, he incorporated some revealing comments which indicate what made him so successful, both before and after his Beamsville experiences:

More than once during my service with the Air Force did I congratulate myself on the knowledge I had of machine guns. I must say that I was fortunate in receiving no less than five machine-gun courses during the war. With this knowledge, which I considered imperative at times, and used to its fullest extent, I always looked after my own guns, in fact was most particular about this and gained in the long run, as I never had a stoppage in the air due to gun or ammunition.

I would strongly recommend young observers and scout pilots to almost live with their guns until to handle and operate them become second nature.

On many occasions during the war I remember incidents when formations were on patrol they were caught in rain or snow storms and invariably broke up their formations; the majority lost their way and had forced landings. In most cases the cause was through inexperience in low flying in bad weather. To overcome this pilots should be trained in low flying under bad weather conditions; it would be useful not only in war, but in peace flying as well.

Only once during my career with the Air Service did I have the opportunity of seeing the Commander of the Air Force. It gives one the impression that there is a tendency among the senior officers to completely overlook the existence of the junior officers. The same conditions prevail among the junior officers, as I have noticed, much to my regret, how a great many of them completely ignore the existence of the men. In my opinion there is nothing that keeps up the spirit of the personnel more than occasional visits from senior officers.[27]

Godfrey joined the postwar RCAF. In 1926, in company with a wealthy American, James D. McKee, he undertook a flight from Canada to Montreal. Shortly afterwards, McKee created a trophy to be awarded annually to the Canadian who contributed most to aviation in the preceding year. Godfrey undertook another lengthy flight (Montreal to Vancouver) in 1928; he commanded schools and bases, and ultimately was appointed Air Officer Commanding, Eastern Air Command, and then Deputy Inspector-General.

In this last role he often piloted his own aircraft (an Avro Anson) as he checked various bases. On one occasion he landed as the welcoming parade was forming up. An NCO approached and shouted, "The CO said to get the hell out of here and take this aircraft, too; we're expecting the Inspector General." Godfrey (who was wearing ordinary flying clothes) asked where he was to go. "I don't know – he didn't tell me that," came the reply. "Maybe I'd better leave it here," Godfrey suggested; that upset his one-man reception committee terribly. Finally, Godfrey climbed out of the Anson, followed by his aide; he removed his flying helmet, put on his service cap replete with "scrambled egg," and strolled over the inspect the parade.[28]

Captain Albert E. Godfrey, MC, AFC, photographed in 1919. He wears the original AFC ribbon with horizontal stripes. In the second photo, as a squadron leader wearing RCAF mess kit in 1928, he wears the "authorized" ribbon of his AFC. (Canadian Forces Photograph RE-17475-2, National Aviation Museum of Canada)

Curiously, he received no awards for his Second World War service, although other senior officers were created Commanders of the Order of the British Empire or Companions of the Order of the Bath. Perhaps Godfrey's politics were held against him – he ran for Parliament as a Co-operative Commonwealth Federation candidate in 1945. On the other hand, by retiring early to seek office he may simply have left the RCAF too soon; honours for senior officers cascaded down immediately following VE-Day. In any case, the last formal honour granted him was the McKee Trophy, presented in 1977 at the 50th anniversary of this prestigious award. He died on January 2, 1982, in Kingston, Ontario.[29]

Godfrey was one of several instructors decorated for their services in Canada in 1917-1918. Lieutenant John Owen Leach from Toronto had been decorated with the Military Cross as an infantry officer, then transferred to the Royal Flying Corps. He became a fighter pilot in France but was wounded on May 25, 1917; one leg was amputated below the knee. This could not keep him on the ground. He persuaded his superiors to keep him on the flying list as an instructor. He was posted to Canada, where he served at Armour Heights, then Deseronto.

Isolated newspaper stories reveal a little of Leach. On June 1, 1918, he participated in a flight of 12 JN-4s from Leaside to Beamsville to coincide with an inspection of the latter base by the Governor General. On that occasion he was described as "the best flyer in Canada." Although one may detect some journalistic hyperbole, he was nevertheless good enough that General Hoare had Leach pilot the "Jenny" that returned him from Beamsville to Toronto. On July 25, 1918, as the senior training officer at Armour Heights, Leach was called as an expert witness before a coroner's inquest investigating a crash that had killed a student pilot. He testified as to how records were kept on students and aircraft, the hazards of looping, and the general causes of aircraft accidents. Late in 1918 he was posted back to England to help organize a Canadian Air Force, but the new force never saw action.[30]

A native of Metcalfe, Ontario, John Alfred Sully had served in the Canadian Expeditionary Force before transferring to the Royal Flying Corps on February 14, 1917. He went to France as an observer, joining No. 70 Squadron on March 25. On May 9, 1917 his aircraft was attacked by about 15 enemy fighters. While his pilot took evasive action, Sully fired a burst which sent one of the fighters down in flames.[31] Soon afterwards he returned to England to train as a pilot. He was Mentioned in Despatches in June 1917, no doubt for his recent display of fine gunnery in France. Afterwards, Sully was employed at the School of Special Flying (August 1 to December 1, 1917) before assignment to the British Aviation Mission to the United States (January 1 to December 14, 1918). His particular task was to help introduce the Gosport system of training to the United States Army Air Service; he later described himself as an "instructor of instructors" at Brooks Field, New York. He was promoted to major in the course of his assignment. Apart from the Air Force Cross (*London Gazette* of January 1, 1919) he was accorded an American honour, the Aviation Medal of Merit, issued by the Aeronautical Society of America.

Between the wars he was engaged in the insurance business in Winnipeg, where he also kept in his hand as a private pilot and organized the Winnipeg Flying Club. He was also a militia officer until the RCAF Auxiliary was formed in 1932, when he took command of No. 12 (Army Cooperation) Squadron. He was mobilized for wartime service, recruited, commanded Station Trenton, and ultimately became Air Member for Personnel at AFHQ with the rank of air vice-marshal; he retired in April 1945.

Major John Scott Williams (born in Goldenville, Nova Scotia, 1892) had been a truck driver with the Canadian Expeditionary Force when he transferred to the Royal Flying Corps in 1916. As an observer with No. 22 Squadron he was awarded a Military Cross. Late in 1916 he went to England, trained as a pilot, and remained to instruct. In April 1920, when applying to the Canadian Air Board for a commercial pilot's certificate, he described his activities as follows:

The standard RAF training machine in Canada was the Curtiss JN-4, popularly known as the "Jenny." The aircraft were supplemented by training aids, including the earliest flight simulators and cameras married to machine guns. Sophisticated training techniques were forgotten between the world wars and had to be reinvented in 1938-1939.

I left France in November 1916 after doing 480 hours flying with 22 Squadron and was posted to Gosport. I was one of the originators of the Gosport School of Special Flying and I remained there as Flight Commander until July 1918. Was then sent to Ayr, Scotland to organize and command the Flying Instructors School for Scotland and Ireland. Originated the Travelling Flight System of instruction adopted shortly before the Armistice by the RAF. Personally instructed all the senior Naval officers for duty on Hush Hush machines and commanded the only two official Aircraft Exhibitions.

Williams may have exaggerated (for purposes of his application) his contributions to the development of the training program, but his award, coupled with his rapid promotion, indicated he had been a significant figure. The "Aircraft Exhibitions" were RAF static and flying displays staged at Newcastle, Leeds and London in the spring and summer of 1919. The Newcastle show included possibly the earliest formation aerobatics in the world, using Avro 504s. Immediately after the war he essayed commercial flying in British Columbia under the name of Aircraft Manufacturing Limited, in company with Captain E.C. Hoy, DFC, and backed by several Vancouver businessmen. He stressed his supporters (who included the Lieutenant-Governor) to prove that the firm was no "joy-riding, fly-by-night concern."[32]

In July 1920 Williams was appointed to command the Canadian Air Force training wing at Camp Borden with the rank of lieutenant-colonel – further proof that his association with the Gosport schools had made him a valuable asset to any training scheme. In January 1921 he finally received his Air Force Cross – in the mail. The CAF, a part-time air force at that time, released him, in July 1921 and he returned to civil flying. Aircraft Manufacturing Limited failed, and from 1926 forwards he was engaged in mining and general contracting. In September 1940 he joined the RCAF as an administrative officer, serving at Calgary, Lachine and Regina. He died of natural causes on New Year's Day 1944.

Malcolm Millard Sisley was born at Ellesmere, Ontario, in August 1891 and educated at Markham. In May 1915 he attended the Curtiss Flying School in Toronto, after which he was accepted by the Royal Flying Corps. In July 1916 he was posted to France, where he flew approximately 216 hours on bombing, photography and artillery direction duties with Nos. 10 and 16 Squadrons. A typical mission was one flown on January 26, 1917, in a BE.2e; he dropped two bombs (each weighing 20 pounds) on a road near the enemy front and reported the results as having a "moral effect" on the enemy.[33]

As of June 1917 he was instructing in England, but later that summer he was posted to Canada and the RFC training establishment, which was now well under way. The records are unclear; he may have flown as little as 280 hours or as many as 500 hours whilst so employed; his major postings were to No. 80 Canadian Training Squadron, Leaside (August 1917), No. 88 Canadian Training Squadron, Armour Heights (September 1917, moving to Evermeyer, Texas, for the winter of 1917-1918), No. 42 Wing, Deseronto, as examining officer (May 1918) and No. 81 Canadian Training Squadron, Armour Heights (July 1918). He had attained

G/C Malcolm M. Sisley, AFC, taken in 1941. His AFC work in Canada may have had as much to do with disciplinary investigations as with actual flying.

the rank of captain in June 1918 and major in November 1918. Along the way, while serving at Armour Heights, he had taken his 65-year-old father up in a JN-4.

While serving in Canada, Sisley was given a thorough medical examination. The tour in France had strained his health; on October 19, 1917 he was advised that he was "fit for service in Canada only, not to be allowed to fly above altitude of one thousand feet." We can be sure that he ignored that limitation. He subsequently took an advanced course for instructors emphasizing the theory of flight, spin recovery and other difficult manoeuvres. Applying the course in the context of Canadian training probably earned him his AFC.

Meanwhile, the RFC and RAF in Canada was having peculiar difficulties – that of men impersonating officers. In February 1918 the British Air Mission in Washington complained that many civilian instructors at American flying schools were claiming previous service with the RFC or RNAS; the imposters wore uniforms in towns (where they were bound to have an impact on ladies and bartenders) but made sure not to wear them on an army base. At least one was known to have been an RFC officer who had been released from the service in 1916 for having failed to be an "efficient pilot."[34] Just as hostilities ceased, Major Sisley was appointed an assistant provost marshal and attached to the British Embassy in Washington. His assignment was to locate Canadian and British soldiers who were absent without leave or who had become "confidence men" using their uniforms to gain credibility. He received a certificate of commendation for this work, deemed to have been for "the maintenance of British prestige."

Sisley had three brothers who joined the flying services; two died in action (Arthur in September 1917, Donovan in March 1918). He retired in September 1919 and became a car dealer. He rejoined the RCAF in October 1939, remaining until January 1946. He was given the job of organizing provost services within the RCAF, eventually becoming Provost Marshal with the rank of group captain. In January 1946 he was recommended for an OBE, but it failed to reach the Priority List for such awards. He died in March 1957.[35]

James Stanley Scott, like Sisley and Godfrey, was involved in First World War training in North America. His was an odd career. Born in Roberval, Quebec, in 1889, he attended private schools in Quebec City and was commissioned in the Canadian Expeditionary Force upon the outbreak of war. He went overseas as a gunnery officer, but in October 1915 he was seconded to the Royal Flying Corps. After training as a pilot he went to France flying reconnaissance missions as a Corps pilot (i.e., army co-operation work), first with No. 5 Squadron, then No. 6 Squadron. In July 1916 he was awarded a Military Cross, having strafed enemy trenches at low level and returned to Allied lines with his aircraft shot about like a colander. Soon afterwards he was severely injured while landing at night.

When the Royal Flying Corps established its training programme in Canada, Captain Scott was posted to Camp Borden. He was successively staff officer in charge of training, station commander when part of the training program was located in Texas, and commander of No. 44 Wing, Camp Borden, a post he held until the Armistice. Scott was innovative; he adapted the JN-4 to skis to enable training to continue in the winter months. He was promoted to major on June 18, 1917, and to lieutenant-colonel on September 1, 1918. Although no recommendation or citation for his AFC has been found, his duties and rapid rise in rank clearly indicate an instructor and staff officer of exceptional merit. In January 1918, Brigadier Hoare described Scott as "an admirable officer." In November 1918 he went further in a letter to Air Ministry:

I have an officer at Borden (Major J.S. Scott, MC) who has run a Wing about the size of Netheravon and Upavon together for a year. He is an administrative officer of considerable ability, very much beyond the average Wing Commander in the RAF, and there is no question about his flying ability.[36]

Piecing together his wartime flying is difficult, but on July 26, 1920, he prepared a list of aircraft types he had flown to that date. With hours flown in brackets, they were as follows:

England (1915)	France (1916)	Canada/U.S. (1917-1918)
Farman Longhorn (12)	BE.2c (115)	Curtiss JN-4 (600)
Farman Shorthorn (12)	BE.2d (190)	
Caudron (20)	BE.2e (25)	
Avro (25)	Morane (2)	
BE.2b (10)	De Havilland (2)	
RE.8 (5)	FE.8 (3)	

After the war he returned to civilian life, but in November 1919 he was appointed Superintendent, Certificates Branch of the newly-formed Canadian Air Board, November 4, 1919. Soon afterwards the post became that of Controller of Civil Aviation in Canada under the Air Board. He held this position from April 1920 to the end of June 1922. He was also a member of the Air Board (April 1920 to July 1922). From July 13, 1921, to June 30, 1922, he was a wing commander and commanding officer of the semi-permanent Canadian Air Force. After some months in command at Camp Borden, he went overseas to take the RAF Staff Course at Andover before becoming head of the Air Service (Director, RCAF), May 19, 1924, to February 14, 1928. Scott was promoted to group captain on April 1, 1925; he was also appointed Honorary Aide de Camp to the Governor General. His RCAF service number was the easiest to remember; it was "C.1."

Scott was respected by other senior officers. In March 1924, at Andover, Air Commodore Hugh Brooke-Popham assessed him as "capable, keen, active and hard working ... thoroughly popular ... of great value in expressing the Canadian point of view on many subjects." Major-General James MacBrien, as Canada's Chief of the General Staff (and Scott's superior) was equally happy in April 1925: "Good capacity for command. Energetic, self reliant. Good eye for the country. Habits of life good. Fond of sport. Is performing the duties of his present appointment with ability and good judgement."

Perhaps he was all these things – but as the top air officer in Canada he had nowhere to go. In 1928 he accepted a good paying job in private business. When the Second World War

(Left) Major J.S. Scott, MC, AFC, photographed as a civilian when applying in 1920 for a position with the Air Board. (Right) G/C J.S. Scott on his return to the RCAF. (Canadian Forces Photographs PMR 70-215, HC-10381)

broke out, he rejoined the RCAF with his former rank, group captain, and spent the rest of the war at that level, commanding training schools and holding staff appointments. He was *not* a success this time around. He was argumentative with superiors, quick to sense a slight, and as diplomatic as a buzz-saw. Air Vice-Marshal Albert de Niverville, writing in March 1943, described Scott as "a charming and pleasant man to meet socially when he is off duty." On the job, he was very different: "A stern disciplinarian. Has obtained good results in that he has raised the efficiency of No. 13 SFTS but has done so by bullying methods, with the result that most of his subordinates live in constant dread of coming under his censure."

Scott softened only slightly when he was assigned to No. 3 Training Command Headquarters, and it is significant that nobody ever recommended him for anything other than an Efficiency Decoration. Only upon his retirement in February 1945 was he promoted to air commodore. He died in Halifax on July 19, 1975.

Probably the best documented Canadian AFCs of this period are those awarded to Lieutenants James Durkin "Jimmy" Vance (London and Ottawa) and Harry Alexander Yates (Ingersoll, Ontario), both former RNAS pilots. Vance had been a Handley-Page bomber pilot until June 1918, when he force-landed in Holland and was interned. The genesis of their AFC actions lay in Middle East politics. Immediately after the war the situation was tense. Britain had promised Arab leaders many things to enlist their help against the Turks, but European power plays at the Versailles Conference were prompting a good deal of British hedging and backtracking. A renewed Arab revolt, now directed at Britain rather than Turkey, appeared imminent. To counter this threat, a total of 51 Handley-Page O/400 bombers of Nos. 58 and 216 Squadrons were despatched to Egypt. They departed in April, but not all arrived owing to weather, accidents and diversions, and by the end of October the force was down to 26 serviceable aircraft. At least 15 had been written off, and the government was launching a special inquiry "to investigate recent losses on the Egypt route."

At the despatch of aircraft, Colonel T.E. Lawrence had decided to leave the Peace Conference and return to Cairo. He was a passenger in a Handley-Page dogged by ill-fortune. It was damaged when landing at Pisa; at Centocelle, near Rome, the aircraft overturned, killing both pilots. Lawrence was hospitalized with a broken collar bone and ribs and a mild concussion. At the earliest opportunity he virtually escaped from hospital, boarded the first British bomber available and continued his journey.

Lieutenants Yates and Vance had been serving as transport pilots in No. 86 Wing, shuttling conference passengers and mail between Paris and London. In June 1919 they were given two hours notice to prepare their O/400 (serial number F318) for a trip to Cairo, carrying two mechanics (Air Mechanic E. Stedman and Leading Aircraftman C.F. Hand) and one VIP. Their urgent passenger would be Harry St. John Philby, an expert on Arabian affairs.[37]

The two pilots met Philby at Lympne Airfield in Kent. They asked him if there would be any objection to their attempting to set a London-to-Cairo record. Philby answered, "The sooner I get to Cairo, the better." He personally had no qualms, but his wife must have been upset when a taxi driver said, "Don't worry, my dear, they don't always come to grief."[38]

They left England on June 21 and landed in Paris. On the 22nd they pushed on to Lyons, refuelled the bomber themselves and continued to Marseilles. Yates described the airfield as "the worst aerodrome" he had ever seen. He punctured two tires while taxying, and again the crew had to refuel the air-craft unaided. Given the urgency of their mission, they took off again, flying through low cloud and rain to reach Pisa, where they stayed the night. On the 23rd they reached Rome, overtaking some of the bombers that had been despatched earlier. On the morning of the 23rd, Yates and Vance were air-borne again, headed for Taranto. They passed over mountains 6,500 feet high; Yates described this leg as being "the roughest trip I've ever had." There was worse to come.

They departed Taranto on the morning of the 24th – desti-nation, Crete. When not over water they were skirting rugged shorelines which precluded emergency landings. Their official report described a dangerous ordeal:

We had intended going straight to Suda Bay (Crete), but found that our starboard pump was not working, so that the petrol from the rear tank was not available, there being no equalizing pipe between the two main tanks. We there-fore turned towards Athens which was about an hour closer than Suda Bay.

With barely 15 minutes petrol left we were forced to make a landing about five miles east of Aigion, on the south side of the Gulf of Corinth, in a partially dry river bed. Lieutenant Yates, who was at the wheel, made an excellent landing between two deep fissures, through which the river was running.

Handley-Page 0/400 bomber, the type flown by Lieutenants Harry Yates and James Vance from London to Cairo (National Archives of Canada PA-6378)

Considering the uneven, rocky nature of the ground we were fortunate in breaking only the tailskid and puncturing one tire.

We transferred the three hours petrol which had been lying idle in the rear tank to the front one; repaired the starboard outer wheel by taxying the machine until it hung over the edge of one of the holes in the ground, and replaced the tail-skid while the local inhabitants held the tail up on their shoulders.

The people of the district were very good in supplying food, drink and labour.

Lieutenant Yates took the machine off again in about 50 yards, most of the larger stones having been cleared away beforehand.

The faulty fuel pump had not been fixed; they reached Athens with the two mechanics pumping fuel by hand. The pump was still unserviceable on the 24th, when they appeared otherwise ready to leave Athens. On take-off, both engines failed – "water in the petrol." They spent the day draining tanks and straining fuel through chamois leather.

The Handley-Page was airborne again on the 25th, with Stedman and Hand still manually pumping fuel. En route the aircraft began vibrating; after landing at Suda Bay they discovered that the port propeller had cracked. This was solved by "borrowing" a propeller from an O/400 of No. 58 Squadron which was unserviceable for other reasons. As the 26th

Lieutenant Harry Yates before his remarkable flight to Cairo. (Canadian Forces Photograph RE 68-1539)

broke, Yates and Vance acquired another passenger – Colonel T.E. Lawrence himself, scrounging the first available flight to Cairo. Yates tried to get airborne twice and failed both times when the engines faltered. This time it was water in the carburettors. The flight was delayed by four hours, but at last they took off – mechanics hand-pumping gas again – heading for Sollum. They had to skirt the coast of Crete because the bomber could not climb over the local mountains. Their compasses disagreed with one another. A cross-wind complicated navigation. Most unnerving was their isolation; Yates wrote, "Four hours out of sight of land and not a darn ship in sight. Decidedly not my idea of a good time."

For all their troubles, they reached Sollum on time; Lawrence scribbled a congratulatory note. However, their rudder controls were frayed, and for the last leg of the trip they would have to use rudder sparingly. The final run was 500 miles across a desert populated by nomadic tribes, some of whom were in revolt. When they reached their destination. it was dark, and they circled for 40 minutes before locating the aerodrome and touching down.

The crew were exhausted. Officers and men had worked together on the various problems. Air Mechanic Stedman and Leading Aircraftman Hand had endured the most, averaging two and one half hours sleep each night, working on the ground, eating meals while airborne and pumping fuel from Athens to Cairo. Although the trip had covered five days, only 36 hours had been occupied with actual flying. Some of the bombers they had overtaken arrived weeks later. Let-

Lieutenant Harry Yates, Air Mechanic E. Stedman, Leading Aircraftman C.F. Hand, Lieutenant James Vance. It is difficult to say who had the more difficult task on the flight from London to Cairo – the pilots who took off, flew and landed in terrible circumstances, or the two mechanics who spent most of the flight hand-pumping fuel. (Canadian Forces Photograph RE 68-1538)

ters of congratulations poured in; official honours took a little longer. On April 3, 1920, Air Vice Marshal W.G.L. Salmon (the RAF's senior serving officer) recommended Yates and Vance for the Air Force Cross. In doing so he made a very brief statement; the award was "for conspicuous ability and determination displayed in carrying to a successful conclusion, and in record time, a special flight from England to Egypt from 21/6/19 to 26/6/19." On July 12, 1920, more than a year after their hazardous trip, the *London Gazette* announced the awards, together with Air Force Medals to the two mechanics.

It is difficult to say whether any awards would have been made were it not that Yates had very special connections. His father, George W. Yates, was private secretary to Sir Robert Borden, the Prime Minister of Canada. On December 29, 1919, the elder Yates had written to Borden, complaining that his son and Lieutenant Vance had received no formal recognition nor even any amount of notice in the British press. Reports that honours had been suggested had been followed by no action whatsoever. He compared this with other flights by British officers between England and Africa which had taken more time and brought immediate awards. Yates suggested that Canadians were victims of discrimination, and concluded that such treatment did not augur well for either Imperial relations or aviation in Canada.

Borden, in turn, wrote on January 1, 1919, to his High Commissioner in London, Sir George Perley, urging that the matter of awards be taken up with the Air Ministry. Borden, who was far more nationalistic than many realize, concluded his letter to Perley with a bitter paragraph:

My experience and that of others convinces some that one cannot rely upon the accuracy of statements made by certain officials in the Air Ministry. One Canadian put the case in terse and somewhat brutal form: "First they discriminate and then they lie about it."[39]

What steps Sir George Perley took is uncertain, but, as noted already, action was finally forthcoming in the spring of 1920. Both pilots had returned to Canada by that time. Vance received his AFC in September 1920 at an investiture in Toronto; he described it as "a very impressive little ceremony" but organized at such short notice that he had to attend in civilian clothes, having had no time to retrieve his uniform. A month later, the Governor General formally pinned on Yates' decoration at Rideau Hall.

Vance became a bush pilot; he was killed in a flying accident on Great Bear Lake in July 1930. Yates became a doctor, but he remained active in private flying and in 1961 became chairman of the board of directors of the Royal Canadian Flying Clubs Association. He died of a heart attack in 1968.

For some recipients, the Air Force Cross was a sign of future achievements in aviation. Captain Philip Clarke Garratt of Toronto had taught at Duxford and Northolt from March 1918 until June 1919, with an instructor's course at Gosport thrown in for good measure. In this phase of his career he piloted several aircraft types to compile almost 250 flying hours. His logbook gave only hints of occupa-

tional hazards, such as an entry on April 8, 1918, relating to a five-minute hop in a DH.6 ("Pupil gripped controls"), or an incident involving a BE.2c on April 14, 1918 ("Very windy. Machine turned over landing"). Better known as Phil Garratt, he would help establish de Havilland in Canada and be honoured with the McKee Trophy in 1951 and 1965.[40] Lieutenant Stuart Graham became Canada's very first bush pilot and a senior official in the Department of Transport; during the Second World War he was made an Officer (Civil Division), Order of the British Empire. F/L Harold S. Kerby stayed with the RAF and became an air marshal; F/O George H. Boyce, involved in 1918 with Britain's earliest aircraft carriers (HM Ships *Furious* and *Argus*), also remained in the RAF and ended up an air commodore. F/L Joseph Stuart Temple Fall, DSC, AFC (Cowichan Lake, British Columbia), became an RAF group captain; between October 1943 and November 1944 he commanded No. 34 Service Flying Training School, an RAF unit that had been moved from Britain to Carberry, Manitoba, in November 1940; he died on December 1, 1988; estimates of his wartime fighter score varied from 13 to 36 victories![41]

Others attained high rank in the RCAF: Godfrey, Sully, and Croil (air vice marshals), Geoffrey S. O'Brian (air commodore), Sisley, Scott,

Two AFC winners: Geoff O'Brian, who, when this photograph was taken in 1930, combined purchasing, sales and assistant test pilot duties at de Havilland, and Phil Garratt, who later became the company's manager. (De Havilland Photo 5954)

Harding, plus Fred P. Holliday, John H. Keens and John G. Ireland (all group captains). Captain Jack Leach, MC, AFC, the one-legged instructor in Canada in 1917-1918, wrote himself off in an Ontario Provincial Air Service crash on June 26, 1930. His was a needless death; performing aerobatics in a Hamilton H-47 aircraft, he tried to loop the machine and failed. George Thom became a prospector; looking for oil in 1924, he was drowned when his canoe upset in the Peace River Rapids.

Sopwith Camels aboard HMS *Furious*, one of Britain's earliest aircraft carriers. F/O George H. Boyce, AFC, was a pioneer of carrier aviation. (National Archives of Canada PA-6280)

Chapter 3

INTERREGNUM

The age of chivalry is gone. That of sophisters, economists and calculators has succeeded.

– EDMUND BURKE, *REFLECTIONS ON THE REVOLUTION IN FRANCE* (1792)

Peace is not only better than war, but infinitely more arduous.

– GEORGE BERNARD SHAW (1856-1950), PREFACE TO *HEARTBREAK HOUSE*

From January 1921 through to June 1939 a total of 143 Air Force Crosses and 88 Air Force Medals were awarded to British and Commonwealth service personnel, including seven AFCs and two AFMs to members of the RAAF.[1] Three Canadians serving in the RAF earned AFCs: F/L Archibald James Rankin of Edmonton (AFC awarded July 3, 1926), F/O John Alexander Kent of Winnipeg and P/O George Forbes Rodney of Calgary (both on January 2, 1939). A fourth person sometimes identified as a Canadian, F/L Sidney Leo Gregory Pope, DFC (AFC awarded March 1, 1929), on closer examination appears to have had no connections with Canada until taking command of an RAF training unit in British Columbia from 1941 to 1943. Nevertheless, following that experience, when he left the RAF in 1946 he chose to retire to Victoria.[2]

Rankin was born in October 1896 and had served with the Canadian Expeditionary Force until gassed in August 1917. He transferred to the Royal Naval Air Service and trained as a pilot. Early in 1919 he was sent to Archangel, North Russia, assigned to HMS *Pegasus*, a converted merchant ship, 3,070 tons, accommodating nine seaplanes. On July 20 he was injured when his aircraft crashed into a barge on takeoff. Subsequently, he made the RAF his career. Early in June 1923 he was posted back to *Pegasus*. On September 4, 1923, he was sent to the Calshot seaplane base, from which be was detached to Cattewater, where an expedition was being organized to undertake a photo survey of southern Malaya, including Singapore. The group, including Rankin, was posted to *Pegasus* on March 21, 1924, and sailed for the Far East. They were equipped with five Fairey IIID seaplanes, which was virtually the fleet workhorse of the period. Commanding the air element was S/L E.L. Tomkinson, DSO, DFC.[3]

For much of the work, *Pegasus* was anchored in the Johore Strait, between Singapore Island and the Malay Peninsula. The sheltered waters simplified hoisting seaplanes on or off the ship. Local planters told of extraordinary jungle hazards including fierce tigers and loathsome snakes. The aircrews adopted a special "survival kit" for the region which included a Malay knife, flares, a tool kit, pistols and long ropes to climb down from tall trees should one force-land in them. It was difficult to say what was more unpleasant – the steaming heat or the cockroaches that infested *Pegasus*. Photography, preferably at an altitude of 10,000 feet, was difficult because proper light was not available until about 9.00 a.m., yet by 10.30 a.m. low clouds had begun to form. In all, including preparations at Cattewater and operational flying, the expedition logged a total of 711 hours 35 minutes in the air. The total for Malaya alone was 421 hours 25 minutes, of which the largest block was dedicated to survey photography (301 hours 40 minutes) followed by meteorological work (63 hours 30 minutes) and miscellaneous photography (31 hours 25 minutes); the last category included checks on army camouflage and searches for underwater obstacles.

The Malay survey, related directly to fortress construction at Singapore, was mentioned occasionally in British maga-zines, but with few details; a civilian aerial survey at the mouth of the Irrawwaddy River attracted more coverage. Having completed most of the survey, *Pegasus* visited Borneo and Hong Kong. At the latter port the Fairey aircraft reconnoitred anchorages in mainland China believed to be frequented by coastal pirates. In January 1925 they sailed again, this time for the Dutch East Indies (Indonesia) to "show the flag," on to Singapore for a further two weeks of aerial photography, and then back to Britain where the vessel was paid off. The Malaya project led to Rankin being recommended for an AFC in the following terms:

> For consistent good work and devotion to duty as pilot and photographer in connection with the air photographic survey carried out during the cruise of HMS *Pegasus* in the Far East, 1924-25. The standard of this officer's piloting and photography was of the highest order, and he obtained a vast number of photographs for the air survey which often necessitated flying in a float plane over the jungle out of touch with the sea, and under trying conditions of heat.[4]

He received his AFC at a Buckingham Palace investiture on July 12, 1926. From the Malaya survey he was transferred to the School of Naval Co-Operation at Lee-on-Solent (May 1, 1925). Presumably he was involved in training and some experimental flying, but the records are difficult to trace. At the outbreak of the Second World War he was with the Directorate of Intelligence, Air Ministry. For much of his career he remained close to intelligence duties in various commands. He rose to air commodore rank and was awarded the OBE for wartime duties. Postwar he served with British Commonwealth Occupation Forces in Japan before returning to Britain in January 1949 as Director of Intelligence (Operations).[5]

George Rodney joined the RAF early in 1936. The threat to peace represented by Nazi Germany had become apparent and the RAF was beginning to expand. This included forming No. 148 Squadron at Scampton, Lincolnshire, in July 1937 (transferred to Stradishall, Suffolk, in March 1938). The unit was initially equipped with six Hawker Audax biplanes and one Vickers Wellesley, but the former were disposed of as more Wellesleys became available. Working up on these machines was Rodney's principal task. On September 27, 1938, his commanding officer recommended him for the Air Force Cross in glowing terms:

Acting Flying Officer Rodney has commanded "A" Flight of No. 148 (B) Squadron since 6th July 1937 when the squadron reformed. His ability and enthusiasm in the air and on the ground has formed the standard for some twenty young pilots who have been training in the squadron since that date.

In the absence of a trained C.F.S. [Central Flying School] instructor he has given without mishap the majority of the dual (day and night) to all of these pilots.

He is the pilot of the best crew for Bombing and Rear Gun. His work as a Flight Commander over a long period with the substantive rank and pay of a Pilot Officer is worthy of recognition. The only recognition so far has been the

S/L John A. Kent, DFC, AFC, who tested barrage balloon cables and aircraft cable cutters by flying directly into balloon cables. He was a rarity – a pilot who wrote his memoirs (Canadian Forces Photograph RE 68-1625)

Acting Rank of Flying Officer with an increase of pay of 1/ [one shilling] since 20th May 1938.

The commanding officer at Stradishall agreed, adding his own comments on October 6, 1938: "The achievements of this officer rank high both personally and as a leader. His example has been in every way admirable."[6]

Just before the war Rodney was with the Royal Aeronautical Establishment at Farnborough, working as a test pilot. He went on to fly Wellingtons, Stirlings and Lancasters, was Mentioned in Despatches on January 14, 1944, and was awarded a Distinguished Flying Cross on January 16, 1945. Rodney stayed with the RAF after the war, but following his retirement in 1961 he settled in Victoria, where he died ten years later.

Of the three, the record of John Kent is best known and documented. Having joined the RAF in 1935, he became a test pilot at Farnborough. Part of his job was to fly different types of aircraft into balloon cables, testing first the balloon defences that would soon sprout around British cities, then trying devices that would protect RAF aircraft from balloon cables. He usually flew Battles, Wellesleys or Wellingtons. In two years he deliberately collided with balloon cables some 300 times; once he returned to his field training 500 feet of cable which snagged some high tension wires as he made his landing approach. When recommended for the AFC on September 23, 1938, he had already conducted 60 such flights which were described with classic understatement as "accompanied by a considerable element of risk to the pilot" and requiring "determination and a high degree of skill." His AFC was in recognition of what may have been the most dangerous episode in his career. He went on to a remarkable career as a pioneer of high altitude photo reconnaissance and as a fighter pilot (13 victories, DFC and Bar plus the Polish *Virtuti Militari*, 5th Class). He too remained in the postwar RAF, retiring as a group captain. He died in 1985.[7]

Although not a Canadian, Squadron Leader Francis Victor Beamish (AFC, January 1, 1938) is worth mentioning by reason of connections to this country. From 1929 to 1931 he was attached to the RCAF on exchange duties and flew with the Siskin aerobatic team. This brought him into close association with such men as F/O E.A. McNab (later to have the distinction of being the first member of the RCAF decorated for wartime services) and P/O F.M. Gobeil (a future AFC winner). Beamish's Air Force Cross was awarded for meteorological flying from Aldergrove in Northern Ireland, using an aircraft type, the Bristol Bulldog, that was prone to carburettor icing and radio failures.[8]

Apart from AFCs and AFMs, numerous honours were bestowed upon RAF personnel, engaged as they were in test flying, air route surveys, and limited warfare against colonial rebels. In sharp contrast, from 1920 through to 1941, no member of the RCAF received an Air Force Cross or Air Force Medal. The drought of honours for RCAF personnel was long indeed; from the inception of the force in 1924 no member received a gallantry award until October 1940 (when three RCAF fighters pilots were awarded DFCs for services in the Battle of Britain); no AFCs or AFMs went to RCAF personnel until June 1942, when nine AFCs and four AFMs were awarded for services in Canada. Even formal recognition for services rendered was accorded only briefly (1934-1935).

Why were honours so long denied to air force officers and men? The answer was that the Canadian government was ambivalent, and at times hostile, to granting official honours to anyone, whether civil or military. The principal reason lay in the over-zealous application of a policy laid down in 1918-1919 to distance Canada from some trappings of the British class system. During the First World War more than 800 gallantry decorations had been granted to Canadians serving in the British flying services.[9] Nevertheless, as the war was drawing to a close, a debate emerged in Canada about honours and awards in general, although it was concentrated upon the issue of titles and knighthoods for Canadians. In the House of Commons a Conservative MP, W.F. Nickle, initiated a campaign to suspend the conferring of titular honours upon all Canadians. In May 1918 the House of Commons adopted a resolution that Nickle had presented which urged that the grant of *hereditary* honours to Canadians should be suspended while others should be granted only upon the advice or approval of the Prime Minister.

Nickle and those of like mind returned to the attack in 1919. Prime Minister Sir Robert Borden was absent in Europe, attending the Peace Conference; other ministers in Canada seemed hesitant on this issue. The Minister of Finance reviewed what stood for policy. He argued that war honours had been conferred largely with the approval of Cabinet. However, the New Years List of 1919 was embarrassing because of the large number of civilian nominees named to various grades of the Order of the British Empire, arising out of war work (Red Cross, Patriotic Fund activities, war production). It was decided to suspend nominations until the Commons had weighed the whole matter of civil honours; this inaction was confirmed by Borden himself in a telegram on January 3, 1919. Official inertia permitted radical critics to take the initiative.

Although hereditary titles had been halted, the government and Crown could still, theoretically, bestow knighthoods and other honours. Indeed, with respect to military personnel, this was continuing. These now came under fire. This time there were voices favouring retention of honours; on May 16 the Montreal *Star* opined:

The whole thing is very petty. The majority of opinion in this country is undoubtedly opposed to hereditary distinctions; though logically, hereditary wealth has more dangerous possibilities. But we refuse to believe that Canadian common sense resents awards of honour for honourable public service.

There were few inside Parliament ready to defend honours and knighthoods. Ministers who held knighthoods seemed embarrassed and reluctant to defend their honours. When the matter came up for discussion, the House of Commons followed the lead of Nickle, who chaired the special committee of 12 Conservatives and 13 Liberals. The upshot was the passage of the Nickle Resolution of May 1919, which recommended an Address to the King that henceforth no "title of honour or titular distinction" be conferred upon any person "domiciled or ordinarily resident in Canada." The committee, however, had not sought abolition of all honours. It specifically excluded those that were most dear to politicians – the Privy Council appointments which permitted ministers to be styled "Honourable" or "Right Honourable." It exempted professional and vocational titles; distinguished academics would

continue to be "Doctors" while assorted lawyers would go on receiving the brevet "KC." The committee had also pointedly supported continuance of military decorations, from the Victoria Cross down, which were awarded for "exceptional valour and devotion to duty."[10]

Although a few final Imperial honours were granted in 1920, the practical effect was a suspension of virtually all decorations in Canada. Application went far beyond the letter of the Nickle Resolution, for no services were thereafter rewarded by the state. In the absence of the Nickle Resolution it is quite possible that S/L T.A. Lawrence might have received an Air Force Cross for his leadership during the Hudson Straits Expedition (1927-1928), and one or two other participants might have been recognized as well. Those who organized and flew the Trans-Canada Flight, who pioneered aerial surveys or brought aircraft to the aid of those fighting forest fires – all went unrecognized so far as formal honours were concerned.

This contrasted greatly with Commonwealth practices elsewhere. As already noted, British fliers were decorated regularly for work similar to that done by members of the RCAF. Members of the Royal Australian Air Force also collected occasional awards; an aerial circumnavigation of Australia in 1924 resulted in two pilots, S/L S.J. Goble and F/L Ivor E. McIntyre, being made Companions of the Order of the British Empire (CBE). These were very high honours for such junior officers. Between September and November 1926, an RAAF DH.50A undertook an extended flight through Papua, New Guinea and the Solomon Islands, ostensibly as a survey mission but principally to "show the flag" (including the new, distinctive RAAF roundel) in an area where Australia wished to assert her interests. Ivor McIntyre was again involved, together with a mechanic, Flight Sergeant Les Trist; the RAAF's Chief of Air Staff, G/C Richard Williams, went along as a passenger. At the close of the expedition, Williams received a CBE, McIntyre a Bar to a wartime AFC, and Trist was awarded an Air Force Medal.[11] A rare civilian AFC award, to Lester Joseph Brain, was announced in May 1929 for "distinguished services rendered to aviation by his recent flights in the northern territory of Australia in search of missing aviators."[12] In March 1931 F/L Charles Eaton, RAAF, was awarded an AFC "in recognition of his zeal and devotion to duty in conducting flights to Central Australia in search of missing aviators."[13] In June 1938 F/L William Lloyd, RAAF, was awarded an Air Force Cross for "courageous conduct and devotion to duty" shown in the course of flying in northern and central Australia. Another AFC was awarded to F/O Harry A. Durant, RAAF, on January 1, 1939 "in recognition of his courageous conduct while piloting an Avro Anson aeroplane conveying the Minister of National Defence of the Commonwealth of Australia and other persons from Canberra to Melbourne." Of most interest to Canadians (because of resemblances between RAAF and RCAF inter-war operations) were AFCs bestowed upon F/L Allan M. Charlesworth (1933) for pioneering photographic surveys in Queensland and S/L A.G. Carr (1938), in charge of photographic surveys in Australia for many years and described as having demonstrated "initiative and exceptional devotion to duty while flying under difficult conditions."[14]

In the absence of standard decorations, the RCAF regularly advanced nominations of its personnel for the Trans-Canada Trophy (better known as the McKee Trophy) which had been instituted in 1927. The first RCAF officer whose name was advanced was P/O C.R. Slemon, for the rescue of four occupants of an aircraft that crashed at Cross Lake, Manitoba, on June 9, 1927. The recommendation failed (the first winner of the trophy would be H.A. "Doc" Oaks) but the force would repeatedly suggest potential recipients. Only one such attempt would succeed in the pre-war period – the nomination of S/L J.H. Tudhope (McKee Trophy, 1930).[15]

The issue of awards was raised in the Canadian House of Commons in February 1929. The Member for St. Lawrence-St. George (Toronto), C.H. Cahan, proposed that a committee be established to reconsider the Nickle Resolution. The Prime Minister, William Lyon Mackenzie King, was indifferent to honours, and when a vote was called on Cahill's resolution, it lost 114 to 60.[16]

In 1930 the Liberals were defeated and the King government was replaced by that of Richard Bedford Bennett. The new Prime Minister did nothing about decorations during the first two years of his term but was guardedly favourable to the restoration of state honours, and many who wrote to him felt the same way. In January 1933 Bennett took the first step; upon his request to King George V, Sir George Perley was promoted within the Order of St. Michael and St. George; the venerable old political warhorse, liked and respected by all parties, went from being a KCMG (Knight Companion, Order of St. Michael and St. George, awarded in 1915) to a GCMG (Knight Grand Cross). Late in the Commons Session that year, questions were asked about this promotion and the status of the Nickle Resolution. Bennett finally stated that he did not feel bound by the 1919 declaration; his argument was that titles and honours remained the prerogative of the King. The sovereign, he declared, "can only be deprived of a prerogative right by Statute of Parliament in very special form which the government does not propose to introduce." That flushed out King and his anti-honours views; he asked that before any resumption of honours take place, the House of Commons should be consulted.[17]

The exchange led some to anticipate the next King's Birthday Honours List, released on June 3, 1933. On that occasion no Canadians were mentioned. The shoe dropped with the New Years Honours List of 1934. The *Ottawa Citizen* carried the news on page 14 under a headline, TITLES TO CANADIANS AFTER 14 YEARS. On this occasion Canada gained two new knights: Sir Lyman P. Duff (Chief Justice of the Supreme Court of Canada, made GCMG) and Joseph Tellier (Chief Justice, Court of King's Bench, Quebec, made a Knight Bachelor). There were also four CMGs (Companion, Order of St. Michael and St. George). Lesser but still prestigious honours were also granted; six women were made Commanders, Order of the British Empire (CBE), for work in child welfare, education and health. Eleven further women were made Officers in the Order of the British Empire (OBE). Fifteen people (14 of them women) were made Members, Order of the British Empire (MBE). These numbers were slightly less than the Crown had allowed Canada in the distribution of Imperial honours.[18]

Predictably, the Leader of the Opposition (W.L.M. King) attacked the move, which he described as an attempt "to create in Canada a social order, based on titular distinctions"; it was, he declared, unwise, inconsiderate, rash and unjust, further proof that in the midst of hardship at home and revolution abroad, the government was detached from reality. Almost as an afterthought, King complained that Bennett had not even sought Parliamentary approval to sidestep the Nickle Resolution.[19]

King's outrage was not echoed in the press, although some questions were raised about the principles involved. Bennett, in fact, had given opponents very little to complain about, for the quality of his appointments were very high indeed. Bennett scored again with his nomination of honours for the King's Birthday List (June 3, 1934). Only 12 Canadians were honoured, and again only two knighthoods were conferred; they went to Dr. Frederick Banting (one of the discovers of

insulin) and Charles Saunders (recognition for his scientific work developing seed grains suitable for Canadian conditions). The CMG went to four distinguished civil servants. This time the honours attracted negligible comment.[20]

Bennett recommended a much larger slate of honours for the New Years List of 1935. No fewer than 47 Canadians (eight of them women) were granted awards and distinctions; these included three knighthoods. The 1935 New Years Honours List was notable for the Canadian military; six serving members of the forces received varying honours. They were:

Major-General A.G.L. McNaughton, Chief of the General Staff (awarded CB).

Brigadier W.H.P. Elkins, DSO, Commandant of RMC, Kingston (awarded CBE).

S/L R.S. Grandy, Trenton, test pilot and instructor, singled out for "outstanding services in pioneering air mail routes" (awarded OBE).

Warrant Officer (I) Wenceslas Bilodeau, Royal 22e Regiment, Quebec City, a 29-year militia veteran including CEF service in Siberia, RSM to the regiment since its constitution in 1920 as a Permanent Force unit (awarded MBE).

Chief Petty Officer Charles J.T. Hill of Ottawa, 24-year veteran of RCN (awarded BEM).

Flight Sergeant Harry J. Winny of Vancouver "for outstanding service in pioneer air mail service" (awarded BEM).[21]

The awards to Grandy and Winny are those of most interest to readers of this work and demonstrate one means by which people gained admission to a Bennett Honours List. In the spring of 1934 the Prime Minister approached the Chief of the General Staff (McNaughton) and asked for nominations that would recognize outstanding achievements in Canadian aviation. After conferring with the RCAF's Senior Air Officer, McNaughton wrote to suggest one civilian (bush pilot W.R. "Wop" May), one officer (Grandy) and one NCO (Winny) as outstanding individuals. May was singled out for a series of mercy flights conducted between January 1932 and April 1934; he was subsequently awarded a Civil OBE; Grandy had been the senior RCAF officer involved in a series of 1932 experimental air mail flights between the Strait of Belle Isle and Ottawa; Winny, although publicly linked to air mail work, was recommended for his role in pioneering Arctic survey flights in 1930 and 1931.[22]

The 1935 King's Birthday List (June 3, 1935) was the most massive to date – 107 Canadians honoured including one knightly promotion (Sir William White, whose 1916 KCMG was upgraded to a GCMG) plus eight new knighthoods. While most public attention was directed at the knighthoods, the other awards demonstrated just how much talent Canada possessed and was prepared to recognize (at least under Bennett). Ten CMGs included such figures as Charles Camsell; 23 civil awards of the OBE honoured one celebrity (Dr. Alan R. Dafoe, doctor to the Dionne quintuplets) and others with solid records of achievement (Lester B. Pearson, Lucy Maud Montgomery). Indeed, the arts and public service were more prominent than politicians and jurists.

In this, the last Honours List before Bennett's defeat in the election of 1935, eight members of the Canadian military were honoured. These were:

Lieutenant-Colonel Henry Willis O'Connor, DSO, of Ottawa, a veteran of service with the Princess Patricia's Canadian Light Infantry and aide-de-camp to the Governor General (CBE).

Commander Ronald Ian Agnew, RCN, a member of that force since 1911, currently commanding HMCS *Saguenay* and senior officer afloat in Halifax, "for continuous good service in the Royal Canadian Navy" (OBE).

S/L George E. Brooks, in charge of pilot training at Camp Borden (OBE).

Major E.L.M. Burns, "a noted writer on military subjects" and active in co-ordinating air and land efforts towards aerial surveys (OBE).

Master Gunner Herbert Collings, RCA, of Esquimalt, who had "rendered very efficient service extending over a period of thirty years in the Permanent Active Militia," had previously served six years in the British Army, and had been awarded the Long Service and Good Conduct Medal in 1926 (MBE).

Commissioned Victualling Officer John George Buckner Horne, RCN, of Esquimalt, described as an RN veteran, loaned to the RCN in 1910 and formally transferred in 1917, honoured "for long and faithful service in the Royal Navy and the Royal Canadian Navy" (MBE).

Warrant Officer Anthony Augustine Rabnett, RCAF, of Ottawa, active as a technical NCO and aircraft inspector, described as being "exceptionally thorough, reliable and technically efficient," a member of the RCAF since its inception (MBE).

RSM George Rolfe of Halifax, with 28 years service in the Canadian forces (including the CEF), awarded the Long Service and Good Conduct Medal in 1924, and for five years an instructor at RMC (MBE).

RSM John Wyatt, DCM, of Kingston, a 24-year veteran of

the Permanent Active Militia, awarded the Long Service and Good Conduct Medal in 1928, and since 1933 the College Sergeant Major and an instructor at RMC (MBE).[23]

At no time during his term of office did Bennett or his military advisors seem to consider what we would call "gallantry" (as opposed to "service") awards; hence the granting of honours was confined to knighthoods and awards within the various Orders of Chivalry – the Order of the Bath and the Order of the British Empire – so loved by Anglophiles and so distrusted by those with more democratic tendencies. In any case, Bennett's government went down to crushing defeat in October 1935; his creativity in such fields as banking and broadcasting had not been enough to save him, and his urging of radical reforms in January 1935 had been dismissed as a political death-bed conversion. Depression and division within his party had toppled him. William Lyon Mackenzie King, blandness personified, was back, and honourable Canadians would once again go unhonoured.

The next six years witnessed a drought insofar as honours in Canada were concerned. When King George VI's Coronation occurred in 1937 the only public honour bestowed on a Canadian was admission to the Imperial Privy Council granted to Ernest Lapointe, Prime Minister King's right-hand man. There was a distribution of Coronation Medals to civilians and service personnel – 10,089 in all, with approximately 1,205 going to members of the forces – and military leaders attempted to single out industrious individuals for this award.[24] Various long-service medals continued to be awarded. However, there was no specific recognition of individual merit or bravery such as would have been the case had honours like the OBE been continued. Militia officers were not happy about this; on August 31, 1936, the Adjutant General wrote a memo to the Chief of the General Staff, inquiring about the possibility of reviving the Military Service Medal or the British Empire Medal; he pointed out that the original Nickle Resolution had specifically referred to gallantry awards as being acceptable. The only question in his mind was whether the Canadian government was prepared to submit recommendations to the King. It is not known if this proposal went higher than the Chief of the General Staff; certainly no suggested awards were ever forwarded to the sovereign.[25] Meanwhile, as had occurred from 1920 to 1933, the only Canadians receiving civil honours from the Crown were those who had gone abroad.[26]

The seaplane hangar at Dartmouth with a Stranraer flying boat, November 12, 1939. When first taken, this photograph was classified as "Secret." Even in 1939, biplane patrol bombers were an anachronism. Two years later, these machines were being switched to the Pacific coast as more modern Canso aircraft entered service with Eastern Air Command. (National Archives of Canada PA-136269)

Chapter 4

SECOND WORLD WAR AWARDS

The world continues to offer glittering prizes to those who have stout hearts and sharp swords.

> – FREDERICK EDWIN SMITH, EARL OF BIRKENHEAD, RECTORIAL ADDRESS, GLASGOW UNIVERSITY, NOVEMBER 7, 1931

Courage is the price that Life exacts for granting peace.

> – AMELIA EARHART (1898-1937), *COURAGE*

The higher we soar, the smaller we appear to those who cannot fly.

> – FRIEDRICH WILHELM NIETZSCHE

At the outbreak of the Second World War there was some confusion as to what honours might be bestowed upon Canadian airmen. British authorities understood the non-awards policy, but were unsure of how far it would extend in wartime. There was no question that gallantry awards, pure and simple, could be offered and accepted – the Victoria Cross, Distinguished Flying Cross, Distinguished Flying Medal and so on. There was less certainty about the Distinguished Service Order, which was finally approved by Canadian authorities in November 1940.

The first awards to RCAF personnel raised diplomatic problems. The Air Officer Commanding in Chief, Fighter Command, approved of DFCs to three members of No. 1 (C) Squadron and communicated these to the unit. Word of the honours was immediately flashed home. Unfortunately, no Canadian officer or diplomat was informed, and on October 11, 1940, the Air Officer Commanding RCAF Overseas was asking for details of these awards.[1] On December 2, 1940, Fighter Command Headquarters submitted to RCAF authorities recommendations for four added awards – two for MBEs, two for BEMs – to be granted to other Canadians who had served in the Battle of Britain. This evidently caused some consternation among Canadian "brass," but by December 31 it had been agreed that the two lesser recommendations might go forward; the MBEs would be held up pending clarification of what honours were acceptable.[2]

Awards for gallantry overseas seemed clear enough; by the end of 1941 a total of 23 members of the RCAF had been decorated for gallantry in action. Service awards, whether in Canada or abroad, and gallantry awards for Canadians at home seemed more difficult to resolve. In October 1941 two airmen received the British Empire Medal for bravery exhibited seven months earlier at Patricia Bay.[3] Nevertheless, there was confusion about what could be recommended. Forcing the issue was the fact that since the autumn of 1940 several RAF schools with their officers and other ranks had moved to Canada; British officers wanted to recommend some of their staff for awards, but agreed not to do so as long as Canadians doing the same work were ineligible for decorations. That seemed to provide enough of a case for the first RCAF AFC and AFM awards to be recommended and approved in June 1942. The delays, however, undoubtedly prevented some awards going through; at least one AFC nomination for an RCAF officer in Ferry Command clearly fell through the cracks.[4]

The issue of what ultimately was or was not acceptable remained cloudy until July 24, 1942, when a Special Committee of the Canadian House of Commons recommended that "persons domiciled or ordinarily resident in Canada will henceforth again be eligible for the award of Honours and Decorations, including awards in the Orders of Chivalry, which do not involve titles." This had been reached following three weeks of hearings with evidence presented by representatives of the three services, the Secretary of State and the Department of External Affairs.[5] The way was thus cleared for receipt of all gallantry decorations plus orders up to the level of Companion, Order of the Bath (CB). Anything that bestowed a knightly "Sir" upon the recipient would be forbidden.[6] Significantly, only after that date were RCAF officers cleared to accept status in the junior levels of the Order of the Bath and the Order of the British Empire with the first CBs, CBEs, OBEs and MBEs being gazetted on January 1, 1943. The Canadian policy was understood by most (though not all) British officers; in 1945 Air Chief Marshal Sir Arthur Harris complained bitterly that he had not been allowed to secure a knighthood for A/V/M C.M "Black Mike" McEwen. Harris blamed this on internal RCAF politics; he did not appreciate that the Canadian Parliament itself had forbidden titular awards.

It was this confusion in 1941-42 over what decorations were acceptable to the Canadian government that probably explains one curious AFC award. W/C Lawrence Edward "Larry" Wray (Toronto) had been a member of the RCAF since 1930. Like many other career officers, his most exciting times had been spent on aerial photography in remote areas of Canada; in 1937 he had directed the aerial search for F/L S.W. Coleman and Sergeant J. Forty, who had gone missing in the Northwest Territories. Wray later commanded the Test Flight of No. 7 (General Purpose) Squadron (forerunner of the Central Experimental and Proving Establishment); in February 1939 he was nominated (unsuccessfully) for the McKee Trophy.[7] The outbreak of war brought rapid promotion and frequent postings; on September 5, 1941, as an AFHQ staff officer, he was aboard a naval launch attempting to salvage a Grumman Goose that had overturned in the St. Lawrence near Quebec City. A gale was blowing and it appeared that they were going to fail. In the words of his AFC citation, gazetted on June 11, 1942:

… Wing Commander Wray plunged overboard from the Naval Rescue Launch, made fast and held a line until the aircraft could be towed out of danger into the middle of the river, remaining with the aircraft until 0400 hours the following morning. His action undoubtedly saved the aircraft.

It was a praiseworthy act for one of his rank – but as something that would merit an Air Force Cross the deed seems out of place. Another award, say an MBE (Member, Order of the British Empire) would have been more appropriate. However,

W/C Larry Wray received his AFC for risking his life to salvage an airplane. When captured by the Germans, he showed equal heroism and leadership among his fellow prisoners. (Canadian Forces Photograph PL-8408)

as of that time it was unclear as to whether MBEs and OBEs were "politically correct." With the dead weight of the old Nickle Resolution still restricting awards, Wray's AFC may have been granted simply because no other appropriate decoration appeared available at the time.

Larry Wray received his AFC at a Government House investiture on December 3, 1942. He was posted overseas, promoted to group captain, given command of Station Skipton-on-Swale, and proceeded to fly on operations which, as a station CO, he had no business doing. On March 18, 1944, his aircraft was shot down and he was taken prisoner. Wray arrived at Stalag Luft III shortly after the infamous "Great Escape"; for much of his stay there he was the Senior Allied Officer. In that capacity he worked tirelessly to improve conditions, oblivious to his own safety and comfort. He showed leadership in "bucking" German captors on behalf of POWs during the winter march from Sagen to Lubeck; Wray was reputed to have reduced the German camp commandant to a nervous wreck. He was punished by confinement in a small, over-heated room, yet ultimately he virtually controlled the German officers on the march and in the finally stages had the POWs lodged in scattered barns across the countryside. His work in captivity earned him the grade of Officer, Order of the British Empire (OBE). His postwar career took him to the rank of air vice-marshal and command of No. 1 Air Division in Europe.

CANADIANS IN THE ROYAL AIR FORCE

And everywhere the blue sky belongs to them, and is their appointed rest and their native country and their own natural homes, which they enter unannounced, as lords that are certainly expected, and yet there is a silent joy at their arrival.

– SAMUEL TAYLOR COLERIDGE (1772-1834),
THE ANCIENT MARINER

We shall not cease from exploration and the end of our exploring will be to arrive where we started and know the place for the first time.

– T.S. ELLIOT (1888-1965), *FOUR QUARTERS*

While the greatest number of AFC and AFM awards described in this study were to members of the RCAF, significant numbers of Canadians had enlisted directly in the Royal Air Force before the Second World War or in the first few months of that conflict, when RCAF enlistment standards were still exceptionally strict. Not unnaturally, many of these CAN/RAF personnel were aircrew who, throughout the war, appeared on lists of casualties as well as awards. Wherever the RAF operated, CAN/RAF members were to be found. However, it might be borne in mind that in some cases persons identified as "Canadian" sometimes had very slim Canadian credentials, and the absence at that time of distinct Canadian citizenship (as opposed to being a "British subject") makes it awkward even today to ascribe nationality to certain individuals. Thus, if P.S. Turner (born in Britain, raised in Canada) is considered a Canadian, the same logic would make Max Aitkin (born in Canada, raised in Britain) British. Only since the passage of the Citizenship Act (1947) has it been possible to state clearly who is, or is not, a Canadian.

A case in point is that of W/C Alick Foord-Kelsey. Although born in Alberta in 1913, much of his schooling was in Britain, including King's School (Canterbury), Corpus Christi College and Canterbury University. He enlisted in the RAF in 1934 and was commissioned in 1935. When recommended for an Air Force Cross on May 21, 1943, he had been nine months as chief instructor at the RAF College and Service Flying Training School, Cranwell; apart from being an "exceptional pilot" he was singled out for his "judgement and sense of proportion in allotting to each of the many items of the training syllabus its due amount of time and effort." In spite of his lengthy association with Britain, he was described in RCAF documents as a "Canadian in the RAF."[8]

A clearer case is that of Robert Benvie Fleming, who was born in Stellarton, Nova Scotia, in 1916 and educated in Bonavista, Newfoundland. He joined the Royal Air Force in 1938 and was commissioned the following year. He flew three complete tours with Coastal Command during the war (one on Hudsons with No. 220 Squadron, two on Liberators with No. 547 Squadron). He was mentioned in despatches (June 8, 1944) and awarded the Distinguished Flying Cross (February 6, 1945); in between he received an AFC for work at No. 1674 Heavy Conversion Unit, Aldergrove. When recommended he was described as having flown a total of 1,040 hours including 172 in the preceding six months. S/L Fleming's citation paid tribute to outstanding work away from anti-submarine and anti-shipping patrols:

Since being posted to the unit as Flight Commander, this officer has taken part in, and was largely responsible for, the conversion of No. 220 Squadron to Fortress and Nos. 160 and 86 Squadrons to Liberator aircraft. He operated the first Liberator to be fitted with the Leigh Light and was also responsible for the initial training of two squadrons with aircraft so fitted. Squadron Leader Fleming has displayed the greatest keenness and determination throughout his career.[9]

More orthodox was the training conducted by F/O Philip Henry Knowles. Born in Vancouver and raised in Victoria, he had served in the Canadian Scottish Regiment in 1932-33. Joining the RAF in 1937, he was recommended for the AFC on January 2, 1941; it was gazetted on April 1 of that year. He was then with No. 3 Service Flying Training School in Britain and was described simply as "an instructor of outstanding ability" whose pupils had "always attained a high state of efficiency." Soon afterwards he was posted to Canada, where he continued instructing until switching to Ferry Command.

S/L Royd Martin Fenwick-Wilson was awarded the AFC at the same time as Knowles. Born in Greenwood, British Columbia, he had joined the RAF in 1934. At the beginning of the war he was instructing at No. 12 SFTS in Britain. His skills as a teacher were matched by administrative ability. Shortly after his AFC award he was promoted to wing commander and posted to No. 405 Squadron, succeeding another CAN/RAF officer as CO. He remained with that unit until February 1942 when he was succeeded by an RCAF officer, W/C J.E. Fauquier. Nevertheless, Fenwick-Wilson's most notable contribution to the war effort went unrewarded; on the night of June 5, 1944, commanding No. 218 Squadron he participated in Operation GLIMMER. Sixteen Lancasters from No. 617 Squadron and six Stirlings from No. 218 Squadron, flying precisely timed tracks, dropped bundles of "Window" (aluminum foil strips) across the English Channel, registering on German radar as an invasion convoy advancing upon Calais. Needless to say, the real Allied invasion was commencing further west.[10]

Very different training and combat duties were performed by W/C Harold Hamlyn Burnell of Weyburn, Saskatchewan. A member of the RAF from December 1936 onwards, he saw extensive service in North Africa in 1940-41, then was posted to Canada on instructional duties. Returning to Britain in 1943, he became chief instructor at No. 3 Lancaster Finishing School upon its formation (November 1943). When recommended for an AFC he was praised for having developed the syllabus and solving "many instructional problems." He went on to receive a DSO for services on radar jamming Liberators with No. 223 Squadron (September 1945) but was killed on active service on November 14, 1945.[11]

One of the more travelled of these CAN/RAF personnel was Francis Sidney Powley. Born in Kelowna in 1915, he had been educated in that city. He joined the RAF in January 1937 and was commissioned later that year. He was one of six CAN/RAF aircrew to receive Air Force Crosses in the New Years Honours List of 1942; he was then a flight lieutenant on the strength of the RAF in India. The citation sent through channels (though not published) read:

This officer has shown commendable keenness and energy during the past year whilst employed at the Flying Training School. As an instructor there he has flown 625 hours. He has also been responsible for armament training and has set an excellent example to the numerous pupils that have passed through his hands.[12]

Powley rose to wing commander rank and received a DFC for services with No. 166 Squadron, Bomber Command (January 18, 1944); he was killed in action on April 4, 1945.

Adventures of another sort befell Squadron Leader Alexander M. Jardine of Vancouver. He had joined the RAF late in

1935 and wound up a flying boat pilot. In April 1937 he was posted to Singapore, piloting Singapore IIIs with No. 205 Squadron. With short breaks on Valentia transports, Blenheim bombers and a Sunderland, he virtually toured the area on bi-plane flying boats until March 1941 when Catalinas arrived. From then until November 1941 he was in constant motion. Operating on detached duties out of Koggala Lake (Ceylon), he reconnoitred bases in the Maldive and Seychelles Islands, the Chagos Archipelago, Mauritius and along the east coast of Africa. The work involved photography, taking soundings of water depth, and site line surveys, all the while showing "out-standing zeal, enthusiasm and devotion to duty"; when rec-ommended for the AFC, his superiors wrote: "His navigation, airmanship and flying under all conditions of sea and weather commanded respect."[13] All the while, aircrews were on the lookout for German long range mrchant raiders, but everyone knew that a greater threat lay in the Pacific.

When the Japanese storm broke over southeast Asia, Jardine was swept into the maelstrom. It is a measure of the desperation of those times that apart from searches in the Gulf of Siam, he was called upon to use his Catalina to bomb enemy airfields. Japanese raids drove the squadron from its bases; from mid-January forwards, No. 205 was operating from Dutch East Indian sites. The last two serviceable Catalinas were flown to Australia, but Jardine's machine was out of commission; he nevertheless evaded capture until the end of May. With a party of RAF airmen, Jardine attempted to escape in a Glenn Martin machine, only to find it had been sabotaged. The group moved to the south coast of Java, where they set about building a boat. The Japanese finally caught up to them about May 15, 1942, and he spent 40 months in harsh captivity. Following the war he transferred to the RCAF, retir-ing as a group captain in 1965.

Flight Lieutenant Dudley B. Graeme of Vancouver had travelled to Britain before the war as an agent on behalf of a lumber company. He enlisted in the RAF in August 1940 and trained as a pilot. Having earned his wings, he was posted on May 31, 1941, to No. 11 Group Anti-Aircraft Flight, a unit which was subsequently redesignated No. 287 (Anti-Aircraft Cooperation) Squadron, and spent the next 38 months with that unit. The principal task was to supply targets and drogues for anti-aircraft gunnery practice, although other duties in-cluded simulated low-level and dive-bombing attacks on ground troops. Graeme became flight commander and even-tually was in charge of night flying. His most intensive flying period was a six-month stretch (February to August 1942) when he logged 274 hours. In his long service with No. 287 he flew a variety of types, but the ones he piloted most were the Airspeed Oxford (464 hours), Boulton Paul Defiant (442 hours) and Westland Lysander (116 hours). His superiors thought highly of him; one assesment described him as hav-ing "a good influence and an energising result on his subordi-nates," while another declared, "His keenness and general abil-ity are outstanding." He was awarded an AFC in June 1944. Nevertheless, he must have been relieved when he was finally posted to operational duties, flying 41 sorties with No. 107 Squadron (Mosquitoes) between October 1944 and April 1945. He transferred to the RCAF to speed his repatriation home, but severed all connections with flying after 1946.

Group Captain Charles Ley King was awarded his AFC for services as CO of No. 8 Air Gunner School in Britain. An elec-trical engineer from Sault Ste.Marie, Ontario, he had joined the Royal Flying Corps in April 1917. As a army cooperation pilot in France he had been awarded a Military Cross and then a Distinguished Flying Cross. Like many First World War vet-erans, King had made the postwar RAF his career, and had been mentioned in despatches for operations in Iraq (1928). He was recommended for the AFC for his work in converting the school and its staff to the Blackburn Botha aircraft, one of the most unloveable types ever carried on RAF inventory. Notwithstanding his rank, King logged considerable time, up to 62 hours in a month, giving dual control training to instructors.

Wherever the RAF operated, Canadians were to be found. Some were specialists, like Michael E. Pollard, whose expertise lay in medium bombers – Blenheims at the beginning of the war, Mosquitos at the end. Between operational tours he was chief flying instructor at No. 130 Operational Training Unit, teaching low-level strike tactics. This earned him his AFC to accompany the DFC won in September 1942 and a Distinguished Service Order bestowed in August 1944. Other Canadians performed a variety of tasks. Charles N. McVeigh (further described elsewhere) went from bombers to transport aircraft.

HOME FRONT OPERATIONS

War is a period of great boredom, interrupted by brief moments of intense excitement.

– RICHARD HILLARY, *FALLING THROUGH SPACE* (1941)

The Air Force Cross and Air Force Medal had been instituted specifically to recognize bravery and outstanding services in fields not directly related to contact with the enemy. The Canadian Home War Establishment, charged with defending the country against attacks by enemy ships and aircraft and with protecting the sea lanes of the North Atlantic and Pacific approaches, had only sporadic brushes with hostile forces. Eastern Air Command, for example, in spite of many U-boat sightings, had fewer than 100 direct confrontations with German submarines; only once did a surface warship of the German navy get within 400 miles of Canadian shores (it was undetected by EAC patrols). On the Pacific coast, a submarine shelling a Vancouver Island lighthouse by night and several hundred ineffective unmanned incendiary balloons constituted the only direct Japanese attacks on Canadian soil over a 44-month war. The threat (particularly on the West Coast) was perceived to be greater than was the case, so Canada long maintained excessively large fighter, coastal artillery, torpedo-bomber and patrol bomber forces; the submarine menace in the Atlantic was real enough, but Eastern Air Command was long burdened with inadequate patrol bombers (not overcome until Liberators were introduced in the spring of 1943) while the fighter and coastal artillery aircraft gave aircrews plenty of flying experience preparing to meet non-existent threats.

Not surprisingly, the home front has been little written about since the war; Cy Torontow (AFC, No. 117 Squadron) is a rare bird for having written memoirs that describe, vividly if only too briefly, his experiences in Eastern Air Command and with Canadian-based transport squadrons.[14] Nevertheless, the achievements were there – the development of airports and routes in frontier country, the re-supply of remote bases. The hardships and hazards were also present, from boredom and frustration at flying long patrols which increasingly were known to be pointless, to battling ferocious weather in aircraft like the Canso that seemed designed to produce airsickness. Almost 300 RCAF aircrew belonging to the Home War Establishment bomber reconnaissance squadrons died on active duty during the war. Risks meant rewards; of 427 RCAF recipients of the AFC for wartime services (including one Bar), 377 were based in Canada; of 42 RCAF recipients of the AFM at that time, 38 were based in Canada. Their duties, broadly speaking, were as follows:

	AFC	AFM
Training	258	21
Home War Units	44	10
Transport	31	4
Search and Rescue	10	–
Test and Development	9	1
Meteorology	7	–
Ferry Command	12	–
Other	7	2

There were occasions when service in a Home War Establishment unit might warrant either an AFC or a DFC. S/L Roland Dobson (Hamilton, Ontario) enlisted in the RCAF in 1931. Early in the war he ferried Hudsons overseas, but his principal duties were with No. 7 (BR) Squadron on the Pacific Coast. About September 1943 he was recommended for an AFC; his work as CO of his unit, particularly in training his crews, was stressed. The award was not approved at the time;

he was Mentioned in Despatches in January 1944, and a year later he received a DFC, yet at no time did he ever even sight an enemy vessel, much less attack one. An award was clearly merited; an AFC would have been just as appropriate as a DFC.

Another example of near-interchangeability of some Home War Establishment awards concerned Donald George Selby of Fonthill, Ontario. He had enlisted in Niagara Falls, Ontario, in July 1940 and trained as a Wireless Operator/Air Gunner. On September 5, 1942, he was aboard Catalina Z2140 of No. 116 Squadron when that aircraft exploded and burned at Battle Harbour, Labrador, probably following the accidental release of two depth charges while taxiing. The Court of Inquiry subsequently recommended that "Suitable recognition be shown FS Selby, Sgt [T.L.] Whettell and Mr. Norman Lea [on-shore civilian] for gallant rescue work." Selby was commissioned soon afterwards. On December 13, 1943, he was put up for an AFC, specifically for his actions on this occasion:

Pilot Officer Selby and Pilot Officer Whettell, with other members of the crew and civilian passengers, were blown into the sea. They were able to climb on to the port wing, the starboard wing being in flames. They assisted other survivors, who were suffering from shock and injuries, on to the wing and, due to their coolness, undoubtedly were responsible for saving the lives of at least three survivors.

Nothing seems to have come of this AFC recommendation. Much later, having flown 1,686 hours, including 1,155 on operations (124 sorties), he was recommended for a DFC. This was granted, effective November 3, 1944. The citation made no mention of his brave conduct in 1942, concentrating instead on his more recent duties on long-range patrols:

This officer has proven himself to be a most courageous and resolute member of aircraft crew over a long period of flying operations in the North Atlantic area. His work has at all times been of a very high standard and he has set a splendid example of achievement. His determination and confidence while on operations have been an inspiration to his squadron. He is a wireless air gunner of high merit and skill, and his gallantry and devotion to duty have done much to create high morale amongst the aircrew of his squadron.[15]

I f the line between an AFC and DFC was sometimes difficult to draw, there were instances where the distinctions were clear, and more than one Home War officer received both. The first and most famous of these was S/L Norville Everett "Molly" Small. A native of Allandale, Ontario, born December 1908, he had enlisted at Camp Borden in May 1928. He subsequently trained as a sergeant pilot, receiving his wings at Vancouver in June 1931. He left the force in 1937 and spent two years in commercial aviation, rejoining the RCAF in December 1939. He was posted to No. 10 (BR) Squadron, which was preparing to replace its Westland Wapiti biplanes with Douglas Digby bombers. With airline experience on modern aircraft, Small became a jack-of-all trades – instructor, reconnaissance pilot (looking for airfield

S/L Norville E. "Molly" Small was one of the most dynamic figures in Eastern Air Command. His death in a flying accident deprived that formation of its most effective anti-submarine tactician. (Canadian Forces Photograph PL-6880)

sites in Newfoundland; seeking potential remote anchorages that enemy submarines might try using) and trans-Atlantic ferry pilot (five deliveries to Britain). In July 1941 he moved on to No. 116 (BR) Squadron, just formed and equipping with Catalinas. In May 1942 he became No. 162 (BR) Squadron's first CO, charged with getting it up and running; a month later he moved to Yarmouth to lead No. 113 (BR) Squadron.

"Molly" Small was the most charismatic operational leader in Eastern Air Command; his superiors described him as a "master pilot" and an "excellent tactician." It was natural that the first wartime AFC awards to RCAF aircrew included him (June 11, 1942). He received it at a Government House investiture on December 3, 1942. In the interim he had been nominated for the McKee Trophy; G/C N.S. MacGregor, commanding Station Yarmouth, praised Small for demonstrating that aircraft could now be flown in weather that would previously have resulted in grounding, and for raising the standards of aerial navigation.[16]

During 1942 there had been a radical change in the war; German submarines had moved into the western Atlantic and the RCAF had a fullscale U-boat campaign to tackle. Small led all the way; he was brave, determined and smart. No. 113's Hudsons adopted the latest Coastal Command tactics that had been developed in earlier intensive operations around Britain and Iceland. Other squadrons flew patrols hoping to see a U-boat; his crews often waited for shore-based radio operators to get a "fix" on a submarine, then "scrambled" like fighters to track it down. In four months Small personally conducted five attacks; one of these, on July 31, 1942, sank *U-754*, the first submarine destroyed by Eastern Air Command. As 1942 turned into 1943, Small was turning anything at hand into something better. Canso aircraft had an effective operational radius of 500 miles; he had them stripped of blister guns, ammunition and marginal equipment, and by February 1943 the operating radius had been pushed to 700 miles. On January 1, 1943, Small was awarded a Distinguished Flying Cross; on the 7th he was dead, killed in a Canso crash while taking off from Gander, Newfoundland.[17]

Other pilots in EAC earned AFC/DFC combinations. Barry Haig Moffit, born in Toronto in 1920, was a flight lieutenant operating Cansos and Catalinas with No. 5 (BR) Squadron when he received an AFC on January 1, 1943; the unpublished citation read:

S/L Barry H, Moffit, shown here in a postwar photograph, received both the DFC and AFC for his services in Eastern Air Command. (Canadian Forces Photograph PL-100764)

This officer has displayed unbounded enthusiasm and keen devotion to duty. He has a total flying time of 725 hours, 614 of which have been in 62 operational flights on anti-submarine and coastal patrol work. His efforts in this direction have been untiring and he has set a consistently high standard for the other members of the squadron.

Moffit remained with that unit, fighting the elements all through the winter of 1942-43 as the Battle of the Atlantic intensified. On May 4, 1943, he attacked and sank *U-630* while operating at the limit of his range. Moffit was recommended for a DSO and received a DFC; he remained in the postwar RCAF, rising to group captain before retirement. He died at Stoney Creek, Ontario, in 1992.[18]

Two other Eastern Air Command pilots received AFC/DFC combinations before the war was over. F/L Garrett Munro Cook (Chilliwack, British Columbia) received an AFC on January 1, 1943, for services with No. 116 Squadron; he had been recommended for showing "zeal, determination and devotion to duty" as shown by his having flown 1,550 hours, "850 hours of which were on operational flights covering many hazardous sorties on coastal reconnaissance and anti-submarine patrol." On January 6, 1945, he received a DFC; he was then a wing commander leading No. 113 (BR) Squadron, and his flying was summarized as 2,340 hours of which 1,293 were operational (192 sorties). The award (which could just as easily have been bestowed as a Bar to his AFC) was in recognition of "a splendid record during a long tour on anti-submarine operations" which was characterized by skill, leadership, efficiency, and enthusiasm which made him "an inspiration to other aircrew."

F/O Reginald Ross Ingrams (born in British Columbia, raised in Saint John, New Brunswick) was awarded an AFC at the same time as Cook; he was flying Digbys in No. 10 (BR) Squadron when recommended. As with many other decorations, it was for many hours logged over 82 sorties, none of which had produced a U-boat sighting. His luck changed when the unit converted to Liberators. On the evening of September 22, 1943, F/L Ingrams attacked *U-422* in the Atlantic, inflicted casualties and forced her under; somehow his homing torpedoes missed and he was robbed of a "kill." In March 1945, as a flight commander in No. 145 (BR) Squadron, S/L Ingrams received a DFC; by then he had flown 2,100 hours including 140 sorties (1,325 hours). He was described as "an able leader, whose enthusiasm, courage and devotion to duty have been an inspiring example to those serving under him." Ingrams remained in the postwar RCAF, rising to wing commander and retiring in 1964.

The examples of Eastern Air Command awards just given suggest that in 1942 and early 1943 – when operations were intense, adversity the norm and observable results few – the policy was to award Air Force Crosses with some liberality and restrict Distinguished Flying Crosses to rare instances when a U-boat sinking was known to have been achieved (Small) or the number of attacks had been so high as to indicate a very keen crewman (F/O M.J. Belanger). From mid-1943 to the end of the war, with high flying hours, better equipment and results known with greater certainly, Eastern Air Command cut back AFC and AFM awards, substituting those of the DFC and DFM. The example of No. 116 (BR) Squadron demonstrates the pattern; between June 11, 1942, and January 1, 1943, its members were awarded four AFCs, three AFMs and *no* DFCs; after that, and to the end of the war, squadron personnel would receive two more AFCs but six DFCs and one DFM. For No. 10 (BR) Squadron it is even more striking – five AFCs, two AFMs and *no DFCs* between June 11, 1942, and January 1, 1943, followed by 24 DFCs from January 1, 1944, to February 23, 1946 (no AFCs, AFMs or DFMs).

None of Eastern Air Command's AFM recipients were further decorated, but William Henry Bulmer was distinct from his NCO colleagues. A native of Saskatoon, he had enlisted in February 1941 and trained as a wireless operator. In due course he was posted to No. 5 (BR) Squadron. Bulmer was awarded his Air Force Medal on January 1, 1943; the citation read:

Flight Sergeant Bulmer has at all times displayed courage and devotion in the performance of his duties. He has

W/C Reginald R. Ingrams, DFC, AFC, received the AFC in January 1943 for having flown 601 boring, uneventful yet hazardous hours looking for U-boats in the North Atlantic. Two years later he was awarded a DFC for continued service in Eastern Air Command including one attack on an enemy submarine. (Canadian Forces Photograph PL-133791)

completed 774 hours of flying as observer, 668 of which have been on 69 coastal patrol flights. He is conscientious in his work and has been an example to others at all times. Due to the skill displayed by this NCO in his trade, his aircraft has been enabled to return to base in all types of weather.

Bulmer was later commissioned and posted overseas. On January 1, 1945, he was Mentioned in Despatches. He was then with an Air/Sea Rescue unit (No. 270 Squadron), which would have put a high value on his trade, but details of what work he performed to merit this distinction are not available.

F/O Robert L. Rizon, an American in the RCAF. By the time his AFC had been approved, he had transferred to the USAAF. (Canadian Forces Photograph PL-2654)

(Below) A Supermarine Stranraer, the aircraft type associated with F/O Robert Rizon (AFC) and LAC William J. Hunt (AFM). (National Archives of Canada PA-197484)

Western Air Command operations brought fewer opportunities to engage the enemy; the squadrons that were detached to Alaska in 1942-43 saw only limited action and most personnel who were decorated in that campaign received American awards. Nevertheless, a few AFCs and one AFM were awarded for services on Canada's Pacific coast. One incident gave rise to two decorations. On May 1, 1940, a Seaplane and Bomber Reconnaissance Training School had been opened at Sea Island (Vancouver). In July 1940 its mandate was enlarged to include landplane as well as seaplane training; it was subsequently redesignated No. 13 (Operational Training) Squadron. In November 1940 it was relocated to Patricia Bay, near Victoria. Never employed operationally, it was still considered part of Western Air Command's active reserve, although its few combat aircraft were frequently types one step removed from the salvage shops – Vickers Vancouver and Vedette flying boats, Fairchild 71s and Northrop Deltas, to name a few.

On November 2, 1941, F/O Robert L. Rizon (Los Angeles) was instructing on Stranraer 932. Two years earlier the flying boat would have been considered one of the RCAF's most modern aircraft; now it was being replaced by Cansos in Eastern Air Command and equipping units in this peaceable theatre. As the take-off run began, the port engine burst into

A Supermarine Stranraer, the RCAF's most modern patrol aircraft in 1939. Canadian production of the Stranraer exceeded that of the parent British factory. (Canadian Forces Photograph PL-2729)

flames. Rizon aborted the take-off and set off the fire extinguisher. It seemed to have no effect, so he ordered the crew to abandon the Stranraer. Once they were in the water, however, they noted that Leading Aircraftman A.A. Norridge, a non-swimmer, was missing. He was still aboard the aircraft, searching for his lifejacket.

Rizon, accompanied by Leading Aircraftman William James Hunt (Winnipeg), returned to the aircraft. By now both mainplanes were burning. Hunt gave his own lifejacket to Norridge, then remained to help Rizon who had now decided to fight the blaze. Standing behind the port engine and under the main fuel tanks, now wreathed in flames, he seized extinguishers and buckets of sea water as Hunt passed them up. Eventually the fire died out; the Stranraer was salvaged and continued on RCAF inventory until February 1945. Rizon was recommended for an AFC and Hunt for an AFM. Both were approved, but by the time that occurred (June 1942) the former had transferred to the United States Army Air Forces.

Mention of the USAAF is reason enough to note two AFC recommendations for American personnel that originated in July 1942. Group Captain R.H. Foss, commanding Station Gander, suggested that Major Ryder W. Finn and Captain Bertram C. Martin should be so decorated for a three-month photographic survey they conducted out of Gander in late 1941, covering the Labrador coastline from Hamilton Inlet north to Cape Chidley. Subsequently they had participated in anti-submarine patrols and on February 15, 1942, had been instrumental in the rescue of survivors from a torpedoed steamer. As of this writing (August 2000) it is not known if these awards were approved.[19]

MERCY AND RESCUE WORK

But this she knows, in joys and woes,
That saints will aid if men will call;
For the blue sky bends over all.

– SAMUEL TAYLOR COLERIDGE (1772-1834), *CHRISTABEL*

Out of this nettle, danger, we pluck this flower, safety.

– WILLIAM SHAKESPEARE, *KING HENRY IV, PART I*

In the late afternoon of July 21, 1942, Grumman Goose No. 917 of No. 122 (Composite) Squadron departed Yakataga, Alaska, bound for Anchorage with seven persons aboard. It never reached its destination, and a search was started. On the 29th a report was received of three men having been sighted in a river valley north of Yakataga. That day F/L George L. Preston left Patricia Bay in Goose 940 to investigate. He stopped at Annette Island overnight, picking up a service doctor, F/L W.V. Pepper, before proceeding.

Weather held the Goose at Annette Island until 10.30 a.m. on the 30th, when Preston pushed on to Yakatat. He was advised that survivors had indeed been located at Yakataga, and that an American Hudson had been sent there to retrieve them. No further information arrived, and Preston decided to fly to Yakataga himself, alighting on water. It was well he had used his initiative; on arrival he was told that soft field conditions had prevented the Hudson landing.

Rescue parties moving on foot had brought in a survivor, Aircraftman Maylor, and he told a grim story. Goose 917 had crashed in mountainous country. One passenger had been killed outright; another had drowned during an attempt to walk out. At least two other men were coming on foot, in spite of harsh country and cascading rivers. These two, Sergeant

Francis M. Bailey and Aircraftman T.M. Silberman, reached the coast about 8.30 p.m. From this point onwards, Preston's own report is the most eloquent description of events:

After discussing the procedure for the rescue of the remainder of the crew, we decided it better to locate the aircraft by air, and if there was no place to land near it we would start in from Yakataga by foot which would take five or six days.

The weather closed in that evening and we were unable to take off until noon next day (31-7-42) with three local men, Sergeant Baily and Flight Lieutenant Pepper.

A survivor was located on a hill near the scene of the crash after about forty minutes of flying. Rations were dropped and a note telling him to remain there, that we would be in for him as soon as possible. After scouting around, I located a small lake at the base of the glacier on the opposite side of the mountain where the survivor was located, a distance of approximately two miles. The lake seemed of a fairly good size but there was quite a bit of ice floating and due to the colour of the water I was unable to tell the depth. After searching the lake, a spot of clear water was located which showed fairly good depth, I landed and deplaned passengers,

The rescue party proceeded to the scene of the crash.

The lake was sounded and was found to have plenty of water except at mouth of outlet and near shore.

Approximately ten hours later the rescue party returned to plane with Flying Officer [P.H.] Gault and Sergeant [R.B.] Roberts. We emplaned passengers and took off for Yakataga. The fog was coming in from the sea. I tried to get down to the beach to the landing field but was unable to locate it due to low ceiling, turned out to sea and went up through overcast. The top was 1,500 feet. All places seemed to be filled in. I returned to the lake we had left approximately one hour before and spent the night there, unable to get back to Yakataga Field before noon next day. The weather closed in shortly after.

Sunday we proceeded to the scene of the crash, removed the body of Corporal [Thomas B.] Donald from the crash and buried him in a grave near by, then returned to Yakataga Field.

On Monday, as soon as WX [weather] permitted, we made two trips to Yakatat with survivors as the field seemed too soft to take off with full load. We were held at Yakatat from Monday evening until Friday noon, arriving at Annette Island Friday, August 7, 1942, at 1530 hours. We proceeded to Patricia Bay with the survivors from 917, arriving at 1735 hours, August 8, 1942.

The rescue capped several months during which Preston had performed his various duties in the face of demanding weather and airfield conditions. The *Canada Gazette* of March 2, 1943, announced his Air Force Cross; it also reported that Sergeant Bailey had been awarded a George Medal for his actions following the crash of Goose 917. Preston was in charge of No. 1 Winter Experimental and Training Flight from January 1944 to January 1945; eventually he commanded No. 166 (Communications) Squadron; he was invested with his decoration in Winnipeg by A/V/M T.A. Lawrence on April 15, 1944.[20]

There is a local saying, "God made the world in six days, and on the seventh, sailed inshore and hurled rocks at Labrador." Newfoundland itself has been described as a "piece of rock entirely surrounded by fog." The region beyond the Avalon Peninsula was one of increasing isolation and poverty as one retreated further from St. John's, the capital which at times seemed to have forgotten how to rule its hinterland. When Richard Grenfell arrived in the 1890s he found illiterate thousands suffering from tuberculosis and malnutrition; fifty years onward, struggling with debt through minimal citizen services, the government had done little to supplement the Grenfell Missions.

In 1940 an invasion of Canadian and American forces occurred. Their task was continental protection, but they also brought prosperity to the immediate vicinities of their bases and renewed hope for many inhabitants of outports and camps. The records of bases like Gander and Goose Bay were punctuated throughout the war with reports of mercy missions. Yet the RCAF did not welcome these tasks. It had war work to do, including occasional searches for lost aircrews and resupply of isolated bases; responding to medical emergencies was not only a distraction but also put service aircraft and crews in jeopardy. Sometimes a note of exasperation with civil authorities crept into RCAF reports; on May 12, 1943, following delivery of medical supplies to battle a pneumonia epidemic at Nain, Labrador, the pilot who had flown the mission (P/O S.E. Alexander) complained that the operation would have been unnecessary had the civil power (the Hudson Bay Company and the government of Newfoundland) provided adequate rations and medical stores, backed up by emergency reserves, in the first place.[21]

Few men were busier at exigency flying than F/O Horace William "Jimmy" Westaway. British-born and a First World War veteran of both the infantry and Royal Flying Corps, he had migrated to Canada in 1929 and joined the Ontario Provincial Air Service. He enlisted at North Bay in March 1942 and ended up flying communications aircraft out of Gander. He showed outstanding ability, whether operating on wheels, skis or floats, frequently far from base in marginal conditions.

F/L Horace A. Westaway, AFC, won his decoration at the age of 51, flying mercy missions in Newfoundland and Labrador. (Canadian Forces Photograph PL-25257)

Westaway never refused an assignment; he became a sort of "angel of mercy," alighting in remote communities to fly dangerously ill civilians to whatever hospital might be at hand.

As an ambassador of good will to what was still a foreign community, he made good "copy" for the station's public relations officer. Westaway, it was reported, had insisted on an aircrew medical exam when he joined up, and had amazed the doctors who administered it. "They practically took him apart, bit by bit, but they couldn't find anything that was even slightly worn." He had personally supervised conversion of one of Gander's Norseman into a flying ambulance, accommodating two stretcher cases, a doctor and a nurse. In winter he used ice hillocks to bounce a heavily-loaded airplane into the air on take-off. Late in 1944 the PRO wrote:

> Flying Officer Westaway has a personal war with the stork because he is often called to race the old fellow to the hospital here. So far he has always won, but he is seriously worried about photo finishes. There are many little Newfound-landers who can claim Jimmy for a Godfather and many of them owe their lives to his superior flying skills which enables him to come through in weather that grounds the ducks.

His superiors recommended him for a Mention in Despatches, which was gazetted in November 1944. However, the exploit which gained him an AFC concerned service rather than civilian clients.

On September 6, 1944, two Harvards from Gander were engaged in local flying when one crashed; the accident and location, twelve miles from base, was reported by the other machine on its return. Locating the site should have been easy, but the weather had suddenly turned nasty. Even as search aircraft were being recalled, Westaway took off in a Norseman, located the wreck, and landed on a small lake to let off a rescue party, who reached the two survivors within an hour. Westaway could have sat out the storm there, but instead he returned to Gander to brief any follow-up rescuers. On the morning of the 7th, with no let-up in the weather, Westaway returned to the lake, executing what the Gander diarist described as "one of his famous small area landings," and retrieved both injured men and the ground party. The citation to his

Noorduyn Norseman engaged in training para-rescue personnel, 1943. The Norseman was purpose-built as a bush plane that served the RCAF as a light transport, training aircraft, and rescue machine. (Canadian Forces Photograph PL-13636)

AFC paid tribute to his "outstanding courage and skill ... determination and devotion to duty." Westaway reaped his AFC at the age of 51. His was a rare "immediate" rather than a "periodic" award. He was content to receive it in the mail in August 1945, when he had returned to flying for the Ontario Provincial Air Service at Sault Ste.Marie.[22]

On the night of May 1, 1945, Station Torbay received a message that a medical crisis had arisen in Buchans. A child was dying; penicillin must be delivered at once. The weather was foul – zero visibility, zero ceiling and a 40-m.p.h. wind sweeping down from the north. Three men volunteered to make the flight. After take-off they fought their way through severe icing which interrupted radio communications, and had to grope their way down through cloud until they found a momentary break at 200 feet. The container was dropped successfully and the Norseman struggled back to base. On July 31 W/C Cal Brooker recommended all three aircrew for AFCs, and they were approved. Honoured were F/L Raymond Hoshowsky (pilot, home in Glen Bain, Saskatchewan), F/L Laurence Kauffeldt (navigator, from Ottawa) and F/O Clifford S. Mawhinney (radio operator, from Toronto).[23]

Mercy flights were not confined to the Maritime provinces. No. 6 (Communications) Flight, based in Edmonton, flew many such missions, particularly as Canadian and American air operations extended into the Northwest Territories. However, a particularly dramatic mission was flown closer to home. Early in July 1944, F/O Joseph Sinclair Coombes (Prince Albert, Saskatchewan) volunteered to fly to a bush country farm in the Pembina area, southwest of his base, to pick up a woman experiencing a complicated pregnancy. The challenge for Coombes was the uncertainty of finding a suitable landing site. He took off in a Norseman, accompanied by Nursing Sister Helen M. Brown (Czar, Alberta) and a service doctor, F/L Raymond W. Burnap (Edmonton).

On arrival at his destination, Coombes found that the only open space was a ploughed field. He landed without damage to the undercarriage, boarded the patient, then took off from a hastily improvised runway in a field of scrub brush. Things were just too tight; he scraped through some trees, damaging his elevators and jamming open the throttle. Nevertheless, he regained his base and landed in the dark in spite of damaged controls and having to switch off his engine at the last moment. The patient was hospitalized in time to save her life. The citation to his award stated that Coombes had, "with complete disregard for his own safety, displayed exceptional skill and courage, which is most praiseworthy."

There were honours all around on this mission. Flight Lieutenant Burnap was Commended for Valuable Services in the Air. Helen Brown was recommended for Associate of the Royal Red Cross, a very high honour reserved for nurses. For reasons not apparent, authorities at Air Force Headquarters reduced this to another Commendation for Valuable Services. If the treatment of personnel differed between Coombes' flight and the incident involving Hoshowsky, Kauffeldt and Mawhinney, it should be remembered that the honours system was administered by humans, not computers.

The Pembina flight was Coombes' most notable mercy mission, but not the only one. In mid-October 1944 an American aircraft retrieving personnel on the west coast of Hudson Bay was damaged by storms. Coombes was despatched to pick them up. In three trips spread over two days he ferried 17 men to Churchill. In the summer of 1945 he transported the first in a series of parties that were to locate the North Magnetic Pole; that winter he was involved in aerial resupply associated with Operation MUSKOX. Coombes was nominated in February 1946 for the McKee Trophy. Although he did not receive it, the recommendation itself was a tribute to his services in Search and Rescue, including the RCAF's first training of para-rescue personnel.[24]

At least one non-RCAF American was recommended for an AFC by Canadian authorities. This was a tricky matter when it came to protocol, since the award had to be approved by both the King and the American government. It involved Lieutenant August Kleisch, United States Coast Guard, for an exploit in April 1945. The unpublished citation for his AFC read as follows:

(Left) Lieutenant Kleisch beside his R-4 helicopter.

(Below) Kleisch's base on a frozen Labrador lake. (Both photographs courtesy of United States Coast Guard)

> By co-operation, traditional of the American authorities, Lieutenant Kleisch proceeded to Goose Bay, Labrador, by air, with a dismantled helicopter aircraft. Within twelve hours he had the helicopter serviceable, and in a further forty-eight hours he had completed the rescue, one at a time, of all nine survivors of an RCAF aircraft which had crashed in the bush thirteen days earlier near the border of Quebec and Labrador. The rescue was made with great fortitude and courage under hazardous conditions where any failure of the equipment, comparatively untried under similar conditions, would have left his own chance of rescue very remote, and, at best, have exposed him to prolonged hardships in the severest conditions. But for Lieutenant Kleisch's prompt and courageous rescue, the survivors might have been stranded until spring, with dire results.[25]

The incident described had followed the crash of a Canso of No. 162 Squadron on April 19, 1945, roughly 130 miles from Goose Bay. All nine persons aboard survived, but it was only on the 21st they were located. Supplies and emergency

The RCAF aircrews put their survival training to good use during the two weeks required to effect their rescue. This was their "kitchen," excavated in a 12-foot snowdrift.

When Lieutenant Kleish alighted, he had to put his "chopper" on to a large canvas patch to prevent the H-4 freezing to the lake surface. (Both photographs courtesy of United States Coast Guard)

rations were dropped and two RCAF Norseman attempted a rescue; the first evacuated two injured men; the second, partially mired in slush, failed to attain flying speed and crashed in attempting to take off from the site, fortunately without further injuries. Another Norseman alighted on the 22nd, but was itself stranded by sticky, thawing snow that frustrated take-offs. Eastern Air Command Headquarters appealed to the United States Coast Guard for assistance with a helicopter.

At Floyd Bennett Field, Long Island, a Sikorsky R-4 training machine was dismantled, flown by C-54 to Goose Bay, unloaded and re-assembled. Lieutenant Kleisch flew it to a refuelling site 35 miles from the crash. He could airlift only one person at a time. The first rescue was completed by nightfall of the first day (April 30). However, the R-4's engine froze up during the night, delaying an early start next day. A defroster had to be delivered from Goose Bay before the evacuation could resume; the last marooned flier was removed to Goose Bay on May 3.

Kleisch had joined the United States Coast Guard as a mechanic but had been commissioned as an ensign in February 1942 and promoted to lieutenant (junior grade) in December of that year; as of January 1944 he had been promoted to full lieutenant. He made the United States Coast Guard his career and retired in 1959 as a lieutenant-commander.[26] The case of Lieutenant Kleisch is especially interesting when one compares it to a 1949 attempt by Canadian authorities to secure an AFC for another American Coast Guard officer (see chapter 5).

Overseas, Air/Sea Rescue services were improved throughout the war, with both sides learning from one another. The problems varied with theatre and sea conditions; obviously survivors, be they downed airmen or torpedoed sailors, faced different hazards in the North Atlantic than in the Bay of

Biscay or the Mediterranean. Around the British Isles, and especially the North Sea, the statistics were impressive. A total of 1,684 lives of Allied aircrews were saved in 1943. The two highlights of the year were the week of July 25 to August 1, when 156 were recovered (121 of them Americans) and a single day, September 6, when 131 were rescued (all Americans except the crew of a Sunderland). On Christmas Eve of 1943, Lieutenant-General Ira Eaker (Commanding General, U.S. 8th Air Force) cabled the Air Officer Commanding, Coastal Command:

> Your superlative Air/Sea Rescue Service has been one of the prime factors in the high morale of our combat crews. This organization of yours has picked up from the sea nearly 600 of our combat crewmen since we began operations in this theatre. It is a remarkable achievement made possible only by the highest efficiency and the greatest courage and fortitude. It has our unbounded admiration.[27]

Rescues in 1944 were even more frequent, reflecting the rising intensity of air operations as well increased efficiency of ASR units; the USAAF helped by making available 25 Thunderbolts that served as VHF radio relays and spotters for returning aircraft that were in trouble. A total of 2,364 aircrew were picked up by aircraft and launches based in the United Kingdom, as well as 846 members of other services. Of the latter, 205 were airborne soldiers that had been assigned to the Arnhem airborne assault but had, for various reasons, been forced to ditch.[28]

Perhaps the easiest thing in an ASR operation was to find the survivors, particularly if a clear distress call had been sent out by those in need. Once found, they would have to be kept alive until rescued. At the beginning of the war the RAF used

A drawing from a training manual demonstrates the dropping of Lindholme life-saving gear. (Canadian Forces photograph PL-14806)

Thornaby Bags – floating containers adapted from parachute packs that were stuffed with emergency rations. Dropped by free-fall, they often broke up when hitting the sea, and unless dropped near the survivors they were hard to see and difficult to retrieve.

Staff at RAF Station Bircham Newton developed the Bircham Barrel, tougher, larger and dropped from a bomb rack. RAF Station Lindholme improved on that with Lindholme Gear – five packages, each about the size of a 500-

pound bomb, that were roped together with colourful lines and dropped simultaneously. One unit held an eight-man dinghy; the other four contained medicine, water, food and signalling equipment. The next step was development of the airborne lifeboat, which was introduced into service in May 1943. Although very spectacular, its use and effectiveness were limited; the most sympathetic assessment is that aircraft based in Britain dropped a total of 113 lifeboats; in 61 cases they were boarded successfully by at least one man; in 12 cases the results were not known; in 39 cases no rescue was effected, usually because the lifeboat had been dropped too far from survivors.[29]

While dozens were saved through airborne lifeboats, liter-

Standard dinghy drill practised in an English swimming pool. (Imperial War Museum H.2851)

A few Canadians overseas were decorated for ASR work, but as most received Distinguished Flying Crosses, their achievements lie outside the scope of this book.[31] An exception was F/L John Albert James Murray, flying Warwicks. A pilot in No. 281 Squadron from November 1943 until November 1944, and with No. 279 Squadron thereafter, he was recommended for the AFC when he had logged a total of 680 flying hours, including 180 on ASR duties. He was praised for "loyalty, perseverance and initiative" shown over eight months as a deputy flight commander in No. 279 Squadron.

His most hazardous experience was in June 1944 when he himself was faced with double engine failure near midnight and forced to ditch off Scapa Flow under 10/10 cloud. Nevertheless, he brought the aircraft down precisely and there were no casualties. On another occasion, soon after taking off from Sumbrugh, one engine packed up. He regained the field but weather, topography and the urgency of the situation compelled him to land across and down wind. The aircraft ran off the end of the runway into the sea and caught fire. F/L Murray remained on top of the burning aircraft until all crew members were clear away. He then jumped into the water and assisted a non-swimmer airman who was in danger of drowning.

Although he participated in many searches, only once did

ally thousands were rescued through more conventional means – sometimes by merchant or warships, usually by high-speed motor launch, frequently by Walrus seaplanes dropping out of the sky to pluck survivors from under the very nose of the enemy. Large flying boats could and did make rescues, but not as often as one might suppose; alighting on an ocean swell could be dangerous. Late in 1942 two Sunderlands crashed in the Bay of Biscay trying to retrieve survivors of a third aircraft, and more men died than were ultimately saved.[30]

Murray get to drop an airborne lifeboat, and it was not successful. On September 25, 1944, he was sent far north, off Stavanger, Norway, to search for the crew of a downed Liberator. He located wreckage and one man, believed to be still alive in a dinghy. The lifeboat was dropped, but the survivor appeared too weak even to try reaching it. Lindholme gear was dropped closer, but still the man drifted past the equipment. He was finally observed to fall out of his dinghy and float away, face down. F/L Murray and his crew returned to base; they had been airborne five hours 31 minutes and were heartbroken at their failure.[32]

Coastal Command Warwick aircraft adapted to the Airborne Lifeboat role. This was the type piloted by F/L John A.J. Murray. (National Archives of Canada PA-133287)

METEOROLOGICAL FLYING

Know the enemy, know yourself, your victory will never be endangered. Know the ground, know the weather, your victory will be total.

– SUN TZU, *THE ART OF WAR* (CIRCA 500 B.C.)[33]

A daring pilot in extremity;
Pleased with the danger, when the waves went high
He sought the storms.

– JOHN DRYDEN (1631-1700), *ABSALOM AND ARCHITOPHEL*

In the late 1940s and early 1950s considerable publicity was given to United States Air Force crews who penetrated hurricanes in B-29s and B-50s. In fact, meteorological flying went back much further; it has been supplanted in more recent years by aerial satellites that detect evolving weather patterns in their earliest stages.

The importance of "weather hunting" was increased in wartime because it was impossible to deploy weather ships for long periods lest submarines hunt them down. Moreover, weather data of itself became highly classified information; every effort was made to deny the enemy any knowledge of developing weather patterns in the western Atlantic, even if this complicated communication of what we knew to our own

After the Gloster Gladiator became obsolescent as a fighter, it continued to perform well in the meteorological reconnaissance role. (Imperial War Museum MH-3411)

forces. The Germans were so desperate to obtain meteorological data from points west that in 1943 they landed a robot weather reporting station on the coast of Labrador. The importance of weather reports in modern warfare was crucial, given that huge bomber formations now moved back and forth across Europe; inaccurate information could frustrate raids and endanger hundreds of aircrew personnel. The crucial weight given to weather reports in the timing of the D Day landings in June 1944 has been told repeatedly.

In Canada, the meteorological services were run largely by the Department of Transport until the outbreak of war, when the RCAF became directly involved through training of meteorological assistants and their deployment across the country, first at operational commands and then at the mushrooming British Commonwealth Air Training Plan schools. While much information could be gathered by ground-based devices (barometers, thermographs, balloons and radar), this had to be confirmed by observations in the air. Eastern and Western Air Commands organized meteorological flights to fly far out to sea, gathering data on clouds, winds and changing pressure patterns. The aircraft of choice for these operations was the Canso flying boat, which was capable of very lengthy sorties. Crews engaged in extended over-water flights may have felt a little more secure in a flying boat as well, although a forced landing in the Atlantic or Pacific would have been perilous in any aircraft.

Overseas, aircraft engaged on anti-submarine patrols routinely reported on weather conditions. Early in the war Coastal Command had assumed the burden of seeking detailed meteorological information. This was done through scattered flights equipped with cast-off aircraft – Gladiators and Spitfires for local flying, Hudsons and Hampdens for longer sorties. The latter two were inadequate, both in range and in sophistication of airborne equipment. The RAF admitted that meteorological units were the "Cinderella of the Air Force." In mid-1943 Coastal Command grouped some of the specialist flights into squadrons to scout the weather; this was

A Lockheed Ventura, the aircraft type flown by Western Air Command's Meteorological Flight. (Canadian Force Photograph PL-24334)

followed in October by upgrading of aircraft, principally using Hudsons and Venturas for short-range reconnaissance while Halifaxes flew longer sorties. Fitting the aircraft with proper instrumentation took longer, and in the meantime the Venturas were deemed unsuitable; they were replaced by Fortresses. Special observers were assigned to crews (now numbering eight men in the long-range aircraft) to take the necessary readings, thus allowing navigators to concentrate on their duties.

Meteorological flying was not simply a matter of taking off and looking at weather patterns out to sea. It was specialized and required particular skills. *Coastal Command Review* of August 1944 described these operations in detail:

Briefly, a Met. reconnaissance (as opposed to a vertical ascent) consists of a level flight at the same time each day on a standard track and at a pressure height of 950 milibars – usually between 1,700 and 2,000 feet. At set intervals sea

level pressure, humidity and temperature are found from the special instruments carried. At the end of the track the aircraft climbs to 500 milibars, or about 19,000 feet. The return trip is flown either in a gradual descent or at 500 milibars for a set distance. The observations are coded and signalled back to base, some of these signals containing as many as 80 groups. The navigation can be very tricky as the upper winds are liable to be strong, and at the best they are only forecast winds. Moreover, the pilot is obliged to fly at a set height so that he cannot climb above cloud when he wants an astro sight, nor descend below it when he wants a drift. As often as not he is in cloud for long periods.

Anyone who has served on a station from which Met. aircraft are operating knows that their sorties are very rarely cancelled because of bad weather. Pilots are expected to, and do, take off even when operational aircraft are grounded. Apart from the difficulties and dangers of flying in very bad weather, Met. crews have little excitement to relieve the monotony.

As of January 1944, Coastal Command had a wide array of aircraft and units to gather special information. These were:

No. 1402 Met. Flight, Aldergove – Gladiator, Spitfire VI
No. 518 Met. Squadron, Tiree – Halifax V
No. 521 Met. Squadron, Bircham Newton – Ventura, Gladiator
No. 519 Met. Squadron, Wick – Ventura, Spitfire VI
No. 1407 Met. Flight, Reykjavik – Ventura

At that date, few members of the RCAF were present in these units; No. 521 Squadron had three pilots, three navigators and two air gunners wearing "Canada" flashes; in No. 519

Squadron there were six RCAF pilots, one navigator and ten gunners. These were relatively small numbers when one notes that 903 members of the RCAF were serving in RAF Coastal Command units. One year later, the situation had altered with respect to equipment and RCAF numbers; in December 1944 the organization was as follows:

No. 1402 Met. Flight, Ballyhalbert – Hurricane II, Spitfire VI
No. 518 Met. Squadron, Tiree – Halifax V
No. 521 Met. Squadron, Langham – Fortress II, Hurricane II
No. 519 Met. Squadron, Wick – Fortress II, Spitfire VI
No. 517 Met. Squadron, St. Davids – Halifax V
No. 520 Met. Squadron, Gibraltar – Halifax V, Hurricane II

The enlarged meteorological establishment (including larger crews aboard the four-engined aircraft) also meant more RCAF personnel engaged in this work; No. 518 Squadron had 12 Canadian pilots, 2 navigators and 26 wireless operator/air gunners; No. 1402 Flight had 2 RCAF pilots; No. 521 Squadron had 2 pilots, 3 navigators and 4 WOP/AGs; No. 519 Squadron had 6 pilots, 3 navigators and 19 WOP/AGs; No. 517 Squadron had 7 pilots, 4 navigators, and 10 WOP/AGs. That made a total of 100 RCAF personnel engaged in Coastal Command "met" operations out of 866 Canadians scattered through RAF units in that formation.[34] While their principal task was meteorological, they occasionally drove German submarines under.[35] Even areas not frequented by submarines needed meteorological coverage. Apart from the normal hazards of being far from home in uncertain weather, these aircraft risked brushes with enemy aircraft that were probably conducting similar operations.

That was almost certainly the case with F/L Lyle G.W. Jarvis. A native of Ottawa, he had enlisted in the RCAF in

January 1941, graduating as a pilot in October. Soon afterwards he went overseas and joined No. 519 Squadron. On June 8, 1944, the *London Gazette* announced that he had been awarded the Air Force Cross. No citation appeared, but documents pertaining to his career show that, when recommended, he had flown 941 hours, of which 231 hours had been in the six months preceding nomination for that award. These same documents describe the reason for his being honoured:

This officer has been with the squadron since July 1942. He has carried out no less than 70 long range meteorological reconnaissance sorties, many of which were undertaken in extremely bad weather conditions. He has shown the greatest enthusiasm and persistence in carrying out these sorties and has only once failed to complete a sortie and then because of engine trouble. On many occasions he has carried out flights from Wick to points north of the Arctic Circle. On one occasion, whilst making a meteorological sortie, he encountered and made a determined attack upon a FW.200, damaged one of his engines and only breaking off the attack when the aircraft disappeared into cloud. As Flight Commander, Flight Lieutenant Jarvis has taken great trouble in organizing training and in giving advice and assistance to newly joined air crews. He has proved to be an inspiration to all members of the squadron.[36]

The combat with the FW.200 had occurred northeast of the Faeroe Islands on November 26, 1943, when Jarvis was piloting a Ventura. He had veered in behind the enemy bomber, opening fire with his forward machine guns at 1,000 yards and closing to 400 yards while the Germans replied in kind. The Focke-Wulfe's starboard inner engine was seen to be smoking and the rear belly gun position to be out of action.

The combat had concluded at 3,000 feet as the FW.200 entered cloud; the Ventura was undamaged.

The weather that meteorological crews were to investigate was their more challenging foe. F/O Raymond Hart, a pilot from Midland, Ontario, received his AFC for completing 241 flights (269 hours) in all conditions, including occasions when visibility on take-off was under 200 yards.[37] Flying close to the Arctic Circle, a Fortress of No. 519 Squadron piloted by F/L Donald S. MacNeil (RCAF) was heavily damaged when it was struck by lightning. F/L Marc F. Brunelle (Penetanguishene, Ontario), the radio operator, sustained shock and burns. Nevertheless, working in bitter cold, he improvised an aerial. His exertions aggravated his injuries but contributed to the safe return of the aircraft. Both Canadians received an AFC; their adventure in the electrical storm was one of several which led to their being decorated. MacNeil had flown 52 "met" sorties (450 hours) in the course of his tour.[38]

F/O Charles W. Crawford of Winnipeg was yet another outstanding RCAF pilot engaged in weather reconnaissance. While most AFCs were awarded for long term good work, his was in recognition of an outstanding feat on November 24, 1944. Halifax Q of No. 520 Squadron had been engaged in a long-range sortie over the central Atlantic. Four and one-half hours into the flight, just as they were setting course for base, the starboard outer engine developed trouble in the constant speed unit and had to be feathered. A distress call was sent out; Crawford ordered that all ammunition and some flame floats be jettisoned and continued on at 10,000 feet. In spite of the difficulty, things seemed to be going well; the aircraft was in radio contact with base. Suddenly the port outer engine quit without warning and the Halifax swung violently. The port inner would not give full power; it vibrated furiously when the throttle was applied. The Halifax began losing height at a rate of 200 feet per minute. All non-essential equipment was jettisoned, including the radar transmitter, which had been unserviceable since the failure of the starboard outer engine. An hour after the first sign of trouble, Crawford concluded he could not make base and altered course for Portugal, hoping to land at Lisbon. At 5,000 feet the Halifax entered solid cloud, emerging over water at 1,500 feet, close to Cape Espichel. Contact with base had now been lost, owing to height and distance. The port inner was vibrating worse than ever; Crawford decided to ditch while he still had enough power to control the aircraft. All crew were ordered to ditching stations; before doing so the wireless operator clamped down his key to send a continuous signal.

In the dawn light Crawford could just make out the swell on the sea. He turned to put the aircraft in, along the swell, giving a running commentary over the intercom as he did. The navigator subsequently described events:

At approximately 0750 hours, after what seemed an eternity, the captain ditched the aircraft perfectly, not one of the crew being moved from their position on impact. The nose immediately broke off, and a large wave swiftly rushed through the whole length of the aircraft. A shower of water which entered the front and rear emergency hatches threw the first two of the crew who were already clambering out, back into the aircraft.

After this first onrush of water no more seemed to enter and even when everyone was out of the aircraft, there was only about four feet of water inside.

We salvaged six K type dinghies, two parachutes, dinghy radio and kite, etc., along with two large ration containers, a pair of binoculars and the camera, and also the Nav.bag. The sextant, which I had placed ready to take out with me, had been washed to the rear of the aircraft by the first inrush of water, with our diversion bags in which we had packed our ordinary operational sandwiches, etc.

The impact must have broken a petrol pipe line as the fuselage was soon filled with petrol fumes, and the wireless operator who went back into the fuselage to salvage more kit was so overcome by these fumes that he had to be helped out of the rear escape hatch in an inebriated condition. On being put into the large "Q" type dinghy he completely passed out for a few seconds. Under these conditions it was inadvisable to stay too near the aircraft, so we cut loose the dinghy and paddled about 30 yards away.

Two lights could be seen in the distance, one to the north and the other to the east. As it became lighter we identified these as two ships. We fired a red Very cartridge every five or ten minutes in order to give our position if we had been sighted by either of the ships.

There was a heavy swell running which lifted the dinghy 15 to 18 feet. This made a few of the crew sea sick for a short time. Meantime the six ""K" type dinghies had been blown up and we fastened them to the "Q" type. Into these we transferred part of our equipment. There was a good deal of water in the dinghy so we baled, one of the crew using a boot for the job. Another member of the crew, a wireless operator, took some photographs of the aircraft in the water with the K.20 camera we had salvaged.

About an hour after ditching, one of the ships which we had sighted could be seen heading in our direction, and after spending one hour 40 minutes in the dinghy, we were picked up by this ship approximately 20 miles south-west of Lisbon. It turned out to be a Portuguese fishing trawler, and so we dumped everything into the sea, except the dinghies, binoculars and camera. One of the wireless operators, being first on the trawler, took some more photographs of the crew being helped aboard. He then unloaded the camera and handed the spool of film to the air attache at Lisbon when we finally arrived there.

The crew of the trawler attempted to tow the aircraft into Lisbon, as it was still floating quite well, but after their first attempt the aircraft sank, having floated for two hours 40 minutes. The trawler then landed us in Lisbon, where we stayed for four days before we finally got a passage on an aircraft back to Gibraltar.[39]

Canada's Eastern Air Command needed weather information to deal with submarine hunts in the North Atlantic; in 1942-43 many a Canso had difficultly regaining base in the face of stiff northwesterly winds. Nevertheless, the numerous meteorological stations scattered over North America's great land mass reported conditions reasonably well. It was a different story south and southeast of Nova Scotia; many unexpected weather patterns developed there, notably between the Maritimes and Bermuda.

The Eastern Air Command Meteorological Flight was formed at Yarmouth, Nova Scotia, in October 1943, initially with one Canso; it eventually grew to three Cansos and one Harvard, the latter being used for local weather climbs. Its first commanding officer, S/L Roy D. Renwick of Teeswater, Ontario, remained with the unit until February 1945; he was awarded the AFC on November 3, 1944, for having established a very efficient unit; another founding member, F/L Douglas C. Martin, DFM, a navigator, was subsequently Mentioned in Despatches (July 7, 1945) for "perseverance and devotion to duty [which] have made him one of those instrumental in the carrying out of the original plan and development of this unit."[40]

One writer has described the work in a manner that points up similarities and differences compared to "met" flying overseas:

A typical Met flight consisted of flying a track extending 500 nautical miles SSE from Yarmouth, taking weather observations every 50 nautical miles enroute. At each 100 mile point, descent to the sea was made to obtain an atmosphereic pressure reading using the aircraft altimeter. At the final point a climb to 10,000 feet was made to report on cloud conditions. All observations were coded and radioed back to base. Perhaps one of the most touchy procedures was the letdown to sea level in the thick fog which persisted along the edge of the Gulf Stream. Ones' trust in the radio altimeter had to be stretched even on a clear day if the weather was calm and "glassy" water conditions existed.[41]

The EAC Meteorological Flight had problems throughout its history with aircraft unserviceability. Perhaps it had low priority with Command Headquarters, or Station Yarmouth servicing personnel were less efficient, or perhaps the problems were due to the delicate specialist equipment carried. Faulty engines and leaking fuel tanks were reported frequently, and a notoriously undependable Canso was exchanged for another that proved to be equally unreliable. A low point was recorded in August 1944; 20 meteorological sorties were completed, but two were scrubbed or curtailed by excessively bad weather and nine aborted or cancelled from aircraft unserviceability.

Among those honoured for meteorological flying in Eastern Air Command was F/L William Alden Smith, an American (New York City) who had enrolled in the RCAF in Montreal on August 11, 1941. He trained as a pilot, graduating from No.

8 Service Flying Training School on May 22, 1942. Like many Americans who had joined the RCAF, he chose to stick with the force rather than transfer to the USAAF after Pearl Harbor. If his motives for doing so were potential excitement, he must have been disappointed, for he never left North America. Following further training at Canadian schools, he joined No. 5 (BR) Squadron on July 26, 1943, flying anti-submarine patrols. In the summer of 1944 he went with that unit to Yarmouth, Nova Scotia; he was transferred to the Meteorological Flight on February 13, 1945, and departed on September 18, 1945, only days before demobilization. On December 1, 1945, the *Canada Gazette* announced that he had been awarded the AFC. No citation appeared, but one had been drafted when he was recommended; at that time he had flown 2,025 hours, of which 695 had been flown on operations – anti-submarine patrols with No. 5 (BR) plus weather reconnaissance sorties between Yarmouth and Bermuda. The unpublished citation read as follows:

This pilot and meteorological flight commander has proved himself consistently to be a most keen and efficient captain of aircraft. On one occasion his speedy and accurate reporting of an enemy U-boat enabled subsequent attacks to be carried out against it. Persistently he has taken off on instruments in the face of most adverse weather, making possible the fine record of continuous daily flights which has recently been achieved by the Meteorological Flight. He has displayed praiseworthy skill and devotion to duty.[42]

The diaries of Station Yarmouth and of the Meteorological Flight do not make exciting reading; the entries are sparse and colourless. Read in conjunction with each other, and with those of other units, they offer glimpses of challenges and persistence, though not necessarily of high drama. Thus, the Dartmouth diary entries of April 25 and 26, and 1945 read simply:

[25th] Canso 9832, captained by F/L Smith, took off from base on meteorological flight to Bermuda, being airborne 7 hours 17 minutes.

[26th] Canso 9832, captained by F/L Smith, returned on meteorological flight from Bermuda, being airborne 5 hours 26 minutes.

These are unexciting in themselves, until one looks at the weather. It had been good enough on the 25th, but the following day Smith had returned in marginal conditions, the ceiling varying from 400 to 1,000 feet, with visibility reduced at times to four miles in rain and light fog. More striking, however, are the entries for April 28, 1945. The Yarmouth diary reported:

Canso 11027, captained by F/L Smith, performed meteorological flight for a period of 8 hours 36 minutes.

Other entries, however, showed the true state of affairs. Nos. 5 and 161 (BR) Squadrons, which shared the Yarmouth field, had flown no sorties that day "due to weather conditions." These were further described elsewhere as:

Near zero conditions in fog first nine hours, then gradually improving becoming broken to overcast at 700-1500 by mid period. Visibility less than one mile at first, becoming ten or better second half except briefly five in drizzle. Light drizzle first and third quarters with occasional light rain showers last quarter.

Another example of this sort of determination was on May 18, 1945. The ceiling varied from 70 to 300 feet with visibility ranging from nil to one mile in fog. Other units did not operate that day. F/L Smith took off for Bermuda and completed his mission in 8 hours 22 minutes flying time. Flights averaged about eight hours but on occasion were pushed much longer. On February 13, 1945, for example, Smith was airborne 9 hours 6 minutes; on May 14 he was out for 9 hours 16 minutes, on May 31 he flew an even 9 hours; on June 12, 1945, he flew 9 hours 14 minutes. His persistence was shown on July 22, 1945, when he took off on a weather reconnaissance trip to Bermuda. He was airborne only 48 minutes before engine trouble forced his return. He changed aircraft and departed again, this time flying 8 hours 3 minutes on the outbound leg. The next day, in what must have been a very indirect flight, he returned to Yarmouth in 9 hours 32 minutes. His last "met" flights were on August 9 and 10 (Bermuda and back). On August 13, 1945, a detachment of Liberators from No. 10 (BR) Squadron took over meteorological flying duties. The diary of Station Yarmouth, normally very taciturn, noted the occasion:

> The twin-engined Canso aircraft, long familiar to the residents in western Nova Scotia, finally disappeared from the skies, to be replaced by four-engined Liberators. So ended an era, during which this reliable machine took off in fair weather and foul, departing and returning in brilliant sunlight or dense fog. Many are the flights that terminated in Bermuda, with occasional diversions to New York, Boston, or alternatives, and numerous are the distinguished passengers flown over this route on "joiner" flights, including Rear Admiral Leonard W. Murray, CB, until recently Commanding Officer-in-Chief, Northwest Atlantic, and Air Vice Marshal A.L. Morfee, CBE, Air Officer Commanding in Chief, Eastern Air Command, under whose joint direction the counter submarine measures on the Atlantic Coast were brought to a successful conclusion.

Another pilot honoured for services with the unit was F/L Howard L. Spinney, whose AFC was announced in the *Canada Gazette* of April 14, 1945. Born at Central Argyle, Yarmouth County, Nova Scotia, August 14, 1920, he had been raised in Yarmouth and had enlisted there on October 1, 1940. He graduated from No. 2 Service Flying Training School, Ottawa, on April 15, 1941. It was the beginning of an adventurous career. After a course at the Central Flying School, Trenton, Spinney went on to become an instructor. During this period of his career he had a harrowing experience. In June 1942 he was demonstrating aerobatics to a pupil, descending from 6,000 to 3,000 feet as he did. Suddenly the controls failed and he ordered the student to bale out. The youth was holding his rip-cord when he jumped; the 'chute opened immediately and snagged the leading edge of tailplane. The pupil was killed. Spinney was thrown out before he could turn off the engine. His parachute opened but swung violently and he barely missed a pond and a tree. He was unconscious for a half hour.

He continued instructing; it was not until March 1943 that he was posted to No. 31 General Reconnaissance School at Charlottetown to learn the tactics of maritime reconnaissance. From May to November 1943 he flew anti-submarine patrols with No. 117 (BR) Squadron. He subsequently flew with the EAC Meteorological Flight from November 11, 1943, to February 23, 1945. Later he trained as a transport pilot and served overseas with No. 436 Squadron.

During his tour with the Meteorological Flight he had several memorable flights and one close call. The unit diary includes the following entries:

[July 17, 1944] F/O Spinney took off at 1050Z [Zulu Time or Greenwich Mean Time] in [Canso] 9760 on the Met Flight, returning at 1952Z. This trip was through very turbulent frontal conditions. A request for a diversion to Bermuda was refused because of a tropical storm in the south.

[August 7, 1944] F/O Spinney took off at 1053Z in 11056 on the Met flight, returning at 1903Z. This flight was notable because it encountered a violent cumulo-nimbus cloud at 5,000 feet at 400 miles out. The aircraft was brought out from under at 300 feet.

[December 29, 1944] F/L Spinney took off at 1135Z on the Met flight on 9770. Severe turbulence all the way out coupled with icing and a fifty knot gale forced him to return early from position four at a ground speed of sixty knots. On the climb, one of the outer compartment windows was shattered by ice. Temperature was 0°F. On return to base half an hours work was required to lower the nose wheel, as the doors had become frozen shut. Landing was made at 1620Z, no water base being fit to land in.

On February 7, 1945, an engine failed 100 miles from home. Everything except emergency equipment was jettisoned. He was down to 400 feet when the aircraft finally stabilized and he struggled into Yarmouth. Most disturbing was that although several distress calls had been transmitted, none had been heard at base. When recommended for the AFC, Spinney had flown 2,560 hours of which 330 had been on operations (28 sorties). His superiors had described him thus:

This officer, as captain of an aircraft in a Meteorological Flight, has demonstrated at all times outstanding skill and devotion to duty. On many occasions he has carried out flights in the most hazardous weather conditions, calling for the highest degree of determination and resourcefulness. His initiative and splendid record have been an inspiration and example to all members of his crew and unit.

F/L Spinney left the RCAF in February 1946. He returned to the force in 1951, instructing on Chipmunks at the Moncton Flying Club before taking a second discharge in 1953.

Pilots were not the only ones honoured for their work in the meteorological flights. If one may cite an individual representing another trade, Warrant Officer John C. Henderson is as good as any. He had enlisted in Montreal on December 6, 1940, and trained as an aero engine mechanic. When heavy aircraft became more complex and demanding of pilots, a new aircrew trade was created, that of flight engineer, to assist aircraft captains with such things as fuel systems and balancing engine speeds to required ranges. Henderson remustered to this new trade in August 1943; he was duly posted to No. 116 (BR) Squadron, which he had served in his days as an "erk"; in June 1944 he was moved to Yarmouth and the EAC meteorological flight. The records are not sufficiently detailed to name his crew captain or to provide stories of his sorties. When recommended for an AFC, he had flown 2,388 hours, 1,433 of them operational. The award was announced in the *Canada Gazette* of July 7, 1945, noting that he had since been commissioned. Again, no citation appeared, but documents in the National Archives provide what should otherwise have been made public:

> This warrant officer, as a flight engineer, has completed a very large number of arduous flying hours with a meteorological flight and attached to operational squadrons. Despite adverse weather conditions he has at all times shown great keenness, resourcefulness and devotion to duty. The efficient and reliable manner in which he has carried out his assignments has been an example to all members of his unit.

There were, of course, others in Eastern Air Command's meteorological flight who were recognized with something less than an Air Force Cross. F/L Patrick J. Bruton, for example, was Mentioned in Despatches on January 6, 1945. Bruton is worth singling out, for on January 31, 1945, he undertook a weather flight that lasted 12 hours 37 minutes, possibly the longest such sortie in the history of the unit.

Western Air Command's Meterological Flight is poorly documented in that formation's records. It was formed on December 16, 1944, at Patricia Bay (near Victoria) and used Ventura aircraft. The unit flew one sortie almost daily, each trip lasting a little over five hours. Somewhat more is known about S/L Dalton F. Ritzel, who organized the Western Air Command meteorological flight before moving on to command a communications flight. Born in 1912, he had enlisted in the RCAF in Vancouver on April 2, 1941. He trained as a pilot, received his wings at Calgary in November 1941, and moved on to become a transport pilot in Canada. His posting to Patricia Bay early in January 1945 followed quickly upon formation of the meteorological flight. He was awarded an AFC on February 23, 1946. When recommended he had flown 3,000 hours (210 hours in the previous six months). The citation (unpublished) declared:

> This officer organized and commanded the Meteorological Flight which, although operating under the extremely severe weather conditions that existed in this command during the winter months, completed almost one hundred per cent of its daily flights during the past year. Through his outstanding ability and devotion to duty by personally flying the most hazardous flights, he has set an example to his unit that has made their achievement possible and his untiring efforts in maintaining schedule has been a major contribution towards the safety of flying on the West Coast. On disbandment of the Meteorological Flight, he was appointed Commanding Officer of Western Air Command Communication Flight which he continues to operate with the same zeal and efficiency.

TEST AND DEVELOPMENT

All the business of war, and indeed all the business of life, is to endeavour to find out what you don't know by what you do.

– ARTHUR WELLESLEY, DUKE OF WELLINGTON

Originality is the most vital of all military virtues.

– B.H. LIDDELL HART (1895-1970),
THOUGHTS ON WAR, 1944

Basic research is what I am doing when I don't know what I am doing.

– WERNER VON BRAUN (1912-1977) (ATTRIBUTED)

There were (and are) several types and levels of test flying, from routine checks associated with aircraft serviceability through "first flights" on prototypes, exploring the limitations of aircraft, checking new applications and studying new or improved equipment, as mundane as a compass, as complex as a new navigational system. All have their place; all involve their own peculiar challenges. RCAF test flying and aerial work in support of other research went back to the first days of the force. In the early 1920s, aircrews held small, sticky paddles into the slipstreams of their aircraft, trapping spore samples for the Department of Agriculture, which was investigating the spread and pattern of plant diseases. Aircraft like the Vickers Vedette, developed to meet Canadian needs, had to be test flown. Cold weather tests helped develop heating systems and special lubricants for northern flying. None of this was specifically recognized between the wars.

Even in wartime, most RCAF research and development flying was associated with humdrum tasks; the "cutting edge of technology" was more often being sharpened by manufacturers or advanced technical centres at Dayton or Farnbor-

ough. Early in the war the RCAF Test and Development Establishment at Rockcliffe was testing the adaptability of many types to RCAF needs; it was also examining new equipment such as oil filters, masks that incorporated radio microphones, undercarriage warning horns, cabin heating, cockpit lighting and rear view mirrors. F/O Robert B. Middleton (Fort Frances, Ontario), when on the staff of the Test and Development Establishment in 1940-41, was involved in checking out modifications to Harvards, Yales, Lysanders and Bolingbrokes; his most exciting trials were probably the load, speed, climb and general performance tests he conducted on the Grumman Goblin biplane fighter. One can imagine the excitement that F/O Frederick C. King felt in June 1941 as he flew an Anson, comparing performance between propellers with 75° pitch and those with 80° pitch.

On the other hand, there were moments when staff recognized that they were witnessing something very notable, even if it was not dramatically exciting. The TDE diary of July 21, 1941, recorded one such instance:

First flight of Vidal fuselage Anson 6013X by Flying Officer King. This was an important event. It is the largest moulded fuselage of this type yet attempted. The large fuselage was received in June. The work of assembling commenced on 10/6/41 and was completed 15/7/41. There will now follow a period of testing to ascertain its performance and weathering.

The solid-skin Anson V represented a redesign of the original fabric-covered British Anson. Their durability was increased, so that many Ansons manufactured in Canda survived into postwar service; their earlier counterparts were either burned or became children's play-sites in farm yards.

On October 1, 1943, No. 1 Winter Experimental and Training Flight was established at Kapuskasing, Ontario. The unit diary spelled out the mandate at the outset:

(a) the compilation of operating experiences on individual aircraft types under severe cold weather conditions.
(b) the development of aircraft modifications, lubricants, ground equipment, clothing (as required by Flying Clothing Committee) to facilitate cold weather operation of aircraft.
(c) the establishment of techniques for cold weather operation, servicing and maintenance of aircraft.
(d) instruction of both ground and aircrews in the art of cold weather operations.

The name was misleading; the "training" aspect soon disappeared and the flight concentrated on experimental work. On October 19 F/L Stanley Oklo Partridge reported to take charge of flying operations. A native of Barrie, Ontario, he had enlisted in the RCAF in April 1928 and served as a mechanic. Long service and experience qualified him for better things; in July 1941 he was commissioned in the Aircraft Engineering Branch of the force. Soon afterwards he took aircrew training at No. 2 SFTS and earned his wings. After several months as a check pilot at Nos. 8, 9 and 10 Repair Depots, he was posted to the new testing unit. In January 1945 he would be promoted to squadron leader and given command of the place.

Kapuskasing had few facilities; there were two hangars, one of which was used by No. 124 Squadron. However, it had not been chosen for comfort; quite the reverse. In mid-winter it was just about the coldest corner of Canada. One of the first aircraft delivered to the flight was a Lancaster III, EE182, and although Partridge flew several types of aircraft during his tour with No. 1 WET Flight, this "bird" (which became increasingly temperamental with age) was his specialty. At the beginning the Lancaster was often away in Toronto, where Victory Aircraft was beginning to produce "Lancs"; EE182 was used for tasks ranging from comparative performance trials to public relations flights. Nevertheless, its prime role was to be alternatively parked and flown in cold weather while a stream of experts evaluated modified lubricants, grease, fuel lines, guns and gadgets. To experience the worst that Mother Nature could offer, flights ranged farther north, to James and Hudson Bays. It was not uncommon for Partridge to pilot a Spitfire or a Mosquito on the same day as the Lancaster.

When warm weather came, the test program was cut back, but Partridge continued to fly EE182 on other duties. On April 14, 1944, he and a crew left Kapuskasing with the Lancaster on an extended demonstration tour that culminated on the 30th at Ellis Air Force Base, Florida. There they demonstrated the type to American officers; Partridge also had turns at the controls of a PB4Y, Marauder and B-29; the unit diary reported his return on May 25. Within a week he was off to Wright Field in Ohio for more Lancaster demonstrations (and check flights on a P-38, P-47G, P-60, Sikorski R-4, A-26, P-61, and B-29), returning on July 1. However, his most interesting detached duties were those he performed in April 1945. In

Stanley O. Partridge, whose varied career included test pilot and Arctic survey duties. (National Aviation Museum)

anticipation of Lancaster units operating alongside American bomber units in the Pacific – and with a view to Allied standardization of some equipment – he was to learn and teach as much as possible in a few days. With a full crew he left his unit on April 12, proceeding via Rockcliffe and Washington. Excerpts from his report describe their work:

15 April – Washington to Eglin Field. On arrival the aircraft was thrown open for inspection by the ordnance and armament officers of the Field.

19 April – Bomb loading equipment was demonstrated to the Committee of Standardization of Bomb Suspension composed of specialists from the U.S. Army Air Forces, U.S. Navy and RAF.

While at Eglin Field, the officers and NCOs of the crew were given the opportunity of obtaining useful information and instruction in matters of interest to their trades. Squadron Leader Partridge received 14 hours instruction in very heavy bombers qualifying as first pilot day and night on both the B-29 and B-32. This is attested to by transition slips signed by the appropriate authorities of the Very Heavy Bomber Group at Eglin Field. Flight Lieutenant [G.C.] Peek received instruction in the air on the Norduyn [sic] bombsight. The other members of the crew spent their spare time studying American equipment and methods. Three American officers were given flying instruction in the Lancaster and were checked out with Squadron Leader Partridge.

On April 25 they left Eglin Field and flew to Bolling Field, Washington. Next day, at the request of the British Air Commission,

Lancaster EE182 at Kapuskasing during cold weather tests under the direction of S/L S.O. Partridge; note the special engine tent. (National Archives of Canada PA-196936)

Partridge and his crew flew to the Patuxent River Air Station as part of a show put on for the Secretary of the U.S. Navy before the flight home to Canada.

As mentioned, EE182 had her bad days. One of those was March 27, 1944. The WET Flight was being moved from Kapuskasing to Gimli, Manitoba. Partridge was transporting 17 people to the new base when the port inner engine failed near Sioux Lookout, and he completed the flight on three engines. Another notable day was February 17, 1945; on that occasion the unit diary reported:

Lancaster airborne at 1045 to 1230 hours, Squadron Leader Partridge as pilot. Flare dropping and prop feathering tests carried out. No. 3 engine propeller failed to unfeather. Landing effected on three engines. Airborne again at 1545 to 1730 hours. High altitude (26,000 feet) oxygen test. No. 4 engine of Lancaster failed in flight. Dinghy release tested on Lancaster after flight. Work commenced on changing No. 4 engine of the Lancaster.

Perhaps as a reward for his troubles, Partridge was sent with the Lancaster to England in mid-June 1945, returning to Gimli on July 20. While in Britain he added to the aircraft types in his logbook, including a Typhoon, Tempest, Lincoln, Meteor, Me.323 and Ju.352. He was awarded his AFC while absent overseas. When recommended he had flown 1,423 hours, a third of it on test flying. The citation noted that at various times he had checked out 84 American and civilian pilots on the Lancaster, notwithstanding that the type had no dual controls.

No. 1 WET Flight was stood down on September 22, 1945; on October 1 it was reborn at Edmonton as the Winter Experimental Establishment. Partridge was still with the unit, using EE182 as a freighter when he was not flying a Mosquito. A peculiar entry in the new WEE diary was dated October 14, 1945: "Mosquito KB428 (S/L Partridge) airborne to Vancouver to hunt for tradesmen." Whether he was checking on AWOL airmen or expected to bring people back in the bomb bay was not clear!

The WEE was soon evaluating a far greater range of aircraft than the old WET Flight had known; as of January 31, 1946, they had two Spitfires, two Lancasters and two Meteors plus one each of the following types – Halifax, Liberator, Lincoln, Mosquito, Tempest, Hudson, Dakota. However, the larger establishment compelled Partridge to fly less and administer more; his deputy, S/L E.L. Baudoux, assumed the burden of supervising flight testing; when he was airborne, Partridge was most likely to be checking airfields in the Northwest Territories or flying a Liberator on radio calibration duties.

On June 21, 1946, he was posted to Northwest Air Command Headquarters. That summer he participated in Operation INVESTIGATOR, an extensive survey of potential bases using a Canso and two Norsemans. This was in anticipation of the RCAF's postwar northern mapping. He also found himself on an Arctic jury at the murder trial of an Inuit woman. Partridge went on to technical staff positions at Edmonton, Rivers and Ottawa. He retired in March 1960 and died in 1992.[43]

A frequent visitor to the WET Flight at Kapuskasing and Gimli was F/L James Clayton Snyder of Kitchener, Ontario. He had earned his wings in March 1941. Soon afterwards he was posted to No. 120 (BR) Squadron on the Pacific Coast. In March 1943, however, he was posted to the Test and Development Establishment at Rockcliffe to become staff pilot to the specialist de-icing flight. Beginning with Hudsons and working up to larger types, he was at the forefront of aircraft de-icing techinques until February 1945, when he was posted away to train as a Mosquito pilot. When recommended for an AFC, he had flown 1,845 hours, although how much was specifically with the de-icing flight is not known.

S/L Andrew Robert Leslie McNaughton received his AFC in June 1945. He was the son of A.G.L. McNaughton, Canada's best known general of the war. The father had been a true soldier-scientist (he retired as Chief of the General Staff to become chairman of the National Research Council), and the son was similar. The younger man had been educated at Loyola College and McGill University and was employed as a research scientist by Canadian General Electric when the war broke out.

Andrew McNaughton joined the RCAF in October 1939 as an armament officer on the General List; he attained the rank of squadron leader in July 1943 and was released from the force in January 1946. Almost the whole of his service career was spent at Rockcliffe. When recommended for the AFC he had flown 1,480 hours. Although he piloted aircraft during some experiments, much of his air time was logged with somebody else at the controls. Some experiments, such as comparing the durability of self-sealing fuel tanks under fire

The son of a famous general, F/L Andrew R.L. McNaughton chose the RCAF as his career and became a test pilot. Notwithstanding the job, his career proved to be remarkably uneventful. (Canadian Forces Photograph PL-9211)

from different weapons and types of shells, could be carried out without leaving the ground.

He authored or co-authored at least 29 wartime technical reports while with the Test and Development Establishment; his output was almost certainly higher as he would have contributed to research that was conducted by others as well as experiments held at places other than Rockcliffe. Summaries of sample reports, found in the Test and Development Establishment diary, demonstrate the nature of his duties and the painstaking commonality that constituted most such work:

December 4, 1942: Further report to Report No. 531 on Pattern of Bombs…The purpose … was to investigate the accuracy with which a series of linked bombs can be dropped from an altitude of 30 feet on a full size plan of a submarine drawn on the ground.

January 8, 1943: Report No. 565 on Flares, Aircraft Reconnaissance 4.5-inch Experimental Proof Tests… The purpose of investigation was to proof test certain 4.5-inch aircraft reconnaissance flares by launching them from 20,000 feet above ground level…

July 3, 1943: Report No. 622… Trials on Tow Target Release Hook Incorporating ATFRO [Atlantic Ferry Organization] … Purpose of investigation was to conduct towing tests with towing hook…

Not all experimental work was conducted at the recognized test units. At one time or another, tinkering went on everywhere. However, No. 6 Repair Depot, at Trenton, was particularly busy for several factors – proximity to Ottawa and Toronto (where ideas were so often hatched), the presence of Lake Ontario (suitable for testing everything from ordnance to sea markers) and a variety of aircraft at all times.

F/O Alex Kennedy Miller was an American from New York City. He must have been a colourful character; the diary of No. 6 RD reported on May 30, 1944 that he had gone on leave to fly his own First World War airplane (identified as a "D.H.G.," an apparent misprint for something else) at a U.S. Army air show. Elsewhere he has been described as a barnstormer and a crop duster.[44] Miller was 37 when he joined the RCAF; his wartime service was entirely at No. 6 Repair Depot. The greater part of his duties consisted of checking previously "bent" aircraft after they had been repaired and ferrying them back to their units. Nevertheless, he volunteered in June 1943 to fly a Fairey Battle to its limits while being photographed in various stages of blacking-out. This was part of the work being conducted by W/C Wilbur Franks in developing blackout-inhibiting flying suits. Miller was a "G"-force guinea pig on at least three and possibly five occasions.

Although his AFC citation mentioned the work with Franks, Miller was also remarkable for salvaging aircraft that had force-landed in what appeared to be impossible places. In April and June 1943 he flew out Ansons from what were described as "difficult and inaccessible fields"; on February 2, 1944, he took a ski-equipped Anson off a tiny lake and flew it back to Trenton. He was awarded the AFC on January 1, 1944, and received it at a station parade on April 26. On May 2 he performed a feat that may have caused his superiors to doubt his judgement, if not his sanity.

Anson 7581 had force landed near Rice Lake (close to Peterborough, Ontario) and Miller was sent to bring it out. A fence separating two fields was taken down and he prepared to take off. The base newspaper, the *Sixardee*, tells the rest with flair:

From the take off to the division of the fields he could gain no speed. The aircraft hit the hump between the fields and settled back on the soft ground, where the wheels hit even softer stubble and dug in, resulting in a loss of speed which F/O Miller could ill afford to lose.

At this point F/O Miller was too close to the end of the second field to stop and start over again. So he pulled the aircraft off the ground to avoid the last fence. Due to lack of sufficient airspeed, the tailplane settled and struck one of the fence posts, destroying the port elevator and stabilizer and breaking all elevator control. Because this last field terminated in a steep hill to the lake shore, F/O Miller found himself in a nerve-wracking position. The aircraft started a severe loop. F/O Miller, knowing he had no elevator control, cut all power to stop the uncontrolled plunge and at this point the aircraft dove steeply for the lake. F/O Miller had to give full throttle to both engines and from this point on he staggered across the lake, pulling the throttle on and off to keep the aircraft from ditching.

When last seen he was heading across the opposite hills, climbing very slowly, but through his exceptional ability maintaining steady control by using his throttles only. He climbed to 10,000 feet and prepared to bail out. But, thinking it over, F/O Miller decided to experiment with his throttles and to attempt to bring the aircraft back in a long, slow glide. He judged it from Cobourg so that at the end of the glide he would be just over the fence at the end of the runway of Trenton airport. At about ten feet he cut his throttles and the aircraft nosed straight down and hit the deck of the runway. But once again, F/O Miller kept control and with no brakes he taxied right in to the Test Flight with a few cupfuls of gas to spare.

While test flying is most often associated with aircrew trades, such work involves scientific as well as flying skills. Thus, an early RCAF recipient of the Air Force Cross was W/C George Edward Hall. Born in Lindsay, Ontario, in October 1907, he had attended the Ontario Agricultural College and the University of Toronto. From 1925 onwards he was also an active militia officer. At age 36 he held a bachelor's degree in agriculture, a masters degree in biochemistry, a doctorate in physiology and his medical degree from University of Toronto. At the latter institution he came to know Sir Frederick Banting as early as 1928; by 1939 the latter (famed for his discovery of insulin, a patron of research, but an indifferent administrator) was grooming Hall to take direction of the Banting Institute.

On June 27, 1939, a newly-formed Committee on Aviation Medical Research met in Ottawa with Banting in the chair. The conference established some administrative procedures for an interdepartmental approach to aviation medicine, with the Department of Transport, National Research Council and Royal Canadian Air Force playing the major role. At the same time, some research priorities were outlined. First among these was study of respiration and gas metabolism at higher altitudes, psychological studies affecting aircrew selection, and development of emergency oxygen apparatus. The committee also recommended that a decompression chamber, the first in Canada, should be built at once. This was ultimately designed by Hall (even before he joined the RCAF), Professor W.R. Franks and F/O J. Shortreed, borrowing heavily from American sources; in it, Hall took hypothetical "flights" beyond 35,000 feet, wearing current oxygen equipment. The chamber was fully operational by April 1940, just as the BCATP was getting under way. It proved to be a useful tool in assessing aircrew candidates, so much so that it was used only sparingly for

research. Eventually such matters would lead to a bitter parting of the ways with Banting the scientist, who felt that Hall was putting the needs of the air force ahead of pure research.[45]

Hall had joined the Royal Canadian Army Medical Corps, but on November 16, 1940 he switched to the Royal Canadian Air Force. His early work with that force included participation with two other doctors in a study of electrocardiogram records of 2,000 RCAF aircrew, with results indicating that many apparently healthy applicants had incipient cardial problems.[46] Another of his early assignments, undertaken in December 1940, was a study of air sickness in aircrew trainees, the better to prescribe safe drugs to counter this problem.

He had become a member of the Committee on Aviation Medical Research no later than November 1939. By the autumn of 1941 he was co-ordinating much of the medical research being conducted at many locations but principally at the Test and Development Establishment (Rockcliffe) and Nos. 1, 2 and 3 Clinical Investigation Units, located respectively at Toronto, Regina and Victoriaville. He was concerned with such topics as carbon monoxide levels in aircraft and efficient oxygen masks. Research also took him into design of emergency rations for downed airmen and cold-weather clothing for aircrew and groundcrew alike. In doing this, it was he who laid out the scientific objectives, planned the general line of research, defined operational needs and often participated in the actual tests.

The reports of the committee give some idea of the hazards, discomfort and accomplishments that were part of the job. On May 8, 1941, for example, Hall sat in the turret of a Douglas Digby while it cruised at 10,000 feet for 25 minutes. He wore the standard RCAF summer flying suit over an ordinary uniform. The object was to test the comfort levels in the turret; Hall's body temperature was recorded at five points – on his trunk, arm, thigh, leg and rectum. Only at the last-noted position was body temperature maintained. A need to redesign clothing and turrets was indicated. When a new electrically-heated flying suit was developed, Hall checked it out during a 14-hour sortie in an RCAF Liberator (August 1943).

The process of investigation through to operational adoption was described by one newspaper, taking as an example the curve-fingered flying glove that was developed during the war.

Flying scientists, searching out problems, noticed the old standard glove gave airmen little comfort in sub-zero temperatures and greatly reduced efficiency. They saw pilots grope, all thumbs, over control gadgets, navigators stumble their fingers over maps and slide rule; flight engineers fingers stick to cold steel, and air gunners spend precious minutes trying to adjust jammed guns.

G/C George E. Hall was particularly proud of his AFC, for it proved that he had been accepted by the flying community, even though he, as a doctor, wore no aircrew badges. (Canadian Force Photograph PL-25041)

A glove was needed that combined warmth, flexibility, durability, economy and efficiency. Quiet men like Group Captain Ed Hall, chairman of an air force research committee, got around a table and talked things over. At the table sat a physiologist, physicist,

geologist, textile chemist, textile engineer, medical officer, and a member of air crew – the latter for practical advice.

The investigating scientist presents the problem and his colleagues – civilian and service – go to work. Skin and blood temperatures are measured at sub-zero temperatures and clothed in various thicknesses of material. But the ideal material, when found, is of little use when the fingers, in assuming their natural bent positions, cause a pressure at the joints and subsequent loss of warmth. Then one scientists hits upon the bright idea of modelling the glove fingers in the natural curved position.

But the glove must be easily removed in case of emergency at temperatures down to 40 below. So a zipper is handily installed from forefinger and then to wrist. A thin, firm-fitting rayon glove and a wool glove, smooth on the inside, complete the assembly.

Even the design of a flying glove could be a challenge to those like Hall who were engaged in aviation medicine. (Canadian Force Photograph PL-14822)

Now the airman can yank the zipper and pull off the wool insulating glove. The rayon affords enough protection in the chilling cold for the two minutes emergency work required with the slide rule, instrument panel, jammed gun, radio knob or engine gadget. Then back goes the hand into the snug covering and the guy from Winnipeg or Toronto is nearer top efficiency than his poorer equipped opponent.

The prototype complete, 100 pairs or so are turned out and sent to operational crews, together with a comprehensive questionnaire. Any modifications necessary are applied and the glove is sent to the air chiefs of staff for approval. From there it goes to production and is made available to the Allied air forces.[47]

Hall's work took him to England several times. Late in 1941, returning to Canada by ship, he was thrown out of his bunk as the vessel lurched. He suffered a painful back injury which troubled him for years thereafter. Trans-Atlantic flights were equally uncomfortable, as he with his fellow passengers huddled in unheated bombers, breathing oxygen from equipment that sometimes failed.

Hall was as good an administrator as he was a scientist. In 1942 the Canadian Army tried to borrow him to organize their own research staff dealing with protective clothing. On July 10, 1942, his superior, A/C R.W. Ryan, recommended Hall for an award – Companion, Order of the British Empire (CBE). This was actually a decoration reserved for senior officers, and would almost certainly have been downgraded to an OBE (Officer, Order of the British Empire). However, at some point in the chain of command that ruled on such matters, the suggested honour was further switched from an "order" to a "decoration" – possibly because (as in the case of Larry Wray) the acceptability of honours within the Order of the British Empire was still in doubt, or perhaps because the quota for OBEs had been filled.

On January 1, 1943, W/C Hall was awarded the Air Force Cross. He was then on the strength of Air Force Headquarters (Directorate of Medical Services, Air) in Ottawa. Again, no citation was published, but RCAF documents include an unpublished citation that fully explains how he came to be singled out.

Since the outbreak of war, this officer has been applying Physiology and Physics to the problems of maintenance of aircrew personnel, and he has been co-ordinating all medical activities from an operational point of view. He has spent 300 hours in the air, mostly on test and development work, and on operational flights to get first hand information for safe-guarding the wellbeing, efficiency and safety of flying personnel. He has been the first on all occasions to undertake the risks entailed in development work, particularly in the fields of decompression sickness, high altitude flying, and the testing of oxygen equipment and protective clothing at high altitudes, actually in the air. The risks to which he has exposed himself are the determining elements for eliminating those dangerous factors which may militate against the efficiency, maintenance and safety of aircrew personnel. He was responsible for the erection of the first low pressure low temperature chamber, and his work on anti-glare glasses has been of the highest order.

Hall was intensely proud of the award for several reasons. As a non-flying member of the RCAF, it signalled his acceptance by the aircrew community. Moreover, over the years, he had often argued with colleagues about "theoretical" vs "practical" research; his dedication to the latter had led him to break both with the army and with Banting. His award was proof that he had followed the right path. However, the sight of his ribbon (with no accompanying flying badge) led some to look at him in wonderment. One Canadian pilot (overtired and on stimulants during trans-Atlantic flying) even accused him of being an imposter! Further recognition would follow – promotion to group captain and award of the RCAF's Efficiency Decoration, in appreciation of nearly 20 years of service in the militia and the air force.

Late in 1943 the University of Western Ontario had approached the RCAF, asking that Hall be released to assume the duties of Dean of Medicine, as that faculty was being reorganized and a man of his reputation was needed to head the department. He was too valuable to be spared at once, but so anxious was the university to have him that they simply accorded him the title of Dean of Medicine, then waited until early 1945 when he returned to Canada, resigned his commission and assumed his new duties.

His research work had taken him to Dayton, Chicago and Washington; in October 1946 it was announced that the United States had made him an Officer in the Legion of Merit. He had been singled out for this specifically for his wartime co-operation with the Americans in the development of protective clothing and oxygen equipment. After the war he actively promoted RCAF Reserve activities at the University of Western Ontario and for many years he was president of that institution. He continued to be consulted on service medical matters until the early 1950s; on October 26, 1953 he was awarded the Queen's Coronation Medal. Doctor Hall died on February 11, 1972; his papers are held by the university archives, awaiting a biographer.[48]

Philip Livingston was born on March 2, 1893, at Cowichan Bay, Vancouver Island. He severed his links with Canada in 1912 when he embarked upon medical studies in Britain, and it was 42 years before he visited Vancouver Island again. His subsequent career was with the Royal Navy and the Royal Air Force; when he left the service in 1951 he was A/M Sir Philip C. Livingston, KBE, CB, AFC. Because of his birthplace he is normally listed as a Canadian in the RAF, and even a British writer has described him as "a tall, athletic

Philip C. Livingston (shown here as a group captain) was prominent in RAF aviation medicine. Although he entered that force as a doctor, he earned pilot's wings to experience at first hand the stresses imposed on those he studied. (Canadian Force Photograph PL-14177)

Canadian," though this country's claims to him were tenuous. Nevertheless, he chose to retire to Duncan, British Columbia, where he died in 1982.

Livingston was a specialist in ophthalmology; he also trained as a pilot. From the mid-1920s forwards he concentrated on problems relating to vision in flying. A visit to Germany in 1937 convinced him that the RAF must devote more resources to medical research; how, he asked, were British pilots to fare against Germans having better oxygen masks, goggles and flying clothes? He urged construction of a low pressure chamber to simulate high-altitude flying; officials said it was impossible; his reply was that Germany had already built one. One day, while giving an eye examination to a member of Parliament, he mentioned Britain's relative backwardness in aviation medicine. His words found their way back to the Air Council, and Livingston was called on the carpet for bypassing normal channels in the presentation of his views.

Simple matters included determining standards of vision expected of aircrew and the design of goggles that did not fog and reduced glare during flight. More complex subjects were detection of ocular defects including colour blindness, the effect of diet and drugs on vision, improving night vision, and

Decompression chambers such as this one at No. 1 Initial Training School, Toronto, were very much in demand for medical research, aircrew evaluation and training. (Canadian Forces Photograph PL-3425)

the impact of rapid decompression on the eye. He studied matters as subtle as how a switch from standard to tricycle undercarriages affected aircrew perceptions. In the course of his work, Livingston frequently was both guinea pig and researcher. For repeatedly putting his health and personal safety on the line, he received the Air Force Cross on June 11, 1942. At war's end his OBE (awarded in 1938) was upgraded to a CBE; he was knighted in 1950.[49]

Another "hands-on" person in experimental work was John Fulton, a CAN/RAF pilot. Born in Kamloops, British Columbia, on November 4. 1912, he had been educated in that city and served briefly with the Canadian militia before joining the RAF in 1935. His career was one of the most interesting of the CAN/RAF people. Soon after commissioning he was posted to No. 10 Squadron and then to No. 9 Squadron. With these he flew the last generation of biplane bombers used by the RAF. He also acquired the sobriquet of "Moose," partly because of his robust build, but chiefly because his colleagues felt that a Canadian had to have a nickname, and what could have been more Canadian than a moose?

At the outbreak of war he was a test pilot at Farnborough. His duties were so hazardous that he might well have regarded a June 1940 posting to No. 99 Squadron (Wellingtons) as a form of relief. Nevertheless, Bomber Command was embarking on intensive operations to hinder German invasion plans. Fulton carried out 26 missions with the squadron. His work there led to promotion to squadron leader, a special message of thanks from the Admiralty and award of the DFC.

Fulton was posted from No. 99 Squadron in mid-October 1940 and rejoined the Experimental Section of the Royal Aeronautical Establishment, Farnborough, for another stint at test flying. He was appointed head of the Instrument and Armament Defence Flight. In the course of his tour he was injured when a Spitfire he was flying suffered engine failure; he force-landed in a field and the aircraft overturned. His AFC recommendation was unusual in that it was supported by two agencies – Army Co-operation Command and the Ministry of Aircraft Production. It read:

This test pilot has had two tours of duty with the experimental section, interspaced with a period of operational flying during the course of which he was awarded the Distinguished Flying Cross. During the first posting to the experimental section he was in the research department flight at Exeter in the days when impacts into balloon cables first began in earnest. He carried out 38 actual impacts into cables, two of which were of unusually original nature in Wellingtons. He also carried out very successful and important de-icing work in Blenheims and Harrows. Since his return to the experimental section he has been successful in completing a large number and variety of experiments, particularly at night, in connection with aids to night flying. He has set a splendid example and has shown initiative, determination and courage.[50]

Fulton left the Royal Aeronautical Establishment in November 1941; on December 21 he was promoted to wing commander and given command of a new RCAF bomber unit, No. 419 Squadron. A born leader and daring pilot, he received a DSO and organized the unit into a magnificent fighting team. He was killed in action on July 28, 1942; thereafter, No. 419 was called the "Moose" Squadron, and its wartime personnel proudly described themselves as "Moosemen."

Several members of the RCAF were engaged overseas in operational research and development. F/L Donald Ian MacQueen Fink (Hamilton, Ontario) was a pilot serving with the Airborne Forces Experimental Establishment; the unit in turn had close ties to the Ministry of Aircraft Production. After an abbreviated tour in Bomber Command, he had joined his new unit in July 1942. His logbook showed him towing two light Hotspur gliders (with a Miles Master) on July 29. On August 4, 1942, he was in a Halifax crew towing *three* Hotspurs. Two days later he was piloting a special stripped-down Halifax towing a huge Hamilcar glider, a type which figured with greater frequency in his log entries. The glider loads increased gradually until the Hamilcar represented 18 tons of towed load for the Halifax.

There were problems along the way, ranging from failed communications between tug and glider to bad weather and including Stirling, Halifax and Lancaster tugs. The work also included towing a Hamilcar on April 24, 1943, while photographers in another aircraft snapped pictures from all angles for use in recognition manuals. Some flights, which should have been routine, were not. On June 6, 1943 he was piloting an

W/C John Fulton, DFC, AFC was a heroic bomber pilot, a brave test pilot, and a charismatic leader. He was the first commanding officer of No. 419 Squadron; when he was killed in action, the unit took his nickname, "Moose," as its own. (Canadian Forces Photograph PL-7742)

Hamilcar heavy gliders marshalled for D-Day operations. The development of these craft proved difficult; F/L Donald I.M. Fink received an AFC for his work in finding the right tug and towing gear for these motorless monsters. (National Archives of Canada PA-175174)

Halifax C.VIII, sometimes used as a freighter, sometimes as a tug for the largest Allied gliders carrying light tanks and field guns. (Imperial War Museum MH.4931)

Albemarle and towing a heavily loaded Horsa glider when almost everything went wrong. His hydraulic system failed, depriving him of flap controls, and he began losing height. The glider release mechanism also refused to function until they were down to 50 feet. Fink had to struggle to avoid stalling. At 75 feet altitude he scraped over tall trees and high-tension wires, yet he managed to avoid a crash. "Nearest I've been to six feet under," he wrote in his logbook, yet paradoxically he added, "It was a new experience. I don't feel shaken" – as though he was surprised at how well he had handled the crisis.

Following 18 months service with that the AFEE, Fink was recommended for an AFC. It was noted that he had "taken part in many trials of major importance," singling out his duties as tug pilot during the Hamilcar trials. This large, heavy glider challenged Stirling and Halifax tugs; even rocket-assisted take-off was considered to get fully-loaded Hamilcars off the ground. Eventually the most powerful versions of the Halifax managed to drag Hamilcars to Normandy, Arnhem and the Rhine. Equipment for the airborne forces were Fink's speciality; he also towed Hadrian and Horsa gliders using a surprising range of aircraft that included Bostons, Hudsons, Wellingtons and Warwicks. The submission for his award concluded by saying that he had "performed onerous and often hazardous duties with great devotion, setting a fine example to all."[51] In late 1944 and early 1945 he was transferred to the Far East to continue experiments with glider operations, including "snatches" from remote jungle clearings.

Test and development work often went beyond the experimental and into its practical application. Two RCAF radar officers became AFC recipients in Coastal Command because they took their theories and gadgets to the very heart of the Battle of the Atlantic. First overseas was F/L Clark Kitchener Burlingham of Winnipeg. Enlisting in April 1941, he was taught the new science of radar at McMaster University, then at No. 31 Radio School. He was posted overseas in March 1942, served in various Coastal Command units, then joined the Coastal Command Development Unit in October 1943. His job was to adapt sensitive radar devices to the realities of real aircraft, harsh field conditions and standard unit servicing. When recommended for an award he had flown 845 hours (how much with squadrons as opposed to the CCDU is not known) and endured two crashes; he was singled out for the clarity of his reports on radar equipment. Apart from his AFC (which he received at an investiture in September 1947) he was mentioned in despatches.[52]

F/L Herbert Dudley Davy of Holland Landing, Ontario, enlisted in Toronto in April 1941 and was initially classified as a radio mechanic. After training at the University of Toronto he became a technical instructor at No. 31 Radio School. He was posted overseas in November 1942; commissioning followed in July 1943. Virtually from the moment he arrived in Britain, Davy was involved in radar experimentation. He tested the latest radar devices, taught Coastal Command crews how to use them, and flew on 19 sorties, at least two of which led to attacks on submarines. Apart from his AFC, Davy was twice mentioned in despatches. He left the RCAF in November 1945, and his award was sent to him by registered mail four years later.[53]

Recruiting posters such as this were surprisingly rare; the RCAF got all the men it needed without aggressive advertising. (Canadian Forces Photograph PL-3028)

TRAINING

We must remember that one man is much the same as another, and that he is best who is trained in the severest school.

– THUCYDIDES, *HISTORY OF THE PELOPONNESIAN WAR*, CIRCA 404 B.C.

The Romans are sure of victory, for their exercises are battles without bloodshed, and their battles bloody exercises.

– FLAVIUS JOSEPHUS (37-100 A.D.), JEWISH SOLDIER, STATESMAN AND HISTORIAN

Thou shalt love thy instructor as thyself – or more so. He may have a wife and children at home.

– FIRST OF "TEN COMMANDMENTS FOR BUDDING AVIATORS," PRODUCED BY THE BORDER CITIES AERO CLUB AND PRINTED IN *CANADIAN AVIATION*, OCTOBER 1931

It would be easy to exaggerate the hazards of being an instructor; one did run risks, but most pupils were conscientious, caution at knowing how little they knew cancelling out many rash impulses. It was not just the instructors who steered them away from reckless behaviour; as the war progressed there was advice from their peers. Flight Sergeant Gerald C. Burns of Outremont, Quebec, on learning that his younger brother had been accepted for aircrew, wrote from England to counsel as well as congratulate:

Don't have to tell you that I'm very pleased to hear you've made Air Crew in the RCAF. When it comes to the showdown and they ask you what you really want to be, insist on pilot. It's just like driving a car so you'll catch on easily enough. Just remember to work steadily – don't go wild when you get away from home as I've seen so many do and also remember that while you are in the initial stages the instructor is always right and you can't beat the rules and regulations of flying. Don't try anything stupid at fifty or a hundred feet from the deck – it looks good to the local inhabitants but don't – you don't live very long when you start showing off. No matter how boring the exercise may get do only what you're told. Too many guys have tried to be different but a good majority of them didn't live to tell about it.

Flying is the safest game in the world provided you treat your aircraft properly and obey the rules of the game.

This is not big brother talk, just common sense as I've found out for myself and from watching others. There will be time enough to fly all over the sky and get in there low when you get over here. In the meantime, no foolishness, and particularly no low flying unless you're authorized to do so. All the best of luck and keep me posted as to how you get on.[54]

Signs like this dotted Canada during the Second World War. This one was at Brantford, Ontario. (Canadian Force Photograph PL-3306)

Instructors risked ham-handed pupils, but they were just as liable to yield to temptation themselves, especially if they were frustrated and champing at the bit for an overseas posting. A court of inquiry, investigating an August 1941 Anson crash at No. 3 SFTS that killed an instructor and two pupils, noted that the tragedy had arisen out of unauthorized low flying while the officer was at the controls. The board recommended that schools operating twin-engined aircraft be provided with one or more single-engined aircraft set aside for instructors to "let off steam" (the suggestion was rejected out of hand by senior officers). Following another fatal crash, this one of a Fleet Finch in November 1942, a report declared that "Low flying among pupils cannot be cut down until low flying by instructors with pupils is completely stamped out." That document went on to recommend that in the case of delinquent instructors (those that survived), the culprits should be discharged or remustered to general duties for a year, that the punishment be publicised, and that if they were discharged, it should be made impossible for them to get a flying job for the duration of the war.

Such pronouncements may have cautioned some but not

all. Probably the stupidest tragedy was one that occurred on April 26, 1943. A truck and crew from No. 35 Elementary Flying Training School was salvaging parts of wrecked aircraft from farmer's fields when a unit Tiger Moth began buzzing the truck. It made several passes; on the last one the aircraft collided with the truck, crashed and burned. The RAF instructor died of injuries four days later; two civilians were injured but recovered.

The frustration of instructors who wanted to be on operations was expressed in a poem that was widely circulated within the RCAF:

THE FLYING INSTRUCTOR'S LAMENT

"What did you do in the war, Daddy,
How did you help us to win?"
"Circuits and bumps and turns, laddy,
And how to get out of a spin."

Woe and alack and misery me! I trundle around in the sky.
And instead of machine-gunning Nazis, I'm teaching
    young hopefuls to fly.
Thus is my service rewarded, my years of experience paid,
Never a Hun have I followed right down, nor ever gone
    out on a raid.

They don't even let us go crazy, we have to be safe and
    sedate.
So it's nix on inverted approaches, they stir up the C.F.I.'s
    hate.
For it's oh such a naughty example, and what will the
    A.O.C. think!
But we never get posted to fighters – we just get a spell in
    the Link.

So it's circuits and bumps from morning till noon, and
    instrument flying 'till tea.
"Hold her off, give her bank, put your undercart down,
    you're skidding, you're slipping" – that's me.
And as soon as you've finished with one course, like a
    flash up another one bobs,
And there's four more to show round the cockpit and four
    more to try out the knobs.

But sometimes we read in the papers of the deeds that old
    pupils have done,
And we're proud to have seen their beginnings and shown
    them the way to the sun.
So if you find the money and turn out the planes, we'll
    give all we know to the men
Till they cluster the sky with their triumphs and burn out
    the beast from his den.[55]

Some instructors fought unseen battles. F/L Guy Everett Moore (Marshall, Saskatchewan, and Vegreville, Alberta) strove vainly to get an overseas posting; he was more successful in concealing back troubles. Only at war's end, while he was under instruction at No. 6 OTU, Comox, to become a Dakota pilot, was his condition discovered. Moore's logbook, coupled with an unusual set of albums, reveal a fascinating story of one man's war as an instructor. Prior to the war he had participated in exploration parties tramping through the rugged border areas between the northern Alberta and British Columbia. Then he had attended the University of Alberta. He enlisted in Edmonton in June 1940 and received his basic training at No. 2 ITS, Regina (August 1940). Following ITS there was a problem – insufficient space in the Elementary Flying Training Schools. Pupils were regularly being sent in

(Above) The Fairey Battle (foreground) failed as a bomber in Europe (1939-1940) but became a valued instructional machine in the British Commonwealth Air Training Plan. The Avro Anson was an equal failure as a maritime patrol bomber, but was widely used and much loved as a "flying classroom."

Oops! A Harvard aircraft that did not quite make a successful landing.

An earnest-looking instructor, F/O Guy Moore. (via Mrs. Ruth Moore)

Leaves from Guy Moore's album: (Above) Cessna Cranes with the foothills of the Rockies in the background. (Below) The Avro Anson was the best known of the BCATP twin-engine trainers. Unlike the Crane, this type served into the postwar years. (via Mrs. Ruth Moore)

batches of five to civilian flying clubs for *ab initio* flight training. Moore subsequently recalled his introduction to flying instruction.

The Edmonton and Northern Aero Club was one of these and I promptly opted for the city where I had attended university for three years. My four buddies were agreeable to the move once I promised to introduce them to the prettiest girls in the West.

We reported on September 14th, 1940, and commenced flying two days later. Five aircraft, so we were informed, were available for training – a Gypsy Moth, two Tiger Moths and two Fleet Fawns. Unfortunately, as we crossed the field to report in, the Gypsy Moth was involved in a landing accident leaving only four aircraft. I drew the Fleet, CGF, on which I did almost all of my training. It had an

The Fleet Finch was a delightful elementary training machine; there was a special delight pilot biplanes with wires and struts that evoked images of First World War flying. (via Mrs. Ruth Moore)

Westland Lysanders had failed as army cooperation aircraft but found new lives in the training, air/sea rescue, and communications fields. (via Mrs. Ruth Moore)

open cockpit and was without brakes or tail wheel. Consequently all my flying with it had to be from the grassy part of the field.

Of his four companions at the Edmonton club, one was killed in action (Frank Boroski), one became a prisoner of war (Frank Mills), one earned a DFC following a tour on Typhoons (Brian Clacken) and one was seriously injured overseas in the crash of a Mustang (Norman Rettie). Moore went on to Ansons at No. 5 SFTS, Brantford, attended the Central Flying School at Trenton, and then, with one brief interruption for skills upgrading, instructed continuously at No. 3 SFTS, Calgary from April 1941 to March 1945.

On most flying days he recorded two or three flights, but Moore's logbook reveals instances of exceptionally gruelling work. On June 3, 1942, for example, he logged the following:

Cessna 8164 – one hour 15 minutes (instrument flying with LAC Myttuk).

Cessna 8164 – one hour (instrument flying with LAC Nagy)

Cessna 8163 – one hour 20 minutes (formation flying with LAC Gordon).

Cessna 8163 – one hour (night circuits with LAC Gordon)

Cessna 8151 – one hour (night circuits with LAC Haakenson)

Cessna 8152 – 15 minutes (night circuits with LAC Gall).

Even by Moore's standards, that was a heavy day, but there were others almost equally demanding. On September 25, 1942, for example, he was airborne eight times (twice on airframe/engine tests, six times with different pupils) for a total of 3 hours 15 minutes; on October 5, 1942 he logged 9 hours 35 minutes, of which 30 minutes was devoted to testing aircraft; the balance was supervising pupils engaged in night circuits, night cross-country flights, formation flying and practising turns.

By a curious turn of events, his instructor from the Edmonton Aero Club, Art Haldin, turned up at No. 3 SFTS as a pupil, converting to twin-engine aircraft so that he could fly with Ferry Command. Moore watched his mentor's progress, though other pilots were directly responsible for Haldin's course. Some of his pupils went on to distinction (LAC Robert Gall, under instruction at No. 3 SFTS in the spring of 1942, became F/L Gall, DFC, No. 408 Squadron).

More than his logbook, however, his scrapbook recorded accomplishments and friendships. It was filled with letters from Canadian and Australian students who had graduated as well as fellow instructors who had moved on to operations. They included apologies for having proved troublesome while at SFTS. One ex-pupil wrote that he had considered Moore his favourite instructor, "probably because you allowed me some freedom."

F/O William L.E. Walker, who had served at No. 3 SFTS, wrote a particularly interesting letter from England. It showed how Moore influenced fellow instructors as well as pupils:

Looking back on what I considered then to be wasted time, I feel now that I was a very lucky boy to have put in a hitch

An instructor's office – the cockpit of a Fleet Finch.
(Canadian Forces Photograph PL-3292)

as an instructor. I know more about flying now than I ever would have if I had come directly overseas. Just in case you have any more duff types like me to control in a flight, tell them that they're damn lucky, and if they put up with it for awhile, they'll feel grateful for it when they finally get here... A word or two of thanks to you for all that you did for me when I was kinda foolish about instructing. I know now that I was a damn fool for being so silly, and for beefing so much, and now that I'm finally here, I'm sorry for the trouble that I caused... Thanks for keeping me in line, and especially thanks for keeping my records from being absolutely ruined.[56]

A few notes, originating from Britain, had been heavily censored, with whole phrases cut out by a razor blade; ultimately, some letters arrived with German stamps and POW camp cancellations. At least one ex-pupil correspondent, Pilot Officer R.G. Bell (J9673), was killed in a flying accident in Britain five months after writing Moore.

In April and May 1943, Moore took courses in Standard Beam Approach procedures; thereafter he was No. 3 SFTS's specialist at instrument flying. The training, and his subsequent duties, led him to add a poem to his scrapbook. The writer was anonymous; the title was simple; the theme was one of progress from trials to triumph:

S.B.A.

Is it a dot? Or is it a dash? What does the kicker say?
Do we come? Or do we go? Are we so far away?
Nothing ever seems to tell just what it ought to say,
When first attempts are being made, to cope with S.B.A.

In and out the twilight, up and down the beam,
Dashes, dots and beacons are never what they seem.
Is the aerial up or down? Inter comm or mix.
Volume weak, or volume strong? What a box of tricks!

First along the Q.D.M., then the Q.D.R.,
Plus or minus, more or less, near and yet so far!
Big corrections into wind, small the other way,
Counting more or counting less, adding all the way!

Sitting in a pool of sweat, trying might and main,
Drift has changed with loss of height, round we go again.
Gremlins rasp the perspex, thoughts flow thick and fast,
Stick to the Sperry panel; those thoughts might be your last!

Subconsciously, yet so precise; how easy when you know,
Reactions are so rapid now, where once you were so slow.
So now you fly on Q.B.I., and whereas in the past,
You scraped above the undergrowth, now through the overcast.

Though he became a senior instructor with increased administrative duties, Moore spent only slightly less time in the air. On August 29, 1944, for example, he was airborne four times, logging 4 hours 40 minutes. Throughout his instructional career he registered only one mishap, on November 30, 1941, when he momentarily lost control of a taxying Anson in high winds and collided with another aircraft.

Moore attained the rank of squadron leader. His back problems ruled out a postwar RCAF career, although he did return to flying via a glider pilot's licence in 1977. Instead, he entered the Ontario civil service. From 1957 to 1964 he was Deputy Minister of Tourism and Information; he figured prominently in the development of St. Marie-Among-the-

Hurons, the Penetanguishene Military and Naval Museums, Fort Henry and Upper Canada Village. He subsequently moved to Manitoba to become that province's Deputy Minister of Tourism and Recreation. He spearheaded development of the Manitoba Archives and the Western Canada Aviation Museum. His accomplishments earned him the Canadian Centennial Medal in 1967. He retired from public service in 1980, but remained active in community affairs until his death on October 12, 1994. His logbooks and scrapbooks are treasured by his widow and three children.

Even a good instructor – one worthy of an AFC or AFM – could come to grief through mischance or misjudgment on his part. Edward B. Gale (Asbestos, Quebec), then a flying officer at No. 1 SFTS, was demonstrating forced landing procedures on June 2, 1941. The routine typically was to descend to low altitude over a farmer's field with the engine idling, then pull up just before one had to commit to a touchdown. At 300 feet he applied power, but the Harvard's engine did not respond. Gale made a gliding approach into the field, but he struck a fence and then ran into a stream. He had been wearing his Sutton harness loosely, and the impact threw him against the instrument panel; he needed surgery to repair his nose.[57]

Another instructor making a similar mistake was F/O Norris Howard Russell of Regina. On May 18, 1942, while instructing at No. 10 SFTS (Dauphin, Manitoba), he took a Crane down near Gilbert Plains to demonstrate forced landing procedure. At 50 feet he stalled the aircraft and mushed into a field. Although he and his pupil were only slightly injured, the aircraft was written off; the accident was investigated and ruled as being caused by "Error in judgement."

Although John Gavin Showler of Winnipeg earned his AFC with No. 164 (Transport) Squadron – and would later receive the McKee Trophy for postwar aerial mapping work – his service as an instructor was unusual for the number of accidents he was involved in. The Air Accidents Investigation Branch at AFHQ kept a card file on pilots listing such episodes; Showler's made very interesting reading, even though

Two Ansons that had a "fender bender" at a Canadian Training Station. (Commonwealth Air Training Plan Museum, Brandon)

no mishap was worse than an air force "fender bender." The first incident was on January 25, 1941, at No. 9 SFTS (Summerside) when his Harvard ran off the runway and tipped over on its nose. W/C Elmer G. Fullerton concluded it was due to an error of judgement on Showler's part for having allowed the pupil to land too far down the runway; he was forgiving in that Showler was still inexperienced. On April 7, 1941, two Harvards were taxying out; Showler, in the rear, was to take his pupil up for instrument flying training. The student was having trouble securing the hood that would restrict his vision; Showler turned to speak but continued to taxi. The aircraft ahead had stopped just prior to commencing its takeoff run and his Harvard ran into its tail. Fullerton was less tolerant of this incident; Showler was paraded before his superior and lectured; his logbook was endorsed for careless taxying. Two days later it was endorsed again following another ropey touchdown which saw Showler and student swerving into a snowbank and ground looping. On April 10, 1941, another Harvard taxied into Showler's machine; this time it was the other pilot whose logbook was endorsed.[58]

He had gone directly from getting his wings to instructing; twice inexperience had been cited as mitigating circumstances. In the summer of 1941 he was sent to the Central Flying School, Trenton, and there, on September 12, he was involved in another mishap. As he touched down one tire went flat; he applied rudder to compensate but the aircraft swung so badly that a wingtip was damaged. Somebody wrote on the crash card, "If this pilot has another accident I want to see the card immediately." Showler kept out of trouble for several months, but on July 14, 1942, while demonstrating forced landing procedure in a Fleet Fawn, the engine failed to pick up and he wound up in a field with the aircraft on its nose. An anonymous hand noted, "Show next accident to S/L Reeves" –

but there were no more. In December 1943 Showler was posted to No. 164 Squadron.

One cannot tell the story of a "typical" instructor in this book; because they received formal recognition the men featured were by definition above-average individuals. When access to their files is allowed, the researcher discovers successive laudatory evaluations by superiors. An example is Flight Sergeant (later F/O) Edmond David Fleishman of Vancouver. He had left school with Junior Matriculation, hoping to study medicine at the University of British Columbia but eventually dropping out of that. Times were hard and employment sporadic; when he could find work it was as a logger. Finally, in October 1939 he was hired as a mechanic by Fairchild Aircraft, and in December 1939 he moved on to Noorduyn Aviation. By night he studied aero engine mechanics through the Curtiss-Wright Technical School. However, he finally opted to join the RCAF in June 1940.

Fleishman did not shine as a student; at Initial Training School he was 60th in a class of 244; at No. 8 Elementary Flying Training School (Vancouver) he stood 19th in a class of 23; at No. 4 Service Flying Training School (Saskatoon) he was 21st in a class of 38. Although he acquired his wings, he did not immediately qualify for a commission.

Nevertheless, he was sent to the Central Flying School, the RCAF's instructor factory, where he turned in an excellent performance. His prior experience as a mechanic helped him, for on tests concerning airframes and engines he earned marks of 96 per cent. The chief instructor, S/L G.D. MacAllister, granted him a "C" Category Instructor's Ticket, though he may have damned Fleishman with faint praise when he wrote, "With a little experience should become a capable instructor." Posted to No. 4 Service Flying Training School (Cranes), he was checked almost immediately and did

Sergeant Stephen A. Sanderson, AFM, risked his life to save a pupil and his aircraft following a fire in the air; he died in an air accident in October 1943.

not impress; F/L John C. Wickett tested Fleishman on taxying, take-offs, turns, single engine flight, forced landings, precautionary landings, circuits and proper landings. Fleish-man, he concluded, was below average; his instructional techniques were sometimes wrong; the instructor's "C" category should be revoked unless he improved – and the quality of his students would be the measure of his success.

It was probably the last time that anybody wrote anything critical of him. Thereafter, his assessments were laudatory and his superiors periodically suggested he be commissioned. "An excellent flying instructor," wrote S/L A.E. Thompson (Chief Flying Instructor) on December 31, 1941; on March 2, 1942, a year after Fleishman's arrival as an instructor, W/C C.F. Newcombe described him as "well above the average as pilot and flying instructor … he has been able to obtain the confidence and respect of his students in a very marked manner." S/L Thompson recommended Fleishman for an Air Force Medal on February 13, 1942; Newcombe agreed the same day and A/C A.B. Shearer gave No. 2 Training Command's ap-

proval on May 2, 1942. Fleishman had become an officer on April 10; somebody might have changed the award to an AFC, but news of the commission obviously trailed behind the recommendation; A/M Breadner sent the latter on to Government House, final approval was granted, and the award was announced on January 1, 1943. By then, Fleishman was dead.

Throughout his instructional tour at No. 4 SFTS he had let it be known he wanted an overseas posting; to his credit, he had never allowed his disappointments to affect his work. He was posted out on May 19, 1942, flown overseas, trained to fly Wellington bombers, and then sent to the Middle East. On November 20 he reported to No. 37 Squadron. Three days later, on his first operational sortie, he went to bomb a German airfield on Crete. His Wellington was hit by anti-aircraft fire and shot down in flames. He was 22 years old.

Most instructional AFCs and AFMs were for exceptional performance of routine duties. Sometimes a single brilliant piece of flying brought an award. Sergeant Stephen A. Sanderson, a native of London, Ontario, was instructing at No. 14 SFTS (Aylmer, Ontario) on November 17, 1941, when the Harvard caught fire. He ordered his pupil to bale out. Having assured himself that the student was safe, he brought the fire under control and executed a successful wheels-up forced landing.

Investigation of the incident confirmed his skill and bravery as well as absolving Sanderson of any blame. On February 14 he was recommended for an AFM. Although his coolness had made him a deserving candidate, other considerations were weighed; the school's CO wrote, "It is felt that this award would bolster the morale of Sergeant instructors." Other factors were his skill as an instructor; he was assessed as a superior teacher, frequently chosen to help difficult pupils. He received his medal and a commission; on November 14, 1942, he was posted to No. 10 (BR) Squadron; he was lost on October

P/O John B. McRae is invested with the AFM by A/V/M Heakes, Victoria, January 1946. McRae was decorated for courage and skill following a mid-air collision at No. 1 Bombing and Gunnery School; he was a sergeant at the time. (National Archives of Canada C.145112)

20, 1943, when a Liberator crashed en route from Gander to Dorval.

Sergeant John B. McRae of Vancouver was piloting an Anson of No. 1 Bombing and Gunnery School (Jarvis, Ontario) on April 23, 1944; two students were to practice night bombing on the Lake Erie range. His aircraft was struck by an Anson from No. 16 SFTS that had strayed into the area. One-third of McRae's starboard wing was sheared off, rendering his machine almost unmanageable. He struggled back over land; the two students baled out; McRae succeeded in returning to base and force-landed with his undercarriage retracted. Both

pilots were ruled to have been negligent in keeping a lookout, but McRae was deemed less guilty and his flying skill brought him an AFM.

Throughout the war the RCAF strove to fit the right men into the right jobs – not always successfully. Some men never found their proper niche; others took a long time and a lot of effort to discover theirs. S/L Herbert Collier Stewart of Calgary was such an officer. He had been attending Royal Military College before the war and recived his flying badge early in 1940. He went overseas in October 1940 with No. 112 Squadron, later switched to No. 110 Squadron and finally to No. 414 Squadron. He was unhappy in all three; flying Lysanders, Hurricanes and Tomahawks offered no challenges. He secured a transfer to No. 409 Squadron and flew 31 uneventful sorties (68 hours 45 minutes operational time) on Beaufighters. The low combat time subsequently made it very difficult for him to be granted operational wings.

Stewart thought that he might like test flying; when A/M Lloyd Breadner visited his unit, Stewart (who was still only a flight lieutenant) went over his commander's head to speak directly to the Chief of Air Staff. He had expected to be sent to the RAF Test Pilot School at Boscombe; his exasperated superiors had a more drastic idea – "Send him home without the course." He was posted to Canada; the first two months of 1943 were spent at the School of Administration in Trenton. His career did not look promising. Early in March he went to No. 1 Operational Training Unit at Bagotville, Quebec, flying Harvards and Hurricanes. W/C E.M. Reyno recognized talent as well as limitations. Stewart was in the wrong place; he had no day fighter experience. Still, he had above-average ability. Reyno concluded that he would do a good job in the proper environment.

Accordingly, he was posted to No. 36 OTU, Greenwood, to

familiarize himself with the Mosquito. From August 15 to September 15, 1943 he took the senior instructor course at Trenton; on completion of that he returned to No. 36 OTU (later designated No. 8 OTU). Initially he was not keen about instructing, but he must have realized that his unpopularity with officers overseas had prejudiced his adventurous ambitions. He now applied himself to the job at hand; by June 1944 his superiors were recommending him for promotion and assignment to the job of Chief Flying Instructor.

S/L Stewart was recommended for the AFC on December 29, 1944, when he had flown 1,350 hours, 547 as an instructor. W/C C.C. Moran suggested the award; G/C E.M. Reyno supported it; A/C W.A. Orr agreed as of March 8, 1945. The citation that went to Government House (but which was unpublished) read:

F/L J.E. "Jock" Palmer brought a unique background to his RCAF duties; he had been a First World War instructor and then a Prairie barnstormer. (Canadian Force Photograph DND 65-43)

During a two year period of duty as flight commander and latterly as chief flying instructor at a Mosquito Operational Training Unit, this officer has performed his duties with great zeal and enthusiasm. He has maintained excellent flying discipline in the unit and his efforts have ensured that graduates were of the highest possible calibre. His example has been an inspiration to all instructors and pupils. Throughout, his devotion to duty has been outstanding.

He made the RCAF his postwar career, with postings to Vancouver, Toronto, Ottawa and Washington. In 1956 he took the Sabre course at No. 1 OTU, Chatham, then took command of No. 413 Squadron. When that unit was stood down to become a CF-100 squadron, Stewart became CO of No. 434 squadron, No. 3 (Fighter) Wing, Zweibrucken, Germany. On May 31, 1957 he was killed trying to crash land after engine failure at low level.

Many pupils at No. 5 Elementary Flying Training School must have looked at a portly instructor with some curiosity. His First World War ribbons were easily recognized – many veterans of that conflict were serving again – but what was that curious ribbon that took precedence over all the others? F/L John Ender "Jock" Palmer had been born in Cambridge, England in 1898 but emigrated to Canada before the First World War. He lied about his age to join the Canadian Expeditionary Force; at age 17 he earned the Distinguished Conduct Medal as a machine-gunner at Festubert (1915) – apart from the Victoria Cross, the highest award available to a non-commissioned rank. He later transferred to the Royal Flying Corps, trained as a pilot, and served as an instructor in England (1917-1918).

Palmer was a barnstormer and commercial pilot between the wars; he claimed on joining the RCAF to have flown 9,881 hours on 98 types of aircraft. Initially employed as a civilian instructor, he attended Flying Instructor School, Trenton, in the summer of 1940. As an aircrew type, his age seemed to confuse those who administered his career. He was commissioned in the RCAF at Calgary on December 3, 1941, posted to No. 5 EFTS on December 17, 1941, granted leave without pay, then continued as a civilian instructor. Early in 1942 he was appointed chief flying instructor. On December 1, 1942 he was re-instated in his commission with the rank of flight lieutenant. He took another course at FIS, Trenton (March-April 1943) before resuming his duties at No. 5 EFTS, wearing an RCAF uniform that was steadily challenged by his girth.

Palmer was awarded the Air Force Cross in November 1943. The citation was typical of many applicable to instructors:

Having been connected with flying training for the past twenty years, this officer, for the past two years, has capably fulfilled his duties as an Assistant Chief Flying Instructor and a Chief Flying Instructor. His experience and unfailing devotion to duty have inspired confidence and respect in both trainees and Instructors. Through his untiring efforts as Chief Flying Instructor all courses graduated on time with all sequences completed despite the difficulties that had to be overcome.

Many Canadian fliers, decorated for gallantry in the First World War, received new honours in the Second World War. However, their awards in the latter conflict were for staff and administrative services rather than active duty. Thus, Captain George Howsam was decorated with a Military Cross as a fighter pilot in 1917-18; as organizer and commander of No. 4 Training Command and then of North-West Air Command, A/V/M Howsam would be made a Companion, Order of the Bath; the United States would bestow on him the degree of Commander in their Legion of Merit; Belgium would make him a Commander of the Order of the Crown; Czechoslovakia would admit him to the Order of the White Lion.

Palmer was different. Although his DCM was achieved as a foot soldier, the combination of a DCM and an AFC made him the only member of the RCAF to be decorated for active duty in each of the two world wars. Jock Palmer was retired from the RCAF in September 1944, as the British Commonwealth Air Training Plan was being reduced in size. He died in High River, Alberta, on November 19, 1964.

Training became ever more specialised as the war progressed, and instructors had to be found to meet the evolving needs of the program. The career of Howard Norris (Regina) illustrates the process. Having earned his wings at Camp Borden in January 1941, he attended the Central Flying School before taking up instructional duties at No. 10 SFTS. He served at that unit from February 24, 1941, to October 15, 1944, and was routinely praised for his abilities. Starting with a "C" category instructor's rating he was upgraded to A.2 category by January 1943.

In May 1943 he took a specialist course at No. 1 Instrument Flying School, Deseronto. This included intensive ground instruction as well as practice in Oxford aircraft. The program consisted of five parts: Instrument Flying Under the Hood, Beam Approach Flying (Link Trainer), Beam Flying (Day), Beam Flying (Night) and Weather Flying (flying accurately on instruments in cloud or limited visibility). Norris received 219 marks out of a possible 300. He returned to No. 10 SFTS, specializing as a Beam Approach instructor. When he finally left that school it was to become an instructor at his *alma mater*, No. 1 IFS, where he served (though it moved bases several times) until 1948.

F/L Norris was recommended for an AFC on May 10, 1945. By then he had flown 2,863 hours 40 minutes; of that, 2,670 hours had been as an instructor, first as an NCO, then as an officer. He was singled out for organizing the RCAF's Instru-

Training on the broad, sunny prairie. A Fairchild Cornell over No. 19 EFTS, Virden, Manitoba. (Photo by Nicholas Morant. National Archives of Canada PA-169141)

ment Rating Qualifying Course. The recommendation was approved successively by G/C A.B. Searle (May 10, 1945), A/C A.D. Ross (May 28, 1945) and A/C M. Costello (July 9, 1945) before going to Government House and final gazetting on August 11, 1945. Norris remained close to instrument and all-weather flying throughout his life. He finally became a wing commander and qualified as a CF-100 pilot. On March 5, 1957, he was given command of No. 432 Squadron. On September 5, 1957, while demonstrating solo aerobatics at the Canadian National Exhibition, his aircraft flamed out one engine; the "Clunk" went into an inverted spin and crashed, killing Norris and his navigator, F/O R.C. Dougall.

If it took a good man to teach another to fly, navigate or shoot, what can be said about those who instructed the instructor? They were sometimes denied the challenges of operational postings because they were deemed too valuable at home. Although they were teachers, they never stopped going to school themselves, constantly improving their instructional techniques and striving to lower accident rates. Increasingly, the RCAF monitored their performance through analysis of statistics and on-the-spot inspections. Some of the sharpest RCAF aircrew of the war never left the country.

An example was F/L Hugh Francis Darraugh. Born in Regina in April 1920, he was an accountant before the war, working in Canadian Pacific Railway hotels. He enlisted in Vancouver on December 19, 1940 and soon proved a thorough learner. At No. 2 Initial Training School (Regina) he ranked second in a class of 87. Going on to No. 18 EFTS, he emerged second in a class of 28; his overall assessment (which included rating for academic skills as well as flying proficiency) read, "Brilliant student. Fine attitude and appearance. Steady type. Good leader. Definitely superior." Yet on the practical side he was only mildly impressive; he was graded aver-

age on instruments, average in the Link Trainer, poor at steep turns, yet very good at aerobatics. At No. 12 SFTS, however, he emerged second in a class of 46 and was immediately commissioned (September 25, 1941). His superiors wrote, "Would make a good instructor or reconnaissance pilot."

Thus, following a specialist course at Trenton, he became an instructor. Between December 1941 and August 1942 he logged 800 hours on Cranes at No. 12 SFTS. For a month he flew Cornells and Cranes at No. 2 Flying Instructor School (Vulcan, Alberta); then he moved on to No. 3 Flying Instructor School (Arnprior, Ontario), where from September 1942 to April 1943 he flew roughly 500 hours on Cornells and Finches, teaching others how to communicate and fly at the same time.

Throughout these postings he performed well. At No. 12 SFTS he was described as "a high average instructor who flies and demonstrates well." When inspected at Arnprior, he was depicted as a model mentor: "An above average instructor who is outstanding in his flight. He is an excellent organizer and always graduates his pupils a full week prior to other instructors. He is a very good officer and has a rather interesting personality."

One might wonder what constituted an "interesting personality," but there is nothing on record to suggest eccentricities of any sort. From Arnprior he was posted to the Central Flying School at Trenton where he became an examining officer with the CFS Visiting Flight. This was a corps of experts who travelled throughout BCATP establishments to check up on the schools. Darraugh was a specialist in assessing Elementary Flying Training School staff; between April 1943 and March 1944 he flew 75 hours piloting the Lockheed 10 and Lockheed 12 used to shuttle around the country, plus 300 hours on Cornells and 1,000 hours on Tiger Moths with pupils and instructors.[59] F/L Darraugh was next assigned to No. 2 Training Command Headquarters. His duties thereafter were those of a staff officer. He was industrious at paper work as well; on August 9, 1944 he was recommended for an AFC and it was gazetted on January 1, 1945. The citation read:

> This officer, throughout his career in flying training, has proven himself to be an outstanding pilot and instructor. He is most reliable and keen and can be depended upon to carry to a successful conclusion all tasks allotted to him with determination and ability. The energy, initiative and devotion to duty of this officer are outstanding.

He flew very little after that; he remained at No. 2 Training Command Headquarters until May 1945, supervised the closure of No. 18 SFTS at Gimli, instructed a little, worked with Air Cadets, and for three years (1949 to 1952) was executive assistant to the Chief of the Air Staff. Having made the RCAF his career, however, he was going to have to get back to flying if he was to advance. After learning to fly Sabres he was posted to No. 444 Squadron in Europe, promoted to wing commander, and given command.

On March 12, 1954, Darraugh was assessed as being a good leader, even if he was still inexperienced on Sabres. Three days later he took a Sabre up on a routine familiarization flight. From 22,000 feet he began a GCA approach. His last radio contact with base was when he was eight miles off and at 2,000 feet. Controllers noted that his descent was slightly faster than desired and radioed this to him; he did not reply. Witnesses reported that at 150 feet he blew the Sabre's canopy, but he was still in the cockpit when the aircraft hit the ground with its wheels retracted, killing him instantly. Afterwards it was concluded that he had sustained a total engine failure on the approach and had been trying to force-land the aircraft. Some said he had stayed with the Sabre beyond the point of safety so as not to risk its crashing into the village of Ifforzheim. He left a widow and three children.

Towards the end of the war many instructors in Canada were sporting the ribbons of gallantry awards awarded overseas. Not all were great teachers; Guy Moore's letters include a note from a person signing himself only as "Sandy" who, at No. 8 OTU, Greenwood, wrote:

> The instructors here are mostly ex-operational blokes, the majority of whom have gongs... They are all real good types, although as far as instruction goes it's mostly "Now watch this" and "Oh hell, you've got more hours than me, you know how to fly this – – – thing."

Nevertheless, a few would be further recognized with an Air Force Cross, proof that they were as good at organizing and training as they had been in combat. Among these were:

W/C Harry Malkin (Verdun, Quebec); as Chief Instructor at No. 5 Operational Training Unit he was "largely responsible for the success of this unit in training bomber crews, often under the most adverse weather conditions." Malkin knew of which he taught; he had been decorated with the DFC and Bar with No. 35 Squadron; his aircraft had been repeatedly damaged; he had been wounded at least once. According to an RCAF press release, Malkin, as a mere flight sergeant, had commanded his unit for one day because he was the senior surviving pilot following three nights of exceptionally heavy losses!

S/L William Robert Francis Grierson-Jackson (Guelph, Ontario), No. 5 Operational Training Unit, "a very capable air observer and instructor ... most efficient in carrying out his arduous duties... The operational information he has been able to pass on to the pupils has been invaluable..." Like Malkin, a veteran of No. 35 Squadron, he had earned a DFC when such awards were particularly hard to come by, navigating to distant targets such as Trondheim.

F/L James Robert Feir Johnson (Omemee, Ontario), No. 7 Operational Training Unit; "... has proven invaluable in imparting to his pupils his knowledge of operational flying tactics in the gunnery squadron of this Operational Training Unit ... contributing to a high standard of gunnery training..." Flying low-flying intruder Mosquitos with No. 418 Squadron, Johnson had received the DFC for destroying four enemy aircraft.

(Above) Sergeant Carl C. Harris (Sydney, Nova Scotia) and Flight Sergeant Harry Malkin (Verdun, Quebec) in a Halifax bomber of No. 35 Squadron, RAF. Malkin would be commissioned, win a DFC and Bar, then gain an AFC at an Operational Training Unit in Canada. Harris was reported missing on June 20, 1942. His body was never found, and his name was duly recorded on the Runnymede Memorial (near London) for air force personnel with no known graves. (Canadian Force Photograph PL-7177)

(Right) F/O R.I. Tricket and F/L W.R.F. Grierson-Jackson, DFC. The latter went on to win a DFC as an instructor. (Canadian Forces Photograph PL-23668)

F/L Arthur George Lawrence (Brandon, Manitoba), No. 8 Operational Training Unit; "... a highly efficient and competent chief instructor ... invaluable to his pupils because of the operational knowledge he is able to pass on to

F/L Arthur G. Lawrence, DFC, AFC turned his operational experience as a night fighter pilot into lessons at an RCAF Operational Training Unit. (Canadian Force Photograph PL-58067)

them…" A successful night fighter pilot when airborne radar was unreliable, Lawrence had been awarded a DFC with No. 406 Squadron, being credited with three confirmed "kills"; he had added a fourth victory after the award.

S/L Elmore Hugh McCaffery (Winnipeg), No. 5 Operational Training Unit; "… an outstanding navigator … has given generously of his skill and operational experience, imbuing the instructors under him with his own determination that their pupils shall be as fit for combat as is humanly possible…" McCaffery had received a DFC with No. 15 Squadron (Stirlings), taking the aircraft deep into Germany and over the Alps to Italy. Although invested with his DFC, he was content to receive his AFC by registered mail in April 1946.[60]

S/L Donald Philip MacIntyre (Saint John, New Brunswick), No. 5 Operational Training Unit; "… an outstanding Chief Flying Instructor … through his general knowledge, tenacity and resourcefulness he has raised the flying on this unit to a

S/L R.C. "Moose" Fumerton, photographed while flying Beaufighters with No. 89 Squadron in Egypt, 1942 (Canadian Forces Photograph PMR 555)

(Below) W/C R.C. Fumerton, DFC, while commanding No. 406 Squadron in Britain, 1944. Soon afterwards he was back in Canada to instruct others in night fighting and mastering Mosquito aircraft. (Canadian Forces Photograph PL-28865)

very high standard … a natural leader both in the air and on the ground…" A veteran Halifax bomber pilot, MacIntyre had earned a DFC with No. 35 Squadron and an American DFC in North Africa with No. 160 Squadron. His most remarkable feat was in April 1942 when he force-landed his flak-damaged bomber on a half-frozen Norwegian lake. His crew were unhurt, escaped to Sweden, and made it back to England. The Halifax sank into the lake; its remains were salvaged forty years later and are now displayed in the RAF Museum, Hendon.[61]

W/C Robert Carl Fumerton (Fort Coulonge, Quebec), No. 7 Operational Training Unit; "… very effectively reorganized discipline and flying training to the present high standard of efficiency … raised morale to unprecedented levels … valuable crews and aircraft were saved from destruction…" In 1941 Fumerton had been the first member of the RCAF to score a radar-directed night fighter victory; by mid-1944, with 14 confirmed "kills," he was the RCAF's top night fighter pilot with the DFC and Bar.[62]

S/L Peter Joseph Oleinek (Edmonton), No. 6 Operational Training Unit; "… displayed great ability as an organizer … has planned and developed new and improved flying exercises, the effectiveness of which he frequently

F/O Stanley J. Kernaghan, DFM, a veteran of Coastal Command, who won an AFC instructing at No. 8 Operational Training Unit in Canada (Canadian Forces Photograph PL-24135)

checks by acting as both screen pilot and navigator with students on exercises…" One of the first BCATP graduates overseas, he had received his DFC with No. 12 Squadron when they were still flying Wellingtons; he had once escaped flak and searchlights by hedge-hopping at 50 feet.

F/O Stanley John Kernaghan (Cartwright, Manitoba), No. 8 Operational Training Unit, a ex-Beaufighter pilot (Coastal Command and the Mediterranean) who had been honoured with the DFM in the course of 67 sorties (four enemy aircraft destroyed). As an instructor on Mosquitos from the time of their introduction into Canada he had "displayed superior judgment and skill whilst so employed" as well as providing "… an example and an inspiration to the many pupils who have passed through his capable hands."[63]

One of the most obscure tasks at training establishments was that of drogue operator – the men who winched aerial targets out for fighter pilots, gunner trainees and the occasional anti-aircraft gun crew to practice. It was a tiresome chore, usually carried out by General Duties personnel with no specific trade – the "odd-job" boys of the RCAF.[64]

Given that the target was streamed at least 400 feet behind the tug, there was minimal danger and maximum tedium associated with the job. There were stories of occasional hazards. A popular tale was that of a tug crew working with an ack-ack battery; some shells burst *ahead* of the tug, whereupon the pilot radioed, "Please remember I am

LAC Francis R. Duggan receives his AFM from the Governor General, the Earl of Athlone, at a Government House investiture. As a drogue operator, Duggan was one of many whose work was important but routine. Awards to persons of such junior rank were rare. (Canadian Forces Photograph PL-13972)

(Below) A Lysander used for target towing is refuelled at Patricia Bay, B.C. The distinctive stripes were to ensure maximum visibility, so that practising gunners (whether in the air or on the ground) did not mistake the tug for the target! (National Archives of Canada PA-197486)

pulling this thing – not pushing it." It is difficult to say if this ever happened; it may have been an air force legend. Certainly there were increasing difficulties as the war progressed because the most common target tugs, Lysander Mark IIIs, were aging and showing it through frequent engine malfunctions. One real hazard was that of tow cables fouling aircraft controls in the event of winch failures or sudden manoeuvres. Probably the greatest risks were when fighter pilots practised deflection shooting, but even this was minimized when camera guns eliminated the need for a passive towed target.

Nevertheless, four RCAF drogue operators were decorated with Air Force Medals. Of these, the most junior was Leading Aircraftman Francis Robert Duggan of Niagara Falls, Ontario. He had enlisted on October 26, 1940, at the age of 20 and received his AFM on January 1, 1943, while serving at No. 2 Bombing and Gunnery School. The citation read:

LAC Duggan is employed as a drogue operator. This airman has flown a total of 400 hours. He is most energetic

and reliable. His skill in the performance of his duties whilst flying, and his keenness and untiring efforts, have been a splendid example to all others in his trade. His services have been invaluable in the carrying out of training at this unit.

Curiously, the four drogue operators received their awards between January and May 1943. Subsequently, from 1944 to 1946, five other RCAF drogue operators were singled out for distinction, but their work merited only Commendations for Valuable Services in the Air.

Before leaving awards relating to training, one might pay tribute to a relatively unknown aspect of the BCATP – the British and ANZAC component. The bulk of Australian, British and New Zealand personnel in Canada arrived as trainees, but several hundred were present as staff. Most were British who came following the 1940-41 relocation of several RAF schools to Canada, but Commonwealth personnel were scattered across the Dominion, at every level from AFHQ down to schools.

Numerous awards were distributed among them including 58 Air Force Crosses (56 RAF, one RAAF, one RNZAF) and eight AFMs (all to RAF personnel). Most were for routine instructional duties performed in outstanding fashion over many months, not unlike the awards to RCAF personnel in

S/L E.A.H. Bacon, AFM. A Canadian who had enlisted directly in the RAF, he was back in Canada as an instructor when he rescued two men from a burning aircraft. He later transferred to the RCAF and made it his postwar career. This photograph was taken about 1961. (Canadian Forces Photograph PL-142822)

Canada. One Air Force Medal, however, was for an outstanding display of courage by Sergeant Ernest Augustus Holmes "Gus" Bacon, who was stationed at No. 34 Service Flying Training School, Medicine Hat. His AFM was gazetted in June 1942, shortly after he had been commissioned, and he received the medal at a Government House investiture in Ottawa on December 2, 1942. The incident surrounding his award makes for dramatic reading:

On the night of 28 April, 1941, a crash occurred at Holsom Relief Landing Ground and the aircraft, a Harvard, caught fire. Sergeant Bacon in company with others ran to the scene, across a ploughed field, through barbed wire fences, for a distance of about half a mile. Sergeant Bacon outstripped the others and without any protection immediately proceeded to extricate the instructor and pupil from the burning aircraft. In spite of the fierceness of the fire he managed to get both clear. He then remained and comforted the pilot, an officer, until he died on the way to hospital. Sergeant Bacon has shown similar courage and devotion to duty together with initiative on subsequent occasions. He has shown exceptional ability as an instructor and has shown great devotion to duty while flying. His tireless energy in that direction is outstanding. He well deserves recognition not only for his gallant act but also for the great and exceptional services rendered as a flying instructor.[65]

Bacon was unusual; although he was a member of the RAF, he was Canadian by birth and education. He had been training as an aircraft engineering apprentice in England when the war broke out, and had signed up immediately. Having received his wings, he was posted back to Canada as an instructor; it was only in 1943 that he returned to Britain where he flew operationally with Coastal Command. He left the RAF in 1947, only to join the RCAF the following year. Bacon finally retired in 1966 with the rank of squadron leader.

Of the various Air Force Crosses awarded to RAF personnel in Canada, one was for a particularly notable feat of airmanship. P/O Peter Henry Ludlow, on the staff of No. 6 Operational Training Unit, was flying a Dakota from Patricia Bay to Smithers, British Columbia, on November 28, 1944. The aircraft was heavily loaded with cargo and 14 passengers. Forty minutes out from Patricia Bay and at 12,000 feet, he ran into turbulence and icing so severe that the de-icer boots could not clear it away. The aircraft turned completely over three times in 20 minutes. Ludlow finally regained control and cleared the turbulent area; he was awarded an AFC for "cool courage and almost superhuman efforts."

It is worth noting that two recipients of AFCs awarded to RAF personnel in Canada were, in fact, Canadians who had joined the RAF but whose careers, like Bacon's, brought them back to Canada on instructional duties. One was S/L Kenneth G. Taylor, of Port Elgin, New Brunswick, who had enlisted in the RAF in 1938. After two tours in Coastal Command, flying Hudsons and Beaufighters, he had been posted to No. 1 General Reconnaissance School, at Summerside, Prince Edward Island. When recommended for his AFC he had flown 2,381 hours (an extraordinary figure then), of which 1,330 hours had been on instructional duties. The other Canadian coming home, temporarily, was W.A. Waterton, whose story is outlined further on.[66]

Flight Sergeant James B. Anderson, AFM, was a member of the RAF serving as an instructor in Canada. He received his decoration in January 1943 for instructional work at No. 31 Elementary Flying Training School, De Winton, Alberta. His superiors noted that he was "an unassuming person who does his work well but in an unspectacular manner." (Canadian Forces Photograph PL-16061)

Training did not end when aircrew left Canada. On arrival overseas RCAF aircrew were thrust into rigorous programs that taught the latest tactics, introduced them to new equipment (from radio aids to advanced technology such as jet engines), grouped them as teams and sent them off to their squadrons. Aircrew who had completed a tour of operations were frequently assigned to British-based schools as instructors, and as was to be expected, a few members of the RCAF gained awards for this type of work (see R.S. Turnbull, below). Three RCAF graduates of the BCATP followed very different paths – Sergeant Rodney Stewart Clement, F/L Arthur Favrance Green and F/L David Robb. For reasons not clear, this trio, upon arrival in Britain, were assigned duties as primary flying instructors, a task they might just as easily have performed before going overseas.

A native of Russell, Manitoba, Clement had joined the RCAF in May 1941, trained as a pilot, and received his flying badge in January 1942. He was duly posted to Britain, but instead of continuing on to operational training he was himself

(Right) A Harvard trainer at No. 14 Service Flying Training School, Aylmer, Ontario. This particular machine remained on RCAF strength until October 1957, when it was sent to France under a NATO mutual aid program.

(Below) A Fairchild Cornell peels away from a de Havilland Tiger Moth at Virden, Manitoba. (Photo by Nicholas Morant. DND/National Archives of Canada PA-169140)

A Tiger Moth (probably at No. 20 Elementary Flying Training School, Oshawa) in an embarrassing pose. Accidents such as this were seldom fatal – except, perhaps, to a pupil's hope of graduation!

No. 5 Operational Training Unit, Boundary Bay, British Columbia.
Bomber crews, intended for Pacific operations, trained on twin-
engined Mitchells to learn the intricacies of tricycle undercarriages
before moving on to four-engined Liberators. Four members of the
RCAF – all decorated following overseas services – received AFCs for
work at this unit. (RCAF Photo)

assigned to instructional duties at a British School, No. 4 Elementary Flying Training School (Brough, Yorkshire). Little is known about his activities, but on January 1, 1944 he was awarded an Air Force Medal. When recommended he had flown 687 instructional hours, 475 in the previous six months – a very intensive schedule. The unpublished citation gives only the barest clue as to how he merited the award: "This airman is an enthusiastic and capable flying instructor who has set a very fine example."[67]

Eventually he was commissioned and entered Bomber Command's "pipeline" that led him through operational and heavy conversion training to No. 626 Squadron. In October 1944, on his first mission, his aircraft was hit by anti-aircraft fire, damaging the mid-upper turret. F/O Clement (as he now was) continued the mission, attacked his target, but then had to deal with fires in both wings; one was extinguished, the other subsided to a threatening glow that persisted for the rest of the sortie. Alerting the crew to a possible bale-out, he flew the bomber home to England. Clement was awarded a Distinguished Flying Cross.

F/L Robb (Winnipeg) and F/L Green (Alberton, Prince Edward Island) both earned their wings in Canada in January

The Honourable J.M. Ulrich, Lieutenant-Governor of Saskatchewan, presents the DFC and AFC to David Robb at an investiture in Saskatoon on November 8, 1948. Although recipients of decorations were allowed to wear the appropriate ribbons upon announcement of the award, months and sometimes years passed before they received the actual medals. (National Archives of Canada C.144696)

1942, went overseas, and were assigned to No. 7 EFTS, Desford, where they trained a succession of pupils on Tiger Moths. Both men were awarded Air Force Crosses on January 1, 1944; when recommended, Green had flown 1,020 instructional hours and Robb 1,075. Both then went to operational units (Green to No. 582 Squadron, Robb to No. 100 Squadron, both flying Lancasters) and both were decorated with the DFC. They also survived the war. Green's career was particularly notable; he made the RCAF his career, rising to the rank of group captain, and upon retirement (April 1969) became a school teacher. He died in Ottawa on January 9, 1997.[68]

Prewar RAF squadrons had been reponsible for the final training of their aircrews. Once hostilities began, unit resources were stretched in trying to perform two tasks. To bridge the gap between attaining "wings" standard and "combat" standard, the Operational Training Unit was created. Apart from single-seater fighter OTUs, these assembled crews, then taught them the specialized skills required for their particular commands (Coastal, Bomber, Transport).[69] From late 1942 onwards the last stage of training before reaching a Bomber Command squadron was normally a Heavy Conversion Unit. Aircrew who had learned night bombing on

Whitleys and Wellingtons were brought together to learn the ways of Stirling, Halifax and Lancaster bombers. Initially a four-week program, courses at HCUs had become, by mid-1944, three weeks of ground school, followed by four weeks of training that approximated battle conditions, with long sorties using the latest electronic equipment to practice navigation, bombing, and air fighting tactics; it included fighter affiliation drills (learning evasive tactics), and searchlight exercises (mock raids that tested searchlight crews while acclimatizing bomber crews to those potentially blinding beams). Particular emphasis was given to instruction in "corkscrew" manoeuvres (clear hood and on instruments); this gut-wrenching stratagem was the best means of escaping night fighters. In 1943 and early 1944 there were occasional shallow penetrations of Europe to carry out a raid or leaflet drop, but these were discontinued as Bomber Command's front-line strength grew and the business of crew training took priority at the HCUs. Heavy Conversion Units turned out from 20 to 35 crews per months, depending on weather, serviceability and the demands imposed by casualties; in the summer of 1944 as many as 46 crews per month were trained.

Although not exposed to enemy action, the HCU instructors and pupils were otherwise subject to the usual hazards of night flying over blacked-out countryside. Aircraft flew into high ground or crashed on takeoff or landing; in March 1944 No. 6 Group's *Monthly Summary of Operations* reported:

Another accident was a pupil on a Bullseye [searchlight exercise] who got himself so far off track that he was shot down by the London Defences during an enemy air raid when he should have been tracking between Portland Bill and Bristol.

The level of activity at an HCU was tremendous; almost every waking hour was devoted to work in a classroom, whether on the ground or in the air. In November 1943, for example, No. 1659 HCU flew 1,288 hours; in July 1944 the same unit flew 1,943 hours. No. 1664 HCU flew 1,022 hours in November 1943, 1,783 hours in July 1944; No. 1666 HCU logged a mere 197 hours in November 1943 (the month it commenced work); by July 1944 this had risen to 1,992 hours. Unfortunately, the aircraft themselves were usually old bombers that had been retired from squadron use. They may have carried state-of-the-art radio and radar equipment, but their Merlin and Hercules engines were aging, delivering sluggish performance.[70]

A point debated at various times was what type of aircrew should be instructing at Heavy Conversion Units – tour-expired personnel or men who, though lacking operational experience, might still be skilful teachers with better communications skills. Robert Byers, who had received his AFC in 1942 as a BCATP instructor, toured No. 1674 HCU (for Lancaster crews) in May 1944 and reported on some of the debates then in progress:

Instructors One point that did come out was that men returning from operations for a rest were not getting the rest at this type of unit due to the heavy pressure of work caused by the lack of instructor personnel. Further it was bad for morale of u/t [under training] crews to come in contact with some of the personnel fresh from operations suffering from nervous fatigue…

Flight Engineers Difficulty experienced with air sickness of flight engineers. Consider they should receive flying experience prior to coming to HCUs. Lengthy discussion developed on who should act as emergency pilot, the Bombardier or the Flight Engineer. The C.I. [Chief Instructor] considered that inasmuch as the Flight Engineer was beside the pilot and also knew the engine limitations, he was the logical man to assume the pilot duties in emergency, and so should be given limited flying training. The point came up, why not put back the second pilot?

Among the Canadian AFC winners at conversion units, two examples may be singled out – one for bravery, one for ingenuity.

Arthur Adelbert Bishop had already received a Distinguished Flying Medal flying Stirlings with No. 7 Squadron. He had been commissioned, assigned to No. 1651 Heavy Conversion Unit which was turning out fresh Stirling crews and attained the rank of flight lieutenant. On June 8, 1944, it was announced that he had been awarded an Air Force Cross; no citation appeared and his unit was not even identified. Nevertheless, Air Ministry documents identify the school and tell much of the story. When recommended he had flown 985 non-operational hours, 139 in the previous six months. He had given a total of 535 hours of dual instruction and was described as "an outstanding pilot and instructor." However, it was for a singular act of skill and courage that he was being decorated:

On 13th October, 1943, Flying Officer Bishop was detailed to give dual instruction to a pupil. Shortly after the take off, the starboard wing suddenly dropped. Flying Officer Bishop, taking over the controls, was able by great skill to keep the aircraft on a level keel by using full left aileron and full power on his starboard engine. He was able to complete a circuit and put his undercarriage down but was unable to put his flaps down. Despite this he made a good flapless landing. The main spar was found to be fractured inboard of the starboard inner engine and the whole wing out of alignment. Had it not been for Flying Officer Bishop's outstanding skill, in the face of extreme danger, a crash would have been unavoidable.[71]

Robert Fred Miller of Marshall, Saskatchewan, was a wireless air gunner. After an operational tour he became a ground instructor, commencing in October 1942, and rose to squadron leader rank. He was not content simply to lecture and demonstrate; he followed his students into the air to check both their progress and his own techniques, thus acquiring some 200 hours of non-operational flying, 150 of them in a six month period. Miller took an interest in all aspects of training, be it for navigators, gunners, wireless operators or flight engineers. He had created the job of chief ground instructor at No. 1659 Heavy Conversion Unit when the outfit was formed out of a flight of No. 405 Squadron. Later he assumed the same duties upon the formation of No. 1666 HCU late in 1943.

Not content with existing training aids, he tinkered and improved much of the equipment at hand including turret and cockpit simulators; eventually the units were also using these devices to train radar operators. The importance of these latter may be gauged by a few figures. In December 1943, Air Bombers at No. 1659 HCU ran up 973 hours and 55 minutes of training; at least 145 hours were spent using simulators; an uncertain portion of 228 hours devoted to training with "Gee" was also done without leaving the ground. Navigators at the same unit were reported as having carried out 676 hours training on the ground as opposed to 426 hours in the

Turret training simulator used to train air gunners. Even after reaching operational squadrons, aircrew continued to practice their skills using simulators and other special aids. Their lives depended on being sharp and competent. (Canadian Force Photograph PL-3624A)

(Right) W/C Robert F. Miller of Marshall, Saskatchewan, decorated for services with Heavy Conversion Units overseas. (Canadian Forces Photograph PL-36363)

air. The importance of these devices grew as more were developed and built.

Miller was recommended for an AFC in June 1943. That did not go through. Another submission for an AFC was submitted in January 1944; again, it did not reach the appropriate list, although he was mentioned in despatches on June 8, 1944. His superiors tried again, on July 25, 1944. G/C N.S. MacGregor, in advancing Miller's name for a decoration, wrote in part:

> His example of industry and enthusiasm have at all times been a marked incentive to all those with whom he has been associated, both on the ground and in the air. A truly brilliant mind, coupled with tireless energy which deserve tangible recognition as an incentive to others.[72]

This time the recommendation went through; his name was included in a long list of intermediate awards announced on September 1, 1944. Miller remained with the postwar RCAF and retired as a group captain.[73]

James Albert Hanway of Lunenburg, Nova Scotia, was a very different type of instructor. A pre-war lawyer, he joined the RCAF on August 14, 1940. Having earned his wings in July 1941 and gone overseas in November, he received advanced instruction on Beauforts at a Coastal Command Operational Training Unit. He was posted to No. 39 Squadron in Egypt and flew 12 sorties (60 operational hours). Although his tour was brief, the CO, W/C A.J. Mason, was impressed, describing him as "an outstanding officer who is worthy of accelerated promotion," adding that "with experience he should make an excellent squadron commander."

In September 1942 a Beaufort Flight was formed at No. 5 Middle East Training School, Shallufa, Egypt, and Hanway was posted to it. By July 1943 he had risen to squadron leader; the CO, G/C G.M. Knocker, wrote of him as "a brilliant pilot, a good instructor – a leader – runs his flight well." About that time he was put up for an AFC. The recommendation describes his overseas flying to that time:

This officer has been an instructor on Beaufort aircraft and since his arrival at the school 120 Beaufort pilots have completed the course. Flight Lieutenant Hanway has carried out over 400 hours on Beaufort torpedo bomber instruction, most of the flying being performed at 60 feet above sea level. Since December 1942 he has taken over the instruction on Marauder aircraft and during a period of three months 32 Marauder pilots completed a course under his instruction. It has been entirely due to his skill and courage as an instructor that many torpedo pilots have gained confidence in their aircraft. Flight Lieutenant Hanway has displayed fine ability as a pilot.[74]

Hanway's tour at No. 5 METS was not without incident. On February 24, 1943, he was flying a Beaufort from Shaffula to Port Said when the starboard engine began vibrating violently, then lost power. He lowered his wheels and flaps in anticipation of an emergency landing at El Firdam. He was at 200 feet, commencing a turn towards the field, when the engine failed completely; smoke and flames appeared, faded, then appeared again. He put the aircraft down and extinguished the fire immediately.

A more dicey incident occurred on October 2, 1943. He was approaching Shandur airfield in a Beaufighter. At 1,000 feet, without warning, the port engine delivered a series of loud bangs and then packed up. He was in no position to choose; he lowered his wheels, banked slightly to port, and approached the field on the downwind side. He intended to land beside the runway, but a Baltimore pilot who had just landed could not know that; he obviously saw Hanway's aircraft approaching with undercart down and assumed that the Beaufighter was going to descend on the runway. The Baltimore veered off the hard surface, directly into the Canadian's path. Hanway applied full power to his good engine, gained a little height (he just missed the Baltimore) but lost airspeed. He touched down very hard and tail first, bounced, and crossed the runway diagonally. Just when everything seemed to be under control, the port tire burst; the port undercarriage collapsed, followed by the starboard undercarriage. The aircraft was a mess – but neither Hanway nor his observer was hurt. The accident investigator wrote, "Pilot made best possible landing considering all factors."

At the end of his instructional tour, Hanway estimated that he had flown 20 hours on Marauders and 70 hours on Beaufighters (he was self-taught on the type); the rest of his time had been on Beauforts. When asked about his posting preferences, he stated that he would like either photographic reconnaissance or Beaufighter operations. He was given leave in Canada, but arrived back in Britain in mid-March 1944. On April 7 he joined No. 404 Squadron. On August 26, 1944, he was reported missing while attacking German warships fleeing the Bay of Biscay ports; his body was recovered and buried in France.

(Above) A group of BCATP graduates from the Maritimes, July 1941; James A. Hanway is first on the left, front row. This group of new pilots must have been lucky; only five were killed in the course of the war. (Canadian Forces Photograph PL-3891)

(Right) The saddest investitures were those at which next-of-kin received the medals awarded to deceased personnel. S/L James Hanway's AFC was presented at Government House, Ottawa, to his widow and his sister. Unhappily, neither was fully identified by name or position in the photograph. (Canadian Forces Photograph PL-37613)

FERRY OPERATIONS

Victory is the beautiful, bright-coloured flower. Transport is the stem without which it could never have blossomed.

– WINSTON CHURCHILL (1874-1965), *THE RIVER WAR* (1899)

Ferry Command was an exceptionally cosmopolitan organization stitched together by the Royal Air Force in 1940-41 with assistance from Canadian and American authorities as well as commercial flying services. By late 1941 it was providing a steady flow of aircraft to Britain which grew with every passing month. Although many aircraft were delivered by pilots going overseas to assume operational duties, the bulk of Ferry Command work was performed by its cosmopolitan staff. Sometimes the aircraft were flown directly from Gander or Goose Bay to Scotland; more frequently they went in stages via Greenland and Iceland. This route, in the latter portion of the war, was administered by No. 112 Wing. An alternative route across the South Atlantic (run by No. 113 Wing) was much used to get machines to the Middle East and India. Crews that had delivered aircraft overseas returned to North America by ship or air. The rest period before another delivery flight was normally about two weeks (much of which was taken up in briefing or training on new equipment), but it might be as brief as 36 hours.[75]

F/L Lawrence Latham Jones of Saskatoon was a CAN/RAF officer. He had joined the RAF in 1937 and became a skilled navigator as well as pilot while flying Sunderlands with No. 228 Squadron. He went through incredible adventures and narrow escapes during the Norwegian campaign of April and May 1940 for which he was awarded the DFC. Early in July 1940 he participated in reconnaissance flights supporting Royal Navy operations that neutralized the French Fleet at Oran.[76] Jones began his ferrying service in February 1941 when he flew a Catalina from Montreal to Britain via Halifax. In March and again in May he piloted Catalinas from Bermuda to Britain, and twice in August 1941 he took Hudsons overseas, followed by two more in September. He was posted to No. 45 Group Headquarters, Dorval, in October 1941, where administrative duties took up most of his time thereafter. Soon after reporting there he was recommended for an AFC as follows:

> This officer is employed on ferry duties and has set a very fine example to all pilots in the command. He has completed seven delivery flights with Catalina and Hudsons and, owing to difficulty in turning our civilian pilots round, he made a complete journey from Prestwick to Prestwick in 62 hours, a very fine performance.[77]

Not all of his deliveries were to Britain; "Slim" Jones also brought Catalinas to Eastern Air Command units in the summer of 1941. In 1944 he made Atlantic crossings in a Martin Mariner and a Consolidated Coronado.

Records of Ferry Command crews are incomplete and sometimes contradictory. One of the top pilots was F/L George Gordon Wright of Tisdale, Saskatchewan. A press release credited him with 70 Atlantic crossings and six trips across the Pacific. These figures obviously include returns when he was a passenger aboard somebody else's airplane; up to the end of 1944 he was known to have delivered 28 aircraft across the Atlantic and to have undertaken two round-trip missions in Liberators across the Pacific.

Wright had received his wings in March 1942 and reported to Dorval in April. His first delivery was of a Ventura, flown to Britain between May 26 and 29, 1942. His subsequent delivery

Ferry Command bases such as Dorval witnessed the passage of many aircraft types. The keen-eyed aircraft recognition expert will detect nine types – Lancaster, Fortress, Ventura, Havoc, Marauder, Norseman, Harvard, Canso and Mitchell. (Canadian Forces Photo PL11070)

flights took him as far away as Iraq and northwest India (now Pakistan). Most deliveries were of Mitchells, Liberators and Dakotas, but he also flew a Mosquito to Britain in March 1944 (Montreal-Goose Bay-Greenland-Iceland-Scotland) and in May 1944 he took a Canadian-built Lancaster X (KB758) overseas. His two known Pacific expeditions were flown via San Diego, Hawaii, Fiji, New Zealand and Australia, with dangerous side trips on both occasions to Canton, China.

F/L Norman Edward Greenaway of Camrose, Alberta, as shown on his Ferry Command Crew Card. He was navigator of a Hampden bomber that crashed off the coast of Greenland in 1943. After several days of privation, the crew were rescued. While recovering from frost-bitten feet, Greenaway made himself useful by compiling data for ferry route manuals and an airfield gazetteer. His AFC, announced in September 1945, recognized valuable services both in the air and on the ground.

When not engaged on Ferry Command work, Wright was attached to No. 168 Squadron, assisting them in converting to Liberators. Apart from his Air Force Cross (awarded on September 1, 1944), he was awarded the Czechoslovak Medal of Merit, First Class (November 2, 1946). He remained briefly in the postwar RCAF, flying with No. 12 (Communications) Squadron, but resigned in 1947.

F/L Lewis Benjamin Wyman of Edmonton was almost as busy as George Wright when it came to trans-oceanic ferrying. In fact, the two had been classmates at Initial, Elementary Flying and Service Flying Training Schools; their graduation dates were identical and they reported to Dorval within days of one another. Wyman's first delivery involved a Hudson; he departed Dorval on June 9, 1942 and touched down in Britain on the 12th, having flown via Goose Bay and Reykjavik. From then until the end of December 1944 he was known to have completed 26 deliveries across the Atlantic.

Several entries on his crew card indicate interesting trips. On February 18, 1943, he was involved in an experimental glider tow from Dorval to Houlton, Maine (see below). On several occasions he returned from Europe aboard Pan-American Airways "Clippers" (Boeing 314 flying boats). He was frequently listed as flying Baltimores, Dakotas and Venturas from Nassau (Bahamas) to Accra (Gold Coast, now known as Ghana). He twice delivered Lancaster Xs to Britain (KB705 in November 1943, KB737 in March 1944); like George Wright, his deliveries took him to Iraq and India. As of the summer of 1944, however, he had become principally a VIP pilot. Lewis Wyman was twice Commended for Valuable Services in the Air (June and September 1944) before being awarded the AFC; he waited until January 24, 1956, to be invested with the decoration at Government House. Postwar he was a senior pilot with Trans-Canada Airlines.

In the winter of 1942-1943 the Air Officer Commanding, Ferry Command, Air Chief Marshal Sir Frederick Bowhill, conceived the idea of delivering supplies to Britain aboard gliders towed across the North Atlantic. A team assembled at Dorval to test his idea, using a Douglas Dakota as towplane and a Waco CG-4A cargo glider. Considerable investigative work was done beforehand; the glider was towed

P/O George G. Wright was one of the busiest Canadians in Ferry Command.

P/O Lewis Benjamin Wyman of Edmonton, from his Ferry Command Crew Card.

with various loads, then long-range tows were flown between Dorval and North Bay (a round trip on April 23, 1943), Dorval to Houlton, Maine, then between Dorval and Goose Bay, and finally from Dorval to Nassau and return (May 7 to 9, 1943). New records for distances flown under tow were set – 1,187 miles on a return leg between Nassau and Richmond, Virginia – and approval was given for the Atlantic attempt.

On June 23, 1943, the expedition began. Dakota FD900 was piloted by F/L William S. Longhurst (CAN/RAF); his co-pilot and navigator was F/L C.W.H. Thompson (New Zealander in the RAF). H.G. Wightman, a Canadian civilian, manned the radio while P/O R.H. Wormington (RAF) served as flight engineer. The Waco glider (FR579, named "Voo-Doo") was piloted by S/L R.G. Seys (RAF) and S/L Fowler M. Gobeil (RCAF). A Catalina accompanied this duo, to effect a rescue if the glider were forced down in the Atlantic, although it is

doubtful that it could have alighted in rough seas. The trio subsequently flew four legs as follows:

June 23, 1943 – Dorval to Goose Bay – 850 miles – 6 hours 47 minutes.

June 27, 1943 – Goose Bay to Bluie West One, Greenland – 785 miles – 6 hours 13 minutes.

June 30, 1943 – Bluie West One to Reykjavik, Iceland – 1,000 miles – 7 hours 20 minutes.

July 1, 1943 – Reykjavik to Prestwick – 865 miles – 7 hours 43 minutes.

S/L F.M. Gobeil as a Ferry Command accident investigator early in 1943. (Courtesy the Canadian War Museum)

These figures do not begin to describe the dangers and difficulties of the flight. Gobeil later claimed that in the days prior to departure, odds of seven to one had been laid by Dorval personnel against a successful crossing.

Consider the problems. It was necessary that both aircraft be flown all the time; not for a minute could anyone relax. If the glider got too far below the tug it might stall the Dakota; if the Waco got too high it might tip the Dakota into a dive. Maintaining just the right height relationship was difficult enough in clear visibility, but with 350 feet of rope separating them there were times when fog and cloud cut off visual contact. It then became especially important for the glider pilots to watch the angle at which the tow cable fell away from their craft (the "angle of dangle") as this was the only indication of their position relative to the tug. During the run from Greenland to Iceland the Dakota and Waco were out of sight of one another for more than an hour.

Then there was the matter of turbulence; this could (and did) threaten to disrupt the height ratio between tug and glider. During one severe session between Dorval and Goose Bay the cargo shifted noticeably; Seys and Gobeil had to use to their combined strength to control the Waco. Gobeil described this portion of the flight vividly:

At one moment the tow rope would be hanging like a limp, inert string; at the next if would be snapped straight, as taut and unquivering as a violin string. We feared the fittings would give way or the tow rope break. We were flying over the still-frozen waste of tundra in inner Labrador. Ice began to form on the wings of the glider and hoarfrost in the interior. The temperature dropped below zero. We had to detour around heavy, black rainstorms. We could not avoid all these

W/C F.M. Gobeil, AFC, about 1960. The 1943 glider tow across the Atlantic rescued his stagnating career.

W/C R.G. Seys (RAF) and S/L F.M. Gobeil inspect (for the cameras) the tow rope which had to be spliced repeatedly during the Atlantic glider tow.

F/L William S. Longhurst (a Canadian in the RAF, piloted the Dakota tug on the Atlantic glider tow; F/L C.W.H. Thompson (New Zealander in the RAF) was co-pilot and navigator.

storms and were forced to fly entirely on instruments for varying periods. Several times we considered turning back, but we decided to carry on. Finally, after three hours of this fearful pounding we sighted the Hamilton River and shortly after, the great aerodrome at Goose Bay. With a sigh of thanks we cut loose from the tug at 1,000 feet and landed.

Concerns about the tow rope intensified; at Bluie West One they discovered that one strand in three had worn clear through, and the rope had to be respliced before continuing. Further rope repairs were needed at Reykjavik when Longhurst had to drop the cable on the runway rather than risk dragging part of it over houses that encroached on the field.

"Voo-Doo" delivered 3,000 pounds of cargo to Britain – serum, truck parts and radio components. C.G. Gray, editor of the *Aeroplane* dismissed it as an impractical stunt; the Dakota alone could have delivered as much in less time. The fact that the effort was never repeated proves his point. Some lessons might have been learned that later benefitted airborne landings in Burma and Normandy, but proof of a connection has not been found. Nevertheless, it was a triumph of ingenuity and courage; Seys, Gobeil and Longhurst all received Air Force Crosses.[78]

Ferry Command was, of course, a multi-national organization, and many others were honoured besides Canadians. Two in particular merit special attention. S/L Richard J. Ralph of London, England, was chief instructor at North Bay, Ontario, where from July 1942 onwards crews were trained for transoceanic hops. Ralph was recommended for his AFC on July 14, 1943; it was gazetted on August 31. As of that date he had flown more than 6,300 hours. By then he had left North Bay and returned to routine trans-Atlantic delivery operations; at war's end he was commanding in Lagens (the Azores).

Another AFC gazetted on August 31, 1943, was to F/O Keith Edward Robinson, DFC, Royal Australian Air Force, who had been born in Lismore, New South Wales. From July 1942 onwards he was stationed at Dorval, where he gave trans-Atlantic crews specialist instruction on modern American types, including instrument flying and landing procedures using tricycle undercarriages. Robinson was described as "an exceptional pilot and a hard working instructor." He subsequently took up similar duties at No. 111 OTU, Nassau.[79]

"Voo-Doo" was the CG-4 glider that was towed across the Atlantic in stages in 1943 . (National Archives of Canada PA-193257)

TRANSPORT[80]

For I dipt into the future, far as human eye could see,
Saw the vision of the world, and all the wonder that would be;
Saw the heavens fill with commerce, argosies of magic sails,
Pilots of the purple twilight, dropping down with costly bales.

– ALFRED, LORD TENNYSON (1809-1892), "LOCKSLEY HALL"

It is to the credit of many senior RCAF officers that they worked hard to see merit rewarded, even if it meant recommending a person repeatedly for a decoration before it was granted. The story of Humphrey Oliver Madden is but one example. Born in Langford, England, in 1906, he was already an experienced pilot when he enlisted in the RCAF in October 1939. After service with No. 12 (Communications) Squadron, Rockcliffe, he wound up commanding a flight delivering aircraft to schools and bases throughout Canada; this eventually became No. 124 (Ferry) Squadron, which he led from its formation in January 1942 until the end of April 1943. He was subsequently promoted to wing commander and posted to No. 165 (Transport) Squadron upon its formation at Sea Island.

Some of his early work was unusual. In November 1941 the RCAF was contemplating winter deliveries of Stranraer flying boats from the east to the west coast. With interior waterways likely to be frozen, the force sent Madden to the United States with Grumman Goose 944 to review alternative routes. Between the 2nd and 15th he appraised some of the most spectacular American terrain, looking for appropriate sites. Between Cheyenne and Salt Lake City he flew through broad though relatively dry valleys, the floors of which were already 6,000 feet above sea level, and for 60 miles he manoeuvred down narrow passes, flanked by 12,000-foot mountains. Further west he found stretches cloaked by smoke and fog and plateau lakes that froze about the same time as those in Canada. He checked American bases from San Franciso to Los Angeles, then turned eastward, reviewing the reservoirs behind dams in the American southwest through to Fort Worth, following large river routes northwards thereafter. Madden concluded that a southern ferry route was more practical than one through Utah, and within ten days of his return the first Stranraers were heading for British Columbia.[81]

In December 1942 an American member of the RCAF was

A Lockheed 10A Electra, one of many civilian aircraft secured by the RCAF to modernize its transport fleet at the outbreak of war. (Canadian Forces Photograph RE 64-1906)

ROYAL CANADIAN AIR FORCE

Name.......... MADDEN, Humphrey, Oliver

Rank.......... Squadron Leader

Age.. 35   Height. 6 '   Weight. 175 lbs.

Hair.. Light   Eyes. Brown   Hair on face. Trimmed Mustache

Marks, scars, etc.......... None visible

H.O. Madden (Signature of holder)

R.W. Kennedy F/Lt. (Signature of issuer)

Place. RCAF Station, Rockcliffe.   Date. June 4th, 1942.

134416
Card serial number..........

The identity card of H.O. Madden. Whether he was surveying air routes, searching for lost aircraft or just conducting transport operations, Madden was a dependable officer whose AFC recognized his years of quiet but useful work. (National Archives of Canada PA-204874)

reported overdue in northern Ontario while ferrying a Hurricane. S/L Madden, accompanied by another pilot, promptly flew to North Bay in a Lockheed aircraft. In spite of bad weather and darkness they commenced a search; at 11.30 p.m. they spotted a light on a frozen lake. Their man had loosened a landing light on the Hurricane and was using it to signal. Madden sized up the situation, dropped emergency rations and went on to Kapaskasing, returning in a ski-equipped Norseman to effect the rescue.

That sort of gung-ho approach (displayed on at least one other occasion) was characteristic of the man. He was recommended for an AFC in February 1942 for services rendered between October 1939 and October 1941. That did not go through. In May 1943, when Madden was transferred to Western Air Command, G/C J.G. Bryans tried again, praising his man for skills in training and organizing No. 124 Squadron as well as his bush prowess. Western Air Command authorities put him up for a Mention in Despatches on September 3, 1943; by then he had flown 1,634 hours in the force (409 in the

previous six months). This time RCAF Headquarters took a good look at the file; the MiD was bumped up to an AFC, awarded on January 1, 1944, and presented to him at a station parade on April 15 of that year.

The RCAF's transportation organization developed slowly during the war, responding to events rather than being shaped by a master plan. Communications flights scattered across the country served well enough for half the war; No. 12 Squadron, based in Ottawa, moved people and occasional freight around; No. 170 Squadron ferried aircraft to schools and squadrons within Canada. The need for heavy transport capability became apparent only in 1942. Two ships carrying construction materials to Goose Bay were sunk by U-boats; the submarine menace showed the need for special aerial services in the east and led to the formation of No. 164 Squadron. The war in the Pacific (and especially the Aleutians campaign) resulted in movements to Alaska accompanied by construction of the Alaska Highway, and No. 165 Squadron was formed with the triple purpose of linking Western Air Command bases, transporting men and material north from Edmonton, and providing aircraft to train paratroops at Rivers, Manitoba.

A good transport squadron was one that had nothing to report except routine pickups and deliveries, be the cargo canned goods, spare engines, or fire-fighting pumps; No. 165

Squadron was certainly good in that respect; its wartime diary is exceedingly dull; its principal woes were connected with crowded accommodation, outdoor servicing of aircraft, and occasional mass posting of crews to build new squadrons. It had one tragedy, on July 18, 1944, at Port Hardy, when Dakota 966 crashed on takeoff, killing six. A typical entry, for January 30, 1945, shows the routine:

At Edmonton 29 passengers emplaned on schedule and special. At Rivers, three aircraft used for 35 jumps. At Sea Island, trip 47 off with 14 passengers and 3,058 pounds freight; returned with 24 passengers and 1,590 pounds cargo. Special Lodestar out with eight passengers and 434 pounds freight, returned with four passengers and 100 pounds cargo. To pick up Station Commanders for Command Conference.

No. 165 had been formed with W/C Madden in charge; most of the route trials were flown personally by him, and he was kept busy visiting his detachments. In the latter part of 1943 the squadron flew several times to Anchorage and beyond. The Aleutians campaign had wrapped up in August; RCAF and army units remained a few months before withdrawal. On August 21, Madden departed Edmonton in a Lodestar, carrying A/V/M L.F. Stevenson and staff for a look at the region. In stages they flew through Alaska and down the Aleutian chain, then retraced their steps, arriving back at Edmonton on August 29. The unit diary reported the highlights of what had otherwise been an uneventful journey:

S/L Harry Marlowe Kennedy learned to fly with the interwar RCAF, but when the force was cut to the bone in 1932 he became a civilian pilot, first with Western Canada Airways, then Mackenzie Air Services, and finally Trans-Canada Airlines. He rejoined the RCAF in 1940 and stuck with the force thereafter, retiring as a group captain in 1956. He was awarded an AFC for helping establish No. 12 (Communications) Squadron and organizing the flight arrangements for a 1941 Canadian tour by His Royal Highness the Duke of Kent. Kennedy was admitted to Canada's Aviation Hall of Fame in 1978. (Canadian Forces Photograph PL-945)

In connection with the flight of Lodestar 558, it is of interest that contact was made by the aircraft with Western Air Command every day, at times over a distance exceeding 2,500 miles. Hours of best reception were between 1630-1900 hours (Bering War Time). On one occasion the radio operator contacted No. 2 Group at Patricia Bay and gave position, and over excellent reception listened to No. 2 Group having difficulty in contacting Vancouver. The aircraft flew over Kiska on an unusually fine day and observed the damage caused by bombing and sea bombardment.

Plodding as it may be, the diary of No. 165 Squadron sparkles compared with that of No. 12 (Communications) Squadron, yet this unit also played a significant wartime role. Originally formed as No. 12 Communications Flight on September 10, 1939, it attained squadron status on July 17, 1940. No. 12 (C) Squadron was based at Rockcliffe. Throughout the war it performed many functions; initially it did some test flying; many American pilots applying for RCAF service in 1940-41 were checked out by unit aircrew; for much of the war a flight provided aircraft for AFHQ staff officers to practice while holding down desk jobs. However, No. 12 (C)'s main job was VIP flying. Generals, admirals, air marshals, cabinet ministers, visiting diplomats, the Duke of Kent, the Governor General himself – all were shuttled about as their duties required.

Given the multiplicity of its tasks, No. 12 (C) flew a variety of aircraft – Harvards, Yales, Fairchild 71s, Norseman, Dakotas, and Lockheed transports. At least two of its aircraft (Lodestar 567 and Dakota 663) were modified to luxurious standards. Its VIP work was concentrated in central Canada, but special trips ranged to San Francisco, the Yukon and Southampton Island.

The most famous incident in the squadron's history was a tragic Hudson crash on June 10, 1940, which killed three crewmen and the Minister of National Defence, the Honourable Norman Rogers. Thereafter the unit had a flawless safety record, its only significant accident being on March 28, 1942, when Lockheed 7646 carrying the Honourable J.L. Ralston (Rogers' successor) made a belly landing at Farquier, Ontario; this time there were no injuries. The work was serious but unspectacular. Cy Torontow, who served briefly with No. 12 (C) Squadron, remembered the regular flights in a Grumman Goose, transporting Air Marshal W.A. Bishop (regularly drunk) between Ottawa and Bishop's Muskoka cottage.[82] One of the most unusual trips was undertaken in December 1945 when S/L Andrew Tilley (Toronto) flew Canada's ambassador to the United States to Los Angeles; the mission was to present plaques to American film stars who had assisted in Canadian war bond drives over the past six years.

In the summer of 1943 Canadian forces abroad were expanding but also dispersing. The despatch of the 1st Canadian

Flying Fortress 9203 of No. 168 Squadron, used as a trans-Atlantic mail plane. This particular machine vanished during a crossing in December 1944. (National Archives of Canada PA-133286)

Infantry Division to the Mediterranean was just the beginning of a major deployment of Canadian soldiers to the Italian campaign. Mail services were important in maintaining morale, but existing carrier systems were inadequate. Surface mail sent by sea was not only slow; it ran a great risk, up to April 1943, of being lost through ship sinkings. Trans-Canada Airlines was contracted to fly a trans-Atlantic mail and VIP service, using converted Lancasters. This was not enough. On October 18, 1943, the RCAF formed No. 168 (Heavy Transport) Squadron for the specific task of flying mail and priority freight between Canada and Europe. Based at Rockcliffe, just outside Ottawa, its first long-range equipment consisted of six aging Flying Fortresses delivered in December. The inaugural "Mailcan" flights began on December 15, and soon the squadron was running regular two-way services, which improved when the Fortresses were joined (but never wholly replaced) by Liberators.

No. 168 Squadron flew chiefly between Ottawa and Britain, with distribution to the Mediterranean (and later to the European mainland) carried out by RAF and RCAF Dakotas. However, the Dakotas did not come into play until the spring of 1944; up to that date the Fortresses regularly flew loads from Britain to Gibraltar for onward movement to Canadians in Italy and other Mediterranean points.

On the night of January 23, 1944, Fortress 9205 departed Prestwick for Gibraltar; possible interception by German fighters over the Bay of Biscay had ruled out daylight flights to "Gib." The crew consisted of F/O Horace B. Hillcoat, AFM (Amherst, Nova Scotia, pilot), P/O Eli M. Rosenbaum (co-pilot), F/O Frederick B. Labrish (Regina, navigator), F/O Cecil

The Earl of Athlone presents Corporal Albert de Marco with his AFM, awarded for bravery following the collision of Fortress 9205 with a Wellington over the Bay of Biscay. (Canadian Forces Photograph PL-25151)

F/O Frederick B. Labrish, navigator aboard Fortress 9205, receives his AFC from the Governor General. Labrish was lost with Fortress 9203 in December 1944. (Canadian Forces Photograph PL-25149)

A. Dickson (Edmonton, radio operator) and Corporal Albert de Marco (Lakeview, Ontario, crewman). They were briefed to fly at 5,000 feet, just below icing level. They were cruising not far from Brest when the aircraft lurched violently amid terrible sounds of breaking perspex and tearing metal. The Fortress had collided with a Coastal Command Wellington, the wing of which knocked out two engines and bent all four sets of propellers. The "Wimpie" vanished; Hillcoat and Rosenbaum fought for control and finally regained it at 1,200 feet. Rosenbaum and de Marco then dumped all the mail and anything else that was loose in four minutes flat.

There followed a two-hour ordeal as the Fortress struggled back to Britain. Every crewman gave his utmost, calling up every skill they had learned in their respective trades. With aerials gone, Dickson managed to maintain radio contact with England; Labrish, forced out of his wrecked compartment in the nose, navigated with only half his normal aids from the wireless position; de Marco, a trained mechanic, advised on how to get the most power from the damaged engines. As Fortress 9205 landed at Predannack, in Cornwall, nobody knew if the undercarriage would hold up (it did). All four officers received the Air Force Cross, and de Marco was awarded the Air Force Medal.[83]

No. 168 Squadron was later involved in a much-publicised relief operation. In September 1945 the United Polish Relief Fund appealed to the Canadian government to deliver several

F/O John L. Plant, photographed in 1936. His distinguished wartime work, first on maritime reconnaissance, then air transport, led to exceptionally detailed recommendations for awards. (Canadian Force Photograph AH-640)

tons of penicillin to Poland. There were problems, including clearance for aircraft to a country now under Russian occupation. Ottawa reluctantly agreed. The first shipment, 5,556 pounds, was flown to Prestwick on October 19/20 in a Fortress (the pilot, F/L William G. McElrea, later received an AFC). The RAF delivered the cargo to its destination. Another Fortress, despatched on October 30 to go all the way, crashed near Munster on November 4, killing all five crewmen aboard.[84]

Loss of that cargo increased the need for another delivery; on November 16 a third Fortress left Ottawa, this time with 2,235 pounds of precious cargo. Air Commodore John Plant captained the aircraft to Warsaw and back. The swift delivery in the face of adverse weather was one incident in his career leading to his being awarded an AFC; others included successful landing of a Fortress with undercarriage problems and establishing a transport speed record between Vancouver and Ottawa (January 16, 1946). The RCAF would have been happy to deliver another shipment, particularly as little publicity had been given the flights in Poland itself. However, all subsequent penicillin cargoes went via the RAF.

Hundreds of RCAF and CAN/RAF personnel flew on overseas transport operations, both in RCAF and RAF squadrons. Flying in the teeth of enemy opposition could earn an entry in the *Book of Remembrance* or a combat gallantry award. Following the Arnhem air drop (September 1944) there had also been a generous distribution of Dutch and American awards. Sometimes, as Air Ministry officials weighed the recommendations before them, the question arose as to how far one had to be from the shooting war before a recommended transport DFC became an AFC instead. This became particularly germane in mid-1943, as transport crews shuttling between Gibraltar, Malta and Cairo were exposed to declining risks from enemy aircraft. Shortly after the invasion of Sicily (July 1943) several DFC nominations were converted into AFCs and Commendations, reflecting the changed circumstances. Even so, it was still difficult on occasion to decide which decoration was more appropriate. As personal pilot to Sir Arthur Tedder during the North African campaign, F/L Fred G. de Sieyes (CAN/RAF, from Winnipeg) often flew into the battle zone, particularly while the Battle of El Alamein was raging. Had he been recommended for an award at the time, it would almost surely have been a DFC; by early 1944 only an AFC could be contemplated.

Charles Norman McVeigh of Calgary enlisted in the Royal Air Force in 1937 and trained as a pilot. In September 1938 he joined No. 12 Squadron, flying Fairey Battles. His unit went to France a year later; for much of the "Phoney War" period he conducted occasional reconnaissance missions and dropped leaflets on German border areas. Suddenly, on May 10, 1940, the enemy launched their major offensive in the west. In the next month his unit suffered appalling losses. Six days after the offensive began McVeigh was destroying the fuel dump at Amifontaine prior to retreat; he survived at least nine sorties (one involving combat with six enemy fighters) before No. 12 was evacuated to England. That autumn it converted to Wellingtons.

McVeigh flew several missions on the new type, but on August 16, 1941, he crashed on returning from a raid. He broke a leg. Thereafter he served as an instructor in Britain at assorted schools, including a transport OTU. As a squadron leader he joined No. 48 Squadron in February 1944. Formerly a Coastal Command unit flying Hudsons, No. 48 was now converting to Dakotas under another CAN/RAF officer, W/C J.A. Sproule; McVeigh was in charge of conversion training. On the night of June 5 he led No. 48's aircraft over Normandy as they dropped paratroops. With 1,204 flying hours in his logbook, 140 in six months, he was recommended for the Air Force Cross. It came through on September 1, 1944. Days later he joined No. 437 Squadron and participated in the Arnhem air drops.

S/L Charles N. McVeigh receives his AFC from the Honourable J.M. Ulrich, Lieutenant-Governor of Saskatchewan, on November 8, 1948. As a member of the RAF, McVeigh took part in some of the earliest bombing raids of the war. He switched to transport work following a crash that nearly cost him a leg. (National Archives of Canada C.144694)

Another transport AFC recipient was F/L Alexander C. Wanlin of Winnipeg, shown receiving the medal from the Lieutenant-Governor of Saskatchewan. He had been recommended on October 27, 1945, at which time he had flown 2,514 hours (510 on transport duties, 350 in the previous six months). The CO of No. 435 Squadron noted that Wanlin had considerable experience in Britain and Southeast Asia and that he had been invaluable at "instructing new crews with the polish expected of a transport captain."

He transferred to the RCAF in October 1944 and continued to fly resupply missions between England and the continent. On May 10, 1945, braving weather that defeated many other crews, he flew to Oslo with the task of bringing German delegates out for surrender arrangements. McVeigh was later promoted to wing commander and led No. 435 Squadron from September 1945 to April 1946. He remained in the postwar RCAF and retired in Vancouver. Apart from his AFC he was twice Mentioned in Despatches (January 1, 1941, and January 1, 1946).[85]

Among the double-award recipients was F/L Hardie Emerson McNeil, a native of Drayton, Ontario. He had first experienced the military as a COTC trainee while attending Queen's University, enlisted in August 1941, and graduated as a pilot in May 1942. He was retained in Canada as an instructor, but finally went overseas where he was posted to No. 436 Squadron (the Flying Elephants), supporting the British 14th Army in Burma. He was an outstanding pilot. His

work routinely consisted of dropping supplies at low levels to troops already in contact with Japanese infantry. On one occasion McNeil alighted on a newly captured landing strip and calmly directed the unloading operation while being subjected to Japanese artillery and machine gun fire. On January 15, 1946, he was awarded a DFC.

No. 436 Squadron, with its sister unit, No. 435 (Chinthe) Squadron, moved to Britain after VJ-Day where they joined No. 437 (Husky) Squadron. The three Dakota units constituted No. 120 (Transport) Wing. They were helping support the Allied Occupation Forces in Germany, which at that time included 21,500 Canadian soldiers. Many of the veteran crews had been repatriated, and those like McNeil who remained were kept busy training new crews from men who often had been flying Spitfires or Lancasters a few months earlier. His superiors evidently relied upon him as a deputy flight commander. Having logged 2,735 flying hours (2,050 on operations, 220 in his last six months) he was recommended for an AFC; it was gazetted on June 13, 1946. He received both his DFC and AFC at a Toronto investiture held on November 30, 1949.

Arthur Leland Brown was a similar DFC/AFC transport pilot. A native of Hawarden, Saskatchewan, he had enlisted in May 1941 and recived his flying badge in December of that year. His next postings, to Charlottetown and Debert, suggested a maritime patrol assignment, but in June 1942 he was switched to Ferry Command and in September he was posted overseas. Following four months of further training he was

The Douglas Dakota transport was ubiquitous; it was as important to Allied victory as any gun-toting, bomb-dropping aircraft. (Imperial War Museum CNA 3328)

an AFC; it was awarded in April 1945. The citation (like many others, unpublished), read:

This officer has served the squadron with distinction, earning the Distinguished Flying Cross for work with the squadron detachment in India. On one occasion when one engine on the Dakota he was piloting failed, he safely made a single engined circuit at night. On another occasion when an engine cut he made a successful forced landing on a disused desert landing strip. This officer has set an excellent example in the squadron by his deportment and enthusiasm for his work.[86]

posted to No. 216 Squadron, flying Dakotas. No. 216 was probably the best known RAF transport unit of the war. Its history extended back to the 1920s when its big biplanes had ferried British troops to trouble spots throughout the Near and Middle East. Early in the war its Bombay aircraft had served both as transports and bombers in Egypt. Brown's work with the squadron ranged from North Africa through the Eastern Mediterranean to India. In May 1944, during the seige of Imphal, he dropped supplies to isolated units while Japanese ground fire peppered his Dakota.

As a flight lieutenant he was awarded a DFC in September 1944. He continued with No. 216 Squadron; promotion to squadron leader and responsibilities as a flight commander altered his duties but did not slow his pace. With 2,033 hours in his logbook (124 in six months) he was recommended for

Brown had returned to Canada in January 1945. He instructed at No. 6 Operational Training Unit (Comox), then engaged in training Dakota crews for continued operations in the Pacific. He subsequently flew with No. 412 (Transport) Squadron before going on to other duties in the postwar RCAF. He received both his DFC and AFC at an investiture held on April 1, 1949 (the RCAF's 25th birthday).

One further transport DFC/AFC combination merits

W/C John G. Showler, the Honourable J.C. Bowen (Lieutenant-Governor of Alberta) and Lieutenant-Colonel P.D. Baird at the close of Operation MUSKOX. Between February and May 1946 a convoy of special army vehicles had gone from Churchill to Edmonton via the Arctic coast, supplied by aircraft and gliders. Showler and Baird were experts in their respective fields (air transport and Arctic travel). (National Archives of Canada PA-195913)

description. S/L Frank E.W. Smith (Vancouver) commanded the Edmonton detachment of No. 165 Squadron for much of 1943 and 1944; this was the portion of the unit which faced the most demanding problems in terms of climate, inadequate airfield services, and frequent cargo backlogs that had to be cleared. When the Canadian Army held winter exercises in the Rockies, Smith worked out supply dropping routines. He was awarded an AFC in November 1944. By then he was slated for

overseas service. In Burma, with No. 436 Squadron, he further distinguished himself, particularly by flying weather reconnaissance trips in a Dakota during the monsoon season. He received a DFC in January 1946.

Two transport pilots who received the AFC are worth mentioning not so much for their wartime work as for their postwar achievements. F/O Robert Thomas Heaslip (Uxbridge, Ontario) had spent most of the war on Canada's Pacific coast with communications units; when nominated for his award he had flown 1,775 hours and was flying with No. 166 Squadron. In 1947 he was one of the first RCAF pilots trained to fly helicopters; in 1956, as a squadron leader, he formed No. 108 Communications Flight which operated chiefly from Bagotville, supporting construction of radar sites along the Mid-Canada Line. This had been another form of bush flying, living under canvas, refuelling from drums, occasional forced landings in the wilderness, plus searches for other aircraft that became lost during the airlift. The operation was without precedent, and it brought him the award of the 1956 McKee Trophy.[87]

S/L John Gavin Showler (already met as an accident-prone instructor) became a pilot in No. 164 Squadron, with which he was as much a teacher as an operational pilot. When recommended for the AFC he had flown 3,122 hours – an amazing wartime total. Nevertheless, a greater honour came when he was awarded the McKee Trophy for 1957; as CO of No. 408 Squadron since 1954, he had been responsible for the greater part of aerial mapping in Canada in that period.[88]

FIGHTER PILOT AFCS

The time will come when thou shalt lift thine eyes
To watch a long drawn battle in the skies,
While aged peasants, too amazed for words,
Stare at the Flying Fleets of wond'rous birds.

– THOMAS GRAY (1716-1771), *LUNA HABITALIA* (1737)

Fighter pilots did not normally qualify for Air Force Crosses, but four members of the RCAF received the award in fighter-related duties – one on Home Defence work and three overseas.

James Adamson Thompson of Listowel, Ontario, enlisted in April 1940 at the age of 25. He earned his wings in October and was posted overseas almost immediately. Details of his tour are not readily available; by April 1942 he was back in Canada, beginning a succession of postings through various Canadian squadrons – No. 125 (Hurricanes), No. 135 (Kittyhawks) and finally No. 132 Squadron (Kittyhawks).

Thompson assumed command of No. 132 Squadron in November 1943. The unit was at Boundary Bay, with nothing to do but practice and train, then train and practice. A typical month, January 1944, saw them fly 67 hours 25 minutes on operations (chiefly scrambles), 9 hours 51 minutes non-operational time (ferrying aircraft between fields) and 396 hours 40 minutes of training. This included practice interceptions, air-firing at drogues, cine gun attacks, dogfighting, flour-bombing troops on exercises, and the occasional mock attack on a passing aircraft carrier. On the ground they constantly studied aircraft recognition; skeet shooting was promoted to supplement aerial gunnery instruction. There were occasional flashes of excitement, invariably followed by anti-climax. On December 18, 1943, a Class One Alert was called and four Kittyhawks were despatched from Boundary Bay to Patricia Bay; an unidentified vessel was reported as shelling the west coast of Vancouver Island. Next day the alert was cancelled. No. 132 Squadron's diary reported the circumstances: "The shelling on the west coast was accidental, and carried out by a friendly vessel. The shells apparently landed near an important military installation through an oversight or by mistake."[89]

Thompson's job was to keep the men sharp; No. 132 Squadron was virtually an Operational Training Unit from which pilots were slowly drawn for overseas service. Thompson led regular formation flights and sometimes conducted vertical climb meteorological flights. Under him the squadron looked sharp as well; on June 19, 1944, the unit diary reported they had been congratulated for their smart appearance the previous day during a formal parade. He remained in charge of No. 132 until its disbandment at the end of September 1944. At that time he was recommended for an AFC (gazetted in January 1945); he was reported as having flown a total of 848 hours, of which 112 were operational (102 sorties). The citation read:

This officer, as officer commanding this squadron, has shown exceptional ability as a pilot and leader. By his own very fine personal example of skill and devotion to duty, he has maintained a high standard of efficiency and keenness within his squadron. He is responsible in no small part for the successful operations of the unit. The excellent qualities displayed by this officer are praiseworthy.

S/L Thompson held several staff and flying appointments over the next few months, including a period at No. 6 OTU at Comox, learning to fly Dakotas. He was released from the

RCAF in May 1946, the only Canadian Home Defence fighter pilot to have been awarded an AFC.

F/L William Lloyd Marr of Langley, British Columbia, was serving in No. 409 Squadron when he was recommended for an AFC (November 6, 1944). Earlier in the war he had been an instructor in Canada; his tour on No. 409 (a night fighter unit flying Mosquitos) had been eventful for all the wrong reasons. On five occasions he had been compelled to make single-engine landings by night; in none did he damage an aircraft. Twice he had closed on enemy aircraft, only to have his guns jam. With over 2,100 flying hours and 51 sorties behind him, Marr was deemed worthy of a "gong" for effort and endurance alone.

F/L Leslie Albert Moore, though born in Hamilton, was an American citizen when he enlisted in the RCAF. He would have preferred to join the U.S. Army Air Corps but in August 1941 he lacked the formal education required. Moore flew a lengthy tour with RCAF Spitfire units (Nos. 402 and 411 Squadrons, January 1943 to July 1944). During this time he participated in the destruction of seven enemy aircraft (four shared with other pilots, three solo victories) and was awarded the Distinguished Flying Cross. In August 1944 he was posted to No. 53 Operational Training Unit to pass on his knowledge to aspiring fighter pilots. He was singled out for an AFC. The citation was drafted when he had flown 795 non-operational hours including 183 instructional hours in the previous six months; it read:

> This officer was posted to No. 53 Operational Training Unit as a flying instructor and flight commander in August 1944. He has carried out his duties with the greatest keenness and enthusiasm. He has maintained the highest standards in his work which is of a most exacting nature. He is largely responsible for the excellent morale and spirit of the Advanced Training Squadron.[90]

This was clearly written at the time of his departure from No. 53 OTU; he rejoined No. 402 Squadron on February 22, 1945. Moore's AFC was gazetted on April 3, 1945, but he never saw the notice. On March 25 he was shot down and killed while strafing a train in Germany. His DFC and AFC were presented to his mother on April 29, 1949.

S/L Dominic Joseph Dewan of Ottawa spent much of the war as a staff pilot at a British air armament school while lobbying furiously for an operational posting. He flew one tour on Spitfires, mostly spent escorting American B-17 formations, then went back to another boring non-operational stint. He finally wangled a second tour and managed to shoot down a FW.190 on April 19, 1945, while with No. 412 Squadron. On May 30, 1945, he was promoted to squadron leader and given command of the unit. No. 412 Squadron had been designated as part of the British Air Forces of Occupation. Dewan faced a job as formidable as any combat assignment; keeping the unit sharp and the flying up to scratch when the war was over and everybody wanted to go home. He laid down a program of instruction and air exercises that succeeded admirably until No. 412 was disbanded in March 1946. His Air Force Cross was recognition for maintaining professional standards under enervating circumstances.

EXCEPTIONAL MEN – EXCEPTIONAL CASES

Most saints have been almost unbearable nuisances in life. Some were reformers, some were sages, some were visionaries, but all were intensely alive, and thus a living rebuke to people who were not. So many got martyred because nobody could stand them. Society hates exceptional people because such people make them feel inferior.

– ROBERTSON DAVIES (1913-1995), QUOTED BY JUDITH SKELTON GRANT, *THE ENTHUSIASMS OF ROBERTSON DAVIES (1979)*

The RCAF had sustained a 20-year drought in honours between the wars, and it would seem that at least one Air Force Cross was awarded to honour a beloved "character" as much for his interwar work as for his wartime services. G/C Frederick Joseph Mawdesley had been a successful commanding officer of No. 5 Bombing and Gunnery School when he received the AFC in January 1945. His performance in this and other commands had been outstanding, but what really made "Mawdie" different was the sum of his experiences – he had almost 5,200 flying hours to his credit, more than 1,100 as an instructor – and his personality.

Born in Tyrone, Ireland, in 1891, he had immigrated to Canada in 1914 to work on the Grand Trunk Railway. Soon he was sailing east again, this time with the Canadian Expeditionary Force. In 1918 he transferred from the army to the Royal Flying Corps as an observer, serving briefly in No. 49 Squadron (August 12 to 25, 1918) before he was wounded. He joined the interwar Canadian Air Force, retrained as a pilot, and embarked upon a varied career as staff officer, instructor and photo survey pilot. All of this seemed normal enough, but there was more. "Mawdie" was a colourful eccentric in a relatively bland mix of peacetime officers.

Retraining as a pilot, he had induced despair in his instructors. In 1924 a normal instructional session was only about 30 minutes. In October 1924 , S/L N.R. Anderson, who commanded the flying school at Camp Borden, was up with his special pupil for as much as 110 minutes practising forced landings. Yet even with 43 hours solo time, there were doubts that Mawdesley would ever improve on his erratic landings, and soon afterwards his training was discontinued – even though he had not crashed or damaged any aircraft. Yet his keenness was clear, and the head of the RCAF, G/C J.S. Scott, ordered that "Mawdie" be given three more hours of dual instruction *with any pilot that Mawdesley selected.* He chose S/L R.S. Grandy, who did his best, passed his pupil in some areas, but still insisted that Mawdesley was below par; although determined to be a pilot he had little natural flying ability. They kept at it, until "Mawdie" qualified for his wings in March 1925. Colonel Henry Logan, who witnessed these events, subsequently remarked that "Mawdesley got his wings and Grandy got the OBE" (true – but, as noted above, Grandy got his award in 1935 for pioneer air mail investigation flying).

Collecting "Mawdie" stories became an air force pastime. In command of small units, such as photographic detachments, he insisted on strict adherence to flying regulations, yet he blithely ignored the rules when in the cockpit himself. A pilot leaving one remote location by rail was disappointed that his CO had not turned up to say goodbye – until Mawdesley buzzed the train in an Avro floatplane! In the course of a pioneering two-plane flight to the Arctic Ocean in 1930, Mawdesley was on such bad terms with the civilian surveyor who went along that the latter insisted that they should never share the same airplane. His personal life was bohemian; he was a gambler and a bachelor. Tragically, his reputation as a "character" overshadowed his solid merits and achievements.

NOT IN THE FACE OF THE ENEMY

On October 16, 1924, at the height of Mawdesley's training crisis, S/L Anderson had assessed progress to date and written:

He has been very keen on flying, and his pluck and perseverance have been commendable, but I do not feel that I should ever be happy in advancing him to the stage where he might be placed in charge of a machine carrying passengers whose lives would depend on his judgement.

Five years later, Anderson was CO of Winnipeg Air Station and F/L Mawdesley was in charge of the Cormorant Lake detachment. On January 18, 1930, Anderson submitted a long report to AFHQ, describing Mawdie's activities of the year just past. It was a remarkable story. Between March 12 and December 12, 1929, Mawdie had flown 533 hours. He had supported one battle against a forest fire by making 11 trips to the site, delivering fresh men to fight the blaze. He had landed a wheeled aircraft on the only ice available in thawing lakes – ice pans in the middle of the lakes – to deliver forestry employees to the first forest fires of the season. An aircraft detailed to transport surveyors had been grounded when a propeller cracked; Mawdesley had flown a Varuna 200 miles to Barens River, strapped the big four-bladed prop to the mid-section on the upper wing of his aircraft, and brought it out for repairs. He had conducted a mercy flight on March 31. Between May 3 and 6 he had flown a series of medical missions in poor weather. Anderson concluded his report with words very different from his earlier assessment:

He has flown through storm and smoke and darkness in carrying out the work of his Sub-Station… He has demonstrated to officials of Government Departments in a remarkable manner the great assistance which air transportation can be to them in their work, when arranged and supplied by a well organized, well equipped and efficient Air Service like the Directorate of Civil Government Air Operations.

Sergeant Harry Bryant and F/L Fred Mawdesley confer during 1932 air operations. The colourful "Mawdy" was long overlooked when honours were being distributed. He was awarded an AFC for command of a training establishment, but his greatest contributions to Canada had been made in the 1930s, when formal state honours had been either banned or severely rationed. (Canadian Forces Photograph RE-19227)

He has also proven that there is no other manner in which the Government of the country can win and hold the gratitude, admiration and loyalty of the people in outlying settlements of Canada more quickly than by keeping Government aircraft available to supply their needs in times of distress and sickness.

It is considered that Flight Lieutenant Mawdesley has done more in a practical way to further the cause of sound, sane sensible aviation in the Dominion of Canada during 1929 than any other pilot, and is respectfully recommended for the award of the Trans-Canada Trophy.

He did not receive the McKee Trophy (W.R. May got it for 1929), but he went on doing remarkable things – the flight to the Arctic Ocean in 1930, participation in a series of mail flights between Ottawa and the Strait of Belle Isle in 1932. Seconded to the RAF, he delivered flying boats to Singapore. In 1937 he was at the centre of an aerial search and rescue operation in British Columbia and piloted the Governor General around portions of the Northwest Territories.

There was a downside to his career. In 1931 he had resisted a desk job so forcibly that W/C G.O. Johnson described his actions as "wilful and deliberate disobedience." That assessment – and some mysterious "black marks" – blighted his subsequent career, which was largely spent on the fringes of the RCAF, far from AFHQ and the Air Command postings that brought high rank to others. Even when the "honours drought" ended and the war was forcing many promotions, Mawdesley was held back. He had come near to being retired on account of age in 1938. His career from 1939 to 1945 was curious. Superiors seemed ready to praise him, but not too much: "Keenness might tend to influence his judgement at times" wrote A/C A.H. Hull on December 14, 1942; now *there*

was an ambiguous assessment! A/V/M A.B. Shearer was more generous: "Wing Commander Mawdesley has given good and faithful service to the RCAF over a long period of years and is a well qualified and informed officer."

G/C Gordon McGregor was generous in his praise of Mawdesley, especially following a 1943 stint as acting commanding officer at Patricia Bay. Holding down a temporary post, Mawdie had been given no incentive to do anything but "hold the fort." Instead he had improved appearances, performances and morale; he had even cleared up old problems that McGregor had never hoped to see resolved. Wherever he went, Mawdie was described as smart in appearance, excellent in management and an officer who cared deeply about the welfare of his subordinates. If he was under a cloud, he did nothing to betray personal disappointment or bitterness.

It was as commanding officer of No. 5 Bombing and Gunnery School that he shone most brightly. Dafoe, Saskatchewan, was a harsh, isolated place by BCATP standards. Promoted to group captain (at last) and given charge of the school, he took a keen interest in the welfare of all, creating recreational and physical fitness facilities where none had existed. Morale soared; late in 1943 the unit was singled out as the best school in the BCATP.

Early in 1944, A/V/M T.A. Lawrence recommended Mawdesley for a CBE (Commander, Order of the British Empire); it did not reach the priority list for the Birthday Honours List. Late in August 1944, A/V/M Ken Guthrie put Mawdie up for an MBE; on September 8 this was changed to an AFC, which finally went through. It is possible – nay, probable – that Mawdesley's AFC was part recognition for services long past and part consolation prize.

He retired in 1945, but his reputation continued to obscure his talents. In the 1950s S/L Rick Mignon, then editor of

Roundel, collected dozens of "Mawdie" stories which he intended to publish as a booklet. Unfortunately, Mawdesley saw the text and was offended to the point of being heart-broken; the man who loved a joke was either too prickly or too old to appreciate one on himself. The book was never published (the manuscript seems to have been lost or destroyed). To make amends, the RCAF named a training centre in Winnipeg "Mawdesley Hall." The old man came for the opening ceremonies, when tributes were paid and old times recalled, but the photographs show him smiling without much conviction. He was, in fact, very much alone. He had never married; he outlived whatever family he had known. When Mawdie passed away at Orange, New Jersey, on May 13, 1968, he was solitary and penniless.[91]

Although Mawdesley's award was virtually a "catch-up" honour, his case was not unique. The AFC to G/C Joseph Menard William St. Pierre was another instance of belatedly honouring an officer who should have received earlier recognition, perhaps with a different award. He had been born in Chicago in 1912 to French-Canadian parents and lived in the United States until he was 19. When he came to Canada it was to work for Imperial Oil. In 1937 he joined the RCAF Auxiliary. The war brought rapid promotion, and by 1942 he was a wing commander with considerable instructional experience.

W/C Joseph St. Pierre, photographed in North Africa when he commanded No. 425 "Alouette" Squadron. He wears the ribbon of an American DFC. St. Pierre's AFC, awarded in 1945, was tardy recognition for earlier services in organizing the Alouettes. (Canadian Forces Photograph PL-18346)

W/C St. Pierre was posted to Britain early in 1942. After flying several missions with No. 419 Squadron, he was given command of No. 425 Squadron, then forming as a French-Canadian unit in Bomber Command. He was an excellent organizer, blending English- and French-speaking personnel into a team. Although he performed no outstanding feat of gallantry, his work might have been recognized with an MBE or an AFC. However, Canadian authorities overlooked him in 1942. In the summer of 1943 three RCAF squadrons – Nos. 420, 424 and 425 – were despatched to North Africa to assist in the invasions of Sicily and Italy. The units operated alongside American bomber squadrons. Major-General J.H. Doolittle, commanding the 12th Air Force, recommended St. Pierre for an American Distinguished Flying Cross, and its award was announced in October 1943.

Late in 1943, RCAF authorities suddenly woke up to W/C St. Pierre's abilities. They proposed a DFC for him, but the Air Ministry frowned on the suggestion – a Commonwealth DFC and an American DFC seemed like giving a man two medals for the same work. A/M Lloyd Breadner, writing in February 1944, noted that an AFC recommendation might have been entertained at an earlier date. A/M Harold Edwards promptly suggested that such an award be granted. Nothing happened; either existing quotas were filled or the timing was too late.

Nevertheless, when St. Pierre was promoted to group captain and given command of No. 9 Bombing and Gunnery School, his superiors would have been aware that his work at forming No. 425 Squadron had not been recognized sufficiently, and that an AFC recommendation would be in order at the first opportunity. A/V/M Adelard Raymond, Air Officer Commanding No. 3 Training Command, put St.Pierre up for an AFC on January 31, 1945, and it was gazetted on April 24 of that year. The citation stressed his work at No. 9 BGS, but it paid belated tribute to his earlier accomplishments overseas:

Since returning from commanding an operational squadron overseas, this officer has been actively employed in bombing and gunnery instructional duties. As Commanding Officer of this Bombing and Gunnery School, he has devoted considerable time and energy in becoming thoroughly conversant with all phases of his work. His sound judgement, knowledge and pleasing personality have won for him the respect of all personnel under his command. Group Captain St.Pierre's devotion to duty has been an example and inspiration to all ranks. By his ability he has made a marked contribution to bombing and gunnery training.[92]

On January 1, 1944, the *London Gazette* announced the award of an AFC to W/C Robert S. Turnbull, DFM. His unit was given as No. 427 Squadron and as usual, there was no citation. In fact, the award had begun as a recommendation for an OBE (Officer, Order of the British Empire) on June 21, 1943 when Turnbull was commanding No. 1659 Conversion Unit, which turned crews from twin-engined aircraft into competent teams operating four-engined bombers. The recommendation had described the recipient's work in glowing terms:

Since completing his tour of operations in April 1942, Wing Commander Turnbull has shown exceptional ability and devotion to duty both as a flying instructor and as Commanding Officer of the Conversion Unit. He has done 396 hours instructional flying and built the unit up from a flight of 405 Squadron to a very efficient full-sized Conversion Unit. He sets a high standard for his officers and is an outstanding example to all pilots screened for instructional duties after a tour of operations.[93]

Further up the chain of command, this had been refined and edited; at Air Ministry the citation now read:

This officer has shown exceptional ability and devotion to duty both as a flying instructor and as Commanding Officer of the Unit. He sets a high standard for his officers and is an outstanding example to all pilots screened for instructional duties after a tour of operations. He has shown fine ability in the building of this Conversion Unit.[94]

The story of Robert S. Turnbull is remarkable for the fact that the AFC was only one of an impressive array of decorations he won. Born in Winnipeg in 1918 and raised in Govan, Saskatchewan, he enlisted in the RCAF in Regina on June 19, 1940. He duly graduated as a pilot from No. 4 SFTS, Yorkton, Saskatchewan, but his marks were not sufficient to bring him a commission. As a sergeant pilot he was posted overseas. After operational training, he joined No. 476 (RAAF) Squadron. He immediately made his mark; during a raid on Nuremburg he circled the target area for an hour, trying to identify his objective before bombing. That brought him a Distinguished Flying Medal and an immediate commission. Promotion came fast. By war's end Turnbull was a group captain. On Sep-

W/C Robert S. Turnbull, DFC, AFC, DFM was as brilliant in combat as in training bomber crews. He evidently should have been commissioned immediately upon receiving his wings; as it was, his DFM was won while holding non-commissioned rank. (Canadian Forces Photograph)

tember 4, 1945, at an investiture in Canada, he received the DFC, Bar to DFC and AFC to accompany the DFM that had been presented to him earlier. As CO of No. 427 Squadron and later of No. 64 Base, he had been recognized as one of the RCAF's most daring bombing leaders. To these awards was added the French Croix de Guerre with Silver Star in 1947.[95] G/C Turnbull remained in the postwar RCAF; he retired in 1970 and died in Victoria in 1977.

If Turnbull's AFC was only one of many honours he received, S/L John Hone was an exceptional officer in another way; he was the only member of the RCAF to win the Air Force Cross twice. For ten years before the war Hone was a Manitoba bush pilot; his firm, Arrow Airways, ranged as far as the Arctic Circle, with geologists and prospectors as its special clients. He was one of the earliest Canadian commercial pilots to qualify for instrument flying. In 1936 he was commended

for running "the soundest and most efficient aircraft operating company in the Dominion of Canada." Just before enlistment he had saved two lives and was pioneering flight insurance. Hone joined the RCAF at Camp Borden on October 3, 1939; he received his air force wings there on December 30, 1939, following what author Tom Coughlin describes as "what must have been the shortest pilot course on record."[96] From student he turned instructor, specializing in instrument flying, but it was as a salvage expert that he initially earned formal recognition. His first AFC, announced on June 11, 1942, was unusual for the fact that a formal citation accompanied the gazetting:

This officer displayed the greatest ingenuity and tenacity in the matter of the rescue of Battle aircraft No. 1306 from March 10th to March 16th, 1940, from the ice in the neighbourhood of Parry Sound, Ontario. This aircraft was considerably damaged during a forced landing on the ice which was rapidly deteriorating and, working against time and in very bad weather, he supervised the temporary repair of the aircraft and managed to get it in flying condition and returned it to its base at No. 1 SFTS, Camp Borden. His flying capabilities as displayed on this occasion were of the highest order. In addition to this, Flight Lieutenant J. Hone was responsible for the salvage of a De Havilland Moth in June, 1940, under trying circumstances, in which he displayed a resourcefulness of the highest order.

It may be observed that the Hone received his AFC at the same time as W/C L.E. Wray, and that both were decorated for essentially salvage rather than flying exploits. As with Wray, it may be argued that the 1942 award should have been an MBE – but the political admissibility of an MBE was still up in the air at that time, while an AFC was acceptable.

Hone went on to a variety of other tasks. He flew Stranraers and Catalinas with No. 5 (BR) Squadron out of Dartmouth, Nova Scotia. He commanded No. 2 Air Navigation School at Pennfield Ridge, New Brunswick. He served briefly with Nos. 12 (C) and 168 (HT) Squadrons. Between January 4 and 8, 1944, he was involved in a mercy flight around Kapuskasing involving evacuation of a stretcher case by Norseman. He went to No. 7 Photo Wing, based at Rockcliffe, then mapping portions of Canada in anticipation of the postwar survey program which would be among the RCAF's greatest contributions to Canada. In the summers of 1943 and 1944 he piloted a Canso, often accompanied by two Norsemans, to Ungava, Baffin Island and other Arctic islands.

For the historian the diary of No. 7 Photo Wing is frustratingly vague. Aircraft would be reported as departing for Winisk or Churchill, with little information about what they are doing. References to individuals were rare, but in July 1944 S/L Hone was reported engaged in searching for a lost American aircraft as well as checking ice in a Canso. The diary entry for August 31, 1944, was particularly intriguing; without describing his mission it stated that Hone had flown a Canso from Churchill to Nottingham Island to Southhampton Island – he was airborne 11$^{1}/_{2}$ hours – and that the ceiling at Nottingham was 200 feet. The document failed to state his mission, which had been to pick up a badly burned Inuit child and a companion.

S/L John Hone was the only member of the RCAF to be awarded the AFC twice. His air force career was merely an interlude in what was otherwise a life of bush flying. Hone was also a valued assistant during a 1948 air search (Operation ATTACHE). (Canadian Forces Photograph PL-9099).

On January 1, 1945, it was announced that Hone had been awarded a Bar to his AFC. This time the citation was not made public, but Governor General's records reveal the work that had brought additional recognition:

This officer, for two successive seasons, has organized, equipped and taken survey parties into unmapped territory surrounding Hudson Bay and extending far to the east and the west. Due to his vast knowledge of flying in Canadian bush and unexplored territories, triangulation stations have been so well established that subsequent mapping by air surveys can proceed without loss of time. Of the party who accompanied this officer on the first season's operations, all volunteered to accompany him the following year despite the fact that such an expedition is far removed from civilization and depends for its food to a large extent upon the natural resources of the territory. During the last season this officer undertook a search for a lost United States aircraft, last heard from near Churchill on Hudson Bay. He found the aircraft on the second day of the search, although the occupants had perished. The outstanding success of the two years of exploration work can only be attributed to Squadron Leader Hone's outstanding leadership, initiative and ability under the most trying circumstances. This officer's skill, resourcefulness and devotion to duty are outstanding.

He left the RCAF in 1945. Frobisher Exploration Company, impressed with his record, promptly hired him to continue explorations in the Ungava and Baffin Island regions. His performance was so thorough that the company nominated him (without success) for the 1945 McKee Trophy.

Jack Hone was briefly called back into service in 1949 to help in the search for missing military diplomats in northern Manitoba (Operation ATTACHE, see pages 174-175). His knowledge of Cree was especially important in gathering reports from natives about aircraft noises and sightings close to the time that the Beechcraft aircraft involved had been lost. With the mission successfully completed, he was discharged again and resumed the life of a bush pilot.[97]

Two other Canadians have received the AFC and Bar; both did so as members of the Royal Air Force. G/C Edward Mortlock Donaldson was awarded his first AFC on September 30, 1941, for instructional duties in Britain; the Bar was added on June 12, 1947. Donaldson is another "CAN/RAF" representative whose Canadian roots were sparse; if three years' attendance at McGill University makes a Canadian, then he was one; otherwise, he may be considered as a transient Englishman.[98]

S/L William Arthur Waterton (Edmonton) was decidedly Canadian. Having joined the RAF before the war, he served briefly with No. 242 Squadron before being sent back to Canada as an instructor. He received an AFC for services at No. 39 Service Flying Training School on January 1, 1943; his Bar was added on June 12, 1947 for work as a test pilot and speed record holder on Gloster Meteor aircraft (Donaldson's Bar to the AFC was for essentially the same work).

In his memoirs, Waterton describes his experiences with the RAF's High Speed Flight in great detail. Formed in June 1946, it was intent on keeping the world's speed record in Brit-

F/L William A. Waterton receives the first of his AFCs at a Government House investiture. He had joined the RAF before the Second World War and won two AFCs with that force – the first for instructor services, the second for high-speed flight. Later, as a civilian test pilot, he was awarded a George Medal for heroism while testing a prototype British fighter. (Canadian Forces Photograph PL-16036)

ish hands; there was a particular determination to keep it away from the new American P-80 Shooting Star. More than pride was at stake; the British were trying to stake out an international market for their aircraft and were facing stiff challenges from the United States, notably in airline sales. The High Speed Flight's basic tool was the Gloster Meteor IV, although new engines pushed the airframe to its existing limits. On September 7, 1946, fighting for control over a defective port aileron, Waterton made five timed runs in Meteor EE550 at an average speed of 614 miles per hour. Donaldson, flying EE549 a few minutes earlier, averaged 616 miles per hour. Momentarily, the two fastest men in the world were a British pilot (with Canadian connections) and a Canadian pilot (with British connections).

Waterton had almost been disqualified from the attempt because of his Canadian birth. Royal Aero Club officials on hand to witness the record attempt had suggested that he could not be considered sufficiently "British" for purposes of tying an international trophy to the Union Jack. Waterton declared that he considered himself British, that his passport described him as British, and that if a Canadian named Lord Beaverbrook could organize wartime aircraft production, then this Canadian was good enough to fly them in any circumstances.

Authorities did not question his "Britishness" on February 6, 1948. On that date, flying a Meteor IV, he established a world speed record over a 100-kilometre closed course – 542.9 miles per hour. He raised the world record a full 46 miles per hour over a mark previously held by G/C John Cunningham in a Vampire. At that time, however, records were swiftly broken; on February 26, 1948, the prototype Supermarine Attacker raised the mark to 560.6 miles per hour.[99] Waterton eventually left the RAF to become chief test pilot for Gloster Aircraft; he was loaned to Avro (Canada) for early testing of the CF-100. Along the way he had numerous hare's breath escapes; he received a George Medal in 1952 for sticking with the Gloster Javelin prototype when it appeared ready to kill him. He retired in 1954 and moved back to Canada.[100]

(Left) F/O John D. Anderson receives his AFC from A/V/M F.V. Heakes, Victoria, January 1946. A native of Quesnel, British Columbia, Anderson had been an outstanding instructor at No. 2 Wireless School.

(Right) F/L Norman S. Baldwin of Toronto received his AFC for outstanding work as an instructor at No. 10 Elementary Flying Training School, Hamilton, Ontario. (Canadian Forces Photograph PL-117282)

(Left) No. 8 (Bomber Reconnaissance) Squadron in Alaska, 1942. F/O J.B. Morgan, Flight Sergeant F.W. Johnstone, Flight Sergeant J.G. Evernder, P/O Jack Attle, posed beside a Bristol Bolingbroke. As the gunnery leader of the squadron, Attle was responsible for training others and ensuring their continued efficiency. AFCs to wireless air gunners were rare; his was such an award. (Canadian Forces Photograph PL-13003)

(Below) F/L Malcolm M. Hay receives the AFC from A/V/M F.V. Heakes, Victoria, January 1946. Hay, who came from Saint John, New Brunswick, was recommended for a Commendation in December 1943, at which time he had executed 13 rescue sorties in addition to his work as a flying boat instructor. No award was approved at the time, but a later recommendation for an AFC was more successful. At No. 3 OTU he had trained RCAF flying boat pilots on Stranraer and Canso aircraft. (National Archives of Canada C.145113)

(Left) Thomas C. Cooke was awarded a DFC for sinking *U-342* on April 17, 1944. In February 1946 he received an AFC for transport work and experimental flying relating to aerial forestry spraying. Soon afterwards he joined the Ontario Provincial Air Service, rising to become the director of that organization. (Government of Ontario Photograph).

W/C Val Patriarche at No. 6 Service Flying Training School, Dunnville, Ontario, December 6, 1940. Born in Winnipeg in 1907, he was by turns an RCAF officer, bush pilot and RCAF officer again. His honours included appointment as an Officer, Order of the British Empire (OBE), Air Force Cross, Legion of Merit (an American award), Efficiency Decoration, and the Queen's Coronation Medal. (Canadian Forces Photograph PL-2369)

Three young provisional pilot officers (white cap bands proclaiming their status) at Camp Borden: R.B. Brown, E.A. McNab and V.H. Patriarche. Brown died in a flying accident at Wasaga Beach (July 1928); McNab commanded No. 1 (RCAF) Squadron during the Battle of Britain and was the first member of the RCAF decorated for wartime services; Patriarche's career included both service and civilian flying. (Canadian Forces Photograph RE-18665)

P/O Thomas E. Reed, AFM, of Richards Landing, Ontario. While serving at RCAF Station Mountain View, he piloted aircraft on assorted duties, including instruction and transportation. In 1942 alone he flew 821 hours. Reed was eventually commissioned; here he wears the distinctive officers' cap. (Canadian Forces Photograph PL-21340)

(Left) Corporal John A. Glover, AFM, of Winona, Ontario, was a flight engineer with No. 116 Squadron, which operated Canso flying boats on anti-submarine patrols. His duties included monitoring engine performance and fuel consumption during long patrols, leaving the pilot free to concentrate on flying and watching for enemy submarines. Flight engineers were usually recruited from the ranks of aero engine mechanics. (Canadian Forces Photograph PL-16083)

(Right) P/O Roy Phillips, AFM, of Verdun, Quebec. As a flight sergeant with No. 13 Squadron in Canada, he showed "unflagging zeal and enthusiasm" which was deemed to be "a constant source of inspiration to his fellow Non-Commissioned Officers." (Canadian Forces Photograph PL-16063)

W/C Archibald P. Walsh, DFC, AFC of London, Ontario, escorts Canada's Minister of National Defence for Air, the Honourable C.G. "Chubby" Power, on an inspection of No. 419 Squadron. LAC J.S. Malloy (Orillia, Ontario) and AC1 J. Morris (British) get the once-over from Power, himself hardly a snappy dresser. Walsh was one of about 1,800 Canadians who enlisted in the Royal Air Force. He received his DFC in December 1940 for bombing operations with No. 214 Squadron, but the circumstances associated with his AFC (awarded in January 1942) are unknown. (Canadian Forces Photograph PL-10636)

Chapter 5

"BRAVERY IN THE PERFORMANCE OF DUTY": 1947–1966

The mind is the standard of the man, and the size of a country is generally measured by the men who are in it.

– JOSEPH HOWE (1804-1873), TO A NEW BRUNSWICK AUDIENCE, NOVEMBER 8, 1851

The Canadian philosophy and tradition of Peace, Order and Good Government is only maintained through Service, Sacrifice and Courage.

– DESMOND MORTON (1937-), ADDRESSING THE ORGANIZATION OF MILITARY MUSEUMS OF CANADA, JULY 13, 1992

In the postwar years Canada did not revert to the situation that had prevailed throughout the 1920s – a policy of no awards for anyone. On the other hand, the granting of honours was severely restricted. As of mid-1946 the army and navy had been instructed not to participate in preparing honours lists; the RCAF was similarly advised in November 1946, following a request that 16 officers and men be formally recognized for work in Operation MUSKOX, a joint army–air force exercise in the Canadian north. Consideration was given to a quota of honours being set aside for annual presentation. The Minister of National Defence did not concur. The Chiefs of Staff Committee, meeting on March 11 and 17, 1947, finally hammered out a policy. The granting of periodic awards in peacetime would be suspended; this, however, would not preclude granting of awards such as the George Cross and Air Force Cross "for individual acts of outstanding merit." This was further refined to "specific acts of gallantry." Henceforth, it would not be enough to serve long and faithfully in routine duties or even to perform an important job in difficult circumstances; only recognizable acts of bravery would entitle Canadians to receive peacetime awards.[1]

A practical application of this came in the summer of 1948.

An RCAF Dakota transport during Operation MUSKOX. Sixteen RCAF officers and airmen were recommended for awards arising from this exercise, but none were approved. The postwar policies for honours and awards were still being hammered out. (Canadian Forces Photograph PL-37482)

In June of that year, fierce flooding occurred in the interior of British Columbia. A Canadian army officer, Captain Ronald William John Grinstead (the Westminster Regiment), risked his life to save stranded civilians amid currents strong enough to sweep a man off his feet. On August 12, 1948, Grinstead was recommended for an MBE, and it was approved. However, three members of the RCAF were recommended for awards that were not granted because the work they had performed, however meritorious, had not subjected them to personal danger. This restrictive policy was not simply the invention of civilians. During the discussion of the awards just mentioned, the Royal Canadian Navy representative stated that his service objected in principle to the grant of awards in peacetime. A/C Riply had his own reservations; in a pencilled minute he wrote:

I am not sure of the policy for peacetime awards but it would appear there must have been hundreds of people from all three services who did their jobs well under trying circumstance. To pick out three in one service who were representative of that service might be satisfactory if that is the policy but I don't think it is easy to do except for bravery cases.[2]

Although the services had adopted a restrictive policy, in at least one instance the RCAF broke ranks, probably for reasons of diplomacy. This followed Operation ATTACHE (already mentioned in respect to John Hone).

On September 12, 1948, a United States Navy Beechcraft 18 carrying one British and four American military diplomats disappeared whilst flying over northern Manitoba. The RCAF started an intense search, scouring the bushland of two provinces. The downed plane was located; all aboard had survived and they had been rescued by September 25. There is no record that any Commonwealth award was recommended (if so, none was granted), but the grateful Americans offered a lavish outlay of their honours, and the Canadian government permitted their acceptance. A/C Martin Costello, G/C Zebulon Lewis Leigh, F/L Robert Vernon Virr and F/O René Joseph Lemieux were admitted to various degrees of the Legion of Merit.[3]

The policies laid down in March 1947 were reviewed at least once by the Defence Council (a body composed of the Minister and Deputy Minister of National Defence plus the three service chiefs) in May 1949. The ban on "service" awards for merit (as distinct from gallantry decorations) was reconsidered, but the Chief of the General Staff (General Charles Foulkes) advised the group that such honours would be unfair so long as they were restricted to military personnel while civilians in other departments were ineligible for those same honours. This was a view strongly held within the Department of External Affairs. In any case, Foulkes conceded, "it would be most difficult to lay down a standard by which outstanding merit might be measured." Awards would continue to be made solely for bravery, with each recommendation to be judged on its own merits, without reference to any arbitrary guidelines to distinguish levels of gallantry.[4]

The policy was not widely known in Canada, and when it was publicised it provoked some hostile opinions. In the summer of 1952 at least two approaches were made to the government for an award to Dr. Roderick J. Macdonald, a 94-year-old country doctor living on Prince Edward Island. On October 27, 1952, Mr. C. Stein (Under-Secretary of State) wrote to Most Reverend Aldred A. Sinnott (Archbishop of Winnipeg) saying in part: "The practice of the Canadian Government since July 1, 1946, is not to recommend the granting of honours and decorations to Canadian civilians except for the saving of life."

Archbishop Sinnott was not impressed; he replied in stinging terms:

It is news to me that the policy of the Canadian Government since July 1, 1946, is not to recommend the granting of honours and decorations to Canadian Civilians except for the saving of life. One might be justified in believing that a Doctor who has practised his profession for almost 70 years and is the oldest living practitioner in the British Empire has done something to save human lives. The policy of the Canadian Government is that a man who saves a tomcat from drowning has rendered greater service and is entitled to recognition. What an absurdity![5]

In October 1956 the Cabinet itself studied the matter and essentially confirmed the standing policy. Apart from support of wartime operations, civilians would be eligible for state honours only for "acts of bravery performed at the risk of death or serious personal injury." Military personnel would be allowed gallantry awards meeting the same standard, as well as medals for long service, good conduct, or marksmanship.[6]

Application of this restrictive policy raised occasional problems; the case of S/L C.E.L. Hare, described below, was one. Like the ATTACHE awards, it involved another government pressing honours upon Canadians. Doubtless there are other instances still buried in the voluminous DND files held by the National Archives of Canada.

Not everyone agreed with the practice adopted. Nevertheless, interservice disagreements ensured its continuance. One problem was that, for non-operational services, the army and navy had no awards that quite matched the AFC and AFM. This was illustrated in October 1954, at a meeting of the Inter-Service Awards Committee, a tri-service body. The chairman that month, W/C W.J. Brodribb, expressed dissatisfaction with the standing policy prohibiting non-operational awards for peacetime services (bravery aside). Army and RCN representatives agreed that wider grants of the AFC and AFM should be allowed, but only if similar arrangements could be made for outstanding services by their personnel. The minutes of the meeting concluded:

> The Members were unanimously of the opinion that the only way this matter will ever be satisfactorily resolved is by the institution of a Canadian Order or of the Canada Medal. However, if this is not possible then participation in British Orders and Decorations for peacetime non-operational service should be permitted.[7]

This was not the first time the issue was raised and the solution provided, but as with other attempts, the proposals died at the senior officer, ministerial or cabinet level; this particular suggestion was shot down before leaving the Department of National Defence. There would be no "service" awards for military personnel until similar awards were created for civilians, and political leaders were loath to become involved in the "honours merry-go-round" which bedeviled British honours such as the Orders of the Bath.

The steps by which postwar gallantry awards were checked were numerous and rigorous. It was not uncommon for officers preparing a recommendation to gather affidavits from witnesses. S/L Fern Villeneuve's AFC, for example, was submitted by the commanding officer of No. 1 Operational Training Unit, but it was also supported by a sworn statement from the duty flying control officer on the night of November 7, 1960. The CO of No. 103 Rescue Unit recommended F/L Raymond W. Cass (Morden, Manitoba) for an AFC, but the submission was accompanied by affidavits filed by two other crewmen who testified to their pilot's courage and professionalism. Similarly, two sworn statements by crewmen were submitted along with the

recommendation for an AFC to F/L Daniel M. Campbell. The duty air traffic control officer at RCAF Station Namao (Edmonton) submitted an affidavit (confirmed by a similar document signed by a corporal) when F/L Kenneth A. Harvey was put up for an AFC.[8] These standards of proof were observed for all awards; a postwar AFC was a rare and prestigious award.

The elaborate steps by which awards were handled is best illustrated by reference to a case. The details of Operation CAPTAIN will be described later; what concerns us here is the procedure that governed awards at this time.

December 23, 1950 – Operation CAPTAIN, the successful rescue of survivors from a Canadian Pacific Airlines crash in the Okanagan Mountains.

Date uncertain – G/C J.A. Easton, commanding No. 12 Group, recommends AFC awards for F/L Paul L. Gibbs and F/O Robert T. Glaister plus a British Empire Medal for Sergeant Delbert Wright.

February 16, 1951 – A/V/M C.R. Dunlap, commanding Western Air Command, approves the recommendations and forwards them to the Chief of Air Staff for consideration by the Senior Sub-Committee of the Awards Co-Ordination Committee (the latter a body composed of senior officers and representatives of such departments as External Affairs and Secretary of State).

April 21, 1951 – The Senior Sub-Committee, Awards Co-Ordination Committee, concludes that the recommendations do conform to the policy of gallantry awards in peacetime in that "bravery was displayed and a saving of lives effected." On this same day the awards are studied and approved by the Personnel Members Committee (senior personnel officers of the three services).

May 7, 1951 – The recommendations are received by the Defence Council.

May 31, 1951 – The Defence Council approves the recommendations.

June 27, 1951 – Major-General W.H.S. Macklin (Chairman, Personnel Members Committee) sends the recommendations for further study to Mr. C. Stein, Under Secretary of State and Chairman of the Awards Co-Ordinating Committee.

July 12, 1951 – Stein replies to Macklin, stating in part, "On the basis of the practice and precedence of the Awards Co-Ordination Committee, I feel no exception would be taken to the proposed awards in these three cases."

July 20, 1951 – The Minister of National Defence (Brooke Claxton) submits the recommendations to the Governor-General.

Date uncertain – The Governor-General transmits the recommendations to King George VI.

August 21, 1951 – Major-General H.F.G. Letson (Secretary to the Governor-General) writes to Claxton saying, "Word has been received from the Private Secretary to The King to the effect that His Majesty has been pleased to approve the Prime Minister's recommendation that the Air Force Cross be awarded to F/L P.L. Gibbs and F/O R.T.S. Glaiser, and the British Empire Medal to Sergeant D. Wright."

September 12, 1951 – A/M W.A. Curtis (Chief of Air Staff) writes letters of congratulations to all three men.

September 15, 1951 – Announcement of the awards is published in the *Canada Gazette*.[9]

All gallantry awards were gifts of the King. This was no mere technicality; George VI took a keen interest in honours (one of the few areas where a constitutional monarch packed some clout) and exercised his prerogative to a considerable degree. The situation was shown following Operation CANON, a dramatic northern rescue attempt.

Late in September 1947 an Anglican missionary, Canon J.H. Turner, was reported seriously injured in a hunting accident at Moffet Inlet, Baffin Island, 450 miles inside the Arctic Circle. A Dakota of No. 112 Transport Flight, Winnipeg, was assigned to the rescue operation. F/L Robert C. Race piloted the aircraft to Moffet Inlet. On October 4, in the face of low clouds and rugged terrain he located a frozen lake where he dropped four para-rescue soldiers led by Captain Lionel G. d'Artois, DSO. The group included a doctor, Captain Ross W. Willoughby, RCAMC.

Captain d'Artois was responsible for contacting Canon Turner's mission, then moving his party and supplies to that site; he established communications with the outside world, selected a landing site for aircraft 23 miles from the mission, collected meteorological data, guided a rescue aircraft to the site (again piloted by F/L Race, who had also flown two re-supply sorties to the paratroopers), and transported the injured clergyman by dog sleigh. This entailed seven weeks of work in harsh weather, limited daylight and brutal topography. He travelled hundreds of miles back and forth as he performed these duties, sometimes over shifting ice; on one such trek he fell through thin ice but extricated himself. On the evacuation flight itself, Race touched down on ice untested except by ground parties and subsequently took off by the light of an improvised flare path. Canon Turner was evacuated to Winnipeg, 1,700 miles away, although he later succumbed to his injuries.

In July 1948, the following awards were announced for personnel engaged in Operation CANON.

Captain L.G. d'Artois – George Medal

F/L R.C. Race – George Medal

Captain R.W. Willoughby – Member, Order of the British Empire

F/O C.C. McMillan – Air Force Cross

Corporal James Paterson Rae – Air Force Medal

Sergeant Howard C. Cook, RCCS – British Empire Medal

F/L B. Morabito – King's Commendation for Valuable Services in the Air

F/O K.O. Moore – King's Commendation for Valuable Services in the Air

Sergeant K.C. Swinford – King's Commendation for Valuable Services in the Air

Sergeant W.W. Judd, RCCS – King's Commendation for Brave Conduct

Corporal L.D. Hawkins – King's Commendation for Valuable Services in the Air[10]

This generous distribution of honours had been achieved only after protracted discussions and correspondence which had virtually pitted King George VI against his Canadian Minister of National Defence, Brooke Claxton. Initially, virtually every active service participant had been recommended for a gallantry award, including four AFCs and three BEMs to RCAF personnel. The army in particular doubted that approval would be given; the long-established custom, followed throughout the war, had been that only a percentage of those participating in an operation would be formally recognized by decorations. As of December 1947 the 11 awards had been reduced to two: George Medals for the senior army and RCAF officers present (d'Artois and Race respectively). Other personnel would receive Commendations.

Brooke Claxton was not so ready to abandon the other participants and at his insistence 11 recommendations went to London for approval by the King. The Governor-General, Field Marshal Alexander, forwarded the documents, even though he, too, felt that the scale of awards was excessive. The King was not prepared to sanction all nominations; he even suggested reducing the two George Medals to an AFC and an MBE. As of March 3, 1948, Claxton was prepared to see that happen, but a week later he had decided to lobby for the full package as originally sent to London – medals for all including two George Medals. When Field Marshal Alexander visited London in May 1948 he discussed the matter with the King, whose views were later summarized:

The King pointed out that such procedure was without precedent. His Majesty further drew attention to the fact that he was called upon in … the role of referee to maintain a balance and standard regarding decorations which were awarded to all parts of the Commonwealth.

A lavish distribution in one Dominion would certainly be attended by an equally insistent demand from others for similar treatment. To refuse one while granting the others would place him in a difficult and possible embarrassing situation.

The King, however, was prepared to offer a compromise – six decorations (including two George Medals) and five Commendations. Canadians themselves would have to sort out who got what among the lesser awards. There was a precedent for this generous offering; following the RAF "Aries" flights of 1945 (described below), all 11 aircrew received some recogni-

F/O Robert C. Race piloted the aircraft used in Operation CANON; Captain Lionel G. d'Artois, DSO led the party that was parachuted into the mission, accompanied by Captain Ross W. Willoughby of the Royal Canadian Army Medical Corps. Every person participating was either commended or decorated, including George Medals for Race and d'Artois and an MBE for Willoughby. Since it happened in Canada, nobody has ever made a movie about it. (National Archives of Canada PA-189545)

(Below) The base at Coral Harbour used as a forward staging area for Operation CANON. (Courtesy of R.C. Race).

(Right) Manual engine start for the Dakota during Operation CANON. (Courtesy of R.C. Race)

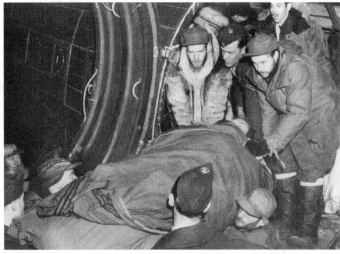

(Above) The "Blizzard Belle," used in all flights associated with Operation CANON. (Courtesy of K.O. Moore)

(Left) The conclusion of Operation CANON in Winnipeg. (Courtesy of K.O. Moore)

(Right) Rear: K.O. Moore, C.C. McMillan, F/L B. Morabito, F.O R.C. Race Front: Corporal L.D. Hawkins, Corporal J.P. Rae, Sergeant K.C. Swinford. The group was photographed just after their arrival in Winnipeg upon the completion of Operation CANON. (Courtesy of R.C. Race).

tion – one Bar to AFC, two AFCs, two AFMs and six Commendations. Claxton reluctantly agreed on June 29, 1948. Of three candidates for an AFC he selected F/O McMillan (Saskatoon); as navigator his duties were more onerous and crucial to the safety of all concerned. Of three AFM nominees he selected Corporal Rae (Cupar, Saskatchewan), a particularly ingenious and industrious tradesman who had started engines in the most difficult situations; however, the Minister had favoured Rae chiefly because the citation recommending him had been the most effusive in its praise.[11]

Canada was, of course, playing by British rules in the distribution of gallantry awards, but American regulations also affected the symbolic rewards that Canada could bestow. This was brought out following a rescue in the mountains of Washington State involving Canadian and American personnel. Fleet Canuck CF-DEJ with two persons aboard was reported missing on the evening of May 2, 1949, whilst flying from Penticton to Vancouver. The RCAF and U.S. Coast Guard instituted a search at dawn of the 3rd. Aircraft swept through rugged mountain peaks, scanning the terrain for the bright yellow machine. Fortunately the weather was good, although turbulence and wind sheers presented difficulties.

On May 6 the Canuck was spotted by Leading Aircraftman Frederick Wesley Hillyer, a crewman in Canso 11005 piloted by F/O Jarvis Hugh McLeod, conducting his fourth sweep through the mountains in three days. The object of their search was just below the summit of Mount Hozomeen (8,080 feet), 60 miles from Abbotsford and two miles inside the United States. The Fleet appeared to be only slightly damaged, but no survivors were spotted until Canso 11087 arrived. It circled while F/O McLeod returned to base. A Coast Guard S-51 helicopter was directed to the scene, piloted by Lieuten-

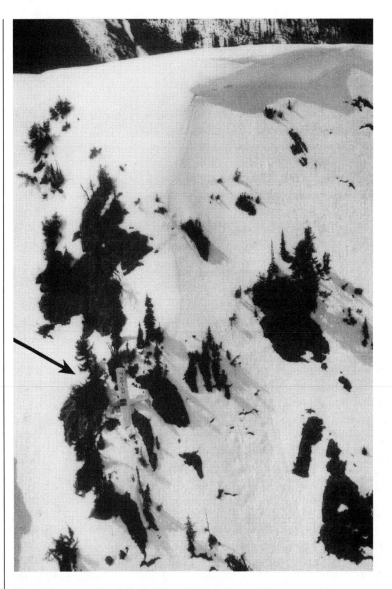

The difficulties of both "search" and "rescue" are evident from this view of CF-DEJ on Mount Hozomeen.

This was an exercise, but Dakotas and para-rescue jumpers figured prominently in postwar mercy missions. (Canadian Forces Photograph PL-124949)

(Below) Lieutenant F. H. Raumer's helicopter manoeuvres over mountainous bush. The photograph cannot show the hidden hazards of wind shear, downdrafts and updrafts encountered in such terrain.

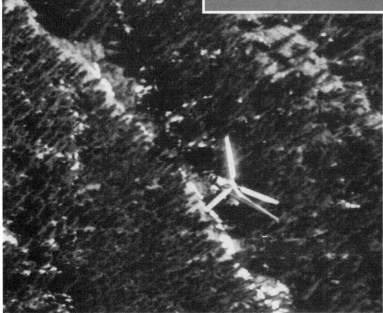

F/O George B. Leckie. As a sergeant he received the AFM for his part in the rescue of survivors from Fleet Canuck CF-DEJ in May 1949. (Canadian Forces Photograph PL-103661)

ant (Junior Grade) Frederick Herbert Raumer, based at Port Angeles, 13th Coast Guard District, Washington. However, he reported that he could not land until a para-rescue team had been dropped to clear a space for him to alight. Raumer proceeded ten miles north of the crash site and landed near a logging camp road.

At 5.10 p.m. of the 6th an RCAF Dakota began dropping equipment as close as practical to the crash area, then followed up with three para-rescue jumpers – Sergeant George Brown Leckie (Winnipeg), Corporal Louis Henri Lionel Binette and Leading Aircraftman Robert Edward Braidner (the first to jump). The area was daunting – heavily wooded terrain interlaced with deep gorges and studded with jagged rocks. They alighted one mile from the crash site but had been scattered because they had been using two different types of 'chutes. It took them an hour to link up and retrieve the equipment previously dropped. By now it was dark, so they made camp for the night.

At dawn of the 7th the team set off towards the survivors, signalling for directions as they went. Lieutenant Raumer appeared with his helicopter, firing a flare to indicate the position of the downed civilians. By now there was something of a race in progress; the para-rescue team, although closing in on the site, was cutting timbers to cross a flooded creek. Meanwhile a civilian party that had struck off through snow and forest from the logging road that had been Raumer's temporary base was making better time and reached the survivors minutes ahead of Leckie, Binette and Braidner.

The crash victims had blistered feet but were otherwise in good shape. Rescuers and rescued camped out that night on the mountain with sleeping bags and extra rations that had been parachuted to them. The slope of the ground was so steep that a level platform had to be gouged before the party could sleep. At dawn of the 8th they set out on foot, bridging once more. Four hours travel brought them to a fire ranger's trail. Three more hours were needed to regain the logging trail. All the while their progress was monitored by aircraft, including the Coast Guard Sikorsky. Once the logging road was reached, Lieutenant Raumer touched down and evacuated the footsore survivors; the other rescuers continued walking to a logging camp, whence they departed by car.

The operation had gone smoothly. Its success obscured the difficulties and dangers of a mountain search and rescue. G/C Z.L. Leigh, commanding No. 12 Group, may have been overly enthusiastic when he submitted recommendations for three Air Force Medals (to each of the RCAF para-rescue team), two Air Force Crosses (to Lieutenant Raumer and to F/L L.A. Harling, who dropped the team and did most of the subsequent resupply work) as well as three Chief of Air Staff Commendations. Air Force Headquarters pondered these recommendations and cut them down to two decorations, with CAS Letters of Commendation to go to all others. The reasoning applied by the RCAF Honours and Awards Committee demonstrated the policies of the day:

It was the opinion of the Board that, although other of the personnel who participated in this particular rescue mission also performed their duties in a brave manner, their individual duties might more justifiably be considered as acts of outstanding merit. It is therefore considered that the element of bravery shown by the personnel in this operation as a whole should be recognized in accordance with the tradition normally followed when recommending awards for combatant operations, i.e. by recognizing only a percentage of those who participated in the actual operation....

Lieutenant Raumer displayed great bravery in operating a helicopter aircraft over extremely rugged and dangerous mountain terrain, without regard for his own personal safety, successfully loading and dropping supplies and other necessities to the ground party. Furthermore, it is considered by the Board that in the light of past assistance and co-operation rendered the RCAF by the United States Coast Guard, it would be in the interests, and a token of reciprocity, that these past services be recognized by an award to this officer.

The bravery of Sergeant Leckie, Jump Master with the para-rescue team, was in accordance with the best traditions of the Service. This NCO on his own initiative, fully recognizing the dangers confronting him, successfully organized and jumped with the para-rescue team to aid the survivors of the crashed aircraft in particularly hazardous terrain.

Getting an Air Force Medal for Leckie was easy enough, although it was not gazetted until December 1, 1951. Processing might have been faster had it not been for the attempt to award an AFC to Lieutenant Raumer – a bid which ultimately failed. The problem lay with American law. Section Nine of the Constitution of the United States declared:

No Title of Nobility shall be granted by the United States: And no person holding any Office of Profit or Trust under them, shall, without the consent of the Congress, accept any present, emolument, office or title, of any kind whatsoever, from any King, Prince or foreign state.

This tough-minded ban extended to decorations from foreign states. An Act of Congress dating from 1881 had modi-fied this, allowing for foreign civil and military honours to be accepted subject to a special Act of Congress. Special statutes had given blanket approval for American military personnel to receive decorations from their Allied counterparts during the First and Second World Wars, but the most recent of these had expired on June 30, 1947. No similar statute had been passed to cover exchanges of awards during the Berlin Airlift (which had been a joint Anglo-American effort), while the Korean War (which would see renewed reciprocal awards) was more than a year away.

It was still possible, in theory, for Raumer to be awarded an AFC, but the procedure was extremely cumbersome. In effect, the Canadians would have to seek approval from King George VI, who in turn would offer the decoration to the American State Department, which would hold the award in trust pending a special Act of Congress covering this single decoration (which act might as easily fail passage as succeed). Since this would make the King's gift of a decoration subject to approval, rejection or revision by a foreign legislature, George VI was unwilling to accept the Canadian government's recommendation of an AFC to Lieutenant Raumer. Only when it was apparent that this award was stalled did the government formally announce Sergeant Leckie's honour.

Major-General H.F.G. Letson, long an advocate of distinctive Canadian honours, was also Secretary to the Governor-General at that time. In a letter to Brooke Claxton dated November 8, 1951, he pointedly remarked that "this is another case which points up the anomalous situation brought about by Canada not having a decoration of its own."[12]

The body which dealt most extensively with suggested awards was the Awards Co-Ordination Committee, renamed the Decorations Committee in November 1956. Its membership represented the armed forces as well as the Governor

General, Secretary of State, Department of Transport, RCMP and the Public Archives of Canada. Normally it supported what had been recommended (i.e., an AFC recommendation usually became an AFC awarded). There were occasional upgrades and downgrades; the George Medal awarded to F/O Race (Operation CANON) had begun as a suggested AFC. F/O Robert E. Sabourin, recommended for an AFC in May 1957, was awarded a George Medal (very rare) in February 1959. In deciding whether to approve, reject, upgrade or downgrade a recommendation, committee members compared past awards with present suggestions, and in some cases (notably involving George Cross and George Medal recommendations) looked at British and Australian awards to determine what constituted Commonwealth-wide standards. Even then, Canadian authorities looked sternly at all aspects of a deed and applied severe tests in determining what was appropriate.

Two particularly well documented recommendations illustrate both the process and the severe standards as they had evolved by the early 1950s. The first involved F/L Terence Jesse Evans (Toronto), a veteran RCAF pilot (commended in 1945 for services as an instructor) who, in October 1950, was detailed to conduct acceptance trials of the first F-86 manufactured by Canadair. Unaware of a faulty modification, he found himself at altitude with the flaps unexpectedly down, jamming the ailerons. Rather than abandon the aircraft, he explored all control options and concluded that it could still be controlled laterally – although at high speed – using aileron trim. He landed the aircraft, not only saving the production prototype but allowing detection of the technical maladjustment that had caused the problem.

Evans' superior, W/C J.M. Frizzle, recommended an AFC and A/C A.D. Ross concurred. Two committees at National Defence Headquarters reviewed this and downgraded it to a King's Commendation for Valuable Services in the Air. The reasoning behind the conclusion, expressed in memos dated March 19 and April 11, 1951, is far more interesting than the decision itself.

(a) Every time a test pilot has occasion to test fly an aircraft, be it a prototype, having been completely overhauled, or modified by new design, there is an undoubted element of risk in his ordinary duties. This case, then, in effect, if approved, could create a precedent for this type of flying, and it might be extremely difficult to deny future recommended cases. Such a precedent could result in lowering the present high standard of the Air Force Cross.

(b) Although not a necessary requirement, this case does not involve the saving of life or lives. This has been a strong factor in recommending previous cases for approval.[13]

Whether or not one agrees with these reasons, the first argument is the most compelling – as a test pilot it was Evans' *job* to take calculated risks. The second point is a little more difficult to comprehend; one would assume that by sticking with the F-86 rather than abandoning it in the neighbourhood of Cartierville, he had ensured that no casualties would be sustained on the ground. The fault may have been with Frizzle, who did not mention this point. Evans received his Commendation and went on to a distinguished career as an RCAF test pilot (he was associated with experiments flying a modified North Star known as the "Rockcliffe Ice Wagon"). Nevertheless, it is worth comparing his case with that of AFCs awarded to other fighter pilots in the 1950s and 1960s, notably F/L K.A. Harvey (see chapter 6).

The other example of restrictive standards (though not

TABLE A: AFC/AFM AWARDS, ROYAL AIR FORCE, REPRESENTATIVE YEARS

	Bar to AFC	AFC	AFM	Remarks
January 1948	3	31	2	Plus two AFCs to RN and six to RAAF.
June 1948	-	21	4	Five more AFCs in July and September 1948 for work in Palestine.
January 1949	-	19	7	–
June 1949	-	31	18	Plus two AFCs to RAAF, one AFM to RNZAF and one AFM to South African Air Force.
January 1950	2	37	18	Plus one Bar to AFC to RAAF, and one AFC each to RAAF, RNZAF and South African Air Force.
June 1950	3	30	12	Plus a second Bar to AFC (RAF) and one AFC to RAAF.
January 1951	1	35	12	Plus five AFCs to RAAF, two AFCs to RNZAF, and one AFM each to RAAF and RNZAF.
June 1951	2	30	15	Plus one Bar to AFC to RAAF, three AFCs to RAAF, one AFC to RNZAF.
January 1952	1	39	15	–
June 1952	3	45	17	Plus one AFC to RAAF.
January 1953	1	50	15	Plus one AFC to RN.[15]

involving an AFC) is even more striking. On December 30, 1953, a North Star crashed at Vancouver. The transport was upside down and in danger of burning. W/C R.W. "Buck" McNair threw caution to the winds and entered the passenger compartment. He restored order, then assisted those aboard to evacuate the aircraft, even searching through the wreckage to ensure that no one had been left behind. All this he did while his clothes were soaked in gasoline from an overturned Herman Nelson heater. Equally striking was the fact that McNair had been badly burned during the war and fully appreciated the hazards he faced.

"Buck" McNair was recommended for a George Medal. In May 1954 the Inter-Service Awards Committee concluded that his actions did not meet the standards for a GM (awarded for "acts of great bravery"). An OBE might still have been bestowed, but the committee also noted that, as a member of the North Star's crew, it was his first duty to look after the safety of his passengers. A Queen's Commendation for Brave Conduct was deemed appropriate.[14]

The standards applied to all Canadian service awards were thus exceedingly high – much more so than in Britain. Even allowing for the size of the RAF, and the scope of its operations (including commitment to British aircraft development, occupation forces in Europe, the Berlin airlift, aerial mapping in Africa and global transport obligations), the AFC and AFM were awarded more generously in Britain, as the figures in Table A demonstrate:

Had the same scale of awards been applied to the RCAF, it is likely that a minimum of five Air Force Crosses and Air Force Medals would have been awarded every year – 100 in the period of 1947 to 1966. The actual number granted in that period was 30 (four AFMs, 26 AFCs). Looking at specific cases, it is clear that some RAF awards were made for work that was nearly identical to that performed by their RCAF counterparts, though the Canadians went without "gongs" because superior performance of ordinary duties was deemed to be part of the job.[16]

British practice continued to be fairly generous. Following the Falkland Islands War, for example, 35 gallantry awards were made to flying personnel (2 Distinguished Service Orders, 13 Distinguished Service Crosses, 1 Military Cross, 9 Distinguished Flying Crosses, 6 Air Force Crosses and 4 Queen's Gallantry Medals). Of the six AFCs, two went to the commanders of naval helicopter rescue squadrons, two to RAF transport pilots and two to crews of Victor tanker aircraft which refuelled Vulcan bombers. They were thus not directly exposed to Argentinean fire, although the Royal Navy AFC recipients were very close to it. The bulk of the gallantry awards were for crews of Harrier jets and tactical air support helicopters that were very much on the front line.[17]

In 1993, however, the British honours system was drastically revised, and in some ways was made consistent with practices that had earlier been introduced into distinctive Australian and Canadian awards. Differentiations between medals based on rank were eliminated; the Air Force Medal and Distinguished Flying Medal were abolished. Henceforth, the Distinguished Flying Cross and Air Force Cross would be awarded regardless of rank. It was also decreed that these honours would be granted only for gallantry in the air; their use to recognize mere distinguished service would be eliminated.[18]

Chapter 6

POSTWAR AWARDS

Peace hath her victories, no less renowned than war.

– JOHN MILTON TO OLIVER CROMWELL, MAY 1652

Nothing is too small to know, and nothing is too big to attempt.

– WILLIAM CORNELIUS VAN HORNE (1843-1915)

A foolish consistency is the hobgoblin of little minds, adored by little statesmen and philosophers and divines. With consistency a great soul has simply nothing to do.

– RALPH WALDO EMERSON (1803-1882),
ESSAYS, NEW ENGLAND REFORMERS

The exploration of awards policy in the previous chapter may have been confusing; comprehension does not improve when one analyzes the AFC and AFM awards in the postwar era. The system was devised and administered by people, not by machines. They might aspire to consistency, but Emerson's words are a warning. If the RCAF (and other Canadian services) sometimes deviated from the standards worked out between 1946 and 1950, they nevertheless strove to avoid dilution of those standards. If they erred, it was on the side of strictness rather than prodigality, as the specific cases show.

La guerre est fini. Avro Anson aircraft, scrapped to become the playthings of children.

OPERATION POLCO

Ask where's the North? at York, 'tis on the Tweed;
In Scotland, at the Orcades; and there,
At Greenland, Zembla, or the Lord knows where.

– ALEXANDER POPE (1688-1744), *AN ESSAY ON MAN*

The whole history of the Canadian North can be divided into
two periods – before and after the aeroplane.

– HUGH L. KEENLEYSIDE (1898-), WRITING IN *CANADIAN*
GEOGRAPHICAL JOURNAL, OCTOBER 1949

I know nothing whatever about courage. I will talk instead on
the vastly more important virtue of adaptability. Everything
you add to an explorer's heroism you have to subtract from his
intelligence.

– VILHJALMUR STEFANSSON (1879-1962)[1]

The *Canada Gazette* which announced awards to those participating in Operation CANON also reported Air Force Cross awards to F/L John Francis Drake (Bender, Saskatchewan) and F/O John Edward Goldsmith, DFC (Halifax), both of No. 413 (Photo Survey) Squadron. They had been, respectively, pilot and navigator on Operation POLCO, a remarkable undertaking to nail down once and for all the location of the North Magnetic Pole, although follow-up work was needed in 1948, in which Goldsmith was again a participant.

The RCAF had a long history of survey flying in the Arctic, but general cartographic photography had been suspended for the duration of the Second World War, when survey was focused on immediate

war aims connected with routes supplying aircraft to Britain, Alaska and the Soviet Union. During this period, Canadian sovereignty was scarcely exercised in the Arctic; American interests were pressed and asserted during construction of the Alaska Highway. An alarmed British ambassador warned Ottawa that the American presence was so great that it came near to constituting an army of occupation. The government of Mackenzie King looked away.

In May 1945 a British aerial expedition consisting of one crew and a Lancaster, "Aries," belonging to the Empire Air Navigation School, undertook an extended expedition (110 flying hours) over the Canadian polar regions. The chief research officer on that occasion was W/C Kenneth Cecil Maclure, RCAF, a Montreal-born former insurance salesman who in wartime had become an expert in navigational problems. For two years he had been studying the difficulties of northern navigation. Working for up to 18 hours at a stretch in unheated compartments aboard the aircraft, over areas where every direction was south, he gathered considerable in-

W/C Kenneth C. Maclure with his parents following investiture at Rideau Hall, Ottawa. Maclure's navigational theories were tested during the "Aries" flights of May 1945. (Canadian Forces Photograph PL-38721)

Lancaster "Aries" in Canada, summer 1945. (National Archives of Canada PA-197490)

time forces and had scant time to assign new duties to those forces that were left.[3]

American interests may have been the most serious threat to Canadian sovereignty, but it was a British proposal that stung the Canadian government into action. In the spring of 1946, Doctor Nicholas Polunin of Oxford and McGill universities proposed through the Air Ministry that an ambitious survey be conducted in the Canadian Arctic. Its aims would be diverse: to "fix" the position of the North Magnetic Pole, determine the existence or non-existence of the Spicer Islands, and search for "supposed pygmy Eskimos still using bows and arrows in central Baffin," to name only a few. The expedition would be composed largely of British aircrew and scientists, but the Canadian government was to be invited to nominate two experts, "preferably a general zoologist and a general geologist-cum-glaciologist."

formation about northern flying. He was awarded an Air Force Cross later that year, and in 1946 the American Institute of Navigation would honour him as well.[2]

The Canadian forces re-asserted the national presence in the north in the winter of 1945-46 when a small army detachment operating tracked vehicles and supplied regularly from the air crossed the Barrens from Churchill to Edmonton amid extensive press coverage. This was Operation MUSKOX. The RCAF was anxious to build on experience gained from the "Aries" flight and from MUSKOX, but the government appeared uninterested; it was intent upon demobilizing the war-

The idea was first shown to S/L John A. Wiseman, AFC, commanding officer of No. 7 Photo Wing and no stranger to Arctic surveys; he had reconnoitred Greenland in 1941 in search of base sites for RAF Ferry Command and had subsequently flown surveys on behalf of the Northeast Staging Route. Wiseman was struck by the extent of the plan, as well as the fact that its British sponsors were very knowledgeable about some subjects and terribly ignorant about other aspects of Arctic flying. Wiseman reported the project to G/C D.A.R. Bradshaw in AFHQ. In a memo to his superiors, dated March 8, 1946, Bradshaw complained bitterly about British intrusiveness. He concluded his remarks with a stinging paragraph:

> The tenor of the proposals would indicate … that this is entirely a United Kingdom idea and that the Canadian Government has been invited to participate. It is respectfully suggested that Canada should have been doing the inviting to our country, rather than the United Kingdom inviting Canada to a British exploration party in Canada.[4]

The British proposal went no further; its sponsors apparently lacked backing at home. The Canadian government, for its part, was initially uncertain as to how it would participate; some thought was given to chartering a Canadian Pacific Air Lines machine to transport the scientists. Meanwhile, the United States was indicating its interest in somebody conducting magnetic surveys in the north. Clearly, Canada must show a willingness to chart its own backyard. The result was a series of expeditions of which Operation POLCO was the most publicised.

Doctor Polunin, having had no success in launching an Arctic survey through the Air Ministry, approached the Canadian government directly. Co-operation was forthcoming immediately. In the summer of 1946 a Canso and three Norseman aircraft were detailed to transport several scientists, Polunin included, to points around Ungava, Foxe Basin and the western shores of Hudson Bay. Numerous objectives were laid down, but some (notably a survey for possible bases in the eastern Keewatin District) were not completed for lack of time in a region where lakes thawed late and froze early. Yet much was also accomplished; magnetic readings were made through

F/O John F. Drake in the Canso used for Operation POLCO.
(Canadian Forces Photograph PL-38488)

much of the Ungava/Hudson Strait area, and the Spicer Islands, first reported in 1877, were finally confirmed to exist. The aircrews involved were all veteran fliers (though not necessarily familiar with northern conditions). The Canso crew was captained by F/L Drake, with F/O Goldsmith as his navigator.

Drake and his crew flew roughly 45,000 miles between June 10 and September 7 of that year; the attendant Norseman aircraft logged 37,300 miles. Uncertain weather was always a problem, but so too was the matter of finding good landing sites. Drake explained this in his report:

> Our first need was a landing and take-off run for the Canso when a dead calm existed, then a beach preferably of sand and long enough to permit the Canso and three Norsemen

to be beached with a wingspan between them and, perhaps most important of all, shelter from the north-west – the direction of the prevailing winds. All this, along with the need for finding an area adjacent to the beach that was suitable for pitching the tents and establishing the other paraphernalia of the main camp, often proved a wearisome and difficult task.

Drake did not dwell on other difficulties inherent in this type of operation. One was propeller pitting from spray thrown up by protracted high-speed taxi runs; at one point, Polunin wrote of the propeller blades as being "jagged almost like a saw." The short-term solution was to file down the pitting, but eventually uneven filing could disrupt the balance between blades and lead to ever-worsening vibrations. Only a complete propeller change would resolve the situation.

The 1946 operation gave everyone valuable experience for their more famous undertaking the following year, Operation POLCO.[5] This consisted of one aircraft (Canso 11060) with a crew of eight (pilot, navigator, co-pilot, wireless operator, flight engineer, electrician, instrument mechanic and airframe mechanic), accompanied by four Dominion government civilian observers qualified in geophysics and geology. They were joined late in the project by a geographer and a botanist.

The initial party left Rockcliffe on July 19, 1947, bound for Churchill. From there they began establishing ground magnetic survey stations at Aberdeen Lake, Yellowknife, Cambridge Bay, Greely Haven (Victoria Island), Takekyoak Lake (King William Island), Guillemard Inlet (Prince of Wales Island), Agnew River (Boothia Peninsula), Allen Lake (on Prince of Wales Island, named on this occasion for the co-pilot), Point Lake and Jully Lake (both on the mainland). At each of these, the horizontal and vertical angles of compasses

F/O J.E. Goldsmith of POLCO, photographed during the follow-up, MAGNETIC. He discusses the project in a staged shot with Mines and Resources scientists John Carroll, Paul H. Jerson, Ralph D. Hutchison and J.L. Jenness. (Canadian Forces Photograph PL-39020)

(Right) A/C A.D. Ross, GC, OBE invests F/O J.E. Goldsmith with the AFC won for work on Operation POLCO. Ross was not left-handed; he lost his right hand in June 1944 while rescuing aircrew from a crashed bomber. (Canadian Forces Photograph PL-50212)

were read. New magnetometers measured the strength and fluctuating factors of the earth's magnetic field.

POLCO was a difficult operation beset by complications throughout. Two geologists taken north were to have been dropped off and brought out by ship. When the vessel, the Hudson Bay Company ship *Nascopie*, was wrecked, the two men were attached to the expedition for its duration. Fog was worse than expected, and coastal ice choked so many intended anchorages that the expedition frequently resorted to uncharted inland lakes.

It had been intended to set up 14 stations; bad weather and ice conditions cut back the program. On July 31 they spent much time locating a suitable beach for the Canso, then rescuing the aircraft when its mooring buoy dragged in a 40-50 m.p.h. gale. Their observations at Greely Haven on August 1 were cut short when pack ice suddenly began drifting into the anchorage. Drake scraped the hull in his hasty departure and repairs were needed at Calgary some days later – a considerable diversion. A possible landing site on Pasley Bay filled with ice in the two days between its discovery and the attempt to use it. In the words of the citation that accompanied Drake and Goldsmith's awards:

The organization and direction of this magnetic survey operation required great ingenuity and daring, for it was the first time in Canadian aviation history that a flying boat had been flown and based for an extended period amongst the treacherous and barren islands surrounding the North Magnetic Pole.

Flight Lieutenant Drake was responsible for taking off and landing his aircraft at numerous hazardous points in the Polar area for the purpose of making scientific observations. In spite of fog, icing conditions, uncharted terrain and unknown currents he pressed the operation with such skill, resourcefulness and courage that it was possible to reposition the Magnetic Pole with greater accuracy than hitherto known. On several occasions he displayed a complete disregard for personal safety in order to save his aircraft from destruction by gale and ice. Without the magnificent leadership and judgement displayed by Flight Lieutenant Drake the operation might easily have ended disastrously.

The navigator, Flying Officer Goldsmith, was responsible for successfully guiding the aircraft through dangerous and uncharted areas in the Arctic Islands. In order to reach observation points surrounding the Magnetic Pole it was frequently necessary to fly above the overcast for many hours. With the minimum of normal meteorological and navigational aids, and in unreliable compass reading areas, this officer invariably directed the aircraft to its destination, often necessitating a let-down through clouds in the vicinity of high hills or dangerous waters. He did not have the assistance of accurate maps and his own sketches of important areas have been accepted for incorporation into official Dominion Government charts. The outstanding manner in which he adapted himself to the difficult methods of navigation required over the pole is worthy of the highest praise.

The successful completion of this pioneering operation was directly attributable to the resolution, direction, integrity and initiative of these two officers, and their skilfullness and courage has set a fulgent example which will be an inspiration to their comrades in the Royal Canadian Air Force.

Besides Drake and Goldsmith, three other members of the crew were given some formal recognition by way of a King's

A Canso on RCAF northern operations in the immediate postwar years. Although this was not taken during Operation POLCO, it may have been on a follow-up job, Operation MAGNETIC. (Canadian Forces Photograph RE-1783-28)

Commendation for Valuable Services in the Air: F/O Gerald W. Allen (co-pilot), F/O Kenneth A. McKoy (radio operator) and Sergeant A.B. Hillman (flight engineer). Hillman may have merited a higher award; his Commendation noted, "He risked his life on two notable occasions at night to save his aircraft from destruction during gales which had torn it loose from anchorage and brought the menace of ice floes." The RCAF felt rather self-conscious about these awards. S/L K.A. Ball, chairman of the RCAF Honours and Awards Committee, declared they were merited – "This was a historic flight and the awards seem quite warranted" – but he was also uneasy – "My only concern is that the civilian observers will not receive any recognition." A half-hearted effort was made to have Polar Medals issued to all participants but the conditions of eligibility were too strict; the civilians would receive no formal honours.[6]

It should be noted that follow-up surveys were needed to confirm findings from POLCO. In 1948 Operation MAGNETIC (July 13 to September 1) again saw a Canso used in the Arctic archipelago. The captain, F/O D.K. Game, had F/O Goldsmith as his navigator. MAGNETIC was resumed in 1949, this time with F/L D.R. Cuthbertson as pilot and F/O A.G. Carswell as co-pilot (both of whom we shall meet again), and once more F/O Goldsmith navigated. Sergeant A.B. Hillman from the original POLCO also accompanied the 1949 MAGNETIC.

WITH THE ROYAL AIR FORCE

Much have I travelled in the realms of gold
And many goodly states and kingdoms seen,

– JOHN KEATS (1795-1821), *ON FIRST LOOKING INTO CHAPMAN'S HOMER*

My road calls me, lures me
West, east, south and north;
Most roads lead men homewards;
My road leads me forth.

– JOHN MASEFIELD (1878-1967), *ROADWAYS*

Donaldson and Waterton aside, with postwar Bars to wartime AFCs, six Canadians received the Air Force Cross in the postwar era while performing duties with the Royal Air Force – five as members of the RAF, the other an RCAF officer on exchange duties in Britain.

In 1946, still facing global commitments, the RAF had decided to recruit former Commonwealth aircrew personnel; since all other air forces were rapidly shrinking, there was no shortage of applicants. At least 38 ex-RCAF aircrew still seeking overseas adventures were scooped up. They eventually served in most of the major theatres frequented by British squadrons and participated in several historic events. One was the Berlin Airlift.[7]

The British called it Operation PLAINFARE; to the Americans is was Operation VITTLES. For all concerned it was a huge operation without precedent – supplying a civil populace of two million for almost a year (June 1948 to May 1949) with every necessity of life, from coal to food. The enterprise involved at least five western air forces and more than 25 civilian companies, with aircraft ranging from Sunderlands and Junkers 52s to C-54 and York transports. It began in impro-

vised chaos when Soviet forces closed all road access to the western sector of Berlin (then under joint four-power occupation); it grew in strength and sophistication, conducted in the face of harassment by the Soviets using searchlights, flares, radio jamming and occasional mock fighter attacks to unnerve the British and American aircrews.

Some crews undoubtedly found these tactics unnerving, although Cliff Wenzel recalled being unfazed; after wartime experiences he considered half-hearted YAK buzzings and searchlight probes fairly tame. Speaking to the Toronto Chapter of the Canadian Aviation Historical Society in 1998, he remarked that current driving on Highway 401 was at least as stressful as flying down the Berlin air corridors. He was almost certainly being modest; air traffic control was primitive, especially in the first six months. Yet compared to problems faced four years earlier, when hundreds of bombers (burning no lights) attacked blacked-out targets in Germany in compressed time/space envelopes, the airlift was relatively simple. Fortunately, the crews' worst fear – that the Russians might ring the city with barrage balloons – was never realized. The main enemy was weather; pilots regularly ignored Ground Control Approach rules, preferring to land under 500-foot ceilings in quarter-mile visibility rather than abort a delivery, then lied about the risks incurred.

It is impossible to describe precisely all the problems besetting the PLAINFARE/VITTLES crews, but high on the list would probably be the York transports that constituted the core of the RAF's lifting capacity; they had persistent oil leaks. Another was Wunstorf airfield itself, a former Luftwaffe fighter base that was initially unsuited to the heavy aircraft which shuttled through. Muddy runways forced the York crews to run their engines at high revolutions even when taxying. Dispersal areas were even softer, churned up by trucks and service vehicles; metal strips laid down to improve the surface wore out tires at a phenomenal rate.[8]

F/O Clifton Leonard Wenzel of Calgary had served in the RCAF during the Second World War. As a bomber pilot in No. 78 Squadron, he had been awarded a DFC. In 1947 he joined the Royal Air Force. He flew Yorks with No. 242 Squadron throughout the Berlin airlift (roughly 400 sorties) and in June 1949 was awarded an Air Force Cross. Although the citation has not come to light as of this writing (February 2000), it was probably related to an in-flight incident over Germany on March 14, 1949. A main hydraulic line broke close to electrical circuits and a fire broke out. He handed over control to his co-pilot, then supervised the emergency. They were in cloud with no hydraulics and no electrical power. His flight engineer put out the fire, and his navigator (Wenzel's brother, Norman) worked out a course and an ETA for Wunstorf. They made base and landed safely. In Wenzel's words, "If you're going to save your own skin, it helps if someone can observe it." One of his passengers was A/V/M Donald Bennett (retired), who suggested to the squadron commander (formerly a Bennett protégé) that Wenzel deserved some recognition. That was almost certainly the genesis of the AFC.

Wenzel's subsequent career was remarkable. From flying Yorks on the Berlin airlift he went to flying Hastings worldwide (1949-50), and then to Malaya (1950-51) for anti-terrorist operations on Lincolns before returning to Transport Command. He switched to the RCAF in July 1951 and rose to the rank of squadron leader. His postings included participation in No. 426 Squadron's trans-Pacific airlift, Chief Instructor at No. 4 OTU and staff duties at Transport Command Headquarters. In July 1961 he transferred to the Auxiliary Air Force, flying with No. 400 Squadron until final retirement in 1969. In civil aviation, Wenzel was employed, either as pilot or manager, for several companies including Pacific Western and

F/O C.L. Wenzel (centre) and Flight Sergeant Frank Smith pick up new parachutes, 1945. When the RAF began recruiting Canadians for their own postwar force, Wenzel joined up and eventually flew York transports during the Berlin Airlift. (Canadian Forces Photograph PL-40656)

F/L Clifford L. Wenzel, DFC, AFC, taken in 1955 after he had transferred back to the RCAF. (Canadian Forces Photograph PL-112588)

Laker Airways (he had met Freddie Laker during the Berlin airlift). Describing his career, he writes: "All in all life has been very good to a farm boy from Medicine Hat. It's nice to look at a globe and know that I've seen most of it from a nice low altitude of 7–9,000 feet at a leisurely 150 knots."[9]

Another of the ex-RCAF aircrew joining the postwar RAF was F/O Lorne Arthur Paul Tapp of Sherbrooke, Quebec. During the war he had earned a DFC as a reconnaissance pilot. On returning to Canada he was loaned to Trans-Canada Airlines before his final discharge from the RCAF. Unhappily, even a veteran RCAF pilot had fewer flying hours than experienced TCA captains, and he became frustrated in an organization where promotion, seniority and flying time were inextricably linked. Tapp accepted an RAF commission. He trained on Avro York transports and ultimately logged 2,500 hours on the type. Posted to No. 40 Squadron, and then No. 99 Squadron, Tapp flew on the Berlin Air Lift, which led directly to his being awarded an AFC on January 2, 1950. Although the citation was never published, Air Ministry records reveal the details of his service that brought him the decoration. When recommended he had flown more than 4,400 hours, of which 600 had been directly related to the airlift and 330 had been logged in the previous six months.

Flight Lieutenant Tapp has been employed as a Captain of a York long range transport aircraft for over two years. Since July 1948 he has flown 335 sorties on the Berlin Air Lift. This officer has shown exceptional enthusiasm, initiative and determination over a long period and this resulted in his being the first pilot at this station [Wunstorf, Germany] to fly 300 Berlin Air Lift sorties. During the past twelve months Flight Lieutenant Tapp has displayed to a high degree qualities of resolute determination, courage and devotion to duty. His enthusiasm and personal example have been an inspiration not only to his own crew but to all the captains in his squadron and have encouraged them to emulate his performance. He is a skilful pilot with a fine record of accident-free flying due mainly to his intense concentration on his task. His personal contribution to the success of the airlift has been most praiseworthy.[10]

F/L Lorne Tapp and A/V/M Larry Wray, October 15, 1962, during the acceptance of CF-104s for No. 1 Air Division in Europe. Tapp won a DFC for reconnaissance work in Burma; as a member of the RAF he was awarded an AFC, having flown York transports during the Berlin Airlift. He then transferred to the RCAF. Wray, of course, had been one of the earliest RCAF recipients of the AFC. (Canadian Forces Photograph PL-147699)

Tapp's logbook for the period gives little more than dates and flying times. Even so, it indicates the intense level of operations. Shortly before PLAINFARE he had been posted to No. 99 Squadron, then engaged in routine transport flying to Iraq, where Imperial garrisons still dominated the scene. For

Tapp, the airlift first appears as a log entry dated July 13, 1948, "Wunstorf–Berlin–Wunstorf," involving a total of 110 minutes flying time (his check pilot and co-captain was Wenzel). That sort of notation became routine as he shuttled back and forth, never mentioning his cargo or any incidents that may have occurred. Twice daily sorties were usual, triple flights were not uncommon, and a week off was rare. Occasionally he had to fly on instruments; this was especially true in February 1949. His last trip on PLAINFARE was on June 20, 1949. A sampling of his daily operations reads as follows:

August 15, 1948
York 238 – self & crew – Wunstorf-Berlin-Wunstorf – 1 hour 45 min (night)
York 328 – self & crew – Wunstorf-Berlin-Wunstorf – 1 hour 45 min (day)
York 141 – self & crew – Wunstorf-Berlin-Wunstorf – 1 hour 45 min (day)

March 9, 1949
York 262 – self & crew – Wunstorf-Berlin-Wunstorf – 2 hours 5 min (night, of which one hour 30 minutes were on instruments)
York 165 – self & crew – Wunstorf-Berlin-Wunstorf – 2 hours 5 min (day)[11]

Soon after being decorated, Tapp was posted to No. 115 Squadron, with which he flew Boeing B-29s (known as Washingtons in RAF service). He rejoined the RCAF in April 1952, served as a transport pilot and instructor, and eventually test-flew CF-104 Starfighters prior to their acceptance by Canada's NATO Air Division. He retired in October 1965 and died in September 1985.

F/O Maurice Arthur Joseph St. Pierre of Ottawa had enlisted in the RCAF in September 1941, trained as a pilot and flown an overseas tour with No. 462 Squadron (Halifax bombers, North Africa and Italy). Further service had taken him to Palestine and Egypt before his return to Britain and subsequent repatriation to Canada. St. Pierre was released from the RCAF in July 1945, but the lure of flying persisted. In August 1947 he boarded the SS *Aquitania*, sailed to Britain and joined the Royal Air Force.

The greater part of his service was as a flight safety officer and instructor at Finningly, North Luffenham and Oakington. From 1949 onwards he was usually found at the controls of a two-seat Meteor VII jet trainer. The type had long been anticipated to convert piston-trained pilots for single-seater jet Vampires and Meteors. Sturdy and efficient, the Meteor VII nevertheless had minor problems. Its short endurance (40 minutes without a belly tank, just over an hour with one) offered little margin for error if the pilot was compelled to fly on instruments or had to repeat an approach following a training

F/L Maurice St. Pierre, AFC. Wartime flying was followed by ten years service with the RAF and an AFC awarded for instructional work on Meteors. Like Tapp and Wenzel, he eventually transferred to the RCAF. (Canadian Forces Photograph PL-141760)

Gloster Meteor T.7, the type flown by F/L St. Pierre. (National Aviation Museum)

mission. The cockpit was unpressurized, which gave rise to canopies misting or freezing. Instructors carried plastic scrapers to clear a peephole during tense approaches! Single engine performance was marginal; early in its career the Meteor VII was remarkable for the frequency of fatal crashes.[12] It was while he was at Oakington, where he was also the instrument check pilot, that he was recommended for an Air Force Cross. The award was approved and announced on June 1, 1953, part of a large honours list published to coincide with the Coronation of Queen Elizabeth II.

New Year and the monarch's birthday had been traditional dates for honours lists in both civil and military fields. Coronations being much less frequent (16 years had passed since the crowning of George VI), officialdom pulled out all the stops to wring the most in pageantry and dignity from the occasion. Queen Elizabeth's 1953 Coronation Honours List,

among other things, recognized aerial service and achievements on the part of dozens of men and women – chiefly British, but including Australians, Rhodesians and New Zealanders. Knighthoods were distributed to aviation pioneers such as Tom Sopwith and aircraft designers such as Sidney Camm (designer of types ranging from the Hawker Cygnet of 1924 to the 1951 Hawker Hunter), as well as to airline managers and senior air force officers. Test pilots Roland Beamont and Joseph "Mutt" Summers were honoured (OBE and CBE respectively). Air Commodore W.A. Stagg (who had given General Eisenhower his famous pre-D-Day weather briefings) was promoted from Officer to Commander in the Order of the British Empire (OBE to CBE). G/C E.M. Donaldson, DSO, AFC (already met as a CAN/RAF winner of the AFC and Bar) also became a CBE. As part of the Coronation Honours, the Queen awarded three Bars to the AFC, 57 AFCs and 18 AFMs.[13] St. Pierre later flew on ferry work between Britain and bases on the Continent. He left the RAF in February 1957, returned to Canada and rejoined the RCAF for a further 11 years, much of it as an instructor at Station Portage.

The Coronation Honours Lists which included St. Pierre's AFC also carried the name of F/O Kelley Aeriel Whynacht,

DFC. Born in Cherry Hill, Nova Scotia, in 1923, he had joined the RCAF in May 1942 and trained as a pilot. Posted overseas, he had received a DFC with Bomber Command (No. 150 Squadron, 34 sorties, 214 operational hours). Demobilized early in 1946, he had, like Tapp and St. Pierre, almost immediately enlisted in the RAF for more adventures. He did not maintain contact with Canada so little of his career is known. In 1949 he attended an instructor's course at the Central Flying School; as of January 1951 he was teaching aircrew to fly Avro Lincolns at No. 230 Operational Conversion Unit. It may be assumed that his AFC, like St.Pierre's, was related to instructional duties. By November 1975 he had attained the rank of squadron leader in the Fighter Operations Control Branch.

Wilfred Jasper Burnett was born in Garden Creek, New Brunswick, in 1915, raised in Fort Frances, Ontario and joined the RAF in 1937. He flew three tours with Bomber Command, winning a DFC in October 1940 and a DSO in March 1945. He remained in the postwar RAF, retiring in 1968 with the rank of air commodore. Although no citation has been found for Burnett's AFC, the general circumstances are readily deduced. The RAF had maintained its interest in northern aerial navigation; the Lancaster "Aries" of 1945-46 had been succeeded by two Lincolns, "Aries II" and "Aries III." New ground was broken in 1954 with "Aries IV," a Canberra bomber. The unit operating her was the RAF College, Manby.

F/O Kelley A. Whynacht, photographed before going overseas in 1943. He won a DFC in Bomber Command, then joined the postwar RAF, where he won an AFC. Little is known of his career in that force other than that his award was associated with flying training.

Flights near, to and across the North Pole were international in scope, involving close liaison with Canadian and Norwegian forces.

As of 1954, Burnett was a wing commander associated with these Polar flights. Sometimes he flew the Hastings transport which carried technicians and other support personnel to Bodo, in northern Norway, the jumping-off site for these excursions; sometimes he piloted a Canberra with two navigators who were being introduced to such flying. On December 16, 1954 he flew "Aries IV" some 2,400 miles to latitude 85°, flying at 45,000 feet; the trip took five hours (average speed 480 m.p.h.) and the student navigators were Lieutenant-Colonel Charles A. North, USAF, and F/L John Tipton, DFC. Several aircrew participating in these exercises received the AFC over time; Burnett's was gazetted on January 1, 1956. In November of that year, in command of Vickers Valiant detachment from No. 148 Squadron, he bombed targets in Egypt as part of the brief Suez War.[14]

The fifth Canadian AFC recipient serving with the RAF, S/L Christopher Edwin Lawrence Hare, was born in Montreal in April 1922, educated in Toronto and enlisted in that city in June 1940. He trained as a pilot, earned his wings in January 1941 and went overseas. His was a most adventurous tour. It began with No. 103 Squadron in Bomber Command, but in September 1941 he switched to No. 458 Squadron and went with that unit to the Mediterranean. In July 1942 he was posted to No. 37 Squadron, but the following month he was shot down and taken prisoner, after evading capture for three weeks. He was held captive in Italy, but when that country quit the Axis in September 1943, Hare escaped and reached Allied lines. After instructional duties in Britain, he joined No. 150 Squadron for another tour on bombers; with that unit he was awarded the Distinguished Flying Cross.

After the war, Hare remained in the RCAF, serving in a succession of air transport units. From January 1949 to June 1951 he was on exchange duties with RAF Transport Command, where he was assigned to the development unit, and eventually he was put in charge of the development flight. This was a very responsible position to give an exchange officer, and there was some concern that it might provoke the resentment of RAF staff. Instead, he charmed superiors, colleagues and juniors alike. The commanding officer of RAF Station Abington, W/C F.C. Griffiths, wrote that Hare had been appointed to lead the development flight at a time when things were not running smoothly. He added that the Canadian had gone on to weld together an excellent team, "brought order out of chaos" and achieved all this without causing jealousy or dispute; he was praised as being a sound "service ambassador" for Canada.

On July 19, 1950, he was recommended for an AFC; he had by then flown 2,370 hours, 250 with the development unit, 177 in the previous six months. It was finally gazetted on June 30, 1951, almost a year after the initial submission. The citation described a tour marked by variety and talent:

This officer has fulfilled the duties of RCAF Liaison Officer and pilot to Air Transport Development Flight in the United Kingdom for the past 18 months. During this time he has acquitted himself as a pilot of outstanding courage and ability, particularly in the following circumstances:

(a) In April 1949 he was captain of a Halifax aircraft which had been adapted for carrying a "Paratechnicon" underneath. This paratechicon was sufficiently large to carry a gun and jeep inside and was fitted to the belly of the aircraft in such a manner that it could be dropped and brought to earth by means of cluster parachutes. Little was known of the handling characteristics of the Halifax with the paratechnicon fitted. On the very first flight from the manufacturers' works Squadron Leader Hare was the captain, when the aircraft suffered a No. 1 engine failure. Squadron Leader Hare would have been fully justified in jettisoning the new paratechnicon as little enough was known of the handing characteristics of the Halifax with the paratechnicon fitted when flying on four engines let alone three. However, having regard to the high cost of the paratechnicon and the fact that on this first flight parachutes were not fitted and thus any jettisoning would have led to the destruction of the paratechnicon apart from danger to people on the ground, Squadron Leader Hare continued to fly on three engines until he felt confident and familiar with the aircraft. He then carried out a successful three engine landing at RAF Brize Norton.[15]

(b) In the spring of 1950 he was appointed task officer in charge of a Lancaster aircraft equipped with prototype cumulo-nimbus cloud warning equipment. During April and May the aircraft was detached to Singapore where trials were to be carried out. The directive suggested that penetration of cloud encountered was desirable if found possible. Under Squadron Leader Hare's leadership over 100 penetrations of cumulo-nimbus cloud were made and some 30 penetrations of thunderstorms in which lightning was present. Four of these latter penetrations were made over Singapore Island in view of personnel at Changi airport. The information which the detachment brought back is of invaluable help towards the progress of safer aviation and the lightning penetrations made over Singapore Island helped considerably to "lay a few bogies" prevalent amongst flying personnel who watched the performance. There is no doubt that the example set by Squadron Leader Hare and his determination to fulfil the task to the utmost of his ability contributed largely to the success of the expedition and his investigations have helped to tear down some of the veils of ignorance which cloud man's knowledge of flying conditions in cumulo-nimbus cloud and thunderstorms.

The promulgation of his award was delayed because Ottawa initially did not want him to have it. British authorities had meant to include Hare's AFC in the New Years Honours List of January 1951. On November 22, 1950, they cabled Air Force Headquarters, stating their intention and asking formal permission to do so. No citation accompanied this communication.

The RAF probably expected that their Canadian counterparts would be pleased. Earlier that year another RCAF officer, F/O Peter B. St. Louis, had been awarded an MBE in the King's Birthday List without objections.[16] Instead, in AFHQ, Ottawa, the proverbial hit the fan. On November 23, 1950, G/C J.G. Stephenson advised the Air Member for Personnel that current government policy precluded RCAF members receiving periodic awards. That same day, a cable was despatched to the Air Member, Canadian Joint Staff, London, trying to block Hare's award while justifying previous inaction (or inattention) with respect to St. Louis:

Regret Canadian government policy precludes inclusion of 19798 S/L C.E.L. Hare in New Years Honours List. Such policy insofar as Canada is concerned has been in effect since 1946. Request Air Ministry to delete this officer's name from their list prior to submission to the King.

Appreciated that F/O St. Louis, RCAF, appeared on last periodic list. However, circumstances this latter officer's case differ inasmuch as he was on non-effective strength at time the services he rendered were recognized by award.

Provided copy of recommendation for S/L Hare con-

W/C Christopher E.L. Hare, DFC, AFC and F/O J.M. Dawson, in 1960, shortly before they were killed in a CF-100 accident. Hare's adventures included a wartime escape, two tours on bombers, and 18 months of dangerous experimental flying while attached to the postwar RAF. (Canadian Forces Photograph PL-77662)

tains evidence of some specific act of an exceptional nature it will be considered here as a special case. Provision is made for such cases (refer AFAO P7/7) but are not included in periodic honours list.[17]

Senior RCAF officers were basing their objections on policy; they probably were unaware of the circumstances that had generated the AFC recommendation. Their protest certainly delayed promulgation of Hare's award by six months, but by June 1951 AFHQ had reversed course. Just prior to gazetting of the AFC, Air Vice Marshal A.L. James wrote to Hare, congratulating him on the decoration and mentioning the "flying skill and courageous actions" which had been demonstrated by saving a valuable prototype, possibly saving lives, and conducting hazardous experimental flights. The AFC was thus deemed to fall within the bounds of earlier directives that awards should be for "gallantry" rather than "service."

After his tour in the United Kingdom, Hare resumed RCAF duties, initially with transport units (Station Lachine and No. 426 Squadron) and later as a staff officer and fighter squadron commander (No. 414 Squadron). He was killed in the crash of a CF-100 near North Bay on November 14, 1960.

SEARCH AND RESCUE

Throw out the life-line across the dark wave,
There is a brother whom someone should save.

– EDWARD SMITH UFFORD, *REVIVALIST HYMN* (1884)

In the immediate postwar period, the RCAF was assigned a national and international role of search and rescue but this was restricted to air traffic only. On July 12, 1951, the Cabinet broadened this mandate to include co-ordination of marine cases on both coasts and in the Great Lakes; Rescue Co-Ordination Centres at Halifax, Winnipeg, Edmonton, Torbay, Vancouver and Trenton supervised air and sea SAR operations.[18]

The size and status of RCAF SAR operations varied and developed, but the situation as of 1956 is worth describing; it stands mid-way between the end of the Second World War and the integration of the Canadian Armed Forces. That year, the RCAF had 151 officers, 324 non-commissioned officers and 472 airmen (total, 947) directly engaged in SAR work; this did not include support staff such as administrators or mess employees. The cost of SAR that year was approximately $6,000,000, and the force had 44 aircraft dedicated to SAR operations distributed as follows:

121 Rescue Unit, Sea Island – 2 Cansos, 2 Dakotas, 2 Otters, 2 helicopters.

111 Rescue Unit, Winnipeg – 2 Lancasters, 4 Otters, 2 Dakotas, 2 helicopters.

102 Rescue Unit, Trenton – 3 Dakotas, 4 Otters, 3 Cansos, 3 helicopters

103 Rescue Unit, Greenwood – 2 Cansos, 3 Otters, 1 Dakota, 2 helicopters.

107 Rescue Unit, Torbay – 3 Lancasters.

Rescue Unit, Goose Bay – 1 Dakota, 1 Otter.

Each unit had aircraft ready to move at 30 minutes notice during normal working hours and one hour standby after working hours or on weekends. All but the Torbay unit had para-rescue teams present and a special school at Trenton gave courses in para-rescue, searchmaster and ground rescue duties.[19]

By the nature of their mission, SAR crews risked becoming objects of searches as well. An instance of this befell F/L K.O. Moore (a veteran of Operation CANON). On January 18, 1948, he evacuated two sick men from Arctic Bay, using a Dakota of the Joint Air Training Centre at Rivers. On the 20th, en route from Coral Harbour to Churchill, the aircraft was forced down on the ice of Hudson Bay; they were located and rescued by a Norseman on the 22nd.

Postwar search and rescue was a joint project of service and civilian organizations, increasingly eased by new technology (homing beacons) and more general use of radios in boats and aircraft. Civilian operators assisting in a search might complicate the process by becoming lost themselves; more commonly their help was welcomed. On March 6, 1964, for example, four seal hunters reported missing in the Gulf of St. Lawrence were located on drifting ice by an RCAF Argus, then picked up by a Kenting Air Services helicopter. On May 1 of the same year a boat with two seal hunters went missing in the same area; it was found by civilian searchers, an Argus dropped supplies and an S-55 helicopter owned by Eastern Provincial Airways completed the rescue.[20]

The traditions of the RCAF included minimal equipment, often of dubious quality. In the SAR

Vertol 42 (H-21) helicopter, a type introduced into RCAF service in 1954. These "choppers" were the backbone of RCAF Search and Rescue work for 15 years. (Canadian Force Photograph PL-100836)

field, this was apparent by 1956, as the Dakotas and Cansos showed their age. On March 22, 1956, Maritime Air Command sent Air Force Headquarters a letter that was blunt and shocking:

1. Reference is made to AFHQ message DSS 466 10 Feb 56 and K 128 11 Feb 56.
2. 103 Rescue Unit at Greenwood out of eighty attempted Canso flights had twenty-six aborted due to unserviceabilities, and in nearly all SAR missions a delay was experienced owing to unserviceabilities. The weight restrictions now imposed on the Canso make it no longer a long-range SAR aircraft.
3. Rescue Co-Ordination Centre Torbay had on eight occasions to rely on USAF or civilian support to carry out SAR missions which required an amphibious aircraft.
4. There is a definite requirement for an SA-16 type of aircraft for SAR operations in the Atlantic Area of Responsibility.

Transport Command, responsible for SAR operations in central Canada, was equally concerned about equipment, especially as its responsibilities extended ever north and traffic in that region grew almost monthly. On November 23, 1956, A/V/M J.G. Bryans urged replacement of Dakotas (now considered too slow and short-ranged for any but local missions), purchase of more helicopters, a minimum of four SA-16 Albatross aircraft to be secured (they were already widely used by USAF Air Rescue units), and that four North Stars be modified for long-range SAR work; this latter suggestion was inspired by another American example of thoroughness:

The USAF Air Rescue Service in its continuing effort to have available the optimum rescue equipment, recently acquired the first of 38 modified SC-54D Rescuemasters specifically tailored for long range, large scale rescue operations. These aircraft have been modified to include such items as IFF interrogators, multipurpose radar equipment, VHF and UHF homing devices, lookout blisters, long range tanks, special doors, etc.[21]

Improvements came slowly but eventually. Although lacking a life-saving capability, the Canadair Argus (introduced into service in 1957) greatly extended the RCAF's maritime search capability. In 1960 the much-sought Albatross joined the force, enabling retirement of the last Canso two years later. Also in 1960 the versatile C-130 Hercules entered RCAF inventory – the greatest friend possible for anyone living "north of 60."

The first of the great postwar SAR flights had been Operation CANON, already mentioned. The second, honoured by an AFC at the same time (July 31, 1948) as CANON personnel were recognized, involved F/O Roland Burgess West, DFC. Born at Medford, Nova Scotia, on January 25, 1919, he had been educated there and in Kentville before becoming a boat pilot in the Bay of Fundy. He had enlisted in Halifax on August 19, 1941, trained as a pilot, then spent most of the war flying Cansos with No. 116 (BR) Squadron on Canada's east coast. After flying 84 sorties (704 operational hours) he was awarded the Distinguished Flying Cross. The work may have been tedious, but West learned about flying in unpredictable conditions.

After the war he elected to make the RCAF his career; he attended the RCAF Staff School in Toronto and shortly afterwards he was posted to No. 103 Rescue Flight at Greenwood. The citation to his AFC describes what followed:

For a period of over two years Flying Officer West has been continuously employed on search and rescue operations along the east coast of Canada. During many hazardous and difficult mercy flights and searches along the eastern seaboard and over the western Atlantic he has proved himself to be an outstanding captain and extremely capable pilot, successfully completing many special missions.

On 1 January 1948 this officer was detailed as captain of a Canso aircraft which had been ordered to attempt the evacuation of a woman who was critically ill at her home at Mutton Bay, Labrador. Although climatic conditions were extremely poor, heavy clouds, fog and driving snow being encountered, and very adverse sea conditions existed in the confined harbour at Mutton Bay, he succeeded in reaching his objective and executed a safe landing. Under substantial difficulties of sub-zero weather, billowing seas, and attendant hazardous circumstances, the patient was safely placed on board the aircraft. Although the aircraft was heavily-laden with ice from flying spray, and water was pouring into the hold from a faulty nose-wheel door, Flying Officer West accomplished a most successful take-off. With the same resolute determination and initiative he fulfilled his return mission, a total distance of nearly one thousand miles, and landed at base where the patient was transferred to the hospital.

Throughout all his operations with search and rescue flight, and in particular the Mutton Bay mission, he has displayed utmost keenness, efficiency, leadership and high devotion to duty. His personal courage and cheerful enthusiasm merit the highest praise and have been an inspiring example, not only to his flight but to all his associates in the Royal Canadian Air Force.

West's AFC was only one of many honours that would come his way; he gained a reputation as one of Canada's top SAR pilots. The Trans-Canada Trophy (McKee Trophy) went to him in 1948 in recognition of more than 2,000 hours flown on mercy missions. Nevertheless, following the SAR flights, he had gone on to further adventures, as the McKee award pointed out:

In addition to his Search and Rescue operations, Flying Officer West was employed as Captain of an aircraft on special flying operations in the far north during 1948. Many of these flights were to landing strips in the Eastern Arctic where he acquired further knowledge regarding northern operations. During the spring floods in British Columbia, Flying Officer West flew many long hours carrying sandbags and other vital materials across the Rockies into British Columbia. In June, 1948, he was chosen to perform the first large-scale "Rain Making" operation in Canada, This operation was successful in producing large quantities of rain over the drought stricken area north of Sault Ste. Marie, Ontario.

S/L Roland B. West, DFC, AFC, receives the McKee Trophy as the most outstanding figure in Canadian aviation in 1948. The Honourable Brooke Claxton, Minister of National Defence, makes the presentation. (Canadian Forces Photograph PL-39949)

Flying Officer West has invariably displayed a keen desire to pass on to other aircrew all the information he has acquired as a result of his various flying operations. In addition, he frequently took inexperienced co-pilots on such flights, in order that they might benefit from his knowledge and instruction. This officer was also responsible for converting many new pilots to the Lancaster, Canso and Dakota aircraft.

There followed a long and varied career that included scientific research and observance of American intercontinental ballistic missile test firings. He retired from the force in 1966, and in 1973 he was admitted to the Canadian Aviation Hall of Fame.[22] Newfoundland and Labrador had been primitive in wartime and their plight did not materially improve after the war – or even after joining Canada in 1949. The annals of RCAF SAR are replete with tales from the Arctic, but also from Newfoundland. As seen in the case of "Rollie" West, a pilot might be involved in multiple mercy flights, frequently in the face of horrendous odds. Like West, F/L Oland Grant Nelson (St. Thomas, Ontario) was a veteran of wartime maritime reconnaissance operations (Coastal Command and No. 413 Squadron, Ceylon). He too ended up in No. 103 Rescue Flight (redesignated No. 103 Search and Rescue Unit in the summer of 1950), flying 1,200 hours with them. Most trips took him to Baffin Island and the eastern Arctic, although he also participated in the

F/L Oland G. Nelson, another Search and Rescue pilot whose AFC was won under hazardous circumstances. The postwar Canadian forces demanded higher standards for AFC awards than prevailed in the RAF. (Canadian Forces Photograph PL-51405)

1948 ATTACHE search. Just as he was about to take up less demanding duties, a call came through for yet another daring mission. The citation for his Air Force Cross read, in part:

On 5 October 1949, Flight Lieutenant Nelson, on the eve of posting from No. 103 Search and Rescue Flight, Greenwood, volunteered to captain an aircraft detailed to undertake mercy flights to remote settlements. On the following day, after flying to Goose Bay, he took off in a Canso for St. Mary's on the Labrador coast but was forced to turn back due to gales and the extremely adverse and hazardous weather and water conditions prevailing when he reached destination.

On the 7 October, under very bad conditions he reached Nutak on the northern coast and picked up a severely injured Eskimo. On the 9th he returned to St. Mary's, picking up a small boy dangerously ill with a ruptured appendix. Although not originally planned, he proceeded to St. Anthony on the northern Newfoundland coast and emplaned several seriously ill Eskimos. Exceptional skill and determination was exhibited landing and taking off on these flights as well as boarding his patients from small boats with heavy seas and cross currents threatening harm to the personnel and aircraft. Flight Lieutenant Nelson landed at Halifax, after completing a total of twenty hours flying during which a distance of twenty-six hundred miles was covered. By his skill and fortitude he was instrumental in saving at least two lives.

This citation, edited and vetted by uniformed bureaucrats, do not catch the full drama of the flights. The original recommendation spelled things out in greater detail. At St. Mary's he had been compelled to land and take off in crosswinds to clear the surrounding hills; at St. Anthony he had not only encountered high seas but had been compelled to manoeuvre in practically open water. The man who drafted that recommendation on March 13, 1950, was himself bound for distinction: the officer commanding No. 103 Search and Rescue Flight on that date was S/L Wallace Angus Grayton McLeish, DFC, a former school teacher from Hamilton, Ontario, who had visited Berlin on four occasions – once as an Olympic rower in 1936, three times as a bomber captain during the Second World War.

Ten days earlier, McLeish had returned from the second of two rescue missions that were to lead to his receiving an AFC; three weeks after submitting a recommendation on behalf of Nelson, his own CO, W/C G.A. Hiltz, (Station Greenwood) was writing up a similar description of McLeish. His adventures were among the most hazardous ever association with an AFC award; his willingness to take risks bordered on the reckless. Danger was no stranger to him; he had earned his DFC with No. 428 Squadron when Bomber Command was taking some of its heaviest losses. He subsequently commanded No. 103 Search and Rescue Flight, and, like Nelson, he participated in Operation ATTACHE.

The first incident began on October 21, 1949, when word arrived that a gravely injured man had to be evacuated from Resolute Bay. McLeish and his crew departed on the 22nd in a Lancaster, flying from Greenwood to Frobisher Bay. On the morning of the 23rd the forecast showed poor conditions all the way to Resolute Bay with a good probability of impossible landing conditions. However as the patient's condition was

S/L W.A.G. McLeish (right) at Rockcliffe, ready to search for a missing Beaver aircraft; he chats with Corporal Ed Burrows (Toronto) and LAC Earl Greenough (Moncton). McLeish was an SAR specialist whose bravery bordered on the reckless. (Canadian Forces Photograph PL-50910)

Swords into ploughshares. In the postwar RCAF, Lancaster bombers assumed many new roles, including Search and Rescue. This one, belonging to No. 408 Squadron, was employed on aerial photography and mapping. (Canadian Forces Photograph PL-102459)

grave, McLeish elected to depart at dawn in a snow storm and gale so strong that the landing flares blew out immediately they were lighted. The headlights of two trucks stationed at the end of the runway were his only guides on takeoff.

At Resolute, with the maximum ceiling at 100 feet, he had to make several passes at the field before landing. Having emplaned the patient, he turned around and returned to base in appalling conditions. The citation to his AFC described these vividly:

> Due to unfavourable weather conditions the flight was accomplished without aid of astronomical observations, visual pinpoints or radar fixes, in addition to a magnetic compass made unreliable by proximity to the North Pole. A total of 24 hours 55 minutes flying time was entailed in this mission, the last 20 hours of which was continuous except for loading and refuelling.

The flight of October 23, 1949, had been a test of skill and navigation. A mission flown on March 3, 1950, was a demonstration of nerves; one can imagine his crewmen staring at their white knuckles. Its object was the evacuation of a ten-year-old Inuit boy from Clyde River on the northeast coast of Baffin Island. The child was suffering from malnutrition and gangrenous frozen feet. A Lancaster was the only aircraft with the necessary range, but no previous attempt had ever been made by the RCAF to land an aircraft of this size on an unknown and unprepared ice surface. Unlike F/O Race (Operation CANON), McLeish would be touching down on a surface that had not been reconnoitred by any expert on the ground.

Ice is notoriously unreliable (ask the ghosts of drowned snowmobilers). Even Arctic ice is tricky, for it may be weakened by currents or pressure shifts; a dusting of snow can hide jagged ridges and deep cracks. The snow itself is difficult to gauge in depth or texture. In these circumstances, the Lancaster crew risked everything from being marooned with the patient to a serious crash. Lowering his undercarriage, McLeish made two passes over the intended landing area, dragging his wheels in the snow to test its depth. Having elected to land, he brought his aircraft down literally an inch at a time, prepared to take off again if the snow drag on the undercarriage became too great. He did not close his throttle until he felt solid ice under the wheels. The ice surface was rough, however, and as the aircraft lost speed, it was subjected to violent jolting. Once down, he had to apply more than 50 per cent power to taxi. The rest was anti-climax. The Inuit patient was emplaned and a direct flight to Goose Bay was uneventful. McLeish and Nelson were awarded their AFCs at the same time (April 14, 1951); McLeish received his decoration at a Government House investiture on February 22, 1952.

Given the feats he performed, it is worth noting what type of officer McLeish was at this time. In April 1949 his commanding officer, W/C. R.O. Shaw, described him as "efficiently commanding 103 S and R Flight; hard but fair; loyal and resolute." Another assessment, this one from November 1950, described an archetypical man of action; W/C G.A. Hiltz wrote:

> This officer is outstanding as an operational pilot. He likes flying and does a lot; while Officer Commanding 103 SAR Flight, he always went on the most difficult trips… I would criticize him only for his questionable administrative ability. I think this stems from beliefs that anything not directly concerned with flying is nonsense…

He had left No. 103 SAR Unit in August 1950. His later postings included Churchill and AFHQ. In March 1957 he was given command of No. 440 Squadron (CF-100s), and he was killed in a "Clunk" crash on June 10 of that year. His family had given much to their country; three younger brothers, John, Bruce and Robert McLeish, had followed him into the RCAF; John was killed in action in August 1943; Bruce was killed in a Sabre collision in Europe in 1955; he was 23 years old.

F/L Lawrence B. Pearson, AFC, shows his son the cockpit of a CF-100.
Pearson was one of several SAR pilots who went on to fly fighters.
(Canadian Forces Photograph PL-105422)

On June 18, 1950, No. 103 Rescue Unit despatched a Canso from Greenwood via Goose Bay and Fort Chimo through failing weather and erratic radio static. The crew were relying on instruments and dealing with severe carburettor icing that led the engines to cut out intermittently. Their mission was to retrieve a seriously ill native boy. Their intended landing area at Payne Bay on the western shores of Ungava Bay was frozen solid far out to sea. The pilot, F/L Lawrence Bell Pearson (Woodstock, Ontario) flew a further 60 miles north to Emilik where the mouth of a river was practically clear of ice, offering a possible landing space, though cramped and ringed by ice. Pearson realized that an attempted landing might end in disaster, yet a boy's life depended on his ability to set the Canso down on the water and take it off again; he accepted the risk. After alighting in open water and anchoring his aircraft he noticed that the swells caused by the landing were breaking off large pieces of ice from the frozen section of the river; these floes began drifting down in the swift current towards the aircraft. If allowed to strike the Canso they could seriously damage the hull and wing floats and possibly jeopardize the take-off.

Pearson showed ingenuity and took every possible precaution. He positioned two men on the wing and directed them to run from one wing tip to the other as necessary in order to raise the wing floats whenever ice was drifting dangerously close. At the same time other crew members fended off floating ice with boat hooks and oars and used sleeping bags as buffers when it was impossible to prevent ice from pressing too close against the hull. He directed his crew with such skill that in the 45 minutes the aircraft was on the water waiting for the boy to be brought out no damage was caused to the aircraft by the drifting ice. With extremely delicate manoeuvring he took off successfully from the treacherous waters and flew his patient southward to hospital. When F/O Pearson was awarded the AFC in June 1951, the citation noted:

> This officer's daring initiative, resourcefulness and undoubted skill and determination in this instance, and in other equally spectacular phases of rescue flying, has set a splendid example and is worthy of the highest praise.

Every major SAR mission was different. Operation HAVEN was remarkable for the extremely high latitudes reached and the use of JATO (Jet Assisted Take Off) during the mission. The central figure, S/L (later G/C) James Frederick Mitchell, originally from Toronto, had been decorated with the DFC and Bar as a bomber pilot during the Second World War. His AFC exploit began on September 20, 1950, when word reached Edmonton that Charles Haven, a weather station staffer at Eureka Sound, had contracted severe blood poisoning and required immediate medical attention. Two dangerous alternatives were offered – either to fly in and drop a medical officer or attempt to land and bring the patient back for treatment.

Eureka Sound lies some 700 nautical miles north of the Arctic Circle and within 500 nautical miles of the North Pole in a rugged, uncharted area. Given the distance and unusual atmospheric conditions, normal radio aids to navigation were negligible. In addition, the proximity of the Magnetic North Pole rendered the magnetic compass useless. Facilities for forced landings en route were non-existent; the nearest alternative suitable for landing in event of an emergency was Thule in Greenland. There was a shortage of meteorological information coupled with a strong possibility of weather unexpectedly deteriorating either en route or at the destination.

S/L Mitchell, Officer Commanding Northwest Air Command Communication Flight, took the risks and volunteered to carry out this perilous flight in a Dakota aircraft. The mission called for accurate planning at short notice; in particular he would have to calculate the correct gasoline load required on the run from Resolute Bay to Eureka Sound. He had to ensure the lightest possible landing weight for a very short runway at the destination and still have sufficient fuel for a flight to the alternative at Thule in case of inclement weather. Mitchell and his Dakota departed Edmonton at 1315 hours on September 20, 1950, after a last-minute weather briefing,

(Above) Airmen fit JATO bottles to a Dakota for Operation HAVEN. (Below) Loading a Herman Nelson heater into a Dakota. Such equipment was vital in Arctic operations to keep engines and fuel lines thawed. (Canadian Forces Photographs PL-49039, PL-49066)

S/L James F. Mitchell and S/L J.R. Jackson, pilot and medical officer in Operation HAVEN. (Canadian Forces Photograph PL-49044)

There was a 40 degree cross wind, gusting to 36 knots, and he was on instruments. All the same, he executed a smooth touchdown. The patient was delivered to hospital at 0530 hours on September 22. During the 40 hours and 15 minutes from the time of take-off until arrival at Churchill, S/L Mitchell had flown 3,139 nautical miles in 28 1/2 flying hours and with only 3 1/2 hours sleep. When the aircraft returned to Edmonton at 2140 hours on September 22, 1950, a total of 3,857 nautical miles in far northern territory had been covered – the longest mercy flight in the history of the Royal Canadian Air Force up to that date. His AFC citation praised Mitchell's "determination, bravery, fortitude and devotion to duty."

It is remarkable that none of Mitchell's crew seem even to have been recommended for awards. The situation was different following Operation CAPTAIN, the rescue of survivors from a Canadian Pacific Airlines crash on December 23, 1950. The DC-3 had been reported missing in the British Columbia interior. A search began; No. 123 Rescue Unit's aircraft were flying *through* the mountains, not over them, scouring the terrain for signs of wreckage.

F/O Robert Thomas Glaister of Prince Albert, Saskatchewan, a wartime veteran of Transport Command, had been bucking mountain turbulence and poor visibility in a Dakota. Dusk was gathering when he detected signal fires on the eastern slopes of Mount Okanagan. He descended to 4,000 feet where peaks 7,000 feet high frowned down; switching on his landing lights, he spotted survivors waving firebrands and improvised signals. Glaister's pinpointing of the downed airplane made possible the next step in the drama.

In the late morning of the 23rd another Dakota, this one piloted by F/L Paul Lewis Gibbs, DFC (Onion Lake, Saskatchewan) arrived to deliver a para-rescue team. Visibility was still

which subsequently proved to be the only complete one received during the entire trip. He refuelled at Baker Lake and Resolute Bay. On arrival at Eureka it was found that the landing surface consisted of a rough strip only 2,000 feet long marked out with oil barrels. Rather than drop a doctor and leave him stranded, Mitchell decided to attempt a landing. This he accomplished very skilfully. Two hours later the aircraft was again airborne with Mr. Haven aboard. A JATO pack boosted the Dakota off the improvised runway.

The return flight was made by way of Resolute Bay to Churchill through extremely trying weather conditions. Mitchell was close to exhaustion as he approached Churchill.

poor, icing conditions severe, and things were getting worse. The survivors were at the 4,000 foot level, the cloud base was at 5,500 feet, and all the peaks above that height were cloaked. Moreover, the clouds were moving in; it was only a matter of minutes before the whole crash site would be obscured. After making one test run at 5,000 feet, Gibbs chose the one possible approach, a dangerous one, and dropped his stick of para-rescuers. Within minutes they were with the survivors. Gibbs was not finished. Extricating his Dakota from the mountains, he landed at Penticton, where he was appointed the local search co-ordinator. Working closely with Canadian Pacific Airlines officials, the Royal Canadian Mounted Police and local civilians, he planned the successful evacuation of the survivors by ground party, showing leadership and organizing ability that matched his flying skills.

F/O Robert T. Glaister, AFC, one of three men decorated for bravery in the course of Operation CAPTAIN, December 1950. (Canadian Forces Photograph PL-112097)

Gibbs and Glaister were each awarded the Air Force Cross on September 15, 1951. Also honoured was Sergeant Delbert Wright of Vancouver, the leader of the para-rescue team, who received a British Empire Medal. The arrival of his men boosted the morale of the survivors. He personally cared for the Dakota's second pilot, who was dying, and afterwards supervised the removal of bodies. Several passengers were evacuated that night, and Wright stayed with the others overnight until the last person had been brought out safely.

Most of the SAR awards for this period went to officers who had considerable wartime experience on twin- and multi-engined aircraft. F/L Donald Reginald Cuthbertson from Brighton, Ontario, was an exception. He had joined the RCAF in May 1941, recived his flying badge in February 1942, then served as an instructor on Harvards until January 1943. Once overseas, he trained as a fighter pilot and flew an extended tour with No. 416 Squadron (Spitfires). During the Normandy campaign he was credited with the destruction of two German fighters plus one damaged.

Cuthbertson remained with the postwar RCAF; we have already met him in connection with Operation MAGNETIC. Afterwards, at Goose Bay, he became a member of the SAR Flight. Copies of signals connect him to missions not otherwise detailed in official records. As co-pilot in a Norseman flown by G/C Leonard J. Birchall (August 23, 1950) he helped evacuate a woman suffering from acute appendicitis from Hopedale Moravian Mission; Leading Aircraftman C.D. McLaughlin was along as crewman. Cuthbertson was alone as pilot on a second flight to the same place (September 5, 1950), evacuating a boy with a fractured arm plus a second patient from Port Harrison. On yet another flight in a Norseman with McLaughlin on September 28, 1950, he evacuated a sick Inuit from Nutuk, 300 miles north of Goose Bay. The return flight was hard due to low clouds over the Labrador hills. Unable to maintain sight of ground, he flew two hours above overcast; approaching Goose Bay Radio Range, he was able to proceed to the Northwest River Grenfell Missions.

This was all "routine"; his most remarkable exploit was on September 28, 1951. Hopedale Mission had asked that a seriously injured civilian be evacuated, and F/L Cuthbertson was the man for the job. Accompanied by LAC McLaughlin, he left Goose Bay in a float-equipped Norseman. The forecast had been bad, and the "met" people had been right. By the time he reached Hopedale strong easterly winds were buffeting the coast, raising five-foot swells. In spite of this, Cuthbertson alighted successfully and emplaned the patient. Just as he was about to depart, another emergency call was delivered. A youth at Makkovik, some 60 miles southeast of Hopedale, had been mauled by huskies and was in critical condition; air transportation to the nearest hospital was urgently requested. Cuthbertson and his crewman, plus the first patient, took off for Makkovik, knowing the wind and water conditions would be equally bad. He landed there without mishap, but, just as the critically injured youngster was placed on board the aircraft, a heavy bank of fog rolled in. Cuthbertson had to take off under a ceiling of only one hundred feet. He returned to Goose Bay in below-freezing temperatures. Twice the engine faltered with carburettor icing, and radio static made radio communications impossible for most of the time. Nevertheless, Cuthertson maintained a steady course, arriving at base amidst heavy thundershowers, an indefinite ceiling of 300 feet and visibility varying from one quarter to one-half mile. He touched down in Goose Bay harbour using a let-down procedure he had worked out himself for such an emergency.

Four days later he was airborne in the Norseman on another mercy flight. His crewman on this occasion was Leading Aircraftman John Warren Malo (Taber, Alberta). Their destination was Saglek Bay, some 375 miles up the bleak Labrador coast, to evacuate a civilian who was in critical condition due to frost-bitten and gangrenous feet. The trip was made with a strong northeast wind blowing, a 500-foot ceiling at Saglek Bay and clouds close to ground level for most of the route. On arrival they faced wearily familiar conditions – heavy swells were rolling into Saglek Bay with waves four to six feet high breaking over the mooring buoy. Cuthbertson completed a successful landing but securing the aircraft was a challenge. LAC Malo tied a rope around his waist and perched on one float to moor the Norseman to a buoy. Twice he was washed off the float and immersed in near-freezing water. Each time he climbed back on the float. On the third try he succeeded.

As the patient was being loaded on the aircraft, it was discovered that the right float had sprung and was leaking badly. Cuthbertson took off immediately in the same heavy sea conditions. After 7 hours and 30 minutes of rough instrument flying and a landing and take-off in practically impossible conditions, the weary crew and patient arrived safely at Goose Bay. Cuthbertson's AFC capped two seasons of SAR work; LAC Malo was accorded a Queen's Commendation for Brave Conduct.

Almost five years passed before another SAR AFC was awarded, this one to F/L Andrew G. Carswell. Born in Bishop, California, in May 1923, he had been residing in Toronto when he joined the RCAF in 1941. He flew with Bomber Command, was shot down and taken prisoner. He left the force in September 1945 but rejoined in November 1948; his first major assignment had been the 1949 portion of MAGNETIC. In 1951 he joined No. 123 Search and Rescue Unit at Sea Island (Vancouver). Occasionally he flew Lancasters on supply drops for army exercises, but his chief duties were as an SAR pilot. His vehicle in this role was the aging Canso.

Carswell was marked out for distinction by two missions.

On June 28, 1956, he landed Canso 11100 in strong winds and heavy seas near Galiano Island to rescue two fishermen from a sinking vessel. He manoeuvred the aircraft into a position where the men could board. The takeoff in rough waves was particularly hazardous as the aircraft had been severely damaged by heavy seas while landing and was shipping water faster than could be handled by the pumps. He flew the survivors to Sea Island without further incident. His flight engineer, Sergeant Ian J. McPherson, had performed heroically with one hand in a cast; perched on the pitching Canso wingtip, McPherson had thrown a line to the fishermen, then kept tension on the rope as they were hauled to safety. Recommended for an Air Force Medal, McPherson was ultimately awarded a British Empire Medal.[23]

On September 6 of the same year, Carswell landed a Canso aircraft (serial 11087) at sea some 600 miles off the West Coast of Vancouver Island to remove a critically ill crewman of the weather ship *St. Catharines*. With considerable difficulty the seaman was transferred to the aircraft and with JATO the Canso became airborne, returning to Victoria, where the man was transferred to hospital. Doctors stated that had the patient not been evacuated by air, he would have failed to survive a sea voyage to Victoria. The citation to his AFC declared, "Flight Lieutenant Carswell's courage, devotion to duty, and skill have served as an inspiration and fine example to fellow aircrew."

The Cansos were finally retired, replaced by the Grumman SA-16 Albatross. On the morning of February 20, 1964, No. 103 SAR Flight, Greenwood, despatched an aircraft to search for a missing seal hunter, Albert Muise, in the Gulf of St.Lawrence. Charlottetown reported the ceiling as 1,000 to 1,500 feet, visibility four miles in light snow showers, and winds easterly at 16 mph. Sydney gave the ceiling as 200-400 feet, visibility one mile in light snow with ice pellets. As so often happened, the search had been launched even as the weather deteriorated.

F/L Raymond William Cass, a veteran of 22 years service with the RCAF, was piloting Albatross 9308. After an extended search, he and his co-pilot simultaneously spotted their man on a large ice pan floating amid hundreds of smaller floes. Cass reported his sighting; the Rescue Co-ordination Centre ordered him to return to base; the weather was worsening and an ice-breaker would make the final pick-up in about six hours. It appeared that the ice pan was breaking up and that Muise would not have six hours. Dropping an emergency kit would serve no useful purpose. Later, Muise confirmed these observations in an affidavit: "The ice was breaking up fast and even the seals were leaving; if I had been there for one hour more I would have been a goner."

Cass made 12 passes over the scene, intent on a rescue but meanwhile polling his crew about their assessment. That in itself united all behind him. F/L Dwight W. Rhodes, the navigator, described the effect of the polling: "His deliberate manner and this obvious consideration for the safety of those with him did much to instil a sense of confidence in his crew which unanimously agreed with his decision." Dodging ice floes and fighting a three-foot chop, Cass put the Albatross down. However, once on the water he could not easily manoeuvre. The next stage was up to Corporal Phillip E. Blank, who launched a rubber boat secured by a line in the direction of Muise's ice pan. Here were further dangers; the boat might be punctured or the line might break and set Blank adrift. The craft's outboard motor was swamped and died. Using paddles, Blank rowed, steered and fended off threatening chucks of ice. Muise finally jumped alongside the boat and was pulled in; after that the Albatross crew reeled the craft back to the aircraft.

Once more, Cass had to use all his skills to dodge floes and take off in heavy seas. He succeeded in what the station CO, G/C R.A. Gordon, later described as a "peerless demonstration of professional flying skill of the highest order." Cass had earned his AFC; Corporal Blank was awarded a British Empire Medal. Nevertheless, when the RCAF chose to cut aircrew later that year, Cass was among those later dubbed the "Hellyer 500."

The last two Air Force Crosses awarded to RCAF personnel were announced on July 29, 1966 – one to a fighter pilot, F/L Kenneth A. Harvey (whose exploit is described further on), and one to an SAR pilot, F/L Daniel Michael Campbell, employing the latest in rescue technology, a Labrador helicopter.

Dan Campbell's exploit was merely the highlight of an illustrious career. He had joined the RCAF in 1948 at the age of 18, having gone solo in a Tiger Moth with the Air Cadet squadron in Saskatoon. Joining No. 123 SAR Flight in March 1949, he became a specialist in the work, flying Canso, Norseman and Lancaster aircraft before learning to fly S-51 helicopters in 1953. Between July 1955 and December 1957 he had operated "choppers" with No. 108 Communications Flight, already described in the context of Bob Heaslip. Back on the Pacific Coast with No. 121 Communications Flight, he flew numerous rescue and mercy flights over mountains and salt water. In January 1962 he and his crew rescued 22 seamen from a grounded Greek freighter in a 50-knot gale. In April 1965 he co-operated with the National Geographic Society and Senator Robert Kennedy when the latter was climbing an Alaskan mountain

F/L Raymond W. Cass, who polled his crew before putting an Albatross down on ice-clogged water to rescue a seal hunter, February 1964.

that had been named for President John F. Kennedy. In the course of this he had landed on Mount Hubbard (Yukon Territory) in a CH-113; at 14,950 feet it was the highest helicopter landing in Canada as of that date. Two months later came the feat for which he was decorated.

A civilian aircraft had crashed in forested mountains near Bramfield, Vancouver Island. Two survivors walked out of the bush, reporting injured colleagues still on site, but they were vague as to exactly where the accident had occurred. Just at sundown of July 18, 1965, the tail section of the aircraft was spotted lodged in the top of tall timber. Darkness was fast approaching as F/L Campbell manoeuvred his "chopper" (Labrador 10402) over the crash site to lower a doctor. The AFC citation is eloquent in its description of subsequent events:

… When the first man was lowered it was found that at the full extent of the hoist cable he was some 20 feet from the ground, due to the height of the timber, the gradient of the mountain slope and the limited length of the hoist cable. It was then necessary for Flight Lieutenant Campbell, if he were to effect a rescue, to nestle the helicopter fuselage in the tree tops. With extraordinary skill, he nestled the helicopter fuselage into the tree tops, successfully lowering the rescue team and their equipment.

To ensure a safe fuel supply and the success of the rescue operation, Flight Lieutenant Campbell then returned to base and although now midnight returned to the crash scene determined to complete the rescue. Again he nestled the helicopter fuselage in the tree tops and safely hoisted the survivors and rescue team to safety.

Had Flight Lieutenant Campbell not completed the rescue that night, rain and fog later closed the area to search aircraft until 21 July, 1965, it is doubtful if one of the injured survivors could have survived another night of exposure as, besides suffering burns to the upper part of his body a lacerated knee and a possible back injury, he was also in a state of shock.

During the entire rescue mission Flight Lieutenant Campbell faced grave personal danger when nestling the fuselage in the trees, as any sudden change of wind could easily have caused the helicopter to crash causing undetermined injury or death to himself and others. This officer's calm professional approach, exceptionally fine airmanship, courage and devotion to duty in an extremely critical situation were major factors in saving human lives.

Campbell remained with No. 121 Communications Flight until August 1967. Posted to Trenton, he developed and promoted a "Defensive Flying Programme" for civilian pilots. For this he received the Gordon McGregor Memorial Trophy for "outstanding efforts and achievements in the field of flight safety and accident prevention." With No. 413 Squadron, Summerside, he continued flying SAR missions; in December 1972 he plucked 13 crewmen from a sinking ship. One year later he was appointed an Officer in the Order of Military Merit. As a major in National Defence Headquarters, he continued to promote flight safety and SAR training until he retired in October 1977.

It is worth noting that the RCAF was not alone in SAR operations, but only RCAF personnel received AFCs and AFMs.

F/L Daniel Campbell in the Labrador helicopter flown during his AFC exploit of June 1965. (Canadian Forces Photograph PL-123757)

Major Dan Campbell, AFC, is invested with the Order of Military Merit by Governor-General Jules Léger, December 1973. Campbell made SAR work his career specialty. (Canadian Forces Photograph IS 74-236)

There was no RCN equivalent of these, although naval aircrews engaged in similar work (helicopter rescues) secured other awards, from Commendations to George Medals.[24]

The case of Lieutenant Wallace Elmer James is worth reciting as one of only two members of the RCN even *recommended* for an Air Force Cross. Two hours before dawn of October 26, 1954, he and a crewman took off in a HUP-3 helicopter (serial number 51-16621) from HMCS *Shearwater*, the naval air base at Halifax. Their mission was to rescue the injured light keeper of St. Paul's Island, who had been caught by a dynamite explosion, sustaining a fractured skull and lacerated arm. They landed at Sydney, picked up a doctor, then headed for the island in the teeth of 25-knot winds, turbulence and snow flurries that thickened until visibility was reduced to a quarter of a mile. Arriving at St. Paul's Island, James alighted in a small valley

(Left) Lieutenant-Commander Wallace E. James, MBE. As an RCN Lieutenant and helicopter pilot, he was recommended for an AFC following a 1954 rescue from St. Paul's Island. Although naval authorities concurred throughout the process, an MBE was substituted for an AFC at the last moment. (Canadian Forces Photograph E.56530)

(Below) A Navy HUP-3 helicopter, the type used by Lieutenant James in his rescue flight. (Canadian Forces Photograph E.59522)

which actually funnelled the winds onto his chopper. He kept the rotors turning 45 minutes while the doctor treated and retrieved his patient. They returned to Sydney on instruments without incident; the mission had taken eight and a half hours of arduous flying.

The Flag Officer, Atlantic Coast, reported Lieutenant James's

feat without suggesting a specific decoration. The Personnel Members Committee, Department of National Defence, meeting on February 25, 1955, and using previous awards as a yardstick, suggested an Air Force Cross. On March 22, 1955, the Awards Co-Ordination Committee agreed; an Inter-Service Awards Committee session, held on April 20, 1955, also concurred in recommending an AFC. All these bodies included RCN representation. However, at some point thereafter (probably at the level of Government House), an MBE was substituted for an AFC; Lieutenant James's award was gazetted on June 4, 1955.[25]

Mercy and SAR flights were sometimes dramatic, and those which resulted in rare decorations for personnel were particularly so. Nevertheless, most such flights were routine affairs, undertaken with cool professionalism. Nothing illustrates this better than a message transmitted from the Halifax SAR Centre to AFHQ on March 22, 1948; the crew are not even identified:

REPORT ON MERCY MISSION TO FORT CHIMO. LANCASTER HELD AT GOOSE BAY DUE TO WEATHER UNTIL EARLY MORNING 21 MARCH AT WHICH DATE AIRCRAFT COMPLETED FLIGHT HAVING EVACUATED TEN ESKIMOS AND INDIANS. NINE OF THE MOST SERIOUS CASES WERE BROUGHT TO HALIFAX FOR HOSPITALIZATION AT HMCS STADACONA. TWO WERE STRETCHER CASES AND THEIR ILLNESS UNCERTAIN. AN RCMP CONSTABLE ONE DOCTOR AND NURSE ACCOMPANIED AIRCRAFT. BECAUSE OF THE LANCASTER THE TRIP WAS MADE IN SHORT TIME OF TEN HOURS. CASE CLOSED.[26]

OPERATION HAWK – NO. 426 SQUADRON ON THE PACIFIC AIRLIFT[27]

The less mobile means of mundane transportation must, for the most part, inevitably give way to these winged carriers of the sky. Such is the law of evolution – the order of the universe.

– "J.A.P.," WRITING IN CADET WING REVIEW, LONG BRANCH, ONTARIO, NOVEMBER 1918

There must be great care taken to send us munition and victual whithersoever the enemy goeth.

– SIR FRANCIS DRAKE TO LORD WALSYNGHAM DURING OPERATIONS AGAINST THE SPANISH ARMADA, JULY 29, 1588

The RCAF's most sustained and significant contribution to the Korean War was made by No. 426 Squadron. As of June 1950 this was the only long-range transport unit in the force; it had been busy earlier that year with Operation REDRAMP (flood relief in Manitoba). When news of the war's outbreak reached No. 426, personnel sensed they would be involved. However, it was only on July 20, 1950, that the unit was ordered to prepare six North Stars with crews and technicians for trans-Pacific operations. The official announcement came on the 21st; on the 23rd the unit diarist noted that Dorval and Lachine had been inundated with "a plague of newspaper reporters, radio announcers, etc." The first six North Stars departed Dorval on the 25th, carrying double crews, 185 ground crewmen and 25 tons of logistical supplies. They flew in formation to Ottawa, where they passed over the Peace Tower, dipping their wings in salute; the body of former Prime Minister Mackenzie King was at that time lying in state in the Parliament Buildings. They continued in formation to Toronto, but proceeded independently after that.

No. 426 Squadron established its West Coast base at McChord Field, Tacoma, Washington, the hub of the USAF's Military Air Transport Service (MATS). Three North Stars departed Tacoma on July 27, arriving at Hanada (Tokyo) two days later; flying time was just under 28 hours one way. For a time it was hoped that the unit could despatch one sortie per day, but this proved beyond the resources of a six-plane outfit. Eventually, No. 426 found it could send off five aircraft per week. On December 3, 1950, the squadron reported its 100th departure for Japan.

A North Star engaged in Operation HAWK, the RCAF's major contribution to operations associated with the Korean War (Canadian Forces Photograph PL-50716)

The varying fortunes of UN forces affected No. 426 Squadron's expectations. On October 17, 1950, with MacArthur's armies apparently winning, personnel speculated that Operation HAWK might soon be ended. By November 9, however, the unit diarist recorded "reversals on the war front," and on December 6 there was speculation that "serious reverses" would compel No. 426 to move its forward base to Japan in anticipation of massive airlift evacuation from Korea itself. Fortunately the situation never became so grave, and No. 426 continued to operate between Tacoma and Tokyo. When the front stabilized in June 1951, airlift requirements declined. This was fortunate, for No. 426 continued to be involved in other tasks, including Arctic resupply, mercy flights and trans-Atlantic transport.

The Korean Airlift brought No. 426 into close and cordial

contact with its USAF counterparts. When MATS despatched its 1,000th sortie from McChord Field (February 4, 1951), an RCAF aircraft was accorded the honour. In May 1951, personnel at Tacoma participated in U.S. Armed Forces Week, culminating in a joint parade through the city. On this occasion, No. 426 provided 50 airmen marching seven-deep (non-standard RCAF procedure) behind an ensign that had been stitched together for the occasion by S/L L.W. Queale and his wife. The unit diarist wryly noted: "It was realized that marching 'seven deep' and flaunting a makeshift pennant were quite unorthodox as far as the RCAF was concerned but it was a case of 'When in Rome – do as the Romans do.'"

For most of Operation HAWK the North Stars flew a northern Pacific route – McChord, Elmendorf, Shemya and Hanada. Alternative fields were used at Adak and Missawa. A few trips were made via the central and south Pacific, but these encountered stronger headwinds. Early in the operation, when trained personnel were in short supply, some crews flew 155 hours a month, almost all of it above cloud. MATS recognized this to be excessive and set a limit of 110 hours a month for crews.[28]

Unfortunately the records are vague as to exactly what was carried from sortie to sortie. When HAWK was wound up on June 9, 1954, the RCAF announced that No. 426 Squadron had flown 599 round trips (four of them directly to Korea itself), logged 34,000 flying hours, carried 13,000 personnel and airlifted 3,500 tons of freight. There is almost nothing to indicate how much Canadian freight was carried as opposed to American materiel. Rarely did the unit's documents give a closer glimpse. An exception was a report filed for April 1951 (before Canada's 25th Infantry Brigade had fully deployed to Korea): "April was a big month in the carrying of evacuees from the Far East. A total of 235 were carried from Itami to Hickam, 19 from Itami to Haneda, 57 from Hickam to Travis. No Canadian Army personnel were airlifted to or from the Far East."[29]

If Operation HAWK was poorly documented in terms of statistics, we do have a contemporary account of the work in progress, as viewed both by the aircrews and their passengers:

Every morning Canadian ground crews applied the final tune-up to one of the North Stars. The pilots, navigator and radio officer received their briefing. The olive-clad troops heading for the Korean battle front smoked their last cigarette before gathering up their rifles and bulky army equipment and climbing into the big plane. Soon they were airborne, heading across desolate mountain terrain for Anchorage in Alaska where a fresh crew was waiting to take over without delay for the next leg of the flight to Shemya in the Aleutians. This was the worst part of the whole flight as far as weather was concerned. Even in summer flying conditions over the Aleutians were bad and in winter they were much worse. Shemya was perpetually blanketed in pea-soup fog and ground control approach was used on nearly every landing. Fortunately the USAF had its most experienced ground-control approach crews stationed there.

At Shemya the crew and passengers stretched their legs, breathed in the fish-foul air and walked to the dimly-lit Quonset-hut mess for a quick meal. After the big transport plane had been fuelled and serviced, a fresh crew took over to fly the 2,100-mile haul to Tokyo. For the navigator this was the busiest part of the flight for continuous fixes were sent out to let the ground stations know the aircraft position along the route. Depending on wind and load conditions the planes went either to Missawa in northern Japan and then to Haneda Airfield or else directly to Haneda. Here the technicians prepared the North Star for its long return journey while the crew enjoyed a 48-hour rest in To-kyo.[30]

Operation HAWK was conducted with no fatalities, but there were some close calls. On April 15, 1951, North Star 17509 (F/L J.A. Watt and crew) was cleared by Ashiya tower to descend from 4,000 to 3,000 feet prior to landing. At 3,400 feet the aircraft hit trees atop a hill that was not even indicated on the airfield map. No one was injured but the aircraft sustained considerable damage to its nose, oil cooler and exterior radio aerials. On the night of December 27 1953, North Star 17505 crashed at Shemya, Alaska, on the homeward run. The aircraft was landing in a 50-knot crosswind and blowing snow. Runway ice reduced braking action and high gusts blew the North Star off the runway into a gulley.[31]

In the course of HAWK, 22 members of No. 426 Squadron received formal recognition in the form of one OBE (W/C C.H. Mussells, DSO, DFC, the commanding officer for most of the operation), one MBE (S/L W.H. Lord, chief technical officer at the outset), four AFCs, two AFMs, two BEMs (Flight Sergeant A.L. Engelbert and Corporal J.B.P.A. Trudel, both of the Ground Servicing Echelon) and 12 Commendations for Valuable Services in the Air.[32]

Given that HAWK was flown in support of a war, the standards governing awards had been relaxed to allow "service" honours to be granted in addition to "gallantry" awards (hence the OBE, MBE and BEMs which were for administrative or technical work apart from flying; at least one of the Commendations appears to have been for duties other than flying). Even so, the RCAF kept a relatively tight rein on decorations. British and Australian air force units operating in and around Korea were permitted "periodic" awards based on flying hours (the system used during the Second World War).

Canada could have participated in the same generous rationing scheme, but apparently chose not to do so. In August 1952, for example, a departmental committee dealing with non-combat Korea awards reduced an "Approved Scale" of 6 AFCs, 6 AFMs, 2 OBEs, 2 BEMS and 12 RCAF Commendations (a total of 28 potential awards) to 4 AFCs and AFMs plus 1 OBE, 1 BEM and 6 Commendations (total of 12); between then and June 1953 there were only 9 awards of all types to No. 426 Squadron personnel. In August 1953, with the fighting over but freighting continuing, another committee suggested a further 2 AFCs and AFMs plus 3 Commendations for the squadron, but no more awards were forthcoming.[33]

None of the gallantry awards granted in connection with HAWK arose from such white-knuckle exploits as were displayed in most other AFC and AFM incidents between 1947 and 1966. The RCAF had reverted – with HAWK alone – to granting "service" flying awards issued in clumps. Even so, the standards for being recommended were very high, as evidenced by the limited number of decorations granted (probably no more than 5 per cent of the aircrew engaged) and the conditions under which they were earned. The plain fact was that HAWK was no piece of cake.

The trans-Pacific Airlift was flown in some of the most appalling weather and airfield conditions in the world. The highest standards of navigation were required; trespassing into Soviet territory would be deadly and sea conditions in the North Pacific were such that a ditching would be a disaster. Virtually every AFC citation relating to HAWK referred to these trying circumstances; that for S/L James D. Dickson (Hammond River and Rothesay, New Brunswick) read, in part:

He has flown a total of 600 hours over the 11,000 nautical mile route, often through hazardous icing and fog condi-

S/L James D. Dickson, DFC, AFC, DFM, died of polio in Britain less than two months after receiving his AFC.

tions, without mishap… His sterling qualities and abilities as a pilot were demonstrated forcibly on a flight from McChord Air Force Base, Washington, to Elmsdorf Air Force Base, Alaska on the 23rd November 1950. As on all trips the aircraft was loaded with troops and vital supplies for the United Nations' effort in Korea. After completing two hours of the eight hour flight the aircraft encountered most severe icing conditions and head winds. In spite of the weather, Squadron Leader Dickson completed his flight, landing at his destination in a 74-knot gale. All other aircraft flying the route that encountered the same conditions, with the exception of another RCAF aircraft, aborted and returned to their points of departure. Had it not been for the superior skill and determination shown by this officer, a vital load would have been delayed….

F/L Robert Martin Edwards (Winnipeg and Lucky Lake, Saskatchewan) was correspondingly cited for his performance on the demanding route:

In his capacity as captain and pilot of North Star aircraft he has in support of the United Nations operations in Korea participated in twenty-six round trips to the Far East over the eleven thousand nautical mile route. Throughout these flights, which have on many occasions necessitated flying

F/L Robert M. Edwards posed in the cockpit of a North Star during Operation HAWK. (Canadian Forces Photograph PL-50553)

through some of the most adverse weather conditions in the world, he has carried out his allotted tasks in an exemplary manner.

S/L Howard Allan Morrison, DSO, DFC, an ex-Pathfinder from Lauder and Winnipeg, Manitoba, had also battled the climate:

As a captain of a North Star aircraft he flew a total of 300 hours from McChord Air Force Base, Washington, over the northern great circle route through the Aleutian chain carrying troops and vital supplies to Japan. These flights were made through weather conditions which are considered to be the worst in the world...

His qualities as a pilot frequently have been demonstrated forcibly. In one instance while carrying a vital load of troops and ammunition between Elmendorf, Alaska and Tokyo, Japan he was forced to carry out an approach and landing with assistance of GCA in the most adverse weather conditions. The visibility and ceiling were reported as being less than 1/8 mile and fifty feet...

F/O Donald Melvin Payne, DFC (Toronto and Hamilton) needed all his skills as an instrument flying specialist:

Flying Officer Payne ... flew approximately 500 hours over the great circle route through the Aleutian chain to Japan carrying troops and vital supplies. Frequently these flights were flown through hazardous weather conditions which are considered to be the worst in the world. His exceptional ability, resourcefulness and leadership were instrumental in the completion of these missions without mishap.

These qualities were demonstrated forcibly on a flight from Shemya in the Aleutians to Tokyo, Japan on the 2nd

G/C Harold A. Morrison, DSO, DFC, AFC, who abandoned medical studies to fight a war and subsequently made the RCAF his career. The eagle on his tunic denotes that he flew Pathfinder aircraft during the Second World War, in which role he had been twice decorated. His later career included duty in the Congo and with NORAD. (Canadian Forces Photograph PL-86532)

October, 1950. When approximately 700 miles southwest of Shemya the number three engine of the aircraft he was flying suddenly went out of control; attempts to feather it proved useless and the only means of reducing the RPM was by decreasing speed. When it became apparent that either the propeller or complete engine assembly might break loose at any moment, Flying Officer Payne sent out a distress signal and prepared his crew for ditching. However, as a result of his outstanding ability, he was able to keep the aircraft airborne without further damage, allowing him to return to Shemya. Had it not been for the superior skill and resourcefulness shown by this officer, a valuable aircraft and crew might have been lost.

The two Air Force Medals awarded during HAWK were both to non-commissioned flight engineers. Flight Sergeant Alfred Arthur Drackley of Birsay, Saskatchewan, had begun his air force career in June 1940; as a mechanic he had accompanied a Stranraer surveying Labrador airfields. Late in 1942 he had remustered to flight engineer. In Eastern Air Command squadrons he flew on 116 sorties (1,311 operational hours), for which he qualified for an Operations Wing with Bar. His postwar service included a stretch with No. 103 Rescue Unit; his post-Korea service would take him to the Middle East with UN peacekeeping units. The citation to his AFM also stressed the importance of his job owing to the weather encountered:

Flight Sergeant Drackley has served on the Korean Airlift since its inception as a Flight Engineer on North Star aircraft, having been attached to the Military Air Transport Service, USAF, on 26 July 1950. He has flown a total of over 400 hours in the Pacific.

On many occasions hazardous weather conditions have been encountered and it was necessary to do instrument let downs or land with the aid of GCA at the destination.

North Star transports entered RCAF service in 1947 and were finally retired in 1966. Apart from Operation HAWK, they were used around the world, sometimes carrying Canadian politicians (and always the Canadian flag) to every continent except Antarctica. The last North Star is now rusting away outside the National Aviation Museum, a victim of governments that have neglected to supply the museum with the facilities befitting a national institution.

Flight Sergeant Drackley's experience, efficiency and co-operation with the captain of his aircraft during these emergencies were in a large part responsible for the success of the operation.

In the performance of his duties Flight Sergeant Drackley has set an example for all airmen by his devotion and loyalty to duty. This non-commissioned officer through his trade proficiency and advice has been instrumental in maintaining a tight route schedule which resulted in a high aircraft utilization and thus increased the squadron's ability to carry vital personnel and material over the 11,000 mile Pacific route…

Corporal Gerald Rexford Reed (North Bay, Ontario) had joined the RCAF in 1943. The citation to his AFM also mentioned weather, but the award was more specific with respect to a particular feat he had performed in the course of HAWK:

Corporal Reed has, during his tour of duty with 426 Transport Squadron on the Korean Airlift, participated in thirty-seven round trips to the Far East, in support of the United Nations operations in Korea. Throughout these trips he has exhibited exceptional skill as a flight engineer and technician. On a flight between Shemya, Alaska and Misawa, Japan, he displayed a typical example of his resourcefulness. This particular flight had taken unduly long as a result of the loss of an engine en route and excessive head winds. Due to a mechanical failure, the nose wheel became damaged on landing at Misawa and the flight was unable to proceed to Tokyo as scheduled.

Unable to obtain the necessary replacement parts and despite the fact he had been on duty for approximately sixteen hours, Corporal Reed proceeded to manufacture the replacement brackets required, carried out retraction tests and finished off the remaining necessary adjustments practically single handed. The aircraft was then able to proceed to Tokyo where permanent repairs were effected. Corporal Reed has been responsible on numerous occasions for keeping his aircraft serviceable under adverse conditions by dint of hard work and constant, unswerving devotion to duty.

As mentioned, HAWK was but one task performed by No. 426 Squadron during this period. RCAF signal traffic reveals that at least one significant mercy mission was undertaken by F/O Payne between trans-Pacific flights. In December 1950 an urgent call reached Lachine; a boy at Lake Harbour, Baffin Island, had contracted double pneumonia and oxygen equipment was needed to save him. The apparatus was flown to Goose Bay, where it was packed for a parachute drop by Corporal R.H. Crebo (Moose Jaw, Saskatchewan), a para-rescue technician who accompanied the mission and supervised the drop. F/O Payne had been detailed for a re-supply sortie to Frobisher Bay; the drop at Lake Harbour was a mere detour. It was executed on December 28 with great precision; the package floated down within 100 yards of the hospital door and was in use within half an hour. Such incidents showed the versatility of RCAF crews.

FIGHTER AWARDS

Gloucester, 'tis true that we are in great danger;
The greater therefore should our courage be.

– WILLIAM SHAKESPEARE, *KING HENRY V*

Seven rare postwar Air Force Cross awards went to members of RCAF fighter squadrons (five pilots, two navigators). Each incident had a common thread – a refusal to abandon a comrade or an aircraft in circumstances where the nominee had free choice but where the possibilities of greater disasters were present. The first of these involved F/O Sydney Edward Burrows of Burnaby, British Columbia. He had enlisted in 1951 and earned his wings the following year. After gunnery training at Macdonald, Manitoba, and attendance at No. 1 (Fighter) Operational Training Unit (Chatham, New Brunswick), Burrows was posted overseas, flying Sabres with No. 434 Squadron out of Zweibrucken, Germany.

On September 13, 1954, he was one of four pilots flying a routine exercise. Some 20 miles from base he sustained a bird strike which shattered his canopy. Fragments of perspex were imbedded in his face and left eye. The citation to his award takes up the story:

> Partially blinded and covered with blood, this pilot retained control of his aircraft and quickly gave the international distress call of "Mayday." He then had to tear off his helmet to clear his face and eyes, thus leaving him with no radio communications. The section leader, on determining the emergency, assigned a wing man to lead Flying Officer Burrows to 4 (Fighter) Wing. Although Burrows was losing blood, suffering great pain and shock, and almost completely blinded by perspex and blood, he safely executed a wheels down landing on the aerodrome. He then taxied his aircraft clear of the runway to enable the remainder of the formation to land. He was lifted from his aircraft and taken to the Wing Hospital for emergency treatment. This young officer, instead of parachuting to safety and losing his aircraft, demonstrated extreme courage and devotion to duty in flying his aircraft back to base to carry out a safe landing while suffering extensive pain and being almost totally blind.

Following the accident, Burrows was assessed as having monocular vision and was grounded; he was assigned Flying Control duties. Refusing to accept this, he lobbied and finally regained his flying category on T-33 and Dakota navigational training aircraft. In 1968 he was appointed CO of No. 440 (Rescue) Squadron. In 1971 he went to No. 424 Squadron Detachment, UN forces, Srinagar, Kashmir, flying a Twin Otter in stages from Trenton to Kashmir. Later he became base operations

F/O Sidney E. Burrows, AFC with a friend, Mrs. Doris Cunningham, just after his investiture. His vision impaired following his AFC exploit, Burrows managed to struggle back to aircrew status. (Canadian Forces Photograph PL-102970)

CF-100s of No. 419 Squadron, similar to the aircraft piloted by F/O Lloyd Thomas Ross when he earned an AFC (Canadian Force Photograph PL-101496)

officer, Station Comox. Burrows retired from the forces in September 1982.

F/O Lloyd Thomas Ross had flown anti-submarine patrols and Canadian-based transport sorties during the Second World War. Demobilized after the war, he rejoined the RCAF in 1951. In April 1955 he joined No. 433 Squadron (CF-100s) at Cold Lake. The squadron subsequently moved to North Bay. Soon afterwards, Ross transferred to No. 419 Squadron, also flying "Clunks" out of North Bay. Ominously, on Friday the 13th (July 1956) he was on a training mission (aircraft 18504) with F/O J.C. Carter in the back seat. While climbing in dense cloud at about 20,000 feet, a heavy explosion occurred in the port engine. The top engine covering was blown off and a fierce fire developed. Ross coolly hit the extinguishers. Although he could not be sure that the fire had been put out, he decided against abandoning the aircraft. He was flying close to North Bay and its populated districts, so his decision probably saved civilian lives.

F/O Ross had difficulty approaching his base due to unreliable ground radar assistance and an erratic aircraft radio compass caused by atmospheric effects. He was flying in solid cloud on instruments, a particularly noteworthy feat because of the considerable weight differential in fuel loads in the two wings, the port engine having been shut down at the time of the explosion. The cloud base was very low on his return and eventually he was forced to make three landing attempts before achieving success.

G/C H.L. Ledoux, CO of Station North Bay, recommended an AFC on September 11; the collection of affidavits concluded on October 30, after which the paperwork moved slowly through departmental channels. Ross was awarded his AFC in March 1957. The citation, after describing his exploit in detail, concluded by saying:

It is considered that Flying Officer Ross' courage, presence of mind and exceptional airmanship resulted in the possible saving of lives, and certainly in the saving of a costly aircraft which he could have abandoned without fear of criticism. He is a most competent and reliable pilot, and his devotion to duty has served as an inspiration and fine example to fellow aircrew.

Ross, in fact, was a true professional. In the original recommendation for this award, G/C Ledoux noted that Ross had previously made *three* single-engine landings after engine failure in twin-jet aircraft.

F/O Charles Maxwell Alexander, a radar officer and navigator, had been born in Scotland and spent six years in the Royal Air Force before switching to the RCAF in Toronto in 1956. He was posted to No. 433 Squadron in December 1957. During an exercise dubbed "Catseye 18" he showed great presence of mind that saved the life of his pilot, F/O W.G. Richards, as well as their aircraft (CF-100 18767). The officer who later drafted his AFC citation showed great literary skill in the process:

F/O Charles M. Alexander, AFC, whose courage in a CF-100 saved his pilot and aircraft in May 1965. (Canadian Forces Photograph PL-133660)

During an Air Defence Exercise on May 24, 1960, Flying Officer Alexander was the navigator in a CF-100 aircraft which was participating in an aircraft interception at 43,000 feet. Shortly thereafter, the pilot of the aircraft suffered extreme anoxia [oxygen starvation]. He was receiving no oxygen whatsoever as the result of a fault in his oxygen system.

Flying Officer Alexander instructed the pilot to descend. The pilot responded and commenced an immediate descent but could not actuate his emergency oxygen supply. Flying Officer Alexander elected to remain with the aircraft and continue to talk the pilot into bringing the aircraft under control from an extremely erratic descent. Flying Officer Alexander noted at one point that their speed was 650 knots and they then entered the cloud deck at 7,000 feet still in a dive.

The pilot gradually responded to instructions and pulled the aircraft out of the dive but the aircraft ended up in an inverted position. Flying Officer Alexander then successfully managed to instruct the pilot to roll the aircraft into a straight and level flight at approximately 10,000 feet.

A ground control landing approach was then commenced. The pilot did not respond to instructions given by the GCA Controller and it was necessary for Flying Officer Alexander to guide the pilot all the way down. The pilot was still under the effects of anoxia upon landing to the extent that he did not round out but flew onto the runway. It was also necessary for Flying Officer Alexander to instruct him on braking action and direction. After a successful landing, the

pilot remembered practically nothing of what had taken place.

Flying Officer Alexander, when faced with the decision of ejecting or remaining with the aircraft, chose to remain in an effort to save his pilot and aircraft. Through coolness and devotion to duty he managed to avert what would have been a fatal accident.

F/O Clive Batcock and his wife outside Buckingham Palace, February 1961. The setting was unusual; most postwar Canadian AFC recipients were presented with their decorations in Canada, but his duties had taken him to Europe and made possible a Royal ceremony. (Canadian Forces Photograph PL-132034)

F/O Clive Charles Batcock of No. 422 Squadron was awarded an AFC at the same time as F/O Alexander. On March 2, 1960, he had been flying a Sabre (serial number 23739) at 42,000 feet and was 50 miles from base (Baden-Soellingen) when his engine failed. He chose to descend through 25,000 feet of solid cloud mixed with frequent rain rather than abandon his aircraft. His was an instance of steely nerves buttressed by a sense of responsibility. He was helped by the approach controller (F/L R.P. Patterson), assistant GCA controller (FS Ken MacMillan) and his own flight leader (F/O Peter Zinkan), all of whom were commended for valuable services.

S/L (later W/C) Joseph Armand Gerard Fernand Villeneuve of Buckingham, Quebec, was the best-known of the post-war fighter AFC winners, thanks to a long association with the "Golden Hawks" aerobatic team. As of 1960 he was on the staff of No. 1

(Fighter) Operational Training Unit, Chatham, New Brunswick. On the night of November 7, 1960, he was practising night circuits on Sabre 23001. He had just completed an overshoot and was midway between base and the town of Newcastle when he experienced rapid deceleration and possible engine failure. Risking a stall, he turned away from the built-up area, preparing to eject. This plan was changed abruptly when he smelled something burning and saw sparks streaming from the tailpipe.

Villeneuve flamed out his engine. By now he was heading for another populated area. He abandoned all thought of baling out; with hydraulics gone he wrestled the Sabre back to Chatham airfield, manually lowering wheels and flaps and deploying dive brakes. Just as

The swept-wing North American F-86 Sabre was a superb fighter airplane; Canadian-built versions with the Orenda engine were even better. The RCAF's "Sabre Years" (1951-1963) were a golden age, epitomized by the respect paid No. 1 Air Division in Europe and the "Golden Hawk" aerobatic team at home. (DND)

he touched down the controls failed altogether. The Sabre hit hard and bounced; he levelled the wings using coarse rudder before the second impact. The aircraft skidded along the runway on fire; he jettisoned the canopy and escaped with a compression fracture of the spine. In the words of the citation:

> Squadron Leader Villeneuve's skill, courage and determination in landing his aircraft rather than ejecting precluded the possibility of the aircraft crashing into a built-up area with tragic results. The actions of Squadron Leader Villeneuve were in keeping with the highest traditions of the Royal Canadian Air Force.

Times changed and so did aircraft; the "Clunk" was succeeded in Air Defence Command by the CF-101B Voodoo. On the morning of April 10, 1963, F/O Donald Franklin Parker was the navigator of a CF-101B aircraft (serial number 17463) of No. 416 Squadron participating in a tactical exercise. While attacking a target aircraft at 20,000 feet, Parker was surprised to find his aircraft turning in the wrong direction for the intercept manoeuvre. On querying his pilot (F/K R.C. Hyslop), he concluded from the replies that the pilot was in difficulty – probably anoxia from faulty equipment.

Parker calmly but emphatically directed the pilot to descend and follow emergency oxygen procedures. Nothing happened, and from further remarks made by the pilot, he

S/L J.A.G.F. "Fern" Villenuve, AFC, was best known for his tour with the Golden Hawks aerobatic team, but in November 1960 he showed cool courage by sticking with his crippled Sabre rather than bale out and risk civilian casualties on the ground. (Canadian Forces Photograph PCN 1116)

realized his colleague was seriously ill. He then began to direct the pilot to return to base and prepare to land the aircraft. Although the situation was dangerous, Parker did not even declare an emergency in his radio transmissions lest he unnerve his comrade completely.

Determined to save his friend and the aircraft, he handled all radio transmissions himself. Meanwhile he soothed, persuaded and encouraged the pilot through the approach and landing in less than ideal weather conditions, in spite of Hyslop's uncertain and often incorrect reactions which caused the aircraft to repeatedly approach critical performance limits. Following the landing, the pilot collapsed almost completely and was helpless. F/O Parker climbed forward, shut down the engines and assisted groundcrew and medical personnel in removing the almost unconscious pilot from the cockpit. Again, the formal citation summed up everything:

> Throughout a dangerous situation, Flying Officer Parker demonstrated exceptional courage, devotion to duty and loyalty to his pilot, in hazarding his own life when he might have safely ejected from the aircraft. His cool and skilful direction, which made full use of the pilot's severely limited ability, was instrumental in saving both their lives and a valuable aircraft.

In the case of Parker's award, documents supporting the recommendation included a

CF-101B Voodoo interceptors, the backbone of Canadian participation in North American air defence from 1961 to 1984. The RCAF did not publicize the fact that the type came with nuclear-armed air-to-air missiles.

statement by Hyslop which gave a moving account of the incident from the viewpoint of the incapacitated pilot. He reported that he felt completely aware yet almost totally helpless, "tendency to close eyes although vision was clear," and too weak even to speak.

One thing was clear; it would be absolutely essential for the navigator to remain if the aircraft was to land safely. I wanted him to stay and yet leave when it was necessary but this idea could not be conveyed verbally as informing the navigator or replying to commands became the most diffi-

cult chore. If conditions deteriorated I planned to call "jump jump" as the word "eject" seemed more difficult for me to say. I would like to add that this was the first flight the navigator and pilot had flown as a crew except for a scramble two hours previous to this flight.

As we let down to TACAN initial point and throughout GCA all checks were clearly called out, the navigator's voice was sharp, clear and commanding with a sincere urgency that cut through my drowsiness and resulted in corrections to airspeed, heading and altitude which at times were reaching critical stages.

I have considerable experience as an A-1 crew member and have endured adverse conditions before in company with "the remarkable navigator." My deepest emotions may some day be able to express the gratitude I hold for F/O Don Parker for his actions during this trying situation. In my opinion his courageous effort more than any other factor resulted in the safe landing of crew and aircraft.

We pay our respect for the Third Party that held the end of the string from which we dangled.

The last of the peacetime fighter AFCs went to F/L Kenneth Abraham Harvey for skill and courage displayed on March 5, 1965, at Station Namao (Edmonton). He was attached to an American experimental unit based there and was flying an F-84F close to the city. Ten miles from base the engine began vibrating and emitting loud bangs. Harvey elected for a downwind emergency landing, although the base was still ten miles distant.

Witnesses reported that the F-84F was trailing thick black smoke. Halfway to the field the noise and vibration worsened; then the engine packed up altogether. By now he was over a densely populated area. Using emergency hydraulics, he maintained the approach and completed a smooth landing. With no brakes, the aircraft rolled nearly 10,000 feet before turning off on the high speed cut-off. As it halted, F/L Harvey climbed out and walked calmly to the rear where the tailpipe was still smoking. Professionalism had paid off.[34]

Chapter *7*

A NEW GENERATION OF AWARDS

Some say the age of chivalry is past, that the spirit of romance is dead. The age of chivalry is never past, so long as there is a wrong left unredressed on earth.

– CHARLES KINGSLEY (1819-1875), *LIFE* (1879)

A society which eulogizes the average citizen is one which breeds mediocrity.

– PIERRE ELLIOTT TRUDEAU (1919-2000), SPEAKING IN WINNIPEG, OCTOBER 1971

Desiderantes Meliorem Patriam (They desire to better their country).

– MOTTO OF THE ORDER OF CANADA

It had been suggested from at least 1866 that Canada should have its own system of honours and awards.[1] Such a step would free the country of the restrictions inherent in using British honours. Over the years, many reasons were advanced for a Canadian honours system. Aside from simple nationalism – of "Canadian awards for the sake of their being Canadian" – there were several reasons advanced. Among them were:

Democracy – The British honours system was hierarchial; the same deed that brought one man a Distinguished Flying Cross would bring another man a Distinguished Flying Medal, the difference being rank rather than the quality of the deed. There were exceptions (awards involving the Victoria Cross, George Cross and George Medal were rank-free), but there were other awards where rank determined the award (as with the Order of the British Empire). Britain herself acknowledged this by introducing new, rank-free gallantry awards in the early 1990s.

Related to the above was that Canada, by foreswearing hereditary honours and even non-hereditary knighthoods for its citizens, had excluded its citizens from the highest service honours of the Commonwealth.

Reciprocity was yet another argument for specifically Canadian honours. During the Second World War, foreign governments had recognized Canada's contributions to victory by bestowing their honours upon Canadians. Thus, the Americans could award General Harry Crerar the Legion of Merit (Degree of Commander); Canada could not return the compliment, as the British had already extended their honours to persons such as Bradley and Eisenhower. Yet repeated suggestions from military and cultural leaders that a Canadian honours system be established were ignored by Conservative and Liberal governments alike.

Prime Minister Lester Pearson was much more bold. In responding to nationalism – Canadian and Quebec varieties included – he embarked upon a wholesale "Canadianization" of symbols, including changing the name of the national air carrier (suggested by a back-bench Member of Parliament named Jean Chretien) and introducing the maple leaf flag. In 1967 his government instituted the Order of Canada. This was overhauled in 1972; the Order now exists in three grades (Companion, Officer, Member). Supplementing the Order of Canada was the Order of Military Merit with three grades – Commander, Officer and Member. The two Orders were to be for *service* rather than *courage* – service as defined in contributions to the nation (i.e., distinguished writers such as Robertson Davies) or to humanity (Jean Vanier).

A distinctive Canadian bravery award had been created in 1967, the Medal of Courage, but no standards were laid down to indicate what degree of heroism was required to win it. When the first recommendations were studied, it became evident that a single medal would not suffice where nominees had faced wide ranges of risk. The armed forces sat on some 20 recommendations while seeking clarification. Interested parties urged an enlargement of the awards system.[2]

As Canada moved towards instituting a range of distinct national awards, concerns were raised about the place of traditional honours. Thus, on January 16, 1970, the Minister of National Defence (Leo Cadieux) was asked to give assurances that previously awarded Commonwealth medals would not be classed as "foreign" honours. This he was prepared to do: "There is no intention whatever to downgrade the awards which gallant and brave Canadians have received in the past from the Sovereign on the recommendation of the government of Canada. It is unthinkable that these would ever be regarded as foreign awards."[3]

This was not enough for opposition MPs. John A. McLean (PC, Malpeque), himself an air force veteran with a DFC, probably overstated his fears when he suggested that the Victoria Cross might have to yield precedence to the Canadian Volunteer Service Medal. He further urged that existing Commonwealth decorations for gallantry in peacetime be retained. McLean specifically mentioned the Air Force Cross, but remarked bitterly that the Liberal government, having "done away with the Royal Canadian Air Force," might now be prepared to "do away with the Air Force Cross as well and thus tidy up the matter." In his closing remarks, however, McLean eloquently put the role of military and civil honours in context:

The traditions and practices of a nation in the matter of awards are part of the symbolism which gives its citizens a feeling of belonging to their country or to their brand of civilization. There are many traditions that members of the Commonwealth, especially the older members such as Australia, New Zealand, Canada and Great Britain, have built up together. We as a country will be poorer if we go on tearing them down on the basis of some narrow-minded bigotry growing out of a shortsighted and provincial immaturity.[4]

The new Canadian gallantry decorations were created in 1972 – the Cross of Valour, Star of Courage and Medal of Bravery. The old British awards were not specifically barred (Canadians serving in British formations may still be recommended for British decorations, just as Canadians attached to American units have regularly been awarded American medals). Nevertheless, recommendations for service and gallantry awards initiated in Canada or by Canadians were henceforth submitted under the Canadian system.

The Cross of Valour, Star of Courage and Medal of Bravery have been granted to both military and civilian recipients without distinction; each has been awarded posthumously in several instances. Nevertheless, the evolution of Canadian honours and awards has continued. The Order of Military Merit (in three grades) was created at the same time as the Canadian gallantry awards (1972) to recognize services not necessarily involving physical hazards; it was roughly a military counterpart of the Order of Canada.

On June 11, 1984, Queen Elizabeth II signed Letters Patent creating the Meritorious Service Cross. This was described as being open to all ranks "for the performance of a military deed or a military activity in an outstandingly professional manner of such a rare high standard that it brings considerable benefit

The Star of Courage, one of the new bravery awards instituted in 1972. (Canadian War Museum 73-18406)

to, or reflects great credit on, the Canadian Forces." The Meritorious Service Cross, as established in 1984, stood for seven years. On July 10, 1991, the original charter and regulations were revoked. A new system was created, the Meritorious Service Decorations, with both a Cross and a Medal plus military and civil divisions. Within the Military Division, those eligible would be members of the Canadian Forces, persons holding honorary appointments within the forces, members of Commonwealth or foreign forces "serving with or in conjunction with the Canadian Forces," and members of military forces of countries allied with Canada. Anyone not falling within those guidelines was deemed eligible for awards within the Civil Division. Distinctions between Cross and Medal would be based on degree of service, *not rank*. Differences between the Cross and the various awards (apart from design) were as follows:

Cross (Military) for "the performance … of a military deed or a military activity in an outstandingly professional manner or of a high standard that brings considerable benefit or great honour to the Canadian Forces."

Cross (Civil) for "the performance … of a deed or activity in an outstandingly professional manner or of an uncommonly high standard that brings considerable benefit or great honour to Canada."

Medal (Military) for "the performance ... of a military deed or a military activity in an highly professional manner or of a very high standard that brings benefit or honour to the Canadian Forces."

Medal (Civil) for "the performance ... of a deed or activity in a highly professional manner or of a very high standard that brings benefit or honour to Canada.

Prolonged lobbying by service and veterans' groups resulted in formal revival of the Victoria Cross (whether, in fact, it has ever been defunct is open to question). It is, however, to be a *Canadian* Victoria Cross. This is to be accompanied by two other decorations, the Star of Military Valour and the Medal of Military Valour, open to all ranks, the awards being based on the degree of hazard. These differ from the earlier Cross of Valour-Star of Courage-Medal of Bravery series in that they are specifically for courage "in the presence of the enemy" – i.e., combat situations. However, "enemy" is so defined that combat itself has a broad meaning that could include peace-keeping situations or even prison riots; specifically, "enemy" is defined as: "A hostile armed force, and includes armed mutineers, armed rebels, armed rioters and armed pirates."

Given the prominence that these awards are likely to have in future, it is worth noting the standards laid down for the award of each:

Victoria Cross
The Victoria Cross shall be awarded for the most conspicuous bravery, a daring or pre-eminent act of valour or self-sacrifice or extreme devotion to duty, in the presence of the enemy.

Star of Military Valour
The Star of Military Valour shall be awarded for distinguished and valiant service in the presence of the enemy.

Medal of Military Valour
The Medal of Military Valour shall be awarded for an act of valour or devotion to duty in the presence of the enemy.

These awards (which received Royal approval on February 2, 1993) are open to members of the Canadian forces or allied service personnel operating with Canadian forces. The regulations create an Advisory Committee composed of one person appointed by the Governor General and five members of the Canadian Forces appointed by the Chief of the Defence Staff. This body, on receiving nominations for awards, weighs the merits of the acts performed, determines whether or not the nominees are eligible, and submits its recommendations to the Chief of the Defence Staff. He in turn may modify the recommendations; ultimately they are passed to the Governor General; final awards are made by instruments (documents) signed by the Governor General. Until awards are made, it will be difficult to gauge the standards of these honours.[5]

The last Air Force Cross to a member of the Canadian forces was awarded in 1966. Nevertheless, acts which previously resulted in receipt of this decoration have continued to be recognized. Thus, in 1981, Captain Gary Louis Flath (Medicine Hat) of the Canadian Forces received the Star of Courage for an act that, two decades earlier, might have brought him an AFC:

Captain Flath of the Canadian Armed Forces was the aircraft commander of a helicopter which, on 13 September 1980, rescued in most perilous circumstances the two survivors of the crew of a crashed U.S. Navy helicopter at Whatcom Peak in Washington State. The wreckage and injured men were located on a rock wall at the 2,200 metre level of the mountain. Forty-knot shifting, gusting winds were blowing around the top, creating down drafts; the cold temperature required engine anti-ice which limited power; constantly alternating cloud conditions and deteriorating weather made the task of deploying rescue technicians extremely hazardous. Captain Flath, in an incredible test of nerves, courage and will power, and with outstanding professional skill, was able to position his helicopter on the edge of the glacier, hovered in and out of cloud for approximately thirty minutes, dangerously close to the mountain rock face, while his crew recovered the injured personnel. The weather closed in immediately after. His gallantry saved the lives of the men who had crashed two days prior, were seriously injured and would not have survived another night on the mountain.[6]

Interesting features of the 1972 gallantry awards were that they were unrelated to the ranks of those being honoured and common to military and civilian recipients. Edward Pruss, a civilian helicopter pilot, executed a mountain rescue on the Alaska–British Columbia border on October 14, 1968; the circumstances were very similar to Captain Flath's exploit. In September 1972, Mr. Pruss was awarded a Star of Courage. Valour did not have to wear a uniform to prove its quality.[7]

While the principle of distinctive Canadian awards is laudable, the current administration and distribution of those same honours may be questioned. Canada now has a bewildering array of crosses, stars, medals, and orders with their various grades. Some are granted only after the most studied consideration; the Cross of Valour has been awarded with a

F/L G.L. Flath and F/O "Bud" Husband on survival training, July 1960. (Canadian Forces Photograph PCN 1921)

frugality that has marked it out as being very special indeed. Lesser awards have been distributed with generosity venturing into prodigality. The most notorious example was the awarding of 193 Medals of Bravery to rescue workers who had entered the Westray Mine after a 1992 explosion; such lavish recognition simply equated the Medal of Bravery with a hazardous occupation badge. There have been other cases, involving lesser numbers but an equal profligate determination to recognize all participants in an event, thereby risking dilution of the honours themselves.

An Atlantic rescue on December 2, 1995, illustrates the problem. A Canadian Forces Sea King helicopter was despatched to a sinking ship, the *Mount Olympus*. In high winds and early morning darkness, Master Corporal Robert Fisher was lowered to the pitching deck, dangerously close to the superstructure, where a crew member was clipped to his harness. Protecting the sailor with his own body, Fisher was then hoisted back aboard the hovering "chopper." Over a span of four hours, he performed this dangerous manoeuvre thirty times.

Fisher was awarded the Star of Courage – fitting recognition for cool fortitude. However, all other members of the rescue crew received an award of some description – a Meritorious Service Cross for Major Daniel R. Burden (pilot of the Sea King) and Meritorious Service Medals for Lieutenant-Commander William K. Erhardt (U.S. Navy co-pilot of the Sea King), Captain Gordon F. Sharpe and Sergeant Frederick Vallis (crewmen working the hoist). While it may be argued that the Star of Courage was for gallantry and the other awards were for professionalism, the incident is reminiscent of the 1947-48 tug of war between Brooke Claxton and King George VI over awards to participants in Operation CANON, resolved by a compromise which saw half the nominees honoured with a medal of some sort, the others receiving formal commendations. One is also reminded of decisions taken in the 1950s, when higher awards to men like "Buck" McNair were turned down because bravery was deemed to be part of the job.

In 2000, Canadian authorities need compromise with no external institution, but must still match deeds to standards of courage and service. Their decisions may sometimes be questionable. Yet a suggested alternative – no awards whatsoever – would be a retrograde step. The Air Force Cross has probably passed forever from the array of decorations that now reward Canadians in the air. Nevertheless, what it represented is timeless, and the current Canadian decorations perpetuate the concepts of selflessness and courage. The name of the medal matters far less than the act that it commemorates.

A hero's repose. Charles L.T. Sawle of Edmonton enlisted in the RCAF in January 1940, received his wings in August 1940, and spent the entire war in Canada, chiefly instructing at No. 12 SFTS, Brandon, Manitoba. He was first recommended for an AFC in March 1942. When none was forthcoming, his superiors recommended him again, describing him as a valuable instructor and examining officer: "His devotion to duty and the conscientious manner in which he has performed his work have been an excellent example to all members of this unit." This time the award went through; it was formally announced on April 13, 1943. Following the war he was selected for duties with the RAF as an exchange officer and attached to the Empire Test Pilot School, Farnborough. On August 30, 1948, flying a Meteor, he dived into the ground and was instantly killed. It was speculated that the Meteor had sustained structural failure, but destruction had been so complete that it was impossible to tell with any certainty. S/L Sawle was buried in Britain.

APPENDICES

Appendix A

CANADIAN RECIPIENTS OF THE AIR FORCE CROSS AS MEMBERS OF THE ROYAL AIR FORCE, 1918-1920

The Directorate of History, Canadian Forces Headquarters, has an extensive card file on Canadians who joined the British flying services during the First World War. It even includes some persons with only tenuous Canadian connections, such as Americans who trained under the RFC/RAF program in this country. The card file has been treated as a primary source for this appendix. The dates in brackets are those of the *London Gazettes* announcing each award.

There have been earlier lists of decorated Canadians from that era, notably those published by Ron Dodds and Dr. John Blatherwick. Nevertheless, three names that appear in their lists of Canadian AFC recipients for this period are dropped from my own tally because the card file mentioned above does not include them. Lieutenant Terence Bernard Tully was Irish by birth and upbringing; he had no connection with Canada until 1922. Lieutenant Paul Richard Chamberlayne and Captain John Alexander Coats (both honoured on January 1, 1919) were instructors with the Royal Air Force in Canada in 1918, but appear to have had no connections with this country before or after their tours of duty here. The former is known to have made the RAF his career and was decorated during the Second World War for organizing air training in South Africa.

ALEXANDER, Lieutenant Alfred Mason (November 2, 1918). Ex-RNAS, 6 January 1917. Canadian connection uncertain.

ANTHONY, Captain Ellis (January 1, 1919). See Chapter 2 for details.

ARMSTRONG, Captain George Hughes (January 1, 1919). Forest Hill, Ontario; ex-RFC; served with Nos. 1, 6 and 19 Squadrons in France. Instructed in No. 43 Wing, 20 July 1917 to 27 July 1919. See *University of Toronto Record of Service.*

BARAGAR, Captain Frank Bell (January 1, 1919); Elm Creek, Manitoba; ex-CEF and RFC; Home Defence pilot with No. 112 Squadron (Camels): killed in July 1943, Port Arthur, flying for Ontario Provincial Air Service, age 54 (7,000 hours flown).

BELL, Lieutenant Stanley (January 1, 1919). Ex-CEF; other Canadian connections uncertain; instructor as of November 1918.

BEST, Lieutenant Louis Edward (February 2, 1919); Victoria, British Columbia. Ex-CEF and RNAS. May have instructed in Canada; as of June 1919 he was with No. 269 Squadron, Aboukir, Egypt.

BOYCE, Captain George Harold (October 10, 1919); Ottawa; ex-RNAS; with HMS *Furious* (July 30, 1918) and HMS *Argus* (November 7, 1918). Remained in RAF and rose to air commodore.

BOYD, Captain Kenneth Gordon (November 2, 1918); Goderich, Amberley and Toronto, Ontario; ex-RNAS; veteran of fighter units; joined No. 217 Squadron, 24 July 1918 but had left by mid-December 1918. Lived in USA from 1925 onwards and as of 1941 was an American citizen.

BRUCE, Lieutenant Walter (November 2, 1919); details lacking.

CARROLL, Captain Reginald Sheridan (January 1, 1919); London, Ontario (bank clerk). See Chapter 2 for details.

CRANG, Lieutenant James Goulding (November 2, 1918); Toronto; ex-RFC; with No. 70 Squadron, April to August 1917; to Home Establishment, August 1917; with No. 3 Aircraft Park, November 1918. Prominent in postwar Toronto Flying Club.

CROIL, Major George Mitchell (June 3, 1919). Born in Milwaukee, Wisconsin, June 1893; family moved to Montreal when he was 11. Ex-British Army and RFC; fighter pilot with No. 47 Squadron, September 1916 to July 1917, then instructed in Egypt. Occasionally flew Lawrence of Arabia. Later RCAF Chief of Air Staff (Air Marshal).

DEVLIN, Captain John Roland Secretan (June 3, 1918). See Chapter 2 for details.

EYRE, Lieutenant Robert Thornton (June 3rd, 1919). Toronto; attended Curtiss School, Toronto, 1916; ex-RNAS; probably a flying boat instructor.

FALL, Captain Joseph Stewart Temple (January 1, 1919). Hillbank, British Columbia. Ex-RNAS; fighter pilot (DSC and two Bars); engaged in training as of 1918; served in postwar RAF.

FRASER, Captain Norman Graham (January 1, 1919). Toronto; attended Toronto Curtiss School; ex-RNAS. Instructor in 1918. Later awarded MBE for services in North Russia.

GARRATT, Captain Philip Clarke (June 3, 1919). Home in Toronto; ex-RFC: served in No. 70 Squadron, July to October 1916 (wounded); various units and schools in Britain until June 1919.

GARRETT, Major Frank George (June 3, 1919). Born in England, 1894; home in Montreal (mining engineer); joined RFC in Canada, May 1916; served in France, 1916-1917; on staff of RFC (Canada), December 1917 to January 1919 (instructor and staff officer, School of Aerial Fighting, Beamsville).

GODFREY, Captain (Acting Major) Albert Earl (January 1, 1919). See Chapter 2 for details.

GRAHAM, Lieutenant Stuart (January 1, 1919). Canada's first bush pilot (June 1919, Laurentide Paper Company); see Chapter 2 for details.

HARDING, Lieutenant David Allen (June 3, 1919). See Chapter 2 for details.

HENSHAW, Captain Albert Goodess (June 3, 1919). Born 1894; home in England but enlisted in CEF in Sarnia, October 1914; transferred to RFC, February 1916. May have been on ferry or check flying in 1918.

HILTON, Captain D'Arcy Fowlis (June 3, 1919). Awarded MC and twice Mentioned in Despatches. In Britain on instructional duties in 1918.

HINTON, Lieutenant Alfred Hyde (June 3, 1919). See Chapter 2 for details.

HODGSON, Captain George Ritchie (2 November 1918). Home in Montreal; joined RNAS, January 1916. Awarded Board of Trade Silver Medal for Saving Life at Sea while on flying boat patrols; seaplane instructor.

HOLLIDAY, Major Fred Parkinson (2 June 1919). Australian-born; settled in Canada and joined CEF; to RFC, November 1915; awarded MC and DSO for services with No. 48 Squadron; instructor in Britain, 1917-1918; served in RCAF during Second World War.

HUDSON, Lieutenant Lionel Augustus Croucher (10 October 1919 - Home in St.John's Grenada, British West Indies (Canadian connection not clear). Appointed 2nd Lieutenant in RFC, 19 December 1917. Served in No. 18 Squadron, 18 July 1918 to uncertain date.

HUMPHREYS, Captain William Rowland Spottiswoode (22 December 1918). Born in England and appears to have lived in Canada only a short time before joining CEF (1914). To RFC, August 1915. Served in Egypt, 1916-17, and in Home Establishment units (defence and training) to end of the war. In postwar RAF to about 1924 when he returned to Canada; served in wartime RCAF.

IRELAND, Captain John Graham (2 November 1918). See Chapter 2 for details.

JOY, Major Douglas Graham (January 1, 1919). Home in Toronto (lawyer); went overseas with CEF, 1916; transferred to RFC later that year.

KEENS, Captain John Henry (January 1, 1919). Born 1896; home in Toronto; joined RNAS, December 1915; served with No. 3 (Naval) Wing and No. 10 (Naval) Squadron; wounded June 7, 1917 (bullet through left lung); employed on instructional duties for balance of the war.

KERBY, Flight Lieutenant Harold Spencer (January 1, 1919). Born in Hamilton, May 14, 1893; home in Calgary where his father was mayor (mechanical engineer); attended University of Toronto; joined RNAS, February 1915. Extensive combat service in Dardanelles and France, 1915 to 1918; on training and staff duties, May 1918 onwards, including Cranwell and Freiston School of Aerial Gunnery. Remained in postwar RAF and rose to rank of air marshal.

LALLY, Captain Conrad Tollendal (November 2, 1918). Home in Wainwright, Alberta; awarded MC and Bar for services in France; no information about work related to AFC.

LEACH, Captain John Owen (January 1, 1919). Home in Toronto; served overseas with Canadian Expeditionary Force and British Army; awarded Military Cross in 1915; to Royal Flying Corps, May 15, 1916. Served in No. 56 Squadron, 25 March to 7 May 1917 (wounded, lost a leg); returned to Canada, where he became an instructor, School of Special Flying, North Toronto; commanded Camp Rathbun in late 1918. Killed June 26, 1930, with Ontario Provincial Air Service.

LeGALLAIS, Captain Philip Edmond Mark (November 2, 1918). Although he has appeared on some lists of Canadians decorated in flying services, records at the Directorate of History state that no Canadian association has been established.

MacKENZIE, Major William Herbert (June 3, 1919). Home in Victoria; joined Royal Naval Air Service, December 11, 1915. Served in Italy,

1917. From February 1918 onwards he was in Britain, instructing aerial torpedo bombing; he likely helped develop either the weapon or tactics.

MAITLAND, Captain James Steel (January 1, 1919). Born 1887 in Scotland; migrated to Canada in 1909 and settled in Montreal. Joined RNAS in Ottawa, December 1916. Seaplane pilot at Calshot and Lee-on-Solent, 1917-1918, instructing at the latter base.

MASON, Lieutenant James Arthur Ryerson (January 1, 1919). Home in Stratford, Ontario. Joined Royal Flying Corps in September 1917. On anti-submarine patrols during the war.

MASSEY, Captain Anrold Bonnell (November 2, 1918). Born 1897; home in Toronto; joined RNAS, March 1917. Seaplane pilot; may have been engaged in experimental work in the summer of 1918.

MILLER, Lieutenant Harvey Allan (October 10, 1919). Canadian credentials weak; was more likely an American from Idaho who joined the Royal Flying Corps in Canada. Details of career poor; may have received Air Force Cross for services in North Russia.

MILLMAN, Lieutenant (Temporary Captain) Norman Craig (June 3, 1919). Home in Toronto; joined Royal Flying Corps in December 1915; awarded Military Cross in June 1918 for work in No. 48 Squadron; nothing known of work that would have led to Air Force Cross.

MITCHELL, Lieutenant Lawrence Newton (June 3, 1918). See Chapter 2 for details.

O'BRIAN, Captain Geoffrey Stuart (June 3, 1919). Home in Toronto. Joined Royal Flying Corps, August 16, 1916; posted to Canada in October 1917, instructing at Camps Leaside and Deseronto.

OSENTON, Lieutenant Charles (November 2, 1918). Born in England; home in Armstrong, British Columbia (rancher); served in CEF; joined RFC, September 1917; with No. 143 Squadron on Home Defence duties, February to October 1918.

PAULL, Lieutenant Joseph Albert (June 3, 1919). Home in Vancouver; joined RFC in Canada, going overseas in November 1916. Served in Nos. 28 and No. 101 Squadrons before posting to Home Establishment for instructional duties, May 1918. Killed in accident, June 12, 1919 while performing exhibition flying at Worcester.

PEACE, Captain Albert Grounds (May 3, 1919). Born in England, 1891; home given as Leicester, England, but he enlisted in the 4th Canadian Mounted Rifles; attached to RFC in September 1916; engaged on instructional duties in England throughout 1918.

PRIME, Lieutenant Frederick Horace (June 3, 1919). Born in Toronto, 1888; learned to fly in 1916 at Stinson School; joined RNAS, May 1916; flying boat and seaplane pilot at Felixstowe, Cattewater and Scilly Isles, 1917-1918.

PROUT, Lieutenant Harold Oliver (November 2, 1918). Home in Croydon, England (contractor) but served in CEF; joined RFC, April 1917; on coastal patrol duties, 1918.

REID, Captain Archibald Cumberland (November 2, 1918). See Chapter 2.

REID, 2nd Allan Douglas (June 3 1919). Home in Toronto. Enlisted in CEF, 1914; attached to RFC, April 1917. There is some confusion over his name, given in records variously as Allan Douglas and Alexander Daniel; award for instructing at a school in France.

RICHARDSON, Lieutenant Robert Reginald (November 2, 1918). Home in Guelph; served in CEF, transferring to RNAS, July 1917. Seaplane pilot.

RUTLEDGE, Lieutenant Wilfred Lloyd (May 3, 1919). Born in 1893; home in Fort William; served with 28th Battalion, CEF (awarded Military Medal and Bar); to RFC, April 1917; served as an observer in France before training as a pilot; instructor, 1918.

SAUNDERS, Captain Kenneth Foster (November 2, 1918). Born 1893; home in Victoria. Trained at Wright School, Dayton, Ohio, and joined RNAS, November 1915. Awarded Distinguished Service Cross, May 1, 1918; probably an instructor in the latter half of 1918.

SCOTT, Major James Stanley, MC (January 1, 1919). See Chapter 2 for details.

SHOOK, Major Alexander MacDonald (June 3, 1919). Born in 1888; raised in Peel County, Ontario but teaching at Red Deer, Alberta;

trained at Curtiss School, Toronto; joined RNAS, November 1915. Awarded DSC, DSO and French Croix de Guerre for services in France, 1917; AFC awarded for staff and instructional duties in England, 1918-1919.

SISLEY, Major Malcolm Millard (January 1, 1919). See Chapter 2 for details.

SMITH, Captain Russell Nelson (June 3, 1919). Home in Leamington, Ontario; joined RFC, November 1916. Wounded while serving with No. 54 Squadron (April 14, 1917); spent the balance of the war instructing; as of August 1918 he was a flight commander at the Flying Instructor School, Shoreham.

STEPHENSON, 2nd Lieutenant Cowan Douglas (January 1, 1919). Commissioned in RAF, April 1918 after training in Canada; went overseas in May 1918; served with No. 251 Squadron. Appears to have been an American (New York State) who preferred enlistment in the RFC/RAF rather than in U.S. forces.

SULLY, Captain John Alfred (January 1, 1919). See Chapter 2 for details.

SUTHERLAND, Lieutenant James Henry Richardson (June 3, 1919). Home in Winnipeg; joined RFC, July 1916; served in France with No. 29 Squadron, March to May 1917 and in England (possibly as a ferry pilot) for the balance of the war. Also MBE (Member, Order of the British Empire), January 1, 1919.

THOM, Captain George (June 3, 1919). Born in Scotland, 1890; migrated to Canada, 1910; became a mining engineer at Merritt, British Columbia; attended Curtiss School, Toronto, and joined RNAS, October 1915. Served in No. 8 (Naval) Squadron; instructed at Cranwell, England, April 1918 to war's end.

TIDEY, Captain Aubrey Mansfield (June 3, 1919). Home in Vancouver; joined RNAS, December 1915. Began as observer but retrained as a pilot, March 1917; flew seaplae patrols, 1917-1918.

TURNBULL, Captain George Mark (January 1, 1919). Home in Pembroke, Prince Edward Island; joined RFC in July 1916; flew with No. 100 Squadron (May 1917 to January 1918) and afterwards with

No. 33 (Home Defence) Squadron; also awarded Belgian Croix de Guerre.

USBORNE, Major George Curzon Osbert (November 2, 1918). Born 1882 in Arnprior, Ontario; educated in Victoria; residing in Hawaii (where his father was a missionary) before the war. Transferred from Canadian Motor Machine Gun Brigade to RFC, December 1915; served in France with Nos. 40 and 60 Squadrons, 1916-1917. Instructor and Home Defence pilot, 1917-1918.

VANCE, Lieutenant James Durkin (July 12, 1920). See Chapter 2 for details.

VINEBERG, Lieutenant Herbert Archer (3 June 1919). See Chapter 2 for details.

WICKENS, Captain Percival (January 1, 1919). Born in England, 1891, migrated to Canada in 1913. Trained at Curtiss School, Toronto, 1916 and joined RNAS; seaplane pilot (anti-submarine patrols, 1917-1918).

WILLIAMS, Major John Scott (November 2, 1918). See Chapter 2 for details.

WILMOT, Lieutenant Charles Eardley (June 3, 1919). See Chapter 2 for details.

WILSON, Captain Hugh Allen (November 2, 1918). Born 1896; home in Westmount, Quebec; joined RNAS, May 1916. Seaplane pilot at Felixstowe and Catforth, 1917-1918.

YATES, Lieutenant Harry Alexander (July 12, 1920). See Chapter 2 for details.

YOUNG, Lieutenant Harold Clare (January 1, 1919)). Born 1893; home in Red Deer, Alberta; transferred from Canadian Machine Gun Corps to RFC, September 1917; apparently for services at No. 3 Aircraft Depot (probably ferry flying).

Appendix B

RCAF AIR FORCE CROSS RECIPIENTS IN THE SECOND WORLD WAR

Guide to abbreviations

AFEE	Airborne Forces Experimental Establishment
AFHQ	Air Force Headquarters
BGS	Bombing and Gunnery School
CCDU	Coastal Command Development Unit
CFS	Central Flying School
ComFlt	Communications Flight
CTS	Conversion Training Squadron
EAC	Eastern Air Command
EACComFl	Eastern Air Command Communications Flight
EACMFlt	Eastern Air Command Meteorological Flight
EFTS	Elementary Flying Training School
Emp ANS	Empire Air Navigation School
FIS	Flying Instructor School
Flt	Flight
GRS	General Reconnaissance School
HCU	Heavy Conversion Unit
IFS	Instrument Flying School
LFS	Lancaster Finishing School
KTS	Composite Training School
METS	Middle East Training School
MFlight	Meteorological Flight
MU	Movements Unit
MView	Mountain View
OTU	Operational Training Unit
O*seas	Overseas (unit unknown)
Penn R	Station Pennfield Ridge
SEAC	Southeast Asia Command
RNS	Reconnaissanace and Navigation School
SFTS	Service Flying Training School
Sqn	Squadron based overseas
Sqn-C	Squadron based in Canada

TCHQ	Training Command Headquarters
TSU	Technical Signals Unit
WAC	Western Air Command
WACComFl	Western Air Command Communications Flight
WACHQ	Western Air Command Headquarters
WETFlt	Winter Experimental and Training Flight
WS	Wireless School

ADAMS, FL Robert Austin	450614	353 Sqn	Pilot
AGAR, FL Carlyle Clare	441114	24 EFTS	Pilot
AINSLIE, FL Thomas Edgar C	450907	420 Sqn	Pilot
AISTROP, PO Charles Sidney	430416	1 SFTS	Pilot
AITKEN, FL George Dennis	450614	2 WS	Pilot
ALEXANDER, SL Ernest A	450101	1 SFTS	General List
ALEXANDER, FL Kenneth A	450614	2 SFTS	Pilot
ALLISTON, FL Edward Arthur	460101	168 Sqn-C	Radio op.
ANDERSON, FO Gordon John	460101	23 EFTS	Instructor
ANDERSON, FO John Devlin	450614	2 WS	Pilot
ANDERSON, WC Norman SA	450101	4 TCHQ	General List
ANDERSON, FL Thomas George	460101	12 SFTS	Pilot
ANDREW, WC Byron	440505	10 SFTS	Pilot
ANNAN, SL Douglas Bruce	460101	13 EFTS	Pilot
ARCHAMBAULT, WC Leon GGJ	460101	1 RNS	General List
ARMER, FO Ross	440505	9 SFTS	Pilot
ARMSTRONG, FL Donald Hadley	440101	2 SFTS	Pilot
ASHER, FO John James	460223	4 Sqn-C	Pilot
ATTLE, FL Jack	450106	8 Sqn-C	WAG
BAILEY, WO1 Wesley Dynes	440618	6 SFTS	Pilot
BAIRD, SL James Harold	460101	18 SFTS	Pilot
BALDWIN, FL Norman Scarlett	441114	10 EFTS	Pilot
BARICHELLO, FO Raymond JE	440618	1 GRS	Pilot
BARRETT, SL Joseph Flavelle	450101	1 TCHQ	General List
BARRON, FL Peter Clarence	460223	168 Sqn-C	Pilot
BARTON, FL Alfred William	450614	14 SFTS	Pilot
BASSO, SL Joseph Antonio	430528	3 BGS	Pilot
BEAT, PO Walter Bruce	430101	10 SFTS	Pilot
BEDFORD, WO2 Ronald F.H.	430101	10 Sqn-C	Pilot
BELL, SL James Frank M.	470101	435 Sqn	Pilot
BELLIS, SL John Whomsley	460101	3 OTU	Pilot

BENSON, FL Thomas	441103	7 Sqn-C	Pilot
BERRY, WO1 Douglas Elliott	430528	2 SFTS	Pilot
BERVEN, WC John L	450421	1 IFS	General List
BEVERLY, FL Edwin Paul	460101	407 Sqn	WAG
BIRCHALL, WC Kenneth	450614	2 BGS	General List
BISHOP, FL Arthur Adelbert	440508	1651 HCU	Pilot
BLACK, FO William Anderson	430101	8 SFTS	Pilot
BLAND, SL Eric Alexander	431026	8 SFTS	Pilot
BONAR, FL James Russell	450421	WACHQ	WAG
BOYLE, FL John Allen	440618	2 SFTS	Pilot
BRAUN, SL Donald Conrad	450811	Edmonton	Pilot
BRODSKY, FL Buddy Karl	440324	112 Wing	Pilot
BROOKER, WC Douglas Jack	460223	CFS	Pilot
BROWN, SL Arthur Leland	450403	216 Sqn	Pilot
BROWN, FL John Thomas	460101	2 TSU	Pilot
BROWN, SL William Russell	450614	1 ACHQ	Pilot
BRUCE, FO Cameron Barrie	440101	12 SFTS	Pilot
BRUNELLE, FL Marc Fernand	460101	519 Sqn	WAG
BUCK, WO1 Percy Lloyd	430528	2 SFTS	Pilot
BUNDY, WC Wilfred John	440618	2 BGS	General List
BURLINGHAM, FL Clark K	440901	CCDU	Radar
BURROWS, FL James Ernest	460223	WACComFl	Pilot
BURROWS, FL Leslie Edward	460223	WACComFl	Pilot
BURTON, FL Elgert	460101	164 Sqn-C	Pilot
BYERS, SL Robert David	420611	4 TCHQ	Pilot
CAHOON, FL Lervae A	451201	4 Sqn-C	Pilot
CALVESBERT, SL Percival S	460101	Penn R	Pilot
CAMERON, FL Archibald M	430101	10 Sqn-C	General List
CARLING-KELLY, GC Fitzroy C	460101	1 KTS	Pilot
CARPENTER, WC Frederick S	430528	WAC	Pilot
CAWKER, SL Charles Mitchell	460101	AFHQ	Pilot
CHESSON, SL Arthur Thomas	430528	6 EFTS	General List
CLARK, SL Frederick Patrick	460101	CFS	Pilot
COHEN, SL Sydney JJ	450106	WACHQ	Navigator
COHOE, FO George Elmer K	450811	3 OTU	Pilot
COOK, FL Garrett Munro	430101	116 Sqn-C	Pilot
COOK, SL John Arthur	450614	SEAC	Pilot
COOKE, SL Frederick George	450614	2 ACHQ	Navigator
COOKE, FL Thomas Charles	460223	124 Sqn-C	Pilot
COOMBES, FO Joseph Sinclair	441114	6 ComFlt	Pilot

COOPER, SL John Harold	460101	CFS	Pilot	FLEMING, WC Arthur	450421	116 Sqn-C	Pilot
COSCO, SL John Eugene	450106	166 Sqn-C	Pilot	FOLKINS, SL Gordon Arthur	431026	11 SFTS	General List
COUSE, WO1 Jackson Murray	430528	2 SFTS	Pilot	FORBELL, SL Harold Cooke	450614	1 CFS	Pilot
COWANS, FL John Cassius	441114	1 CFS	Pilot	FRASER, GC Martin Pare	450421	1 ACHQ	General List
CRAWFORD, FO Charles Walsh	450403	520 Sqn	Pilot	FULLERTON, GC Elmer Garfield	450421	9 SFTS	Pilot
CRICH, PO Howard Clair	450106	4 Sqn-C	Flt Engineer	FUMERTON, WC Robert Carl	460101	7 OTU	Pilot
CRICK, PO William Charles K	450614	3 OTU	Pilot	GAIN, SL Thomas Morley	460101	14 SFTS	General List
CURTIS, FL Joseph Robert	460101	435 Sqn	Pilot	GAIN, FL Thomas William	460101	1 WS	Pilot
DARRAGH, FL Hugh Francis	450101	2 TCHQ	Pilot	GALE, SL Edward Bagley	440505	1 CFS	Pilot
DAVID, SL Paul Emile	430101	11 EFTS	Pilot	GARDNER, WC Edward R	450421	Moncton	Pilot
DAVIDSON, WC Melville AW	450101	1 TCHQ	Navigator	GARDNER, FL Harold Alexander	460223	11 Sqn-C	Pilot
DAVIS, SL Wilfred	460101	CFS	Pilot	GIBB, WC Robert Fred	430101	7 BGS	Pilot
DAVY, FL Herbert Dudley	450614	CCHQ	Radar	GIBBON FL Philip	450101	13 EFTS	Pilot
DAWSON, SL Douglas William	430528	2 EFTS	Pilot	GILBERT, FL George F	430528	4 Repair Depot	Pilot
DE PRET-ROOSE, SL Michel	440324	113 Wing	Pilot	GILLESPIE, SL George M	450907	313 Ferry Flt	Pilot
DEALEY, WO1 Frederick H William	460223	WACComFl	WOP	GILMOUR, SL Walter William	450101	1 SFTS	Pilot
DELANEY, FL Thomas Robert	460101	18 SFTS	Pilot	GLADDEN, WC Richard Fleming	450421	1 ACHQ	General List
DEMPSTER, FO John Henry	431026	2 FIS	Pilot	GOBEIL, SL Fowler Morgan	430817	45 Group	Pilot
DETWILLER, FL Lloyd Fraser	460101	2 EFTS	Pilot	GODSON, WC George Oscar	450101	2 TCHQ	General List
DEWAN, FL Dominie Joseph	460613	412 Sqn	Pilot	GOODERHAM, SL George William	450614	1 FIS	Pilot
DIAMOND, WC Gerald Gordon	450101	12 Sqn-C	Pilot	GOODWIN, WC Ray Walpert	460101	5 SFTS	Pilot
DICKSON, FO Cecil Alexander	440505	168 Sqn-C	WAG	GORDON, SL Charles William	450811	1 ACHQ	Pilot
DREW, PO Charles Cyril	430416	2 SFTS	Pilot	GORDON, FO Thomas H	450614	54 OTU	Pilot
DRYNAN, WC Norman L	450101	16 SFTS	General List	GORK, FL Elgin Graham	450101	413 Sqn	Pilot
DUNCAN, WO1 Wayne Jacob	440505	5 EFTS	Pilot	GRAHAM, FO Edward Bruce	440101	2 (O) AFU	Pilot
DUNLOP, WC Gordon Parker	420611	CFS	Pilot	GRAHAM, FL Jack Ross	450101	St.Hubert	Pilot
DURNIN, FL William Howard	440618	1 IFS	Pilot	GRAHAM, FL William	430528	11 Sqn-C	Pilot
DUTCHAK, FL Joseph	441114	15 SFTS	Pilot	GRANT, SL Malcolm E	430528	17 EFTS	General List
DYER, PO Charles Grant R	440618	10 EFTS	General List	GRAVESON, FO Jospeh Dickson	450421	6 Sqn-C	Pilot
EASSON, FL James Kenneth	460101	Oseas	Pilot	GREEN, FL Arthur Favence	440101	7 EFTS o/s	Pilot
EDGAR, WC Norman Salisbury	450421	12 SFTS	General List	GREEN, FO Cameron Fraser	450421	7 OTU	Pilot
EDWARDS, GC Douglas Muir	430101	1 SFTS	Pilot	GREENAWAY, FL Norman Edward	450907	Dorval	Navigator
ELWIN, FL Louis Billings	430416	16 SFTS	Pilot	GRIERSON-JACKSON, SL William RF	450614	5 OTU	Navigator
ENGLISH, FO Edwin Stamford	450101	1 GRS	Pilot	GRIGG, FL Stuart James	450421	WACHQ	Nav/B
ENGLISH, FL Walter MH	460101	1659 HCU	Pilot	HALE, SL Paul Morrow	450421	Mview	Pilot
EVANS, SL Arthur E	450614	10 AOS	Navigator	HALES, SL Frank William	450614	1659 HCU	Pilot
FARRELL, FL Norman Bushell	460101	4 EFTS	Pilot	HALL, WC Ernest Orchard W	450614	AFHQ	General List
FERGUSON, FL William Thomas	450421	165 Sqn-C	Pilot	HALL, WC George Edward	430101	AFHQ	Medical
FINK, FL Donald Ian McQueen	440608	AFEE	Pilot	HALLWOOD, FL Frederick William	450614	8 OTU	Pilot
FINLEY, SL Eric Duff	450811	14 SFTS	Pilot	HAMILTON, FL James Joseph	441114	12 SFTS	Pilot

HANWAY, SL James Albert	440101	5 METS	Pilot	JAWORSKI, FL Joachim	460101	2 SFTS	General List
HARRISON, FL Donald	460613	Odiham	Pilot	JEFFREY, FL George David	440505	2 EFTS	Pilot
HART, FO James Dalton	450811	8 OTU	Pilot	JENNINGS, SL John Earl	460101	7 BGS	Pilot
HART, FO Raymond Boyd	440608	1562 MFlt	Pilot	JESSUP, PO Clifford G	450421	EACMFlt	WAG
HARTMAN, FL Paul Albert	460101	6 OTU	Pilot	JEWSBURY, SL Herbert Charles	440618	7 BGS	Pilot
HARVEY, GC James Borden	450614	1 SFTS	General List	JOHNSON, FL James Rbt Feir	450614	7 OTU	Pilot
HARVEY, WC Roland John	460101	Penn R	Pilot	JOHNSTON, SL Edward Russell	460223	CFS	Pilot
HARVILLE, FL Charles Gayton	450614	437 Sqn	Pilot	JONES, FO Herbert E	450614	8 OTU	Pilot
HASENPFLUG, WC William Alfred	450811	1 SFTS	Pilot	JORDAN, SL John Joseph	460101	6 SFTS	Pilot
HASKETT, PO Clayton Arthur	450614	14 SFTS	Pilot	JOSEPH, FL Abie Joseph	450811	3 OTU	Pilot
HASTINGS, FL Frederick	450101	113 Wg	Pilot	JOYCE, SL Robert Gray	460212	437 Sqn	Pilot
HAY, FL Malcolm MacMurray	450614	3 OTU	Pilot	KAUFFELDT, FO Lawrence MC	451201	Torbay	Navigator
HAYLETT, WC Arthur Donald	441114	2 SFTS	Pilot	KAYE, SL Thomas Chisholm	450907	1666 HCU	Pilot
HEASLIP, FO Robert Thomas	450106	166 Sqn-C	Pilot	KENNEDY, SL Harry Marlowe	421020	12 Sqn	Pilot
HEMENWAY, FL Harold Cameron	460101	7 SFTS	Pilot	KENNEDY, GC Walter Edmund	450101	15 SFTS	Pilot
HENDERSON, WO2 John Clifford	450707	EACMFlt	Flt Engineer	KENNEY, SL Delford Harold	440101	1664 HCU	Pilot
HERDER, FL Hubert Clinton	450614	9 SFTS	Pilot	KERNAGHAN, FO Stanley John	450614	8 OTU	Pilot
HICKERSON, FL Carl Wendell	430528	124 Sqn-C	Pilot	KERR, WC John Gordon	430528	4 BGS	Pilot
HICKS, FL John Edgar	450614	9 AOS	Nav/B	KIMBALL, SL George F	460223	11 Sqn-C	Pilot
HILLCOAT, FO Horace B	440505	168 Sqn-C	Pilot	KING, FL Frederick Cosford	441114	Rockcliffe	Pilot
HILTZ, WC George Abner	460101	16 SFTS	Pilot	KING, WC Harry Edward	460101	AFHQ	General List
HINDLE, SL Herbert Edward	441114	10 SFTS	Pilot	KJELLANDER, FL Willis E	450614	12 SFTS	Pilot
HODGSON, FO Norman Hedley	451201	167 Sqn-C	Pilot	KNOWLES, SL Charles Ronald	450811	168 Sqn-C	Pilot
HOLLOWAY, FO Peter Wykeham	450106	Yarmouth	Navigator	LABRISH, FO Frederick B	440505	168 Sqn-C	Navigator
HONE, SL John	420611	Camp Borden	Pilot	LAIRD, FL Richard Ewart	440901	650 Sqn	Pilot
HOPE, FO John McIntosh	450811	23 EFTS	Pilot	LANE, FL Edwin Walter	441114	2 BGS	Pilot
HORE, PO Alan Edward	421020	15 SFTS	General List	LANGFORD, WC Herman Hamilton	440618	2 TCHQ	General List
HOSEASON, SL Cecil Henry C	460101	10 Repair Depot	Pilot	LAVERY, FL William Russell	450101	168 Sqn-C	Pilot
HOSHOWSKY, FL Raymond	451201	Torbay	Pilot	LAWRENCE, FL Arthur George	450614	8 OTU	Pilot
HOWDEN, SL John Stuart	440505	10 SFTS	Pilot	LAY, SL Harry Morison	450106	8 Sqn-C	Pilot
HURREN, WO1 George Cecil V	431026	20 EFTS	General List	LEE, FL George Allen	440505	2 FIS	Pilot
HYNDMAN, SL Roy Hall	440101	5 SFTS	Pilot	LEITH, FL George	450421	2 FIS	Pilot
INGRAM, WC George Lew	450421	16 SFTS	General List	LEWIS, GC Alexander	450101	1 GRS	Pilot
INGRAMS, FO Reginald Ross	430101	10 Sqn-C	Pilot	LEWIS, FL Homer Sturr	450101	114 MU	Pilot
IVEY, FL Patrick Barnes	460101	6 Comm Flt	Pilot.	LEWIS, FL John Anson	450101	15 SFTS	Pilot
JACKSON, FL Cyril	450811	13 EFTS	Pilot	LINDSAY, WO2 Thomas	430101	8 Sqn-C	Pilot
JACOX, WC David Ritter	450101	19 SFTS	General List	LINKERT, FO Murray Edward	460101	14 SFTS	General List
JAMES, PO Alan MacKenzie	431126	145 Sqn-C	Pilot	LIPTON, WC Maurice	450614	AFHQ	Pilot
JAMES, SL Clarence A	431026	14 SFTS	Pilot	LOCKHART, PO Andrew Wesley	430101	5 SFTS	Pilot
JARVIS, FL Lyle George William	440608	519 Sqn	Pilot	LOWE, WC Alister Duncan R	450907	1659 HCU	Pilot

LOWRY, SL Romney Hollins	441103	4 Sqn-C	General List
LUPTON, SL Hugh William	460101	11 SFTS	General List
LYON, FL Henry Gordon	450106	4 Sqn-C	Pilot
MacDONALD, PO Ralph James	430101	8 SFTS	Pilot
MacINTYRE, SL Donald Philip	450811	5 OTU	Pilot
MacIVER, FL Norman	450421	19 SFTS	Pilot
MacKAY, FO Donald Robert	450421	8 BGS	Pilot
MACKLIN, SL Douglas Irving	421020	CTSqn	Pilot
MacLEAN, SL Donald James	450614	1 FIS	Pilot
MACLURE, WC Kenneth Cecil	450907	Emp ANS	Navigator
MacNEIL, FL Donald Stewart	460101	519 Sqn	Pilot
MacWILLIAM, FL Dudley LS	460101	1 IFS	Pilot
MADDEN, WC Humphrey Oliver	440101	165 Sqn-C	Pilot
MADORE, FL Andrew Francis	421020	19 EFTS	Pilot
MALKIN, WC Harry	450421	5 OTU	Pilot
MANSON, FL Russell Herbert	450614	2 FIS	Pilot
MARK, SL Cyril Victor	460101	2 FIS	Pilot
MARR, FL William Lloyd	450403	409 Sqn	Pilot
MATTHEWS, FL John Herbert V	450421	2 FIS	Pilot
MAWDESLEY, GC Frederick J	450101	5 BGS	Pilot
MAWHINNEY, FO Clifford S	451201	Torbay	WOP
McALLISTER, FL William Ross	450101	2 SFTS	Pilot
McCAFFERY, SL Elmore Hugh	450614	5 OTU	Navigator
McCALLUM, SL John Donald	460101	1 IFS	Pilot
McCORMACK, SL John Edward	440608	1659 HCU	AO
McCUTCHEON, SL John Terrance	460613	Odiham	Pilot
McDIARMID, SL Maxwell Curtis	450101	3 SFTS	Pilot
McDONALD, SL Stuart Edward	450614	9 SFTS	Pilot
McDONALD, FL William Henry	450403	45 Grp	Nav/B
McELREA, FL William Gerald	460101	168 Sqn-C	Pilot
McKECHNIE, FL Frederick D	440618	16 SFTS	Pilot
McKIEL, FO Arthur Burtis	441114	7 BGS	Pilot
McLACHLIN, FL Harold A	450614	1 AOS	Pilot
McLAREN, FL Donald Howard	450101	5 BGS	Navigator
McLAREN, FO James Matthews	450421	10 SFTS	Pilot
McNAUGHTON, SL Andrew RL	450614	Rockcliffe	Pilot
McNEIL, FO Archibald HF	420611	6 SFTS	Pilot
McNEIL, FL Hardie Emerson	460613	436 Sqn	Pilot
McPHERSON, SL William Grant	450421	2 FIS	Pilot
McRAE, SL Robert Wallace	451201	4 Sqn-C	Pilot
MERRIAM, FO Donald Everett	430528	119 Sqn-C	Pilot
MICHAUD, SL Joseph Ulric A	431026	11 EFTS	Pilot
MICK, FO Paul Alexander	440901	3 AFU	Pilot
MIDDLETON, FL Allan Henry	450421	13 SFTS	Pilot
MIDDLETON, FL Robert Bruce	430101	Rockcliffe	Pilot
MILLER, FO Alex Kennedy	440101	6 Repair Depot	Pilot
MILLER, WC Donald Robert	450907	525 Sqn	Pilot
MILLER, SL Robert Fred	440901	1666 HCU	WAG
MIRABELLI, WC Joseph CJB	440608	17 SFTS	General List
MITCHELL, FL Alvin Wesley	430101	4 Sqn-C	Pilot
MOFFIT, FL Barry Haig	430101	5 Sqn-C	Pilot
MOLES, SL Edward Kendrick	450101	9 AOS	Navigator
MONCRIEFF, WC Ernest HG	421020	12 SFTS	Pilot, CFI
MONTIGNY, FL Laurence S	430101	1 BGS	Pilot
MOODIE, SL Russell Lawson	451201	6 Sqn-C	Pilot
MOORE, FO Allan Whitley	440505	8 BGS	Pilot
MOORE, FL Guy Everett	450614	3 SFTS	Pilot
MOORE, FL Leslie Albert	450403	402 Sqn	Pilot
MORRISSETTE, SL Andre Rene	440618	10 EFTS	Pilot
MULVIHILL, FL John C	430101	116 Sqn-C	Pilot
MURPHY, PO Harry Oliver	450614	3 OTU	Flt Engineer
MURRAY, FL John Albert James	460101	279 Sqn	Pilot
MURRAY, FO Robert Gordon	441114	8 OTU	Pilot
NASMITH, SL Donald Carl	450614	1 SFTS	Pilot
NEALE, SL Arthur Cecil	450106	6 Sqn-C	Pilot
NESBITT, FO John Carleton	450421	Edmonton	General List
NEWSOME, SL George Harvey	450101	23 EFTS	General List
NEWTON, FL Jack Frederick	450811	6 OTU	Pilot
NORMAN, FL Donald Maxwell	450811	7 OTU	Pilot
NORRIS, FL Howard Russell	450811	1 FIS	Pilot
O'CONNOR, WO1 John Edward M	450614	7 OTU	Pilot
O'MARA, FL Earl Francis	450811	Penn R	General List
OLEINEK, SL Peter Joseph	460101	6 OTU	Pilot
PALLETT, FO Bruce Armstrong	460101	9 EFTS	Pilot
PALMER, FL John Ender	431026	5 EFTS	Pilot
PARTRIDGE, FL Stanley O	450614	1 WETFlt	Pilot
PATE, SL William Godfrey	431126	116 Sqn-C	Pilot
PATRIARCHE, WC Valance H	430101	6 SFTS	Pilot
PATTON, FL Archibald	440101	3 FIS	Pilot
PATTON, FL John David M	460101	3 OTU	Pilot

PATTON, FO Joseph	440505	5 EFTS	Pilot	SMALL, FL Norville Everett	420611	116 Sqn-C	Pilot
PAYNE, FL Charles Francis	450614	437 Sqn	Pilot	SMITH, SL Franklin Ernest William	441103	165 Sqn-C	Pilot
PEARCE, SL Francis Henry	460101	436 Sqn	Pilot	SMITH, SL Howard Everett	450811	9 SFTS	Pilot
PETERS, FL William Nelson	460101	14 SFTS	Pilot	SMITH, FL Russell Maynard	450101	413 Sqn	Navigator
PILON, FO Francis Victor	440618	7 SFTS	Pilot	SMITH, SL William Watson	430528	5 EFTS	Pilot
PLANT, AC John Lawrence	460613	WACHQ	Pilot	SMITH, FL William Alden	451201	EACMFlt	Pilot
POLLOCK, GC William Romeo	450421	14 SFTS	General List	SNIDER, PO Harold Lawrence	430416	3 FIS	Pilot
PORTER, SL Robert Edward	450614	9 SFTS	Pilot	SNYDER, FL James Clayton	450614	Rockcliffe	Pilot
POUNDER, WC Elton Roy	450614	Trenton	Navigator	SOMERVILLE, SL Ian	430416	15 EFTS	General List
PRESTON, FL George Delong	430303	122 Sqn-C	Pilot	SORENSEN, FL Paul Elmer	430101	9 Sqn-C	Pilot
PROCTOR, FL Albert Alexander	441114	2 FIS	Pilot	SOUTHAM, WC Kenneth Gordon	450811	1 CFS	Pilot
PURCELLO, FL William Michael	450421	2 FIS	General List	SPARLING, SL John Barry	450614	2 ACHQ	Pilot
RAWSON, FL Clarence Arnold	450421	10 SFTS	Pilot	SPINNEY, FL Howard Lenley	450421	EACMFlt	Pilot
RAYMES, PO Daniel Francis	430101	10 Sqn-C	Pilot	ST.PIERRE, GC Jospeh MW	450421	9 BGS	Pilot
REDFERN, FL Cecil William	460101	1 IFS	Pilot	STADDON, WC Marvin Charles	450101	5 BGS	Pilot
REID, PO Norman Duncan	430101	11 SFTS	Pilot	STEEL, FO Edmiston MM	450101	2 FIS	Pilot
RENWICK, SL Roy Duffy	441103	Yarmouth	Pilot	STEPHENSON, GC John Gay	440618	2 SFTS	Pilot
REYNO, WC Edwin Michael	440618	1 OTU	Pilot	STEVENSON, SL Lewis B	450811	Penn R	General List
RIGBY, FO John James	450106	165 Sqn-C	Pilot	STEWART, SL Herbert Collier	450421	8 OTU	Pilot
RITZEL, SL Dalton Frank	460223	WACComFl	Pilot	STEWART, WC James Gardner	450614	1666 HCU	Pilot
RIZON, FO Robert Louis	420611	13 Sqn-OT	Pilot	STOCKFORD, SL Charles W	460223	CFS	General List
ROBB, FL David	440101	7 EFTS o/s	Pilot	STOVEL, SL Richard Carlton	450101	AFHQ	Pilot
ROBERTS, FL John Henry	420611	116 Sqn-C	Pilot	STOVEL, SL Richard Carlton	450101	AFHQ	Pilot
ROSENBAUM, PO Eli M	440505	168 Sqn-C	Pilot	STUDER, SL Hubert Roy	450421	2 SFTS	Pilot
ROUTLEDGE, FO Robert Henry	450106	4 Sqn-C	Navigator	SWANBERGSON, SL Einor I	460101	20 EFTS	General List
RUSSELL, SL David William	450811	170 Sqn-C	Pilot	SWEENEY, FL Ronald James	450614	10 SFTS	Pilot
RUSSELL, FL Howard Borwick	460101	16 SFTS	Pilot	TAYLOR, WC Carl Clark	450614	3 BGS	AG
SAWLE, FL Charles LT	430416	12 SFTS	Pilot	TAYLOR, FL Frank Edward	460101	Penn R	Pilot
SCOTT, FL Gordon James	460101	1 SFTS	Pilot	TAYLOR, SL William Edward	450614	16 SFTS	General List
SEARLE, WC Arthur Brodie	430416	2 SFTS	Pilot	TERRY, SL Victor Maurice	440101	23 EFTS	Pilot
SEELER, PO George Nelson P	440505	3 FIS	Pilot	THOMAS, FL Kenneth Roye	450811	2 ANS	Pilot
SELLERS, WC George Henry	430528	11 SFTS	Pilot	THOMAS, WC Robert Idris	441103	Uclulet	General List
SHEA, FL Elgar Denis G	460101	13 SFTS	Pilot	THOMPSON, SL James Adamson	450106	132 Sqn-C	Pilot
SHELFOON, SL Anthony AJ	430416	CFS	Pilot	THOMPSON, SL Robert William	460101	AFHQ	General List
SHORT, WO1 James Edgerton	431026	4 SFTS	Pilot	THOMPSON, SL Victor W	450101	16 SFTS	Pilot
SHOWLER, SL John Gavin	450421	164 Sqn-C	Pilot	TILLEY, SL Andrew	450811	12 Sqn-C	Pilot
SIDEEN, FO Oscar	441114	19 EFTS	Pilot	TORONTOW, PO Cyril	430528	117 Sqn-C	Pilot
SIMPSON, FL John Huntington	450811	3 SFTS	Pilot	TOWNSEND, SL Edward Nicoll	450403	231 Sqn	Pilot
SIMPSON, FL John Frederick	460223	EACComFl	Pilot	TRUEMNER, SL Gordon Ross	450614	16 SFTS	Pilot
SIMS, SL Owen Anthony Haig	450101	AFHQ	General List	TUGWELL, SL Samuel Chester	450614	24 OTU	Pilot
				TURNBULL, WC Robert Steele	440101	1659 HCU	Pilot

TURNER, WC William Ronald David	440618	1 TCHQ	Pilot
TWIST, WC Joseph Gainham	431026	CFS	Pilot
VAN HOUTEN, FL John Thomas	450421	7 Sqn-C	Pilot
VINCENT, SL Arthur James	441114	1 CFS	General List
WALLNUTT, FL Thomas	450811	CFS	Pilot
WANLIN, FL Alexander Camile	460101	435 Sqn	Pilot
WARD, SL Bruce Clifford	450614	3 SFTS	Pilot
WARREN, FL William Arnold	450614	1 CFS	Pilot
WARRINER, FL Lloyd Hubert	440901	112 Wing	Pilot
WATSON, FO John Albert	450421	3 OTU	Pilot
WATTS, GC Alfred	440618	3 TCHQ	General List
WATTS, SL John William	460101	4 SFTS	Pilot
WAYAVE, FO Theodore Marshall	430528	120 Sqn-C	Pilot
WEAVER, WC Edward Alfred	441114	4 SFTS	Pilot
WEBSTER, SL Eric Taylor	430528	9 SFTS	General List
WEBSTER, FL Gavin Alexander	450614	18 SFTS	Pilot
WELLS, FL Ronald Gladstone	460101	Penn R	General List
WELSTEAD, WC William Gordon	450421	1 ACHQ	General List
WESTAWAY, FO HW	441201	Gander	Pilot
WICKETT, WC John Cameron	460101	CFS	Pilot
WILKINSON, SL Philip	460223	WACHQ	Pilot and AG
WILLIAMS, FL Clifford F.	430416	6 SFTS	Pilot
WILLIAMS, FL Edwin Mountford	420611	10 Sqn-C	Pilot
WILSON, SL Herbert Malcolm	440101	2 SFTS	Pilot
WILSON, FL Kenneth B	460101	Penn R	General List
WILSON, FL William Robert	450614	2 SFTS	Pilot
WISEMAN, SL James Arnold	450614	AFHQ	Pilot
WITT, FO Reginald	460101	24 EFTS	Pilot
WOOD, FL Willis Glen	441103	164 Sqn-C	Pilot
WOODS, PO George Webster	430101	8 Sqn-C	Pilot
WRAY, WC Lawrence Edward	420611	AFHQ	Pilot
WRIGHT, FL George Gordon	440901	112 Wing	Pilot
WRIGHT, WO Warren Jackson	450614	6 Ferry Unit	WOP
WYMAN, FO Lewis Benjamin	450101	45 Grp	Pilot
YOUNG, SL John Humphrey	460101	5 SFTS	Pilot
YOUNGS, SL George Riley	460101	12 SFTS	Pilot

RCAF Recipient of Bar to Air Force Cross

HONE, SL John	450101	AFHQ	Pilot

Appendix C

RCAF AIR FORCE MEDAL RECIPIENTS IN THE SECOND WORLD WAR

ARNETT, FS James Lawrence	450907	436 Sqn	Pilot
BULMER, FS William Henry	430101	5 Sqn-C	Nav/R
CHANDLER, Sgt Alfred James	420611	5 Sqn-C	AG
CHAUSSE, FS Louis Joseph R	430101	10 Sqn-C	Navigator
CLEMENT, Sgt Rodney Stewart	440101	4 EFTS o/s	Pilot
CORBETT, FS Edward Salter	430101	116 Sqn-C	WOPAG
DADEY, FS Joseph John Harris	440101	1 BGS	Drogue work
DE MARCO, Cpl Albert	440505	168 Sqn-C	General duties
DEEKS, FS Arthur Allen R	420611	8 Sqn-C	Pilot
DUGGAN, LAC Francis Robert	430101	2 BGS	Drogue work
FARLEY, Sgt Thomas Ernest H	441114	6 SFTS	Pilot
FLEISHMAN, Sgt Edmund David	430101	4 SFTS	Pilot
FOWLER, Sgt Harry Wilfred	430101	2 BGS	Pilot
GERMAN, Sgt Harold Wallace	430101	7 SFTS	Pilot
GLOVER, Cpl John Alexander	430101	116 Sqn-C	Flt Engineer
GRIFFITHS, FS Roy	430101	13 Sqn-C	WAG
HAGLEY, Cpl John Henry	430528	5 BGS	Drogue work
HANNA, Sgt Herman Melvin	460101	3 ANS	Radio
HARVEY, Cpl Lloyd George	420611	11 Sqn-C	WAG
HAW, Sgt Victor Alfred	421020	11 SFTS	Pilot
HAYES, Sgt Joseph Anthony	450811	Mview	General duties
HILL, Cpl John Kennedy	430101	2 BGS	Drogue work
HILLCOAT, Sgt Horace B	430101	19 EFTS	Pilot
HOWARD, LAC Thomas Alexander	440101	164 Sqn	WOP
HUNT, LAC William James	420611	13 Sqn-OT	?
JACKSON, Sgt Carl Douglas	430101	11 EFTS	Pilot
LE GROS, FS Philip John	440101	9 (O) AFU	Pilot
MANLEY, Sgt John Alfred	460101	3 ANS	WOP
McCUTCHEON, Sgt William Harold	430416	2 EFTS	General List
McPHERSON, Sgt William John	430528	2 EFTS	Pilot
McRAE, Sgt John Bell	440714	1 BGS	Pilot
MORRIS, FS Arthur John	430101	12 SFTS	Pilot

REED, FS Thomas Edward	430528	Mview	Pilot
SANDERSON, Sgt Stephen A	421020	14 SFTS	Pilot
SCOTT, Sgt William Francis	430528	15 EFTS	Pilot
SMITH, FS James Pender	430101	10 Sqn-C	WAG
STEVENS, Cpl Gillmore V	430528	Coal Harbour	WAG
STEVENS, Sgt William P	430101	19 EFTS	General List
SUTHERLAND, FS Vernon A	430101	122 Sqn-C	WAG
WALKER, FS Bruce Douglas	440101	2 (O) AFU	Pilot
WERRY, Cpl Elmor W	430101	116 Sqn-C	AG and FE
WHIDDEN, Sgt Harold Ernest	430101	7 SFTS	Pilot

Appendix D

CAN/RAF RECIPIENTS OF THE AIR FORCE CROSS AND AIR FORCE MEDAL, 1941-1956

Awarded Air Force Cross

APPLETON, SL James Ronald	430602	?	General Duties
BANKS, WC David Kynvin	420101	203 Sqn	Pilot
BIRCHFIELD, WC Frank EW	410930	234 Sqn	Pilot
BURNELL, WC Harold Hemlyn	440901	3 LFS	Pilot
BURNETT, W/C Wilfred Jasper	560101	RAF College	Pilot
COX, SL Richard Morse	420201	82 OTU	Pilot
DARLINGTON, FL Frank William	430402	??	?
DENISON, WC Richard William	450101	236 Sqn	General Duties
De SIEYES, FL Fred Galt	430608	173 Sqn	Pilot
DONALDSON, WC Edward M	410930	5 SFTS, Tern Hill	Pilot
ENNIS, FL James Moore	420611	204 Sqn	Pilot
FENWICK-WILSON, SL Royd M	410401	12 SFTS	Pilot
FITZGIBBON, SL Basil F	450901	?	General Duties
FLEMING, SL Robert Benvie	440901	1674 HCU	Pilot
FOORD-KELSEY, WC Alick	430831	Cranwell	Pilot
FOSTER, FL George Arthur C	410101	10 SFTS	Pilot
FULTON, WC John	420101	IADFES	Pilot
GRAEME, FL Dudley Brian	440608	287 Sqn	Pilot
GREENSLADE, SL William Roy	420611	21 OTU	General Duties
JARDINE, SL Alex Myles	420101	205 Sqn	Pilot

JOHNSON, SL Steve Nicholas	460101	38 MU	General Duties
JONES, FL Lawrence Latham	420101	45 Group	Pilot
KAYE, SL Thomas Chisholm	450907	1666 HCU	Pilot
KENT, FO John Alexander	390102	RAE	Pilot
KING, GC Charles Ley	420101	8 AGS	Pilot
KNOWLES, FO Philip Henry	410401	3 SFTS	Pilot
LIVINGSTON, GC Philip C	420611	Central Med Est	Medical
LONGHURST, FL William Sydney	430827	Ferry Cmnd	Pilot
MARCOU, SL Harold F	430402	156 Sqn	General Duties
McVEIGH, SL Charles Norman	440901	48 Sqn	Pilot
MILLER, SL John Alexander	440901	107 Sqn	General Duties
PEXTON, WC RD	431026	34 SFTS	General Duties
POLLARD, WC Michael Evelyn	440101	107 Sqn	Pilot
POWLEY, SL Francis Sydney	420101	?	General Duties
RANKIN, FL Archibald	260703	HMS *Pegasus*	Pilot
RODNEY, FO George Forbes	390102	148 Sqn	Pilot
ST.PIERRE, FO Maurice AJ	530601	206 AFS	Pilot
TAPP, FO Lorne Arthur Paul	500102	99 Sqn	Pilot
WALSH, FL Archibald Phillip	420101	9 Sqn	Pilot
WATERHOUSE, WC Richard H	420611	5 SFTS	Pilot
WATERTON, FL WA	430101	39 SFTS	Pilot
WENZEL, FO Clifton Leonard	490603	242 Sqn	Pilot
WHYNACHT, FO Kelley A	530601	230 OCU	Pilot

Awarded Bar to AFC

DONALDSON, WC Edward M	470612	High Speed Flt	Pilot
WATERTON, FL WA	470612	High Speed Flt	Pilot

Awarded Air Force Medal

BISHOP, FS John Franklin	420101	12 OTU	WOP

Appendix E

AIR FORCE CROSS AWARDS – RAF, RAAF, RNZAF IN CANADA, 1942-1946

AMEY, FL John William Thomas	450421	36 SFTS	RAF
BARRETT, SL George Gordon N	450101	1 CFS	RAF
BETTS, FL John Marchbank	440101	35 SFTS	RAF
BICKET, FL Peter Michael	450614	1 IFS	RAF
BROOKS, WC Walter Thomas	460101	39 SFTS	RAF
BROWN, SL Edwin Charles	460101	32 OTU	RAF
BRUCE, FO Robert AP	430101	32 EFTS	RAF
BURNETT, SL Robert Leslie	420611	16 SFTS	RAF
CHESTERMAN, WC Humphrey William	421020	36 SFTS	RAF
CRAWFORD, WO Charles William	430528	31 ANS	RAF
DAVISON, FL George	440505	31 OTU	RAF
DOBBS, FL James Frederick	440101	31 ANS	RAF
DUPONT, WC Richard Evenor	460101	10 SFTS	RAF
EASTWOOD, FL Reginald Frank	440101	31 EFTS	RAF
EDGE, FL Henry Roy	440101	33 EFTS	RAF
FEATHERBY, FL Hugh Frost	440505	33 EFTS	RAF
FOSSETT, FL Ronald Henry	430416	35 SFTS	RAF
FRANCIS, SL Eric Harrison	460101	32 SFTS	RAF
GILLING, SL Kenneth Victor	450614	34 SFTS	RAF
GODSALVE, FL William Herbert L	450101	32 SFTS	RAF
HAMILTON, WC John Stewart	440505	36 OTU	RAF
HARRISON, FO Gordon Wilberforce	450101	31 ANS	RAF
HARRISON, WO John Arthur	440505	32 EFTS	RAF
HAYES, SL Ernest John	440505	31 SFTS	RAF
HAYWARD, WC Frank Bernard Howard	440505	35 SFTS	RAF
HEWITT, SL Robert	450614	14 SFTS	RAF
HIGGINS, FO William	450614	1 RNS	RNZAF
HINKS, SL Stanley Reginald	430416	31 OTU	RAF
JENKINS, FL William Spencer	440101	33 ANS	RAF*
LAMB, WC Peter Gilbert	431026	31 SFTS	RAF
LEA-COX, GC Kenneth	460101	38 SFTS	RAF
LUDLOW, PO Peter Henry	450614	6 OTU	RAF
MacCORMAC, SL John Warner Donald	450811	16 SFTS	RAF
MANNIKIN, FL Ronald Fletcher	450614	31 ANS	RAF
MAW, SL Dennis Mowbray	421020	31 BGS	RAF
MAXWELL, GC Patrick Herbert	450101	6 OTU	RAF
McPHERSON, SL Ian Roy Cardew	450421	6 OTU	RAF
MILLIGAN, SL Frederick Moir	420611	32 SFTS	RAF
MORTON, FL Ronald Vivian	450614	2 FIS	RAF
NORCOTT, FL Dennis Owen	450614	7 OTU	RAF
NORTH, SL Gerald Noel	460101	CFS	RAF
PENMAN, WC William Mitchell	421020	2 BGS	RAF
PEXTON, WC Richard Dunning	431026	34 SFTS	RAF
PRESS, PO Leslie George	430101	31 GRS	RAF
RAE, FL John Philip	420611	31 GRS	RAF
RALPH, SL Richard John	430831	Ferry Cmnd	RAF
REID, FL Andrew Keirs M	450421	2 FIS	RAF
ROBINSON, FO Keith Edward	430831	Ferry Cmnd	RAAF
RUB, FO Kevin Herbert	450101	7 BGS	RAAF
SCRAGG, WC Colin	420611	34 SFTS	RAF
SEYS, WC Richard Godfrey	430827	Ferry Cmnd	RAF
SIMPSON, WC James Archibald	460101	35 SFTS	RAF
SMITH, WO Peter Seymour	430528	32 SFTS	RAF
SMITH, SL Roger Patrick	441114	7 OTU	RAF
STOKER, FL Kenneth Richard	450101	33 SFTS	RAF
TAYLOR, SL Kenneth Garth	450101	1 GRS	CAN/RAF
UNDERHILL, FL Arthur Frederick	431026	3 FIS	RAF
WATERHOUSE, WC Richard Henry	420611	5 SFTS	RAF
WATERTON, FL William Arthur	430101	39 SFTS	CAN/RAF
WESTLEY, FL Frederick William	421020	31 SFTS	RAF
WIGHTMAN, WC William Taylor F	450101	34 SFTS	RAF

* Awarded Bar to AFC, January 1946.

Appendix F

AIR FORCE MEDAL AWARDS –
RAF IN CANADA, 1942-1946

ANDERSON, FS James Beattie	430101	31 EFTS	RAF
BACON, Sgt Ernest Augustus Holmes	420611	34 SFTS	CAN/RAF
CAWS, Sgt Richard Allen	430619	32 EFTS	RAF
COLLINS, LAC James Daniel	440608	31 OTU	RAF
CRAIG, FS Eric Spinks	430619	33 EFTS	RAF
MEREDITH, AC1 Jack	430101	31 GRS	RAF
HORNBY, FS Arthur Newlove	420611	31 ANS	RAF
REILLY, Cpl Terence Desmond	430101	31 ANS	RAF

Appendix G

POSTWAR RCAF AWARDS

Air Force Cross

ALEXANDER, FO CM	601029	433 Sqn	CF-100
BATCOCK, FO CC	601029	422 Sqn	F-86
BURROWS, FO SE	550730	434 Sqn	F-86
CAMPBELL, FL DM	660730	121 CU	Rescue
CARSWELL, FL AG	580315	123 SAR	Rescue
CASS, FL RW	640905	103 SAR	Rescue
CUTHBERTSON, SL DR	530411	Portage	Rescue
DICKSON, SL JD	520607	426 Sqn	Korean Airlift
DRAKE, FL JF	480731	413 Sqn	Survey, POLCO
EDWARDS, FL RM	530103	426 Sqn	Korean Airlift
GIBBS, FL PL	510915	123 SAR	Rescue
GLAISTER, FO RTS	510915	123 SAR	Rescue
GOLDSMITH, FO JE	480731	413 Sqn	Survey, POLCO

HARE, SL CEL	510630	ARCHQ	Test work
HARVEY, FL KA	660730	Namao	F-84 F
McLEISH, SL WAG	510415	TCHQ	Rescue
McMILLAN, FO CC	480731	112 Flight	Rescue, CANON
MITCHELL, WC JF	511224	105 CU	Rescue
MORRISON, WC HA	520607	426 Sqn	Korean Airlift
NELSON, FL OG	510415	103 RU	Rescue
PARKER, FO DF	640104	416 Sqn	CF-101
PAYNE, FL DM	520607	426 Sqn	Korean Airlift
PEARSON, FL LB	510630	103 SAR	Rescue
ROSS, FO LT	570325	419 Sqn	CF-100
VILLENEUVE, SL JAGF	610520	1 (F) OTU	F-86
WEST, FO RB	480731	101 Flight	Rescue

Air Force Medal

DRACKLEY, FS Alfred A	520607	426 Sqn	Korean Airlift
LECKIE, Sgt George B	511201	Edmonton	Rescue
RAE, Cpl James P	480731	Rivers	Rescue, CANON
REED, Cpl Gerald R	530530	426 Sqn	Korean Airlift

Appendix H

LOCATION OF SELECTED AFC MEDALS

It may be presumed that most military decorations remain with the recipients or their next of kin. However, some have been purchased by or donated to public museums, where they may or may not be on display. The following is a guide to AFC and AFM medal sets known to be in public hands.

Canadian War Museum, Ottawa
S/L Russell Lawson Moodie
G/C James Stanley Scott
Captain Russell Nelson Smith
W/C John Cameron Wickett

RCAF Memorial Museum, Trenton
F/O Wesley Dynes Bailey
A/C Gerald Gordon Diamond
F/L Charles Grant R. Dyer

ENDNOTES

Plagiarism is the most sincere form of flattery.

– ANONYMOUS

Anyone who has ever written a university essay knows how readily a "bibliography" can be padded with references to works (some of dubious worth) that were never consulted. Readers seeking a scholarly, comprehensive list of books should consult O.A. Cooke, *The Canadian Military Experience 1867-1995: A Bibliography* (3rd edition, Ottawa, Department of National Defence, 1997). The notes that follow here represent both primary and secondary sources actually consulted. Readers are urged to delve into these for greater details and insights than could be crowded into this volume.

Preface

1. The term "CAN/RAF" requires some explanation. A number of Canadians who served in the British flying services during the First World War chose to remain in the Royal Air Force rather than return to Canada. From 1923 forwards, a trickle of Canadians travelled to Britain to enlist in the RAF, as pilots and ground crew. There were very few until about 1934, when RAF expansion enabled increasing numbers of Canadians to join. By 1939 there were about 1,800 Canadians enrolled directly in the RAF. These "CAN/RAF" personnel wore RAF uniforms (although after 1940 they were allowed to wear "Canada" flashes on the shoulders of their tunics), and were paid, commissioned and promoted in accordance with RAF rates and policies. Roughly 775 were killed or died on active service; about 200 survivors transferred to the RCAF; about 50 made the postwar RAF their permanent career.

   Owing to the exigencies of war, Commonwealth personnel were traded back and forth between units. Thousands of RCAF members served in RAF units (where their accents generated some amusement and their higher pay some resentment); hundreds of RAF personnel (including CAN/RAF types) were assigned to RCAF squadrons overseas. Thus, some AFCs won overseas by RCAF aircrew were for services in RAF units; most awards to CAN/RAF personnel were also for work in RAF formations; occasionally, an award was made to a CAN/RAF member whose had been assigned to an RCAF unit.

2. The most important of these were files held in Record Group 24

(principally Second World War documents originating in the Department of National Defence) and Record Group 7 (files from the office of the Governor General).

3. The Diamond and Dyer logbooks are held by the RCAF Memorial Museum, Trenton, Ontario. Diamond's 1940-41 entries are interesting for his army co-operation flying on the West Coast, using Lysanders for varied tasks such as photography, aerial gunnery practice, message pickups, directing coastal battery "shoots," dive-bombing exercises, and anti-submarine patrols. His 1942 entries were dominated by flights in Grumman Goose aircraft throughout British Columbia and as far north as Alaska. His work with No. 12 (Communications) Squadron was uneventful by comparison; apart from his AFC, his skill was recognized by his being chosen as the co-pilot for the Liberator that took Prime Minister Mackenzie King to the San Francisco Conference (which established the United Nations) in July 1945. Dyer's logbooks recorded the compilation of 2,450 hours flying time; the most striking entries were notations by superiors praising his instructional capabilities.

4. The relevant classes in the Public Record Office are Air 1 (First World War) and Air 2 (Second World War). Both are enormous bodies of documents, best approached via the PRO's excellent finding aids and helpful (though overburdened) staff.

Chapter 1: Origins and Procedures

1. Walter E. Gilbert, *Arctic Pilot: Life and Work on North Canadian Air Routes* (Toronto, Thomas Nelson and Sons, 1940), p. 20.

2. This chapter borrows heavily from P. E. Abbott and J.M.A. Tamplin, *British Gallantry Awards* (London, Nimrod and Dixon, 1981).

3. As of that date, only Australia possessed a Commonwealth air arm separate from the Royal Air Force.

4. Signifying "George V, Rex et Imperator" – George V, King and Emperor.

5. Abbot and Tamplin, *op. cit.*, pp. 4-5. The choice of a mythological figure was both appropriate and amusing. Known as Hermes to the Greeks and Mercury to the Romans, he was a messenger for the gods; in his own right he was god of roads, communications, invention, cunning and theft.

6. The inclusion of civilian eligibility was a hasty attempt to provide a "consolation prize" for Harry Hawker and Mackenzie Grieve, who had nearly lost their lives in a failed trans-Atlantic flight. For more

on this, see J. Routledge, "Air Force Cross and Air Force Medal: Awards to Civilians," *Journal of the Orders and Medals Research Society*, Volume 17, No. 3 (Autumn 1978). An instance of a civilian receiving an AFM was that of Mr. Frank W. Sherratt, Rolls-Royce Motor and Aero Engine Manufacturers (awarded May 12, 1920) in recognition of services rendered during a pioneering (though unsuccessful) flight from London to Capetown (see *Aeroplane*, May 19, 1920). A famous civilian AFC recipient was Alan Cobham, recommended by the Air Ministry in March 1926 for numerous long-range flights, including London to Capetown and return (Public Record Office Air 30/66). Charles William Anderson Scott was awarded the AFC "in recognition of the distinguished services rendered to aviation by reason of his recent flights between England and Australia" (*London Gazette*, June 30, 1931). No Canadian civilian was ever awarded an Air Force Cross, but Louis Bisson, a civilian employed in trans-Atlantic route surveys early in the Second World War, was seriously considered for one when it appeared that there might be problems in getting an OBE (Officer, Order of the British Empire) for him. These were resolved, however, before anyone could remind Canadian authorities that by then the Air Force Cross Warrant would have excluded Bisson anyway.

7. Most of the civilian AFCs had been for record-breaking flights, and it became embarrassing as each successive record was broken to recognize the newest "speed king" or "long-distance champion." As a corollary to this change, the Royal Aeronautical Society instituted gold and silver medals to recognize civilian aeronautical achievements. Air Ministry reconsidered its "no civilian" policy respecting AFCs during the Second World War (in conjunction with re-examination of awards to merchant seamen) but made no changes. Again, in 1953, the eligibility of civilians was weighed, but Air Ministry chose to continue the restriction, even with respect to test pilots. On both occasions it was remarked that test pilots were "well paid to cover the risk of their employment." There was also a fear that restoring civilian eligibility for the AFC and AFM would somehow dilute the standards of the award. A senior officer, writing on March 6, 1941, observed, "We could not possibly confine the awards to test pilots only, and we might conceivably receive recommendations in respect of a steward or stewardess on an air liner." The 1941 discussions are found in the Public Record Office, Air 2/

6999; those respecting the 1953 review are in Public Record Office Air 2/12078.

8. C.G. Grey, "The New Decorations," *The Aeroplane*, June 5, 1918.

9. C.G. Grey, *A History of the Air Ministry* (London, George Allen and Unwin, 1940), p. 105. Grey clearly relished the quip about DFC vs. AFC requirements; he also used it in an article about Air Vice-Marshal Charles Longcroft, *The Aeroplane*, November 13, 1929, p. 1146.

10. *Flight*, February 3, 1921

11. See H.A. Halliday, *No. 242 Squadron: The Canadian Years* (Canada's Wings, Stittsville, 1981), pp. 144-145 for a discussion of Cork's award.

12. Extensive correspondence regarding the proposed NFC and NFM is in the Public Record Office, Adm 1/24071.

13. Colonial Office to Governor General, March 29, 1919, found in Governor General's correspondence, National Archives of Canada, Record Group 7, Group 21, Volume 552.

14. Colonial Office to Governor General, July 26, 1919; *Ibid.*, Vol.553.

15. Directorate of History file 181.009 D.3060 in National Archives of Canada, Record Group 24, Volume 20635. Cases have also been found where a recommendation for an AFC resulted in no award whatsoever. On January 25, 1945, the commanding officer of No. 431 Squadron recommended S/L Harold M. Smith, DFC, for an AFC, noting that Smith had been invaluable in training new crews, particularly during the unit's conversion to Lancaster bombers. Although the station commander concurred, the suggestion did not materialize in any award – not even a Mention in Despatches. See DHist file 181.009 D.4364 (National Archives of Canada Record Group 24, Volume 20648). No reasoning has been found for the lack of an award, but it may have been felt that Smith's DFC was already sufficient recognition of his services.

16. The correspondence is in DHist file 181.009 D.3050 (National Archives of Canada, Record Group 24, Volume 20634) and DHist file 181.009 D.1509 (National Archives of Canada Record Group 24, Volume 20599). It is often difficult to draw a line between courage and recklessness. In fairness to EAC Headquarters, it is worth recalling the Duke of Wellington's adage that there is nothing so stupid as a gallant officer.

17. DHist file 181.009 D.3690 (National Archives of Canada, Record Group 24, Volume 20640).

18. Public Record Office Air 2/9019.

19. The specific copy used was found on File 22-5, No. 31 SFTS, Kingston (DHist file 181.009 D.1409, found in National Archives of Canada, Record Group 24, Volume 20598).

20. Western Air Command File C.122-7-1 "Records – Honours and Awards," formerly DHist 181.009 D.1938, now National Archives of Canada, Record Group 24, Volume 20612).

21. DHist file 181.009 D.1688 (National Archives of Canada, Record Group 24, Volume 20605).

22. DHist file 181.009 D.1718, "Western Air Command Honours and Awards." (National Archives of Canada, Record Group 24 Volume 20606).

23. Public Record Office Air 2/9019 and Air 2/9144. The latter document contains some very interesting RAF cases from the 1946 New Years Honours List where a relatively small number of flying hours were ignored because they had been logged in very hazardous circumstances. W/C Roland John Falk, AFC, had flown only 64 hours in the previous six months – but that included time on captured German jet and rocket aircraft "known to have been the cause of a considerable number of fatalities amongst Luftwaffe personnel." He was awarded a Bar to his AFC. F/L Gordon D. Green, RAF, had flown only 41 hours in the previous six months but they had been dedicated to developing airborne rocket projectiles; once a rocket exploded almost immediately on firing and damaged his Mosquito, but he brought the aircraft back to base. Green received an AFC.

24. These limitations appear to have been followed by RAF and RCAF authorities. By contrast, many service awards to members of the Canadian Army stressed First World War services, popularity or position held relative to the individual's rank.

25. See note 21.

26. Public Record Office Air 2/8910, Chief of the Air Staff's minute of May 5, 1942. In at least one RCAF squadron overseas the unit's high proportion of gallantry awards can be attributed in part to the Adjutant's compelling and detailed narratives that accompanied every recommendation for a decoration.

27. Documents in Byer's scrapbook, owned by his son-in-law, Ken Johnston of Orleans, Ontario. Byers later instructed at No. 3 SFTS, Calgary (July 1942 to May 1943), worked at airfield development along the Northwest Staging Route (May to October 1943), returning to instructing at No. 7 SFTS, Macleod (October 1943 to March

1944). Following a course at the Empire Central Flying Training School, he returned to Canada to apply that body's teachings at Canadian schools, including the Instrument Flying School at Mohawk, Ontario. He left the RCAF in March 1946, having flown almost 3,000 hours with the force. Byers remained active in commercial aviation, flying a Beechcraft 18 for H.J. McFarland Construction Company of Picton, Ontario. Experience with small airfields led him to develop radio controlled lighting systems for airports that could not be permanently lit; see his article in *Canadian Flight*, February 1956.

28. Buck was killed in action on September 12, 1944; by then he was a flight lieutenant.

29. RCAF file 305-4-5, Volume 2, held in National Archives of Canada, Record Group 24, Volume 3350. This file deals primarily with presentations at Government House, Ottawa, but includes information on investitures elsewhere.

30. RCAF file 305-4-6, Volume 2, National Archives of Canada, Record Group 24, Volume 3350.

Chapter 2: The Early Years

1. Cited in Robert Harrison, *Aviation Lore in Faulkner* (Philadelphia, John Benjamins, 1985), p. 43.

2. The *Canada Gazette,* July 5, 1919, reported that Sergeant Major Walter Robert Maxwell had been awarded an AFM. This was an error; Maxwell had been awarded a Meritorious Service Medal (*London Gazette* of June 3, 1919). On November 2, 1918, the *London Gazette* announced award of an AFM to Sergeant H. Mitchell of "Renfrew, N.B."; no such town in New Brunswick can be identified. Royal Air Force authorities confirm that Mitchell had been serving in Scotland; it was common British practice at the time to describe that region as "North Britain."

3. *Air Raids, 1917*, compiled by Intelligence Section, General Headquarters Home Forces, August 1917, in Air Ministry file Air 1/646/17/122/360, copied by Directorate of History and now held in National Archives of Canada, MG.40 D.1 Volume 13.

4. Public Record Office Air 1/2054/206/409/13; see also Public Record Office Air 1/477/15/312/230, copied by Directorate of History and now held by National Archives of Canada, Manuscript Group 40 D.1, volume 10.

5. Croil's career is further described in *Roundel,* June 1959.

6. Public Record Office Air 1/1717.

7. Frank J. Shrive, *The Diary of a P. B.O.* (Erin, Boston Mills Press, 1981), p. 57.

8. Karle E. Hayes, *A History of the Royal Air Force and the United States Naval Air Service in Ireland, 1913-1923* (Dublin, Irish Air Letter, 1988), p. 40; see also Patrick J. McCarthy, "The RAF and Ireland, 1920-22," *The Irish Sword*, Volume XVII, No. 68 (1969).

9. The Para Rescue Association of Canada, *That Others May Live: 50 Years of Para Rescue in Canada* (Astra, Air Transport Group, 1994), p. 9.

10. See S.F. Wise, *Canadian Airmen and the First World War* (Toronto, University of Toronto Press, 1980), p. 213. Public Record Office file Air 1/456/15/312/51 (copy held in National Archives of Canada, MG.40 D.1 Volume 9) reports the attack.

11. A.J. Jackson, *Blackburn Aircraft Since 1909* (London, Putnam, 1968), pp. 113-114.

12. File AIR 1/465/15/312/149 held in National Archives of Canada, MG 40 D.1 Volume 9; file AIR 1/726/137/4 held MG.40 D.1 Volume 16.

13. Report dated July 14, 1918, in Air Ministry file Air 1/413/15/242, copied by Directorate of History and now held by National Archives of Canada, MG.40 D.1, Volume 7.

14. Public Record Office Air 1/39 AH15/9/6, copied by Directorate of History and filed in the National Archives of Canada, MG.40 D.1, Volume 2.

15. RCAF file 821-4-47 "McKee Trans-Canada Trophy – Nominations and Presentation – 1947 Competition," in National Archives of Canada, Record Group 24, Volume 17795.

16. Stuart Graham log book (photocopy) held by National Aviation Museum of Canada (LG01.0044). See also Peter Pigott, *Flying Canucks: Famous Canadian Aviators* (Toronto, Hounslow, 1994), which includes brief chapters on AFC winners Carl Agar, A.E. Godfrey, Stuart Graham and Paul Hartman.

17. Air Ministry correspondence dated September 21 and 24, 1918, in Public Record Office Air 1/289/15/226/139, copied by Directorate of History and now held in National Archives of Canada, MG.40 D.1 Volume 7. Correspondence dated June 8th, 1918, Public Record Office file Air 1/461/15, 312/108, held in MG.40 D.1 Volume 9. Relations between British officers and Canadian subordinates appear to have been very strained during the First World War, more

so than in the Second World War. The British may have been insensitive and the Canadians excessively touchy. An incident in May 1916 illustrated the problem. Four Canadians in the RNAS based at Yarmouth demanded transfer to another air station when their commanding officer made disparaging remarks about their accents; the officer in question threatened to charge them with "mutinous assembly"; superiors scolded the CO and quietly dispersed the Canadians to different bases; Air 1/416/15/243/15, National Archives of Canada, MG.40 D.1 Volume 7.

18. Peter Hearne, *The Sky People: A History of Parachuting* (Airlife, Shrewsbury, 1990), p. 40; John Lucas, *The Big Umbrella: The History of the Parachute from Da Vinci to Apollo* (Elmtree Books, London, 1973), pp. 56-71. The Directorate of History, Canadian Forces Headquarters, holds a manuscript, "Draft Narrative – The History of the Parachute Until 1918" by Captain A.W. Strynadka (file 112.3H.003, Docket 78).

19. *Letters From the Front*, pp. 315-318. A card file at the Directorate of History gives some scanty information. He is shown as still with No. 4 Squadron as of October 22, 1916, and his posting to No. 1 Southern Aircraft Repair Depot is given as March 1, 1918 (it is possible that his handwriting was not clear to the compiler of *Letters from the Front* who may have confused "1916" with "1918"). The Directorate of History copied some documents regarding early parachute trials from Public Record Office Air 1/1071/204/5/1637 and Air 1/1079/204/5/1681 (now filed at the National Archives of Canada in MG.40 D.1, Volume 20). However, they mention no names other than that of Major Orde-Lees.

20. *The Aeroplane*, March 3, July 14, July 28, and December 22, 1920; July 4, 1923.

21. Report by Shook dated June 14, 1918; Public Record Office Air 1/73/15/9/55, copied by Directorate of History and filed in the National Archives of Canada, MG.40 D.1, Volume 3.

22. Public Record Office Air 1/57/15/9/55, copied by Directorate of History and filed in the National Archives of Canada, MG.40 D.1, Volume 2.

23. For a detailed account of this unit see H.A. Halliday, "Beamsville Story," *Journal of the Canadian Aviation Historical Society*, Volume VII, No. 3 (Autumn 1969). Lieutenant-Colonel P. Huskinson, RAF, had originally commanded the base (*Beamsville Express*, August 28, 1918) but Godfrey succeeded to that post without the more senior rank.

24. Welland *Telegraph*, August 7, 1918, reprinted in *Beamsville Express* of August 14, 1918.

25. Interview notes, Godfrey-Halliday, November 20, 1962; Godfrey told the same story, in more detail, to officers of the Directorate of History, November 2, 1972.

26. File Air 1/721/48/5, copied by Directorate of History and now held by National Archives of Canada, MG.40 D.1 Volume 15.

27. The full text of Godfrey's remarks is in Air 1/2388/228/11/73, copied by Directorate of History and now held in the National Archives of Canada (MG.40 D.1, Vol.34).

28. Godfrey interview, November 2, 1972.

29. Godfrey's papers have been deposited with the RCAF Memorial Museum, Trenton, Ontario; a full-length biography of this officer has still to be written. See also Alice Gibson Sutherland, *Canada's Aviation Pioneers: 50 Years of McKee Trophy Winners* (Toronto, McGraw-Hill Ryerson, 1978), pp. 288-293.

30. Toronto *Star* 3 June 1918 and July 25, 1918; Kingston *British Whig*, September 23, 1918. The papers of the late Harry Creagen, deposited with the National Aviation Museum, give a great deal of information about First World War aviation, including a mass of detail on the RFC/RAF training scheme in Canada.

31. His pilot was another Canadian, Lieutenant J.G. Crang (awarded AFC, November 2, 1918).

32. Hoy, a veteran fighter pilot, was the first man to fly through the Canadian Rockies. For more on the Newcastle exhibition (which attracted 175,000 visitors) see *The Aeroplane*, February 12 and April 1, 1919. Anther Canadian participating was Captain Norman R. Anderson, who later became an air vice-marshal in the RCAF; his logbooks are held by the Directorate of History and Heritage in Ottawa.

33. Excerpt from file AIR 1/840/204/5/338, copied by Directorate of History and now held by National Archives of Canada, MG.40 D.1 Volume 17.

34. Directorate of History card file on Canadians in First World War flying services, records of 2nd Lieutenant William F. Sullivan.

35. The author is indebted Stuart A.M. Robertson (son-in-law), who supplied considerable information on Sisley (letter dated March 24, 1996).

36. File Air 1/721/48/5, copied by Directorate of History and now held by National Archives of Canada, MG.40 D.1 Volume 15.

37. Philby was described by Lawrence as one of the "Big Four" in Arabian affairs; later he would be British Administrator in Mesopotamia (Iraq).

38. H.St.J.B. Philby, *Arabian Days* (London, Robert Hale, 1948), pp. 180-181.

39. Public Record Office Air 1/110 has extensive correspondence on this adventure. Copies of the Yates and Borden correspondence is in the Canadian Armed Forces DHist, file 72/686. Their flight is also described by Chaz Bower, *Handley-Page Bombers of the First World War* (Aston Publications, Bourne End, 1992), pp. 111-113 and Captain L.S. Pope, "Another Incredible Journey," *Sentinel*, October 1968; Guy Simser, "A Daring Young Man in His Flying Machine," *The Beaver*, June-July 2000. See also Douglas E. Eagles, *Memoirs of a World War I Pilot, Lieutenant Harry A. Yates, AFC* (Sarnia, private printing, 1985). The identity of the officer who remarked about British tendencies to patronize and lie is unknown.

40. See "In Memoriam," *Journal of the Canadian Aviation Historical Society*, Volume 13, No. 1 (Spring 1975); Sutherland, *op. cit.*, pp. 199-205. A photocopy of his wartime logbook is held by the National Aviation Museum.

41. See Bill Cumming, "The Man Who Refused to Die: G/C Joseph Stewart Temple Fall," *Journal of the Canadian Aviation Historical Society*, Summer 1990.

Chapter 3: Interregnum

1. Abbott and Tamplin, *op. cit.*, give slightly different figures using different time frames. The numbers they use are as follows:

	AFC	Bar to AFC	2nd Bar	AFM	Bar to AFM	Civilian AFC	Civilian AFM
1920-1937	97	10	3	65	3	14	3
1938-1939	48	–	–	38	–	–	–

2. One book, *Canadians in the Royal Air Force* by Les Allison, states that Pope had transferred from the Canadian Expeditionary Force. Biographical sketches of him, published in *The Patrician* (a magazine published by No. 32 Operational Training Unit, Patricia Bay) make no reference to Canadian connections; Pope was born in Dublin (1898) and was attending a private British school when he enrolled in the Royal Flying Corps (1916). Nor can any CEF records be found of him in the National Archives of Canada. His retirement plans were laid out in *The Aeroplane*, March 15, 1946, p. 306.

3. *The Aeroplane*, January 16, 1924; see also Vice-Admiral Sir Arthur Hezlet, *Aircraft and Sea Power* (London, Peter Davies, 1970), p. 119. An informal account of the operation is found in the memoires of Group Captain G.E. Livock, *To The Ends of the Air* (London, Her Majesty's Stationary Office, 1973), pp. 76-97. Public Record Office Air 5/820 includes the Air Ministry's report, which gives much operational information and statistics but does not deal with the adventures of the individual pilots or observers.

4. Public Record Office Air 30/66.

5. *The Aeroplane*, January 7, 1949.

6. Public Record Office Air 2/9315.

7. Tom Coughlin, *The Dangerous Sky: Canadian Airmen in World War II* (Toronto, Ryerson Press, 1968), pp. 17-19; Geoffrey Dorman, *British Test Pilots* (London, Forbes Robertson Limited, 1950), pp. 79-83; H.A. Halliday, *The Tumbling Sky* (Stittsville, Canadas's Wings, 1978), pp. 157-164; Lloyd Hunt, *We Happy Few* (Ottawa, Canadian Fighter Pilots Association, 1986), pp. 76-78; J.A. Kent, *One of the Few* (London, William Kimber, 1971); Michel Lavigne, *Canadian Wing Commanders* (Langley, Battleline Books, 1984), pp. 183-194. The text of his AFC recommendation is in Public Record Office Air 2/9315; a copy is held by this author.

8. Details of his nomination are found in Public Record Office Air 2/2489.

9. Many writers (this one included) have stated that some 800 Canadians were decorated. On closer examination, it would seem that about 800 awards were made. As many fliers received multiple honours (William Barker, for example, received nine awards), the actual number of recipients was probably closer to 600.

10. J. Castel Hopkins, *The Canadian Annual Review of Public Affairs, 1919* (Toronto, The Canadian Annual Review Limited, 1920), pp 157-173.

11. C.D. Coulthard-Clark, *The Third Brother: The Royal Australian Air Force, 1921-1939*, pp. 385-392. Trist later became an Australian bush pilot; he died in the crash of a Junkers W.34 in New Guinea in 1931; see Terry Gwynn-Jones, "Flying for Gold," *Aeroplane Monthly*, June and July 1991.

12. *London Gazette*, May 31 and December 3, 1929; the first publication gave his name as Leslie Joseph Brain; the second corrected this to Lester Joseph Brain.

13. *London Gazette*, March 10, 1931.

14. *The Aeroplane*, June 7, 1933, June 15, 1938, January 11, 1939 and June 14, 1939.

15. For the text of the Slemon nomination see volume 1 of RCAF file 821-4, "Trophies for Individuals – McKee Trans-Canada Trophy," in National Archives of Canada, Record Group 24, Volume 17795.

16. House of Commons *Debates*, February 12, 13 and 14, 1929, pp. 74-78, 90-101 and 102-118.

17. Ottawa *Citizen*, January 3, 1933; House of Commons *Debates*, May 17, 22, 23 and 24, 1933, pp. 5126, 5235, 5323, and 5371-5372.

18. Ottawa *Citizen*, January 2, 1934. The Imperial quota (found in Bennett Papers, National Archives of Canada Microfilm M-1068, folio 236555, telegram dated December 18, 1933, from Buckingham Palace to Governor General) had been as follows:

GCMG – 1   KBE – 1   KB – 2   CMG – 4
CBE – 7   OBE – 11   MBE – 16

19. *Citizen, op. cit,* p. 15. See also *Canadian Annual Review, 1934*, pp. 45-46.

20. Ottawa *Citizen*, June 4, 1934.

21. See Bennett Papers, National Archives of Canada Microfilm M-1069, folios 237423 to 237443 for details of specific awards.

22. *Ibid.*, folios 237326 to 237332.

23. *Ibid.*, folios 236178 to 236194.

24. F.J. Blatherwick, *Canadian Orders, Decorations and Medals* (Toronto, Unitrade Press, 1985), p. 84; DHist file 113.302009 D.85, "Coronation Medals 1937."

25. DHist file 113.302009.D86 "Medals and Decorations."

26. Of these, the most famous was Sir Harry Oakes (1874-1943). American by birth, he made his fortune in Canadian mining but moved to the Bahamas in 1935 to escape Canadian taxes. By judicious philanthropy he persuaded authorities to grant him a baronetcy in 1939. One of the last Canadians knighted was Sir Charles F. Loewen, who joined the British Army upon graduation from RMC, Kingston. He had a very distinguished career during the Second World War and in the Far East afterwards; he rose to the rank of general and was knighted in 1951.

Chapter 4: Second World War Awards

1. The recipients were, of course, S/L E.A. McNab, F/L G.R. McGregor and F/O B.D. Russel, who had distinguished themselves in the Battle of Britain.

2. FS J.R. Burdes finally was granted his BEM in June 1942; FS C.M. Gale was Mentioned in Despatches at the same time. The two persons initially recommended for MBEs never received these awards, although S/L W.R. Pollock was awarded an AFC in April 1945 for services with No. 14 SFTS; by then he had attained the rank of group captain.

3. Leading Aircraftmen Peter P. Conlin and Cecil R. James, using an 18-foot dinghy, rescued a Norwegian pilot whose aircraft had crashed and caught fire in the bay. Their exploit took place on March 18, 1941; their awards were announced on October 6, 1941. Norwegian authorities subsequently attempted to supplement the BEMs with a Norwegian decoration, but this stalled somewhere in the bureaucracy of honours. See Western Air Command file C.122-7-1 "Honours and Awards" (DHist file 181.009 D.1938, found in National Archives of Canada, Record Group 24, Volume 20612.

4. Wing Commander Sedley S. Blanchard of Edmonton had been recommended by RAF authorities early in 1942 for services out of Bermuda; he was described as "a skilful, courageous and determined pilot." The award was delayed and never gazetted while RAF officers waited for their Canadian counterparts to work out the policy. Blanchard was killed in action with No. 426 Squadron on February 14, 1943. Public Record Office Air 2/8910 documents his AFC nomination; see also Les Allison and Harry Hayward, *They Shall Grow Not Old* (Brandon, Commonwealth Air Training Plan Museum, 1992).

5. Proceedings of *Special Committee on Honours and Decorations* (House of Commons). National Library Microfiche 160 COPS (COP CA.4.FI.1.26).

6. Much of this is based upon copies of correspondence in Air 2/6100 records, copied and held by the Directorate of History, CFHQ.

7. See Volume 4 of RCAF file 821-4, "Trophies for Individuals – McKee Trans-Canada Trophy," in National Archives of Canada, Record Group 24, Volume 17795.

8. Air Force Routine Order 2322/43 dated 12 November 1943, reporting his being awarded the AFC.

9. Public Record Office Air 2/9019.

10. Public Record Office Air 2/8891. See also Martin Middlebrook and Chris Everitt, *The Bomber Command War Diaries* (New York, Viking, 1985), p. 523.

11. Public Record Office Air 2/8891.

12. Public Record Office Air 2/6269.

13. *Ibid.*

14. Cy Torontow, *Up, Up and Oy Vay !* (Ottawa, private printing 1990).

15. Crash card relating to Catalina Z2140, formerly held by Canadian Forces Directorate of History and now by the National Aviation Museum; DHist file 181.009 D.3060 in National Archives of Canada, Record Group 24, Volume 20635.

16. RCAF file 821-4-41, "McKee Trans-Canada Trophy – Nominations and Presentation – 1941 Competition," in National Archives of Canada, Record Group 24, Volume 17795.

17. Coughlin, *op. cit.* (see chapter 3, note 7), pp. 87-89; see also W.A.B. Douglas, *The Creation of a National Air Force* (Toronto, University of Toronto Press, 1986) for numerous references to Small. See also Torontow, *op. cit.*

18. Governor General's Records, National Archives of Canada, Record Group 7, Group 26, Volume 57, dossier for 1943; see also Douglas, *op. cit.*, pp. 553-554. A detailed account of Moffit's sinking of *U-630* is found in Larry Milberry's *Sixty Years: The RCAF and CF Air Command, 1924-1984* (Toronto, CANAV Books, 1984), pp. 122-124).

19. Correspondence and recommendations are in DHist file 181.009 D.3061, National Archives of Canada Record Group 24, Volume 20635.

20. DHist files 181.009 D.1283 (National Archives of Canada Record Group 24, Volume 20597) has lengthy reports on the incident. See also F.J. Blatherwick *1000 Brave Canadians* (Toronto, Unitrade Press, 1991), p. 125 for the text of Sergeant Bailey's George Medal, and Larry Milberry, *Air Transport in Canada*, Volume 1 (Toronto, CANAV Books, 1997), pp. 159-161.

21. Goose Bay file S-4-2, ""Operations – Mercy Flights," in the Directorate of History (document 181.009 D.1041).

22. See also H.A. Halliday and Larry Milberry, *RCAF at War, 1939-1945* (Toronto, CANAV Books, 1990), pp. 135-136.

23. As of June 1998, Gatewest Coin and Militaria (Winnipeg) were selling Kauffeldt's medals with his logbook for $ 2,200.

24. Halliday and Milberry, *op. cit.*, p. 136. See also RCAF file 821-4-45, "McKee Trans-Canada Trophy – Nominations and Presentation – 1945 Competition," in National Archives of Canada, Record Group 24, Volume 17795.

25. Minister of National Defence for Air writing to Government House, August 30, 1945; see Governor General's records, National Archives of Canada, Record Group 7, Group 26, Volume 59 (File I-190, dossier 7).

26. See Milberry, *Air Transport in Canada*, Volume 1, pp. 315 and 345-346. Additional information supplied by Scott Price (Historian), U.S. Coast Guard Headquarters, December 12, 1995. British authorities occasionally recommended AFCs for American personnel wherever the Allies shared operations. For example, Captain Woodrow W. Dickey, USAAF, was recommended for an AFC for months of service as personal pilot to Field Marshal Sir Harold Alexander, Supreme Allied Commander Mediterranean Theatre (Public Record Office Air 2/9138).

27. *Coastal Command Review*, December 1943 (DHist document 181.003 D.963). See also C.H. Ward-Jackson and Leighton Lucas, *Airman's Song Book* (London, William Blackwood, 1967). ASR aircrews were doubtless gratified at such praise, but leavened their pride with self-mockery. An RAF song, set to the tune of *The Church Is One Foundation*, reflected these attitudes:

    We are the Air-Sea Rescue, no ruddy good are we.
    The only time you'll find us is at breakfast, dinner, tea.
    And when we see a dinghy we shout with all out might,
    "Per ardua Ad Astra – damn you chaps, we're all right."

28. *Coastal Command Review*, January 1945.

29. Stephen Brewis Daniels, *Rescue From the Skies: The Story of the Airborne Lifeboat* (London, Royal Air Force Museum, 1993), p. 206.

30. See Chris Ashworth, *RAF Coastal Command, 1936-1969* (Sparkford, Patrick Stephens, 1992), pp. 170-179 for more on the history of RAF Air/Sea Rescue; W/C R. Birchall, "Air-Sea Rescue in Wartime," *The Aeroplane*, April 5 and April 12, 1946. For a Canadian slant, see "Air-Sea Rescue," *Canadian Aviation*, March 1945.

31. The interested reader is invited to consult Hugh A. Halliday, "Air-Sea Rescue Pilot: The Exploits of John Spencer, RCAF," in *High Flight*, Volume 2, No. 1; H.A. Halliday and Larry Milberry, *The Royal Canadian Air Force at War, 1939-1945* (Toronto, CANAV Books, 1990), p. 322

32. Public Record Office Air 2/9144; Daniels, *op. cit.*, p. 92.

33. Quoted in the Foreword to *History of the Canadian Forces Weather Services, 1939-1989*, DHist document 90/53. This study outlines the development of meteorological services on the ground but gives no details about the airborne weather checks.

34. For more on meteorological flying, see K.A. Merrick, *Halifax: An*

Illustrated History of a Classic World War II Bomber (London, Ian Allan, 1980), pp. 126-129.

35. On April 12, 1944, Halifax "G" of No. 517 Squadron discovered a U-boat at position 49 degrees 28 minutes north, 18 degrees 45 minutes west. G/517 strafed the enemy, scoring hits on the hull and conning tower; the submarine returned the fire but registered no hits on the Halifax, which despatched a sighting report. Captain of the "Hallie" was Warrant Officer S.A. Young (RCAF) whose crew included three other Canadians – F/O L.G. Dunlop, Warrant Officer W.E. Danforth, and Sergeant A.H. Dixon. Although none were subsequently decorated, the incident was one of those rare occasions when a weather sortie developed into a brush with submarines.

36. Public Record Office Air 2/9004.

37. *London Gazette* dated June 8, 1944; Public Record Office Air 2/9004 has recommended citation.

38. Public Record Office Air 2/9144 identified unit and has recommendations; another adventure had seen their aircraft holed by anti-aircraft fire and a return to base with the instruments, oxygen, electrical and hydraulic systems inoperable and minimal radio aids available.

39. *Coastal Command Review*, February 1945, pp. 22-23.

40. Martin had won his DFM overseas in 1941 with No. 42 Squadron (Beaufort torpedo bombers).

41. Hank Reed, *RCAF Station Yarmouth: East Camp/West Camp* (Yarmouth, East Camp Veterans, 1996), p. 66.

42. National Archives of Canada; Governor General's Records (Record Group 7, Group 26, Volume 59, file 190-I, dossier 7).

43. Squadron Leader Partridge's logbooks have been copied by the National Aviation Museum.

44. E.T. Karcut, *The History of 6 RD and the Aerospace Development Unit* (Erin, Boston Mills Press, 1990), p. 32.

45. RCAF Headquarters File S.47-6-3, "Aviation Medical Research: Committee Thereon," in National Archives of Canada, Record Group 24 E.1, Volume 5383. See also Michael Bliss, *Banting: A Biography* (Toronto, McClelland and Stewart, 1981) for scattered references to Hall.

46. W/C G.W. Manning, *World War Two Royal Canadian Air Force Medical Research Reports*, DHist document 90/221. See also G.E. Hall, "Aviation Medicine in the Royal Canadian Air Force," *Journal of the American Medical Association*, August 1, 1942, pp. 1104-1107,

47. Clipping from unidentified newspaper, circa January 1944, supplied by John M. Ward (brother-in-law), March 5th, 1996.

48. For more on the subject of aviation medicine, see George Smith, *Canadian Aviation Medicine, 1939-1945* (MA thesis, University of Western Ontario, 1996); Edgar C. Black, *History of the Associate Commitee on Aviation Medicine Research, 1939-1945* (Ottawa, National Research Council, 1946).

49. Sir Philip Livingston, *Fringe of the Clouds: The Story of an RAF Doctor* (Toronto, Ryerson Press, 1962), a rather plodding autobiography that does not do justice to his career. See also T.M. Gibson and M.H. Harrison, *Into Thin Air: A History of Aviation Medicine in the Royal Air Force* (London, Robert Hale, 1984). The text of his AFC recommendation (found in Public Record Office Air 2/8910) was as follows: This officer is consultant in ophthalmology, and has rendered most valuable services to the Royal Air Force not only in the visual examination of personnel but on vision problems in general, in particular those related to flying. He has given considerable help in improving our night flying and interception by devising means for testing the night visual acuity of personnel, as well as in developing a pre-adaptation goggle to night-adapt our fighter personnel before taking off, so that their night vision is equivalent to the enemy's who have already become night-adapted during flight to this country at night. In addition he has designed and developed anti-searchlight devices for bomb aimers and pilots as well as developing devices to improve aircraft recognition. In all his researches he has spent many hours in the air, both by day and night, to design and prove the practical value of the various devices he has introduced. Furthermore, he has carried out many tests in the low pressure chamber at Farnborough to assess the relation of oxygen-want at varying altitudes to night blindness, as well as the effect of certain drugs on visual acuity, later proving his point by actual flight in the air.

50. Public Record Office Air 2/6269.

51. The author is indebted to Bruce Finch for photocopies of the relevant logbook entries. Additional information from Public Record Office Air 2/9004. See also Alan Wood, *History of the World's Glider Forces* (Willingborough, Patrick Stephens, 1990); Lawrence Wright, *The Wooden Sword* (London, Elek Books, 1967) deals specifically with the Airborne Forces Experimental Establishment in its many projects, though it does not mention Fink. See also Charles

W. Prower, "Gliding Tanks," *Aeroplane Monthly*, July 1993. Canadian association with airborne operations dated back to some of the earliest applications. An RCAF navigator, George L. Court, was involved in dropping paratroops during the Bruneval operation (February 27, 1942).

52. Public Record Office Air 2/9019.

53. Public Record Office Air 2/8771.

54. RCAF file 900-24, "Public Relations, RCAF," Volume Two, in National Archives of Canada, Record Group 24, Volume 17884. R77219 Sergeant G.C. Burns had graduated from No. 6 Service Flying Training School in July 1941; he survived the war, having won his commission and being Mentioned in Despatches for services with No. 433 Squadron.

55. The poem existed in several versions; this one was in a scrapbook kept by W/C Robert Byers. For more on instructors in the BCATP, see F.J. Hatch, *The Aerodrome of Democracy* (Ottawa, Department of Supply and Services, 1983), pp. 115-161.

56. Walker was awarded a DFC in February 1945 for services as a pilot in No. 77 Squadron.

57. Gale was killed in a flying accident on May 25, 1946; he was at Farnborough, diving a Mustang to about Mach .82 in order to explore the behaviour of wing sections at near-sonic speeds. He made eight dives from 40,000 to 20,000 feet; while climbing for another test he mysteriously lost control and plunged vertically into the ground. There was speculation that he had sustained oxygen failure, but the aircraft was wrecked so thoroughly that little remained to prove any theory.

58. In his career, Fullerton was honoured with both the Trans-Canada Trophy and an Air Force Cross; see Alice Gibson Sutherland, *op. cit.*, (see chapter 2, note 29) pp. 76-84; Showler is covered in the same work, pp. 244-247.

59. At the end of the war Darraugh estimated his flying times at various stations; the reader will note that they total 2,825 hours without even counting his own time spent as a student; that would have brought his total flying time to about 3,000 hours. Other documents, however, indicate that his wartime flying totalled between 2,150 and 2,350 hours. His hours at various schools may therefore be assumed as being exaggerated about 25 per cent. Even the lower figures are impressive; Darraugh's rough estimates at least show the intensity of his flying at various stages of his career.

60. McCaffery's career is further described in *Critical Moments: Profiles of Members of the Greater Vancouver Branch of the Aircrew Association* (Vancouver, 1989), pp. 70-73.

61. For his account of this incident see *Flypast*, October 1982.

62. See H.A. Halliday, *The Tumbling Sky* (Canada's Wings, Stittsville, 1978), pp. 95-102; Tom Coughlin, *op. cit.*, (note 82), pp. 40-42.

63. For more of Kernaghan's wartime experiences, see *Memories on Parade: Aircrew Recollections of World War II* (Winnipeg, Wartime Pilots' and Observers' Association, 1995), pp. 124-125.

64. For an interesting description of these tasks, see M.J. Collins, "The RCAF's Flying Ground Crew," *Journal of the Canadian Aviation Historical Society*, Volume 36, No. 4 (Winter 1998).

65. Air Force Routine Order 185/43 dated February 5, 1943. This is a rare instance of an AFM citation which was published in full. The aircraft that crashed was Harvard 3719.

66. FS Arthur N. Hornby and Corporal Terence D. Reilly (both awarded AFMs), W/C R.H. Waterhouse and W/C R.D. Pexton (both AFC winners) have, in various publications, have been identified as CAN/RAF personnel. None appear on lists of such personnel compiled in 1940-1941 for joint RAF-RCAF purposes (DHist files 181.005 dockets 270, 271, 1094, 1095, 1096). At the time of their awards they were serving in Canada, and their home towns were given as the towns near their place of service. In fact, their sole Canadian connections appear to have been their temporary service sojourn in this country.

67. Public Record Office Air 2/8959.

68. A photostat copy of Group Captain Green's logbook is held by the National Aviation Museum in Ottawa.

69. See J.D. Rawlings, "Operational Training Unit," *Air Britain Digest*, Volume V, No. 12 (December 1953), pp. 6-7.

70. William Carter and Spencer Dunmore, *Reap the Whirlwind: The Untold Story of 6 Group, Canada's Bomber Force of World War II* (Toronto, McClelland and Stewart, 1991), p. 57.

71. Public Record Office Air 2/9004.

72. DHist file 181.009 D.2993 in National Archives of Canada, Record Group 24, Volume 20634. See also Public Record Office Air 2/9019.

73. It should be remembered that Canadian overseas training units included many British personnel whose contributions earned decorations as well. One example was F/O Ernest William Tacon (awarded AFC, June 11, 1942). He was first recommended for the

award in September 1941 for his work at training the first 32 Hudson pilots of No. 407 Squadron (plus 17 crews in No. 59 Squadron). The submission stated that "all these pilots are fresh from the School of General Reconnaissance and had not flown as pilots for periods extending from four to eight months. Moreover, some of these pilots had flown less than 100 hours solo on all types.... From 16th July to August 31st, Flying Officer Tacon flew 133 hours, principally on instructional work in Hudson aircraft. During all this time, neither he nor any of his pupils were involved in any accident. In addition he lectured all pilots of the squadron on the handling and operational tactics for Hudson aircraft." When no award was forthcoming, the CO of No. 407 Squadron made another submission (February 9, 1942), this time successful (DHist file 181.009 D.2620, National Archives of Canada RG.24, Volume 20628). His importance to RAF development may be gleaned from his final title – A/C E.E. Tacon, CBE, DSO, MVO, DFC, AFC. Another instance was W/C Robert Thomas Langton, DFM, long the Chief Flying Instructor at No. 1666 HCU, Wombleton. He had been twice recommended for an award (an AFC in June 1943, an OBE in July 1944) before G/C N.S. MacGregor successfully sponsored an Air Force Cross which was awarded in January 1945. Among other reasons, Langton was singled out for skill at instructing pilots in how to deal with some of the worst problems faced by four-engine bomber crews – flying with two engines on one side only (including turns to port and starboard) and coping with engine cut-outs on take off. (DHist file 181.009 D.2993, National Archives of Canada, Record Group 24 Vol.20634). Flight Sergeant S.H. Lewthwaite (RAF) was awarded an Air Force Medal on January 1, 1945, for services as a flight engineer with No. 413 Squadron; in a little over one year he logged over 1,000 hours on Catalinas (DHist file 181.009 D.1751, National Archives of Canada Record Group 24, Volume 20608).

74. Public Record Office Air 2/8959.
75. See Carl Christie, *Ocean Bridge: The History of RAF Ferry Command* (Toronto, University of Toronto Press, 1995), the only thorough history of this formation. A card file of Ferry Command personnel is held by the Directorate of History, Canadian Forces Headquarters (Document 84/44-3) but for reasons unknown it had no entries past December 1944.
76. See H.A. Halliday, "Sunderlands in Norway," *Journal of the Canadian Aviation Historical Society*, Summer 1974; F.W. Hotson, "Big Boat Pilot," *ibid.*, Fall 1996.
77. Public Record Office Air 2/6269.
78. See F.M. Gobeil, "By Glider Across the Atlantic," *Journal of the Canadian Aviation Historical Society*, Volume 14, No. 1 (Spring 1976), pp. 23-29. Gobeil's papers have been deposited with the Canadian War Museum. Seys appears on some lists of CAN/RAF personnel, but in fact he was British whose only connection with Canada was his wartime Ferry Command service here. Longhurst transferred to the RCAF in May 1945; postwar he was a test and development pilot with Canadair. Gobeil died in 1994 and was the subject of a lenthy obituary in the *Journal of the Canadian Aviation Historical Society*, Volume 33, No. 3 (Fall 1995).
79. Recommendations for Ralph and Robinson are in Public Record Office Air 2/8968. For more on both the North Bay and Dorval training facilities see Carl Christie, *op. cit.* Crew cards on Ferry Command personnel, held by the Directorate of History and Heritage, Canadian Forces Headquarters, detail the background and aircraft delivery records of people in that organization.
80. For thorough studies of Canadian air transport services and their development, see Larry Milberry, *Air Transport in Canada* (two volumes).
81. "Survey of Winter Flying Boat Route Across the U.S.A.," in RCAF Headquarters file 1008-1-171, National Archives of Canada Record Group 24, Volume 4897.
82. Torontow, *op. cit.* (see note 14).
83. For a more detailed account, see Carl Vincent, *The Liberator and Fortress* (Canada's Wings, Stittsville, 1975), pp. 124-126. Hillcoat had won his AFM as a flying instructor at No. 19 Elementary Flying Training School, Virden, Manitoba; he was lost, together with Labrish and Dickson, when Fortress 9203 vanished between Rabat (Morocco) and Lagens (the Azores), December 15th, 1944.
84. A plaque honouring those killed was unveiled at Rockcliffe on May 5, 1947; its whereabouts are now unknown. See RCAF file 532-5, "Transportation by Air – Equipment and Supplies – Transportation of Penicillin to Poland, 1945," DHist document 181.009 D.2406.
85. Public Record Office Air 2/9019; see also *Critical Moments: Profiles of Members of the Greater Vancouver Branch of the Aircrew Association* (Vancouver, 1989), pp. 167-171.
86. Public Record Office Air 2/9061.
87. Alice Gibson Sutherland, *op. cit.*, pp. 237-243.

88. Nomination papers for their McKee Trophy awards may be found in RCAF file 821-4-56, "McKee Trans-Canada Trophy – Nominations and Presentation, 1956 Competition" and RCAF file 821-4-57, "McKee Trans-Canada Trophy – Nominations and Presentation, 1957 Competition," both in National Archives of Canada, Record Group 24, Volume 17,797. The former file also contains a detailed nomination (which did not succeed) of W/C Dudley Lyall Sait McWilliam, AFC for his postwar training duties, particularly the operational training of CF-100 crews. This was the sort of work that could not qualify for a "gallantry award" under postwar policies; a few years later it would have earned him membership in the Order of Military Merit.

89. The gun crew of a small Canadian armed merchant vessel, the SS *Maquina*, were apparently in the habit of firing practice rounds without informing authorities of their intentions. On this occasion between two and six shells landed in the water some 100 yards from shore and were observed by soldiers who swept the horizon with binoculars, spotted the vessel six miles distant, and sounded an alarm. The diary of Western Air Command Headquarters noted that the crew of the *Maquina* were going to be interviewed as soon as they docked.

90. Public Record Office Air 2/9061.

91. Mawdesley has been often mentioned and never analyzed; see articles in *Journal of the Canadian Aviation Historical Society*, Volume IV (No. 4), Volume VIII (No. 3), Volume XII (No. 4) and Vole XXXII No. 2 (Summer 1995); Max Hendrick, "What's a Pre-War Story Without Mawdesley?," *Airforce*, Volume IX, No. 2 (July-August-September 1985); Leslie Roberts, *There Shall Be Wings* (pp. 102-105 and 108); W.A.B. Douglas, *The Creation of a National Air Force*, pp. 113-115; Larry Milberry, *Aviation in Canada*, p. 192. The recommendation for the McKee Trophy can be found in Volume 2 of RCAF file 821-4, "Trophies for Individuals – McKee Trans-Canada Trophy," in National Archives of Canada, Record Group 24, Volume 17795.

92. Governor General's Records in National Archives of Canada, Record Group 7, Group 26, Volume 58, file 190-I, dossier 6. Another instance worth noting of considering use of an Air Force Cross as a belated "consolation prize" concerns S/L B.E. Christmas, a Battle of Britain veteran. On December 23, 1943, his colleague from that campaign, W/C Gordon McGregor, then CO at RCAF Station Patricia Bay, inquired of AFHQ is he might recommend Christmas for an award based on overseas actions that had occured more than two years before. A week later, AFHQ replied that the effort would fail. However, McGregor was advised that he might still obtain some recognition for Christmas: "If you make a very strong recommendation on his present work and past work in Patricia Bay, you certainly can get him an Air Force Cross." Apparently, McGregor did not follow through on this suggestion; no AFC recommendation has been found and certainly none was gazetted; McGregor Papers, National Archives of Canada, Manuscript Group 30 E.283, Volume 1.

93. DHist file 181.009 D.2993 held in the National Archives of Canada (Record Group 24, Volume 20634).

94. Public Record Office Air 2/8959.

95. The Bar to Turnbull's DFC was originally intended to have been a DSO, as recommended by A/C J.G. Bryans (DHist file 181.009 D.2609, in National Archives of Canada RG.24, Volume 12627). This was evidently downgraded at the level of Bomber Command Headquarters or Air Ministry Honours and Awards Committee.

96. Tom Coughlin, *op. cit.*, (see note 17), pp. 204-205.

97. Z.L. Leigh, *And I Shall Fly* (Toronto, CANAV Books, 1985), pp. 183-184. See also RCAF file 821-4-45, "McKee Trans-Canada Trophy – Nominations and Presentation – 1945 Competition," in National Archives of Canada, Record Group 24, Volume 17795.

98. One book describing Donaldson's career does not even mention his Canadian sojourn; see Geoffrey Dorman, *British Test Pilots* (London, Forbes Robertson Limited, 1950), pp. 55-58. Donaldson was recommended in October 1937 for an AFC arising out of aerobatic team accomplishments with No. 1 Squadron, but the award was not approved (Public Record Office Air 2/2489); the recommendation for his wartime AFC is in Public Record Office Air 2/9544.

99. *The Aeroplane*, February 13 and March 5, 1948.

100. William A. Waterton, *The Quick and the Dead* (London, Frederick Muller, 1956).

Chapter 5: "Bravery in the Performance of Duty": 1947–1966

1. RCAF File 45-26-1, "Honours and Awards – Recommendations – Operation Musk-Ox," found in National Archives of Canada, Record Group 24, Volume 5379.

2. RCAF file 45-26-1 (B.C. Floods), in National Archives of Canada

Record Group 24, Volume 5378. F/L Lyle Augustus Harling was recommended for an MBE, he having displayed outstanding skill in organizing airlifts of emergency supplies; Warrant Officer John Robert Burdes, BEM, was recommended for a King's Commendation for assisting Harling; Corporal Maurice Harry Rose, recommended for a BEM, had directed messing arrangements at Abbotsford for upwards of 850 flood refugees at a time. All three submissions were drafted on October 15, 1948; as of October 23, 1948, the recommendations had been shot down by Air Force Headquarters, although copies of the recommendations were placed on the files of the three individuals. No subsequent awards went to Harling, but Burdes and Rose later received Queen's Coronation Medals (October 23, 1953); Rose had by then attained the rank of flight sergeant.

3. The official report of ATTACHE can be found in RCAF file 976-3-2 "Search and Rescue – Missing U.S. Naval Aircraft (Operation Attache)," National Archives of Canada, Record Group 24, Volume 18116. A personal account was also published by Captain B.S. Buster, USN, in *Collier's*, January 29th, 1949. See also Milberry, *Air Transport in Canada*, Volume 1, p.421.

The United States has no medal exactly equivalent to the AFC as described in this book; the award they style the Air Force Cross was created in 1960 as a combat award ranking just below the Congressional Medal of Honour. On the other hand, their Distinguished Flying Cross is awarded for bravery in both combat and non-combat situations, and in extraordinary circumstances may even be awarded to civilians (Amerlia Earhart, for example). James Doolittle won two peacetime Distinguished Flying Crosses; Chuck Yeager received a combat DFC during the Second World War and a non-combat DFC when he became the first pilot to fly faster than sound. At least one member of the RCAF (F/L Douglas G. Scott, Russell, Ontario) serving on exchange duties with the USAF has been awarded an American DFC in circumstances that would have justified a Commonwealth AFC. The award was announced without explanation in the *Canada Gazette* of May 7, 1960. American documents have supplied the citation: Flight Lieutenant Douglas G. Scott, Royal Canadian Air Force, distinguished himself by meritorious achievement while participating in aerial flight on 29 June, 1959, 450 miles north of Point Barrow, Alaska, over the Arctic ice pack. While serving as aircraft commander of a WB-50, assigned to the 55th Weather Reconnaissance Squadron, 17 1/2 inches of a propeller blade on the Number Two engine separated and entered the fuselage, severing the control cables, power sources, hydraulic lines and the bomb bay door actuator, causing heavy drag and buffeting. Flight Lieutenant Scott analyzed the serious emergency and calmly made every needed compensation. He regained control and successfully returned his aircraft over 900 miles without additional damage, thereby saving a valuable aircraft and eleven crew members from possible injury or death. By his exemplary performance in the face of extreme danger, Flight Lieutenant Scott reflected great credit upon himself, the United States Air Force, and the Royal Canadian Air Force. For a more detailed account see *Air Weather Service Observer*, July 1959.

4. "Extract from Minutes of Defence Council Meeting No. 40, held 27th May 1949," found in RCAF file 45-26-1 (Fleet Canuck CF-DEJ), "Honours and Awards – Recommendations – Fleet Canuck CF-DEJ," National Archives of Canada, Record Group 24, Volume 5378.

5. Secretary of State file 114-2-01-2 "Awards (Specific) – Order of the British Empire (Submissions)," National Archives of Canada, Record Group 6 D.1, Volume 361.

6. Cabinet Directive, Circular No. 30, dated November 7th, 1956.

7. Minutes of a Meeting of the Inter-Service Awards Committee, October 12 and 19, found in DHist file 75/601, folio 18. The Canada Medal, instituted in 1943, had never been awarded; see H.A. Halliday, "Lost Honour: The Very Strange Story of the Canada Medal," *The Beaver*, August/September 1993.

8. Secretary of State Papers, National Archives of Canada, Record Group 6 D.1, Volume 359, file 114-2-A1-3 "Awards – Specific – Air Force Cross (Granted)"

9. RCAF file 45-26-1 "Honours and Awards – Service Recommendations – Captain," in National Archives of Canada, Record Group 24, Volume 5378.

10. See F.J. Blatherwick, *1,000 Brave Canadians* (Unitrade Press, Toronto, 1991), pp.145-147; "Operation Canon," *Canadian Army Journal*, May 1948, pp.9-15 and 29-32; H.A. Halliday, "Arctic Rescue," *The Beaver*, April/May 1995. Official RCAF and Army reports of Operation CANON may be found in the Directorate of History – files 181.003 D.1526 and 181.003 D.2261. The story is also (with a surprising twist) told by Milberry, *Air Transport in Canada*, Volume 1, pp.419-420.

11. The discussions and negotiations relative to these awards is documented in RCAF file 45-26-1 "Honours and Awards – Recommendations – Operation Moffet Islet," in National Archives of Canada, Record Group 24, Volume 5379. The affair might best be described as an argument between Brooke Claxton and George VI, with Viscount Alexander as an intermediary. McMillan had an interesting background; he had enlisted in August 1940 as a service policeman, remustering to aircrew in January 1942; trained as a navigator, he flew a wartime overseas tour. McMillan stuck with the postwar air force and retired in 1960.

12. RCAF file 45-26-1 (Fleet Canuck CF-DEJ), "Honours and Awards - Recommendations – Fleet Canuck CF-DEJ," in National Archives of Canada, Record Group 24, Volume 5378. This was the second time that Harling had been recommended (unsuccessfully) for a decoration; see note 2.

13. DHist file 75/601, folio 13.

14. *Ibid.*, folio 17.

15. Compiled from lists published in *The Aeroplane*, various issues. The strength of the RAF as of April 1949 was estimated to be between 225,000 and 232,000 (compared to 15,900 for the RCAF Regular and Auxiliary Forces) and 202,000 in April 1950 (19,600 for the RCAF); A.G.T. James, *The Royal Air Force: The Past 30 Years* (Macdonald and James, London, 1976), p.32; John D.R. Rawlings, *The History of the Royal Air Force* (Temple Press, Middlesex, 1984), p.179. Abbott and Tamplin, *op.cit.*, give numbers based on different time frames as follows:

	AFC	Bar to AFC	2nd Bar to AFC	AFM	Bar to AFM
1946-1979	2,242	115	8	384	4

16. No member of the RCAF was decorated for work associated with the postwar aerial mapping of Canada, while similar work by RAF personnel did result in awards. F/L Alfred Lloyd (RAF), for example, was awarded an AFC in January 1948 for services as a navigator with No. 82 Squadron, then mapping East Africa; in the same honours list, F/L Jack E. Major, RAF, was awarded an AFC for work as personal navigator to the Military Governor of the British Zone in occupied Germany. Other pilots were decorated for aerobatic and demonstration flying; see Public Record Office Air 2/9816.

17. *Flight International*, October 16, 1982. For more on British awards in the Search and Rescue role see John Winton, *For Those in Peril: 50 Years of Royal Navy Search and Rescue* (London, Robert Hale, 1992). This book describes many rescues that were recognized by a variety of awards.

18. These changes are outlined in *The Medal Yearbook, 1997* (Honiton, Token Publishing Ltd., 1997), p.80.

Chapter 6: Postwar Awards

1. Frank Rasky, *Explorers of the North: The North Pole or Bust* (Toronto, McGraw-Hill Ryerson, 1977), p.385.

2. See W/C D.C. McKinley, "The Arctic Flights of the *Aries*," W/C K.C. Maclure, "Technical Aspects of the Aries Flights," and W/C Winfield, "Note on the Medical Aspects of the *Aries* Flight," all in *The Geographical Journal*, Volume CVII, Nos. 3 and 4 (March-April), 1946; "Polar Navigation," *The Aeroplane*, December 28th, 1945; W/C R.H. Winfield, "The Royal Air Force North Polar Research Flights," *The Polar Record*, Volume 5, Nos. 33 and 34 (January-July), 1947; see also Bruce Robertson, *Lancaster: The Story of a Famous Bomber* (Harleyford Publications, Letchworth, 1964), pp.91-95; Francis K. Mason, *The Avro Lancaster* (London, Aston Publications, 1989), pp.211-212 and 221-222.

3. For more on MUSKOX see Donald Storr, "Musk-Ox Adventure," *The Beaver*, June/July 1987; H.A. Halliday, "Exercise MUSKOX," *Canadian Military History*, Autumn 1998.

4. RCAF file 945-11-1, "RCAF Research and Development – Polar Experimental Flight, Organization of," in National Archives of Canada, Record Group 24, Volume 3557.

5. The 1946 expedition is described in great detail by Doctor Nicholus Polunin, *Arctic Unfolding: Experiences and Observations During a Canadian Airborne Expedition in Northern Ungava, The Northwest Territories, and the Arctic Archipelago* (Toronto, Hutichinson and Company, 1949).

6. RCAF file 45-26-1 (Polco), "Honours and Awards – Recommendations – Operation Polco," in National Archives of Canada, Record Group 24, Volume 5379. See also F/L E.P. Wood, "Northern Skytrails: Part IX" in *Roundel*, Volume I, No. 11 (September 1948); "Magnetic Observations in the Canadian Arctic, 1947-1949" in *The Polar Record*, Volume VI, No. 42 (July 1951); "Operation Polco" in *The Arctic Circular*, Volume I, No. 3 (March 1948); H. Glenn Madill, "The Search for the North Magnetic Pole" in *Arctic: Journal of the Arctic Institute of North America*, Volume I, No. 1 (Spring 1948). Dr.

Y.O. Fortier, the senior geologist on "Polco," was made an Officer in the Order of Canada in 1980. For some of Goldsmith's wartime experiences, see *Memories on Parade: Aircrew Recollections of World War II* (Winnipeg, Wartime Pilots' and Observers' Association, 1995), pp.90-91.

7. These adventurous gentlemen were William B. Begy (Mentioned in Despatches in March 1950 and awarded DFC, June 1951, for services in Malaya), John P. Benga, Everett L. Brown (DFC), John A. Cline, Peter R. Curran, Joseph W.M. Elie, William I. Gould, Cameron F. Green (AFC), Herbert Hale, Frederick Hastings, Harold C. Hoover (DFC), John H. Huffman (AFC), Joseph Kicak (DFC), Joseph C.L. Labelle, George W. Lloyd, Donald K. Lynch, James R. Marvin (DFC), Roy A. McLeod (DFC), William M. Mitchell, Verne Montgomery, David L. Moore, Guy E. Mott (DFC, Mentioned in Despatches in March 1950 for services in Malaya), Norman E. Patterson (DFC), Arthur M. Plamton, Gordon R. Price, John V. Raymond, Mervin H. Sims (DFC), Maurice A.J. St.Pierre (awarded AFC, June 1953), Frank Sturgess, Lorne A. Tapp (DFC, awarded AFC, January 1950), John H. Tetro, Forbes W. Thompson, William A. Thurston, Henry P. Trudeau, Clifton L. Wenzel (DFC, awarded AFC in June 1949), Norman F. Wenzel, Kelley A. Whynacht (DFC, awarded AFC in June 1953), and Lewis Woloschuk (DFC).

8. See Richard Collier, *Bridge Across the Sky: The Berlin Blockade and Airlift, 1948-1949* (London, Macmillan, 1978); also Robert Rodrigo, *Berlin Airlift* (London, Cassel, 1960). Seven RAF York squadrons made 29,000 flights to Berlin, moving approximately 230,000 tons of supplies – more than half of all cargoes moved by the RAF during PLAINFARE; see M.J. Hardy, "Last of the War-Liners: The Story of the Avro York – Part 1," *Air Britain Digest*, Volume X No. 1 (January 1958), pp.8-9. For those with a maniacal interest in trivia, the only Canadian-built Avro York (FM400) served on the Berlin Airlift with a civilian firm (G-ALBX, *Sky Dominion*, Skyways Corporation); it crashed at Wunstorf on June 19, 1949; see John Stroud, "Postwar Propliners," *Aeroplane Monthly*, February 1993.

9. Letter to the author, January 14, 1998.

10. Public Record Office Air 2/10302.

11. Portions of Tapp's logbook were graciously supplied to the author by Mrs. Deborah Lobb (daughter). At least one of the many Yorks he flew has been identified by lettering as well as serial number – MW294 which carried the letters AF.

12. For more on the type see Steven J. Bond, *Meteor: Gloster's First Jet Fighter* (Leicester, Midland Counties Publications, 1985); Mike Retallack, "Mastering the Meteor," *Aeroplane Monthly*, November 1993.

13. The Coronation Honours Lists (civil and military) may be found in the June 5 and June 12 issues of *The Aeroplane*. The Coronation itself provided a stage for the RCAF; 24 Canadian Sabres participated in the Coronation flypast (almost upstaging 168 RAF Meteors). At Spithead Naval Review on June 15, RCN aircraft from No. 871 Squadron (Sea Furies) and No. 871 Squadron (Avengers) flew in a huge aerial pageant. History was made on June 2 and 3 when film of the Coronation itself was rushed across the Atlantic by RAF Canberra bomber for near-immediate viewing in North American theatres.

14. For more on RAF Polar flights of this period, see "More Flights to the Pole," *The Aeroplane*, April 9, 1954; "Polar Navigation Flights," *Flight*, July 16, 1954; Frank Beswick, "Far North Exercise," *Flight*, August 13, 1954; "Aries IV Over North Pole," *Flight*, October 29, 1954; "Royal Air Force Polar Flights," *Flight*, December 31, 1954; "More Arctic Training Flights," *The Aeroplane*, December 31, 1954; "Arctic Flight," *The Aeroplane*, July 1, 1955. See also "Air Action in the Middle East," *The Aeroplane*, November 9, 1956.

15. Hare flew Halifax PP350 while testing this device. Also called a "Universal Freight Contained, the "Paratechnicon" was a misbegotten idea – an 8,000-pound box virtually slung in the bomb-bay of a Halifax or under a Hastings transport, dangerously close to the ground on take-off and offering massive drag in flight until jettisoned. The idea was rendered irrelevant by aircraft like the C-82 and C-119 which could air-drop loads through large rear-facing cargo doors. See C.H. Barnes, *Handley-Page Aircraft Since 1907* (London, Putnam, 1976), pp.418-419 and 444-446. See also *The Aeroplane*, issues of October 14, 1949 and March 16, 1951. Hare's career is also described by Milberry in *Air Transport in Canada*, Volume 1, pp.416-418.

16. St. Louis had been attached to a British Antarctic relief expedition and had evacuated five marooned personnel of a scientific party; he had flown a Norseman twice between the relief ship and the shore. For more on this event, see Douglas Liversidge, *White Horizon* (London, Odhams Press, 1951) and V.E. Fuchs, "The Falkland Islands Dependency Survey, 1947-1950," *The Polar Record*, Volume

VI, No. 41 (January 1951).

17. Authorities were splitting hairs; St.Louis had been on leave without pay from the RCAF but was still counted as a member of the force. RCAF Administrative Order P7/7, dated September 30, 1949, was the most recent expression of service policy; it read, "Recommendations for honours and awards to service personnel in peacetime are to be restricted to those cases wherein an element of bravery or gallantry existed in the performance of duty."

18. Volume 6, RCAF file 976-1, "Search and Rescue – Policy," in National Archives of Canada, Record Group 24, Volume 18114; various correspondence but especially memo dated July 16, 1958 (Chief of the Air Staff to Chief of the Naval Staff). The reader is recommended G.Y. Smith, *Seek and Save: The History of 103 Rescue Unit* (Erin, Boston Mills Press, 1990) for an excellent unit history which also provides considerable contextual information on SAR work.

19. Volume 1 of RCAF file 976-2, "Search and Rescue – Generally," in National Archives of Canada, Record Group 24, Volume 18114. These figures were supplied by W/C J.G. Showler for a joint RCAF/DoT meeting held on February 10, 1959, to determine if the Department of Transport should assume responsibilities for a portion of SAR duties; at the conclusion of the conference, although suggesting some equipment upgrades, DoT decided to leave matters unchanged, following the philosophy of "If it ain't broke, don't fix it." See also the Para Rescue Association of Canada, *That Others May Live: 50 Years of Para Rescue in Canada* (Astra, Air Transport Group, 1994).

20. *Ibid.*, memorandum dated April 6, 1964 with added annexes.

21. Volume 5 of RCAF file 976-1, "Search and Rescue – Policy" (see note 18).

22. See Alice Gibson Sutherland, *Canada's Aviation Pioneers: 50 Years of McKee Trophy Winners* (Toronto, McGraw-Hill Ryerson, 1978), pp. 182-186.

23. DHist file 75/601, folio 19 and particularly minutes of the Inter-Service Awards Committee meeting on January 25, 1957.

24. See F.J. Blatherwick, *Royal Canadian Navy Honours, Decorations, Awards, 1910-1968* (New Westminster, FJB Air Publications, 1992).

25. See *The Crowsnest*, July 1955, p.3; administrative details including original recommendation are in DHist file 75/601, folder 18. As a Lieutenant-Commander and Commanding Officer of HU 21

Squadron, James found and rescued two stranded duck hunters in the Musquodoboit area of Nova Scotia, January 1961. At least one other RCN pilot is known to have been recommended for an AFC. Late in 1957 or early 1958 the Flag Officer, Atlantic Coast nominated Commander H.J. Hunter for this award, citing the officer's flying skills and organizing ability demonstrated during flight trials aboard HMCS *Bonaventure* (newly commissioned). Had this been advanced in Britain the recommendation might have succeeded. Under the strict Canadian rules requiring "acts of bravery," Hunter's nomination failed to gain approval of the Inter-Service Awards Committee at its meeting held on April 1, 1958; see DHist file 75/601, folder 20. For brief mention of Hunter's work see J. Allan Snowie, *The Bonnie: HMCS Bonaventure* (Erin, Boston Mills Press, 1987), pp.78.

26. RCAF file 900-22, "Public Relations – Mercy Flights," Volume One, in National Archives of Canada, Record Group 24, Volume 17883.

27. Unless otherwise noted, all information relative to Operation "Hawk" is taken directly from the Squadron Diary held at the Canadian Armed Forces Directorate of History. For an overview of this subject see Milberry, *Air Transport in Canada*, pp.415-418.

28. Fred Hatch, "Pacific Airlift" (narrative prepared for Air Historian, filed as DHist document 181.001 (D12).

29. "Operations Reports, Korean Airlift, 426 (T) Squadron, Lachine," filed as DHist document 74/337.

30. Hatch, *op.cit.*, pp.2-3.

31. Larry Milberry, *The Canadair North Star* (CANAV Books, Toronto, 1982), pp.143-158; see also Ray Jacobsen, *426 Squadron History* (Trenton, private printing, 1989), pp.74-86.

32. Commended were Sergeant Frederick Morrison Bowman (flight engineer), F/L Robert Edward Burn (navigator, from Hespeler, Ontario), S/L Charles Endersbe (radio officer), F/L Abraham Finklestein (navigator), Corporal Edward Clarence Grose (air traffic assistant), Sergeant George Howard (flight engineer), F/L James Burton Miller (pilot), Sergeant Ludwig Cyril Potekal (flight engineer), S/L Russell Edwin Ratcliffe, DFC (navigator), F/L William Smith (radio officer), F/O John Pierce Wilson (radio officer) and F/L Edward Raymond Wolkowski (pilot, from Tiny, Saskatchewan).

33. DHist file 75/601, folders 16 and 17. As of August 2000 the author has failed to determine precisely how the RAF/RAAF quota for non-operational awards was determined; it would appear that gallantry

awards to Sunderland and Meteor aircrew in Korea were on a scale of roughly one decoration for every 300 combat hours flown.

34. AFC awards for the late 1950s and early 1960s are thoroughly documented in Secretary of State papers (National Archives of Canada, RG.6 D.1 Volume 359), particularly file 114-2-A1-3 "Awards – Specific – Air Force Cross (Granted)."

Chapter 7: A New Generation of Awards

1. See Hugh A. Halliday, "Symbols of Honour: The Search for a National Canadian Honours System" in *Material History Review*, No. 42 (Fall 1995).

2. See, for example, "Range of Awards Urged for Bravery," Toronto *Globe and Mail*, January 9, 1970; "Various Medals Urged for Canadian Bravery," Ottawa *Citizen*, January 9, 1970.

3. House of Commons *Debates*, January 16, 1970.

4. *Ibid.*, January 29, 1970.

5. "Victoria Cross Reinstated as Top Military Honour," Ottawa *Citizen*, February 26, 1993; *Regulations Governing the Military Valour Decoration* provided by Chancellery Division, Government House.

6. *Canada Gazette*, July 11, 1981. For the texts of many more Canadian gallantry awards, see F.J. Blatherwick, *1000 Brave Canadians* (Toronto, Unitrade Press, 1991). Flath, born on July 27, 1935, had joined the RCAF in October 1956. He flew CF-100s and CF-101s until 1964, when he transferred to the Canadian Army.

7. Blatherwick, *op.cit.*, p.190.

And now I have finished the work, which neither the wrath of Jove, nor the fire, nor the sword, nor devouring age shall be able to destroy.

– OVID (43 B.C-18 A.D., *METAMORPHOSES*

INDEX

NOTE: This index does not contain material from Appendices.

AFC and AFM (general), design, 14, 16; distribution during Second World War, 72; eligibility, 17, 260 (notes 6 and 7); factors of risk, 24; origins, 14; periodic vs immediate, 20; presentation, 25-26; procedures, 19-20; quotas, 21-23, 224; RAF awards in Canada, 133-134; RAF scale of awards, 186-187
Agnew, R.I., 62
Aistrop, S.O., 26
Aitkin, M., 68
Alexander, C.M., 231-232
Alexander, H., 178, 265 (note 26)
Alexander, S.E., 80
Allen, G.W., 195
Anderson, J.B., 134
Anderson, J.D., 169
Anderson, N.R., 161-162
Anthony, E., 30
Argus, HMS, 53
Armstrong, W.A., 25-26
Athlone, Earl of, 132, 153
ATTACHE, Operation, 168, 174-175, 208-209

Attle, J., 170
Australians, awards to, 59-60, 148
Awards Co-Ordination Committee, 184-185, 220

Bacon, E.A.H., 133-134
Bailey, F.M., 79
Baird, P.D., 158
Baldwin, N.S., 169
Ball, K.A., 195
Banting, F., 61, 104, 106
Barichello, R.J.E., 24-26
Barker, R.R., 25
Batock, C.C., 232
Baudoux, E.L., 101
Beamish, F.V., 58
Beaumont, R., 200
Belanger, M.J., 75
Bell, R.G., 119
Bellow, E.D., 18
Bennett, D., 197
Bennett, R.B., 60-61, 63
Berlin Airlift, 196-199
Berry, D., 26
Best, L.E., 18, 29
Bilodeau, W., 61

Birchall, L.J., 215
Bishop, A.A., 139
Bishop, W.A., 152
Bisson, L., 260 (note 6)
Blanchard, S.S., 264 (note 4)
Blank, P.E., 217-218
Borden, R., 52, 58-59
Boroski, F., 117
Bowhill, F., 145
Boyce, G.H., 53
Boyd, K.G., 32
Bradshaw, D.A.R., 192
Brain, L.J., see Australians, awards to
Breadner, L.S., 29, 122-123, 164
Brodribb, W.J., 175
Brooke-Popham, H., 48
Brooker, C., 82
Brooks, G.E., 62
Brown, A.L., 156-157
Brown, H.M., 82
Brown, R.B., 171
Brunelle, M.E., 91
Bruton, P.J., 97
Bryans, J.G., 150, 206
Bryant, H., 162
Bryden, J., 19

Buck, P.L., 25, 161 (note 28)
Buckner, J.G., 62
Bulmer, W.H., 75-76
Burden, D.R., 242
Burdes, J.R., 264 (note 2), 269 (note 2)
Burlingham, C.K., 111
Burnap, R.W., 82
Burnell, H.H., 69
Burnett, W.J., 201
Burns, E.L.M., 62
Burns, G.C., 112, 267 (note 54)
Burrows, E., 209
Burrows, S.W., 229-230
Butts, R.A., 19
Byers, R., 24-25, 138, 261 (note 27)

Cadleux, L., 238
Caham, C.H., 60
Calthorpe, E., 37
Camm, S., 200
Campbell, D.M., 196
Campbell, D.M., 218-219
Camsell, C., 62
CAN/RAF personnel, general, 259 (note 1), 271 (note 7)
Canadian Aviation Hall of Fame, 208
Canadian Honours, 176, 184, 237-242
CANON, Operatio, 177-181, 185, 205-206, 211, 242
CAPTAIN, Operation, 176-177, 214-215
Carr, A.G., see Australians, awards to
Carroll, J., 193
Carroll, R.S., 36-39
Carswell, A.G., 195, 216-217
Carter, J.C., 231
Cass, R.W., 176, 217-218
Charlesworth, A.M., see Australians, awards to
Chretien, J., 238
Christmas, B.E., 269 (note 92)
Clacken, B., 117

Clark, E.E., 17
Claxton, B., 177-178, 184, 207, 242
Clement, R.S., 134, 137
Cobham, A., 260 (note 6)
Coleman, S.W., 66
Collings, H., 62
Conlin, P.P., 264 (note 3)
Conningham, D., 229
Cook, G.M., 74-75
Cook, H.C., 178-181
Cooke, T.C., 170
Coombes, J.S., 82
Cork, Richard, 17
Coronation Honours, 63, 200
Costello, M., 127, 175
Court, G.L., 267 (note 51)
Crang, J.C., 28
Crang, J.G., 263 (note 31)
Crawford, C.W., 91-93
Crebo, R.H., 228
Croil, G.M., 28-29, 53
Cunningham, J., 169
Curtis, W.A., 177
Cuthbertson, D.R., 195, 215-216

d'Artois, L.G., 177-179, 181
Dafoe, A.R., 62
Danforth, W.E., 226 (note 35)
Darraugh, H.F. 127-128
Davy, H.D., 111
Dawson, J.M., 203
de Marco, A., 153-154
de Niverville, A., 49
de Sieyes, F.G., 155
Devlin, R.S., 27-28
Dewan, D.J., 160
Diamond, G.G., 11, 26, 259 (note 3)
Dickey, W.W., 265 (note 26)
Dickson, C.A., 153-154
Dickson, J.D., 224-225

Distinguished Flying Cross (United States), non-combat awards, 269-270 (note 3)
Distinguished Flying Cross, 14
Distinguished Flying Medal, 14
Dixon, A.H., 226 (note 35)
Dobson, R., 72
Donald, T.B., 79
Donaldson, E.M., 168-169, 196, 200
Doolittle, J.H., 164, 270 (note 3)
Dougall, R.C., 127
Drackley, A.A., 226-228
Drake, J.F., 190-194
Draper, J.W., 26
Duff, L.P., 61
Duggan, F.R., 132-133
Dunlap, C.R., 176
Dunlop, L.G., 226 (note 35)
Durant, H.A., see Australians, awards to
Dutchak, J., 26
Dyer, C.G.R., 11, 259 (note 3)

Eaker, I., 85
Earhart, A., 270 (note 3)
Easton, J.A., 176
Eaton, C., see Australians, awards to
Edwards, D.M., 18
Edwards, H., 164
Edwards, R.M., 225
Elkins, W.H.P., 61
Engelbert, A.L., 224
Erhardt, W.K., 242
Evans, T.J., 185
Evernder, J.G., 170

Falk, R.J., 261 (note 23)
Fall, J.S.T., 53
Fauquier, J.E., 69
Fenwick-Wilson, R.M., 69
Fink, D.I.W., 109, 111
Finn, R.W., 78

Fisher, R., 242
Flath, G.L., 241-242
Fleishman, E.D., 121-122
Fleming, R.B., 68
Foord-Kelsey, A., 68
Fortier, Y.O., 271 (note 6)
Forty, J., 66
Foss, R.H., 78
Foulkes, C., 175
Franks, W., 103-104
French, Lord, 31
Frizzle, J.M., 185
Fulton, J., 108-109
Fumerton, R.C., 26, 130-131
Furious, HMS, 53-54

Gale, E.B., 25, 120
Gall, R., 118
Game, D.K., 195
Garratt, P.C., 53
Gault, P.H., 79
George VI, 178-179, 242
Gibbs, P.L., 176-177, 214-215
Glaister, R.T., 176-177, 214-215
GLIMMER, Operation, 69
Glover, J.A., 172
Gobeil, F.M., 58, 146-148
Goble, S.J., see Australians, awards to
Godfrey, A.E., 28, 41-44, 53
Goldsmith, J.E., 190-195
Gordon McGregor Memorial Trophy, 219
Gordon, R.A., 218
Graeme, D.B., 70
Graham, S., 33-36, 53
Grandy, R.S., 61-62, 161
Green, A.F., 134, 137
Green, G.D., 261 (note 23)
Greenaway, N.E., 145
Greenough, E., 209
Grey, C.G., 17, 31

Grierson-Jackson, W.R.F., 129
Grieve, M., 260 (note 6)
Griffiths, F.C., 202
Grinstead, R.W.J., 174
Guthrie, K., 163

Haldin, A., 118
Hall, G.E., 104-107
Hand, C.F., 49, 51
Hanway, J.A., 140-142
Harding, D.A., 29, 54
Hare, C.E.L., 175, 201-204
Harling, L.A., 183, 269 (note 2)
Harris, A., 66
Harris, C.C., 129
Hart, R., 91
Harvey, K.A., 176, 185, 218, 236
Haven, C., see HAVEN, Operation
HAVEN, Operation, 10, 212-214
HAWK, Operation, 221-228
Hawker, H., 260 (note 6)
Hawkins, L.D., 178, 180
Hay, M.H., 170
Heakes, F.V., 25, 123, 169-170
Heaslip, R.T., 158, 218
Heavy Conversion Units, general, 137-138
Henderson, J.C., 96-97
Hill, C.J.T., 61
Hillcoat, H.B., 153-154
Hillman, A.B., 195
Hillyer, F.W., 181
Hiltz, G.A., 209, 211
Hinton, A.H., 28, 31-32
Hoare, C.G., 42, 44, 47
Hobbs, B.D., 24
Holliday, F.P., 30, 54
Hone, J., 166-168, 174
Hornby, A.N., 267 (note 66)
Hoshowsky, R., 82
Howsam, G., 125

Hoy, E.C., 46
Hughes, P.G., 18-19
Hull, A.H., 163
Hunt, W.J., 76, 78
Hunter, H.J., 272 (note 25)
Husband, D., 241
Hutchison, R.D., 193
Hyslop, R.C., 234-236
Ingrams, R.R., 75

INVESTIGATOR, Operation, 101
Ireland, J.G., 31
Irish Troubles, 31

Jackson, J.R., 214
James, A.L., 204
James, A.M., 20
James, C.R., 264 (note 3)
James, W.E., 220
Jardine, A.M., 69-70
Jarvis, L.G.W., 90-91
Jenness, J.L., 193
Jerson, P.H., 193
Johnson, G.O., 163
Johnson, J.R.F., 129
Johnstone, F.W., 170
Jones, L.L., 143
Joy, D.G., 31
Judd, W.W., 178

Kauffeldt, L., 82
Kennedy, H.M. 151
Kennedy, J.F., 218
Kennedy, R., 218
Kenney, D.H., 26
Kent, J.A., 10, 55, 57-58
Kerby, H.S., 53
Kernaghan, S.J., 131
King, C.L., 70
King, F.C., 98

King, W.L.M., 60-61, 63, 221
King's Commendations, created, 18
Kings's Commendations, awards, 133, 155, 178, 185-186, 216, 224, 273 (note 32)
Kleisch, A., 83-84
Knocker, G.M., 141
Knowles, P.H., 69

Labrish, F.B., 153-154
Laker, F., 198
Lane, R.J., 26
Langton, R.T., 268 (note 73)
Lapointe, E., 63
Lawrence, A.G., 129-130
Lawrence, T.A., 59, 79, 163
Lawrence, T.E., 28, 49, 51
Lea, N., 72
Leach, J.O., 44, 54
Leckie, G.B., 182-184
Ledoux, H.L., 231
Leger, Jules, 218
Leigh, Z.L., 175, 183
Lemieux, R.J., 175
Letson, H.F.G., 177, 184
Lewthwaite, S.H., 268 (note 73)
Livingston, P.C., 107-108, 266 (note 49)
Lloyd, A., 270 (note 16)
Lloyd., W., see Australians, awards to
Loewen, C.F., 264 (note 26)
Logan, H., 161
Longcroft, C., 260 (note 9)
Longhurst, W.S., 146-148
Lord, W.H., 224
Ludlow, P.H., 134

MacAllister, G.D., 121
Macdonald, R.J., 175
MacGregor, N.S., 73. 140
MacIntyre, D.P., 130
Macklin, W.H.S., 177

Maclure, K.C., 190-191
MacMillan, K., 232
MacNeil, D.S., 91
Madden, H.O., 149-151
MAGNETIC, Operation, 193, 195, 215-216
Major, J.E., 271 (note 16)
Malkin, H., 128-129
Malloy, J.S., 172
Malo, J.W., 216
Marr, W.L, 160
Martin, B.C., 78
Martin, D.C., 93
Mason, A.J., 140-141
Mawdesley, F.J. 161-164
Mawhinney, C., 82
Maxwell, W.R., 261 (note 2)
May, W.R., 62, 163
Maylor, AC1, 78
McCaffery, E.H., 130
McElrea, W.G., 154
McElroy, V.H., 17
McEwen, C.M., 66
McGill, F.S., 21
McGregor, G., 163, 269 (note 92)
McIntyre, E.E., see Australians, awards to
McKee Trophy, see Trans-Canada Trophy
McKoy, K.A., 195
McLaughlin, C.D., 215-216
McLean, J.A., 238
McLeish, B., 211
McLeish, J., 211
McLeish, R., 211
McLeish, W.A.G., 209-211
McLeod,J.H., 181
McMillan, C.C., 178, 180-181
McNab, E.S., 58, 171
McNair, R.W., 186, 242
McNaughton, A.G.L., 61
McNaughton, A.R.L., 102
McNeill, H.E., 156

McPherson, I.J., 217
McRae, J.B., 123
McVeigh, C.N., 71, 155-156
McWilliam, D.L.S., 268 (note 88)
Middleton, R.B., 98
Mignon, R., 163-164
Miller, A.K., 103
Miller, H.A., 30
Miller, R.F., 139-140
Mills, F., 117
Mitchell, H., 261 (note 2)
Mitchell, J.F., 213-214
Mitchell, L.N., 27-28
Moffit, B.H., 74
Montgomery, L.M., 62
Moore, G.E., 114, 116-120, 128
Moore, K.O., 178, 180, 205
Moore, L.A., 160
Mooris, J., 172
Morabito, B., 178, 180
Moran, C.C., 124
Morfee, A.L., 95
Morgan, J.B., 170
Morrison, H.A., 225-226
Muise, Albert, 217
Murray, J.A.J., 86-87
Murray, L.W., 95
MUSKOX, Exercise, 82, 158, 173-174, 191
Mussells, C.H., 224

Naval Flying Cross (proposed), 17
Naval Flying Medal (proposed), 17
Nelson, O.G., 208-209
Newcombe, C.F., 122
Nickle Resolutions, 58-60, 67
Nickle, W.F., 58-59
Norridge, A.A., 78
Norris, H., 125, 126
North, C.A., 201

O'Brian, G.S., 30, 53
O'Connor, H.W., 62
O'Mara, E., 26
Oakes, H., 264 (note 26)
Oaks, H.A., 60
Oleinek, P.J., 131
Orde-Lees, T., 37-38
Orr, W.A., 124

Paine, Geoffrey, 13
Palmer, J.E., 124-125
Parachute development, 37-38
Parker, D.F., 234-236
Parliamentary Committee of 1942, 66
Partridge, S.O., 99-101
Patriarche, V.H., 171
Patterson, R.P., 232
Payne, D.M., 226, 228
Pearson, L.B. (diplomat), 62, 238
Pearson, L.B. (pilot), 212
Peek, G.C., 100
Pegasus, HMS, 55-56
Pepper, W.V., 78
Perley, G., 52-53, 60
Pexton, R.D., 267 (note 66)
Philby, H.St.J., 50-53
Phillips, R., 172
Plant, J.L., 154
POLCO, Operation, 190-195
Pollard, M.E., 71
Polunin, N., 191-192
Ponsobby, Frederick, 13
Pope, S.L.G., 55
Power, C.G., 25, 29, 172
Powley, F.S., 69
Powley, F.S., 71
Preston, G.L., 78-79
Prime, F.H., 33
Pruss, E., 241

Queale, L.W., 223

Rabnett, A.A., 62
Race, R.C., 177-181, 185, 211
Rae, J.P., 178, 180-181
Ralph, R.J., 148
Ralston, J.L., 152
Rankin, A.J., 55
Raumer, F.H., 182-184
Raymond, A., 165
REDRAMP, Operation, 221
Reed, G.R., 228
Reed, T.E., 171
Reid, A.C., 33
Reilly, J.R., 42
Reilly, T.D., 267 (note 66)
Renwick, R.D., 93
Rettie, N., 117
Reyno, E.M., 19, 123-124
Rhodes, D.W., 217
Rhodesia, 23
Richardson, R.R., 32-33
Ritzel, D.F., 97
Rizon, R.L., 76-78
Robb, D., 134, 137
Roberts, R.B., 79
Robinson, K.E., 148
Robinson, K.E., see Australians, awards to
Rodney, G.F., 55, 57
Rogers, N., 152
Rolfe, G., 62
Rose, M.H., 269 (note 2)
Rosenbaum, E.M., 153-154
Ross, A.D., 127, 185, 193
Ross, J.M., 18
Ross, L.T., 230-231
Russell, N.H., 120
Rutledge, W.L., 28
Ryan, R.W., 106

Sabourin, R.E., 185
Salmon, W.G.L., 52
Sanderson, S.A., 122-123
Saunders, C., 61
Sawle, C.L.T., 242
Scott, C.W.A., 260 (note 6)
Scott, D.G., 270 (note 3)
Scott, J.S., 47-49, 53, 161
Searle, A.B., 127
Selby, D.G., 72-73
Seys, R.G. 146-148
Sharpe, G.F., 242
Shaw, R.O., 211
Shearer, A.B., 122, 163
Shearwater, HMCS, 220
Sherratt, F.W., 260 (note 6)
Shook, A.M., 39-40
Shortreed, J., 107
Showler, J.G., 120-121, 158
Silberman, T.M., 79
Sinnott, A.A., 175
Sisley, A., 47
Sisley, D., 47
Sisley, M.M., 46-47, 53
Slemon, C.R., 60
Small, N.E., 73-75
Smith, F.E.W., 158
Smith, H.M., 261 (note 15)
Smith, N., 26
Smith, W.A., 93-95
Snyder, J.C., 101
Sopwith, T., 200
Spinney, H.L., 95-96
Sproule, J.A., 155
St.Catharines (weather ship), 217
St. Louis, P.B., 203
St. Pierre, J.M.W., 164-165
St. Pierre, M.A.J., 199-200
Stagg, W.A., 200
Stedman, E., 49, 51,

Stein, C., 175, 177
Stephenson, J.G., 203
Stevenson, L.F., 151
Stewart, C.R.H., 33
Stewart, H.C., 19, 123-124
Sully, J.A., 21-23, 44, 53
Swinford, K.C., 178, 180

Tacon, E.W., 267 (note 73)
Tapp, L.A.P., 198-199
Taylor, K.G., 134
Tellier, J., 61
Thom, G., 54
Thompson, A.E., 122
Thompson, C.W.H., 146-148
Thompson, J.A., 159-160
Tilley, A., 152
Tipton, J., 201
Tomkinson, E.L., 56
Torontow, C., 71-72, 152
Townley, Lt., 31
Trans-Canada Trophy, 60, 66, 73, 83, 158, 163, 207, 268 (note 88)
Tricket, R.I., 129
Trist, L., see Australians, awards to
Trudel, P.B.J.A., 224
Tudhope, J.H., 60

Turnbull, R.S., 134, 165-166
Turner, J.H., see Operation CANON
Turner, P.S., 68

U-342 (German submarine), 170
U-422 (German submarine), 75
U-630 (German submarine), 74
U-754 (German submarine), 74
United States Coast Guard, 83-84, 181-184

Vallis, F., 242
Vance, J.D., 49-53
Villeneuve, J.A.G.F., 176, 232-234
Vineberg, H.A., 29-30
Virr, R.V., 175

Walker, B., 26
Walker, W.L.E., 118-119
Walsh, A.P., 172
Wanlin, A.C., 156
Waterhouse, R.H., 267 (note 66)
Waterton, W.A., 134, 168-169, 196
Watt, J.A., 224
Wenzel, C.L., 196-198
West, R.B., 206-208
Westaway, H.A., 80-82
Westray Mine Disaster, 241

Whettell, T.L., 72
White, W., 62
Whynacht, K.A., 200-201
Wickett, J.C., 122
Wightman, H.G., 146
Williams, E.M., 20
Williams, J.S., 44, 46
Williams, R., see Australians, awards to
Willoughby, R.W., 177-178
Wilmot, C.E., 40-41
Winney, H.J., 61-62
Wiseman, J.A., 191
Wormington, R.H., 146
Wray, L.E., 66-67, 106, 166, 198
Wright, D., 176-177, 215
Wright, G.G., 143-145
Wyatt, J., 62-63
Wyman, L.B., 145-146

Yates, G.W., 52
Yates, H.A., 49-53
Yeager, C., 270 (note 3)
Young, S.A., 266 (note 35)

Zinkan, P., 232

Other books by Hugh A. Halliday
from Robin Brass Studio

Wreck! Canada's Worst Railway Accidents

This intriguing book looks at the 30 worst railway accidents in Canada. The earliest took place in 1854 when a Great Western express collided with a work train near Chatham, Ontario, and the most recent was the Hinton disaster in Alberta in 1986. Hugh Halliday not only explains how each accident happened but also how it reflected railroad practices of the time and what the legal aftermath was.

Most accidents involved human error, often compounded by technological or climatic problems. There were despatchers who issued faulty train orders, or engineers who misread them, or an inattentive trainman who threw a switch thinking he was saving his train from disaster only to cause one. Several accidents involved bridges that either were open when the train came to cross them or collapsed. Fire was a danger, especially when passenger cars were built of wood and lit by oil lamps.

Many accidents reflected the hazards of railroading in a large and sparsely-populated country. Before communications and signalling systems improved, trains entered a "black hole" in which a possibly-unreliable timetable was the only guide a crew had to who might be sharing the track. Some accidents were related to the extremes of the Canadian climate: two tragedies involved snow-clearing crews, and others were the result of torrential rains. A recurring feature of earlier disasters was the power of railway management and lawyers to deflect blame from their organizations and employees.

This is a fascinating piece of research and a must for anyone interested in railway history. It is illustrated with photos, newspaper headlines and maps.

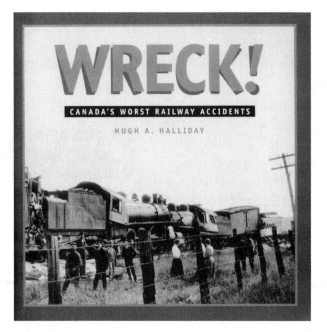

Paperback, ISBN 1-896941-04-4
$18.95 Canada
$16.95 U.S.A.

Murder Among Gentlemen: A History of Duelling in Canada

The formal duel, with its elaborate ritual and code of conduct, was once considered an "honourable" way for self-styled gentlemen to settle disputes involving character and integrity. The law made no special provision for duelling – the winner in a fatal contest was a murderer. But the prevailing sentiment that a duel was "fair," and the fact that upper-crust combatants in the thinly-populated 19th-century Canada were well-connected with the judiciary, meant that duellists usually escaped with little or no punishment. What is surprising is that so many came from the ranks of those whose job it was to uphold the law – lawyers, judges and politicians, including at least two future Fathers of Confederation and several chief justices.

Hugh Halliday not only describes some of the most interesting duels that took place in Canada but looks at duelling in light of our human tendency to ritualize conflicts with codes of acceptable and unacceptable practice. He also examines the steps that often led to a duel, including the public "posting" of allegations, or insults, that was frequently a part of the process.

"An engaging, fast-paced account of duels, both farcical and tragic, which includes a provocative and unflattering portrait of the colonial upper classes." *The Beaver*

"It is a great slice of history." *Ottawa Citizen*

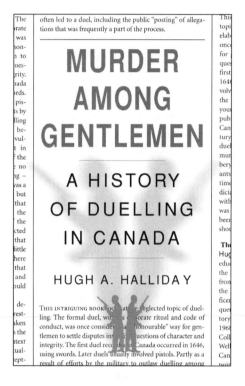

Paperback, ISBN 1-896941-09-5
$17.95 Canada
$15.95 U.S.A.

About the author

Hugh A. Halliday was born and educated in Manitoba. He holds degrees
from the University of Manitoba and
Carleton University. His several careers
have encompassed service as an RCAF
and Canadian Forces historian in
Ottawa (1961-68); teaching political
science, law and history at Niagara
College of Applied Arts and Technology
in Welland, Ontario (1968-74); and
several appointments with the Canadian
War Museum (1974-95), including
Curator of War Art, Curator of Collec-
tions/Research and Curator of Posters
and Photographs. Although he is best known as a military historian, his
broad interests have led him to several fields. For several years he gave a
course, "History They Never Taught You," which dealt with such topics
as Canadian criminals, detectives, disasters, duels, liquor laws, and Métis
history *before* Louis Riel. He continues to write for various publications,
preferring unusual – even unexpected – topics, and he has been employed as a consultant by parties as diverse as Canada Post and the
National Film Board.